HOW AGRICULTURE MADE CANADA

MCGILL-QUEEN'S RURAL, WILDLAND, AND RESOURCE STUDIES
SERIES

Series editors: Colin A.M. Duncan, James Murton, and R.W. Sandwell

The Rural, Wildland, and Resource Studies Series includes monographs, thematically unified edited collections, and rare out-of-print classics. It is inspired by Canadian Papers in Rural History, Donald H. Akenson's influential occasional papers series, and seeks to catalyze reconsideration of communities and places lying beyond city limits, outside centres of urban political and cultural power, and located at past and present sites of resource procurement and environmental change. Scholarly and popular interest in the environment, climate change, food, and a seemingly deepening divide between city and country, is drawing non-urban places back into the mainstream. The series seeks to present the best environmentally contextualized research on topics such as agriculture, cottage living, fishing, the gathering of wild foods, mining, power generation, and rural commerce, within and beyond Canada's borders.

How Agriculture Made Canada

Farming in the Nineteenth Century

PETER A. RUSSELL

McGill-Queen's University Press
Montreal & Kingston • London • Ithaca

© McGill-Queen's University Press 2012

ISBN 978-0-7735-4064-4 (cloth)
ISBN 978-0-7735-4065-1 (paper)

Legal deposit fourth quarter 2012
Bibliothèque nationale du Québec

Printed in Canada on acid-free paper that is 100% ancient forest free
(100% post-consumer recycled), processed chlorine free

This book has been published with support from the Internal Research
Grants Program at the University of British Columbia's Okanagan
campus.

McGill-Queen's University Press acknowledges the support of the
Canada Council for the Arts for our publishing program. We also
acknowledge the financial support of the Government of Canada
through the Canada Book Fund for our publishing activities.

Library and Archives Canada Cataloguing in Publication

Russell, Peter A.

   How agriculture made Canada : farming in the nineteenth century /
Peter A. Russell.

(McGill-Queen's rural, wildland, and resource studies series ; 1)
Includes bibliographical references and index.
ISBN 978-0-7735-4064-4 (bound). – ISBN 978-0-7735-4065-1 (pbk.)

   1. Agriculture – Canada – History – 19th century.2. Agriculture –
Economic aspects – Canada – History – 19th century. I. Title. II. Series:
McGill-Queen's rural, wildland, and resource studies ; 1

S451.5.A1R86 2012   630.97109'034   C2012-906513-7

Typeset by Jay Tee Graphics Ltd. in 10.5/13 Sabon

Contents

Acknowledgments

The research and writing of a book stretch over a long period of time. To the writer it seems a lonely process. But many institutions and people contribute to produce the final product. Returning to Canada in 1989 after twelve years of teaching in the United Kingdom, I had some catching up to do, reading my way back into the prodigious output of Canadian social historians. From that reading, I drew a picture of how the debates over nineteenth-century agricultural history linked together three Canadian regions. In 1992 Okanagan University College (OUC) hired me to teach history and economics. I worked out that synthesis as I taught an upper level course on Canadian social history. I wish to thank OUC and the University of British Columbia for sabbaticals granted to work on what may have seemed disparate lines of inquiry. I also benefited from the responses to papers presented at the Agricultural History Society's annual conferences.

Over these many years, numerous people have helped me in diverse ways. I want to especially thank Donald H. Akenson for his support as editor of *Canadian Papers in Rural History* (alas, now discontinued) and, latterly, as a senior editor at McGill-Queen's University Press. I express my gratitude to the campus library staff, above all Jan Gattrell, who was often more a research colleague than librarian. I also want to acknowledge the help of Michael "Jack" Davis not only for producing the graph included herein but also for working through several iterations to find the clearest picture of Quebec wheat exports. In years gone by, I benefited from the responses (not always positive but always useful) of Fernand Ouellet and J.I. Little.

On the way to publication, I have had an excellent group of editors. Mark Abley at McGill-Queen's University Press shepherded the manuscript through the peer review process and found a home for it as the

first in the Rural, Wildland, and Resource series. Maureen Garvie edited
an ungainly collection of essays into a more coherent whole. Thanks also
go to Eleanor Gasparik, copy editor, for her careful eye in pointing out
infelicities in grammar and language, and reconstructing complex sentences into more flowing prose. Thanks also to David Drummond for
providing the cover design. I benefited greatly from the comments and
criticisms of the anonymous peer reviewers.

And since no man is an island, mine has been shared by my family.
My late parents gave me a model through their writing of local history.
From them I received not only financial support and encouragement but
also their own accounts of growing up on farms in Saskatchewan. I also
thank my wife, Cornelia, for those same three things. But I am much
more indebted to her than words can express. Our three daughters –
Heather, Jane, and Emily – grew up with this project as more than mere
passive observers or rivals for my attention. In the terminology, parents,
spouse, and children formed my personal "domestic economy."

My wish is that this book will find a niche in the world of ideas about
the history of this country of ours.

Abbreviations

AH	*Agricultural History*
CHR	*Canadian Historical Review*
CPRH	*Canadian Papers in Rural History*
Hs/SH	*Histoire sociale/Social History*
JCS	*Journal of Canadian Studies*
RHAF	*Revue historique d'Amérique Français*

BNA	British North America
CPR	Canadian Pacific Railway
HBC	Hudson's Bay Company
NWT	North West Territories
NWC	Northwest Company

HOW AGRICULTURE MADE CANADA

Agricultural Crises in the Canadas in the Nineteenth Century

In German the term *methodenstreit* – "methods-strife" – describes a sterile debate begun in the late nineteenth century, nominally about economic method, driven by personal animosity, which wasted everyone's energy. By contrast, the "good debate" is one that draws in more scholars with new evidence, new sorts of evidence, and new methods that advance our knowledge of the subject. The historiographic debates generated in the study of Canada's agricultural history over the past fifty years – most brief exchanges; some, ranging over decades – have been highly fruitful. This has been especially the case in Quebec, even though those exchanges have also at times been the most acrimonious.

Both Lower Canada and Upper Canada, in the view of at least some historians, are thought to have experienced agricultural crises that profoundly reshaped British North America, their impacts reaching into twentieth-century Canada. By the first half of the nineteenth century, the two colonies confronted a common problem: the limits of good farmland within the St Lawrence lowlands and the consequent need to find alternatives – emigration, migration, or a form of modernization to make farming sustainable on a fixed land base. But they met the problem at different times, in different circumstances, and with contrasting modes of nationalism. How farm families in each community responded to the end of that land frontier is vital in explaining the political and economic choices made by Canadians after mid-century.[1] If these crises were substantially what their exponents have described, then the differing responses of the two Canadas resulted in contrasting approaches to the creation of a new transcontinental state out of British North America. In Lower Canada – which in 1841 became Canada East, and for the sake of simplicity is hereafter referred to as Quebec – the rural crisis is said to have produced a nationalism that was increasingly isolated from the rest of British North America, that sought above all else to ensure that the province remained French. In Upper Canada – then Canada West and hereafter Ontario – the rural crisis is viewed as having helped to produce an expansionist land-hungry nationalism that sought to annex and colonize the North West for British Canadians.

The focus of this book is limited to the agricultural history and historiography of three regions of Canada: Quebec, Ontario, and the Prairies. Each was in turn a large-scale open land frontier in a way that, given the limited extent of their arable lands, the Maritimes and British Columbia never could have been. It is the nature of agricultural frontiers to drive forward until they reach their limits. Farm families' need for ever more lands with each new generation in Quebec and Ontario eventually ran up against the north and south edges of the St Lawrence lowlands. Habitants, starting to farm much earlier, hit the region's limits much earlier, when there were few alternatives in agriculture or industry. One consequence was a long slow economic decline for most. When new lands and jobs became available, habitants' children often faced their options with few resources. While pioneer farming began much later in Ontario, despite that province's greater extent of fertile lands, the settlement frontier moved quickly, driven by both high immigration and strong demand for wheat. The sudden collapse of wheat and land prices in 1857 came at the end of a sustained boom. Many farmers were caught overextended, trying to pay off mortgages on lands whose price had fallen sharply. Unquestionably, the start of the province's industrialization, the accessibility of cheap lands in the American Midwest, and even the possibility of political expansion in the North West created more choices for rising generation. When Ontario entered Confederation, thousands of its sons were primed to migrate West.

At the time of Confederation, the elites in the two Canadas had contrasting goals and motives. Quebec's religious and political leaders wanted Confederation primarily in order to secure undisputed control over what they judged to be the essentials for the nation: education, civil law, natural resources, language. Their primary goal was not to expand beyond their borders but to consolidate *la patrie* within Quebec. Thus they directed more effort to the colonization of the Eastern Townships than to the North West. Ontario's farm and business leaders saw Confederation as a means not just to have a province of their own free of "French domination" but also to acquire room to expand in a new settlement frontier in Rupert's Land, the Hudson Bay drainage basin, nominally owned by the Hudson's Bay Company from 1670 to 1868.

Yet even though the drive to annex Rupert's Land came largely from Ontario, the initial institutions imposed by the new federal government reflected the political power of Quebec. Apart from the impacts of agricultural crises on the farming communities of the Canadas, there was no reason why Manitoba at least should not have become as francophone as it is anglophone. Those initial institutions, however, would be challenged and subverted by the first wave of continental settlers on the Prairies coming disproportionately from Ontario.

In the debates over rural agricultural crises in nineteenth-century Canada, the foremost social historian in Quebec was Fernand Ouellet, who began his arguments from rising and falling wheat export data. His 1962 paper with Jean Hamelin[2] sparked the largest controversy in the history of Canadian agriculture. In two major books published in 1966 and 1976, Ouellet further expounded his thesis of a rural crisis beginning after 1802 and leading to the rise of Canadien nationalism from 1805 to 1837. Yet this central figure in the debate has now disappeared from francophone scholarly discourse. While Ouellet was Canada's foremost pioneer in quantitative history, his critics saw a tendency to present his statistical findings in terms of sharply drawn ethnic characterizations.[3]

For example, he attributed the Canadien withdrawal from the Montreal fur trade after 1783 to an enduring feudal *mentalité* that sought status in land rather than profits in business. Thus he held that the almost complete absence of Canadiens amongst the partners of the emerging North West Company was not due to any belated "decapitation" of the francophone bourgeoisie but to that group's lack of genuine bourgeois values. The problem with such ethnic characterizations of *mentalité* is highlighted by the fact that several prominent anglophone merchants also moved substantial capital into agriculture at the same time. If it was rational for Edward Ellice and Peter McGill to purchase seigneurial lands as investments in the 1780s, it could hardly have been less rational for Canadiens, who could reasonably have considered themselves more qualified to know the sorts of risks the North West trade entailed and the sorts of benefits that could come from owning seigneurial lands. By the mid-1780s Quebec agriculture was expanding its exports, making seigneuries profitable as well as secure investments. In contrast, the attempt to develop a high-cost, long-range fur trade to tie the Prairies to Montreal must have seemed relatively risky, especially to Canadien merchants who could remember the failure of a similar venture a generation earlier by the well-connected and energetic La Vérendrye family. One can accept Ouellet's evidence of Canadiens leaving the fur trade after the American

Revolution without being obliged to adopt his ethnic characterizations of their reasons for choosing to leave.[4] A similar exercise of critical discrimination between statistical data and ethnically charged explanations can also be applied to his analysis of the province's habitants.

Ouellet's work on agriculture provoked several challenges, of which the most sustained came from J.-P. Wallot and Gilles Paquet, beginning in the late 1960s. In 1975–76, T.J.A. Le Goff attempted an analysis of the exchanges, drawing replies from both sides. The debate had developed as both sides sought additional sources of evidence. Ouellet sought to find direct testimony on farm yields in tithe records from church archives. Wallot and Paquet examined a key source that linked the seigneurial area of the St Lawrence Valley with its French ancestry – a notarial document found on both sides of the Atlantic called the "post-mortem inventory" (or "inventory after death"). They maintained that such documents were direct evidence of habitants' improving standards of living, revealing rural patterns of inheritance (including gender issues), trends in standards of living reflected in both household and production goods, and also the degree of market participation implicit in such holdings. Serge Courville advanced an alternative model of agricultural development tied to the rapid growth of villages as a sign of a vigorous rural economy. From across the linguistic divide, other scholars weighed in: John Isbister, Paul Phillips, John McCallum, Frank Lewis, R.M. McInnis, Robert Armstrong. Christian Dessureault, J.-S. Piché, and Allan Greer contributed to the debate at the level of local studies. In the mid-1980s Serge Gagnon undertook a rigorous assessment of the discussion encompassing all parties.

The results of this prolonged academic controversy that dominated Lower Canadian rural history for over twenty years have been positive as well as negative. The lengthy exchanges between Ouellet and his assorted critics led to exploitation of new sources and new methods that resulted in a far more detailed and insightful grasp of the province's rural history than can be found for any other region of Canada. Unfortunately this discussion has been treated in recent Quebec historiography as an embarrassment to be elided rather than a model for refining research methods and conclusions. One goal of this book in carefully reviewing this controversy and its outcomes is to inquire to what extent the harsh ethnic characterizations that led to Ouellet's eclipse can be separated from his quantitative work.

Another goal is to bring Ouellet's work into direct dialogue with the most recent work on Quebec agriculture, which has been largely oriented to comparative studies with European experience. While dealing with issues Ouellet raised, this subsequent work has seldom directly engaged his argument and evidence. Studies using the inventory after death have pursued the degree to which the law promoted equality amongst heirs and rural migration (as related to both levels of family wealth and whether a child was excluded from landed inheritance). While these studies allude to earlier issues in Ouellet's work, such as trends in peasant living standards, systematic direct comparisons have yet to be drawn.

If Ouellet's statistical work is largely correct, then certain things follow. He argues that Quebec-focused nationalism diverted habitants' distress away from its real economic basis (to which they failed to respond by modernizing their farms) into a political dead end in the Rebellion of 1837. The early occurrence of this demographic crisis relative to Quebec's industrialization drove habitants first onto ever more marginal land and eventually to large-scale emigration to forests in or out of the province, or to New England mills where they were lost to *la nation*. Not until the 1890s would there be anything like sufficient industrial jobs within Quebec to begin absorbing the numbers leaving the land. In Ouellet's view, Quebec's agricultural crisis fed a nationalism that sought to retain its habitants, concentrating on "infilling" the province, encouraging young families to start new farms in the Eastern Townships, up the Ottawa Valley, or into the Lac St Jean region (rather than look to the West for new lands). The massive migration to New England and the more limited migrations within the province tell us that Canadiens were not terminally rooted to place. But more than just the relative economics of factory wages and farm-making costs are needed to explain the responses of either francophone elites or the rural masses. Quebec's defensive nationalism produced very different attitudes to the West than did Ontario's aggressive, expansionist land-hungry nationalism. Moreover, Quebec's slow rural recovery left most farm families with few resources for adaptation to modernization, much less westward migration.

In contrast to the controversy surrounding agricultural crisis in Quebec, that around a parallel crisis in Ontario has been influential rather than dominant. The issues have been far smaller, perhaps accounting for the mostly mild temper and more limited scope of the discussion. In the 1970s David Gagan undertook a micro-historical approach to Peel County, one of its hypotheses being that a crisis in agriculture took place in the "critical years" just before Confederation. Gagan took Peel

County as representative of the province, but if it was representative of anything, it was the small crescent of wheat specialist counties around the west end of Lake Ontario. He sought to show how the imperatives of the pioneer family farm required a continuous farm frontier. The end of the open land frontier in the southern part of the province meant that farm families had to adapt.

Both Gagan's fundamental assumptions about farm families and the specific issue of how he handled statistical tools were challenged by José Igartua and George Emery, to whom he replied. Other academics working in micro-histories of other parts of the province have subsequently accepted (D.H. Akenson) or questioned (Glen Lockwood) Gagan's analysis, depending on how it seemed to fit their own locale. A related issue has been the degree of self-sufficiency among pioneer farmers (Leo Johnson) compared to the degree of market participation at different stages in the province's development (Marvin McInnis). Harold Innis's staple theory has been applied to wheat production by some and challenged by others (Douglas McCalla, Marvin McInnis, William Marr). The role of farm families in sustaining staple production has been established (Cohen, Menzies, Derry). There has also been continuing interest in land prices (McCalla) and land speculation (John Clarke).

Gagan's rural crisis hypothesis was grounded in what he saw as the nature of the Ontario farm community. The farmer's dependence upon his sons' labour to clear his farm demanded that he compensate them in some way. His need to reward his sons' work with a start on farms of their own meant that the frontier of farm settlement had to be driven endlessly forward, which produced a drive to annex the North West. Through most of the 1850s George Brown had been the harsh voice of Ontario sectionalism feeding political deadlock that paralyzed the United Province of Canada. While his political moderation in the 1860s may have owed something to personal reasons, in part it might also have been due to the changing priorities of his constituents.[5]

The occurrence of demographic crisis later in Ontario than in Quebec meant that, along with emigration, industrialization within Ontario could be part of the answer to the problem. To the larger size, better soil, and more temperate climate of the average farm in Ontario compared to Quebec must be added the factors of the relative timing of industrialization in each province and consequent market opportunities. Ontario farmers began with greater resources, and then benefited from more fortuitous operations of the market. It can be argued that they also moved away from the wheat staple, to modernize their farms as either dairy or truck farms. Both options required capital investment, which farmers in Ontario were more likely to have had than those in Quebec, depending on the degree to which they had benefited from the wheat booms of the mid-1850s and late 1870s.

The debates over Prairie agriculture have been diverse, but few have generated a sustained historiography such as that in Quebec and Ontario. Some controversy has arisen from models developed outside the region. For example, George Britnell and V.C. Fowke applied the staples thesis, seeing the Prairies dominated by wheat monoculture. Other discussions have centred on issues specific to the region, the apparent decade of delay in settlement after the completion of the CPR perhaps drawing the most attention, from early historians Chester Martin and A.S. Morton to contemporary economic historian Kenneth Norrie. There have been debates over the necessary minimum level of farm start-up costs (Dick, Spry), the roles of women in prairie settlement (Silverman, Kinnear, Cavanaugh), ranching (Jameson, Breen, Evans, Lopfson), and the wisdom of opening the Prairies' driest region to homesteading (Gray, Voisey, Jones). These disparate issues need to be set into a comprehensive account of how farmers, native and non-native, learned to adapt to the specific challenges the Prairies posed to all comers, although not equally to all.

What has attracted less attention in all these debates has been the more wide-ranging consequences for the Prairies of any crises in Laurentian agriculture. While there is a large and still-growing literature on implications such as migration to New England and the francophone colonization of the Townships and other parts of Quebec outside the St Lawrence Valley, questions such as the relative lack of francophone migration to the West have been given less attention. For Ontario, the suggested consequences for Western Canada have been relatively more developed in work on changes in family structures, inheritance patterns, and schooling, as well as migration to urban centres, the American farm frontier, and Western Canada.

For the Prairies, the initial legislation and the initial settlement it attracted reflected the contrasting agricultural developments in the two central Canadian provinces. In the new Dominion, the conservative nationalism of George-Étienne Cartier sought to reserve a place for francophones in the framing of Manitoba's constitution, in the schools, and in the lands to be reserved for the children of Métis and prospective Quebec settlers. The promise was not fulfilled. Several causes have been cited: the failures of the federal government or of the Quebec episcopate, the influence of the Orange Lodge, the weather cycle. But the case made here is that the underlying cause was demographic: relatively few Quebec francophone families had the means and the interest to migrate west in a given year. That province's surplus rural population was already headed overwhelmingly for urban jobs, if not in Montreal, then in New England. Quebec's nationalist and clerical elites strongly encouraged those farmers' sons who wanted to begin a new farm to stay in the province. In the two decades following Confederation, several thousand Quebecers did migrate to the West, not only to Manitoba but also to southern Alberta and the valleys of British Columbia, where they established ranches and fruit farms. But these Quebecers were overwhelmingly English-speaking, many coming from the Eastern Townships, drawn by the prospect of continuing extensive farming in a new, low-cost area.

In Ontario the end of the land frontier and the decline of the staple came at a time when capital reserves were high (from the high prices of the mid-1850s) and urban employment opportunities were on the increase. The indebtedness of Ontario farmers reflected asset acquisition rather than consumption. Not only did they *want* a new land frontier, they had the means to settle it. Between 1870 and 1890 tens of thousands Ontario farmers and their sons moved to Manitoba. Their migration tipped the balanced constitution of Manitoba from a bilingual openness to Canadian duality to an exclusively English-speaking framework. Thus when the third force arrived from Eastern Europe, the context into which it was assimilated was devoutly English. But even as Ontario and British settlers changed the political landscape, the literal landscape and climate forced those settlers and all others to adapt their balance of subsistence and market-oriented production to severe new realities on the Prairies.

This book examines the implications of agricultural crises in nineteenth-century Canada through a detailed review of historiographical debate. In doing so, it not only sifts the arguments over whether or not such crises occurred or to what extent but also examines whether the responses to those situations have been fully or accurately described. From an analysis of these extended controversies, I have sought to trace the connections that show – as never before – the economic, social, and political links that bind together the histories of Quebec, Ontario, and the Prairies.

In preparing the ground for that appraisal, Chapter 1 lays down an analytical framework to refine our understanding of the key terms, above all "farms" and "markets." Chapter 2 takes the reader step by step through the debates stemming from exchanges between Fernand Ouellet and his critics and supporters. Chapter 3 looks at the work of the historians who have compared the agriculture of Quebec and Ontario. Chapter 4 steps back to assess the larger scholarly controversy over the use of the staples thesis in Canadian economic history, while Chapter 5 focuses on David Gagan's thesis of an agricultural crisis in mid-century Ontario and critical responses to his work. Chapter 6 draws together the historiography of early Prairie settlement, particularly that on ethnic conflict between French and English, and the impact of the resolution of that conflict on subsequent European arrivals on the Plains. Chapter 7 reviews the widespread false assumption in the scholarly literature that Canadian land allocation to farmers and railways followed that of the Americans. Canadian land granting practice was not only strikingly different but also produced very different outcomes in the disposal of public lands. Chapter 8 reveals that native peoples under the numbered treaties made the first large-scale attempt to apply European sedentary farming to the Prairies. Their failures tell as much about the government's attitudes toward them as about the suitability of wooden ploughs with iron shares. Chapter 9 examines five contentious issues around delays in settlement, start-up costs, farm families, livestock, and opening the Palliser Triangle. The conclusion draws together the assessments of all the controversies covered in this book about the history of nineteenth-century Canadian agricultural history to state directly my own interpretation of how they interconnect.

Farm Families and Markets – Peasants, Pioneers, and Profit Maximizers

The debates in the history of Canadian agriculture reflect several conceptions of what a farmer was. Some are specific to various times and regions and relate to emerging commercial markets. Before beginning to examine those debates, it is useful first to clarify some of these differing concepts that underlie and perhaps exacerbate them. It is also useful to clearly formulate the "ideal types" of farmer found in the historical literature and locate them on the spectrum of market relationships, in order to relate the usage of those ideal types to the work of several leading social and economic historians of farming. By putting farmers' relations with markets on a spectrum, we gain at once a more flexible framework to deal with the great variety of market relations revealed by empirical research and a ready way to compare and classify those differences.

FARMING AND INDEPENDENCE

Until well past the mid-nineteenth century, the primary motive for European settlement of North America was the acquisition of land as the path to independence. In terms of the society left behind, land ownership meant the achievement (maintenance or restoration, in some cases) of "independence." Migrants aspired to the immediate social status of landowner and the eventual economic status of persons who were not dependent on the personal will of any other individual. By the mid-eighteenth century, the habitant of New France held himself to be superior to the *paysan* of old France. For the settler from Britain taking up land as property owner, under the 1791 Constitution Act he was a voter, a status to which only a small minority in the British Isles could have aspired before 1832 or even 1867.

Once sufficient forest had been cleared, the settler could hope to add economic independence to political and social standing.[1] Although the search for higher wages and more regular employment had motivated substantial numbers of Europeans to migrate, aspiring farmers in Canada saw regular dependence on wage labour as unworthy of their new (or prospective) status.[2] Although at times it might be necessary, persistent resort to it undermined the independence they sought.

Historians have applied several classifications in seeking to understand how newly transplanted Europeans sought to farm the land. Some have argued that at least some of Europe's rural migrants sought to recreate the peasant communities they had left behind.[3] Others have seen them as representatives of the rising commercial order in Europe, seeking land as capital on which to grow and sell cash crops for the Old World.[4] Almost all have recognized that initially the making of a farm would be the primary occupation, whether it was clearing trees to convert forest into farmland in the St Lawrence lowlands or breaking sod on the short-grass prairie.[5] The most contention has not been produced by the attempts to define the ideal type of the farmer but rather by the attempts to apply terms such as "peasant" farmer, "pioneer" farmer, and "profit-maximizing" (or "commercial" or "capitalist") farmer to North American agriculture.

IDEAL TYPES OF FARMERS

What do we mean when we refer to certain persons in the nineteenth century as "farmers"? What did they mean when they called themselves "farmers"? Today, we use the term to mean those who derive their principal livelihood from farming, that is, from the operation of a farm.[6] In Canada in the nineteenth century the term may sometimes have been used rather differently. Its meaning was certainly tied to social status.

At that time, social status depended to a substantial degree on one's relation to property, and especially to landed property. Two men working in Upper Canada to clear the forest on another man's land might have had quite different social standings, though their *economic* positions may have been nearly identical. One bedded down in a lean-to next to the landowner's log house after eating the supper provided by the landowner's wife. The other went home to the lean-to on his own lot to eat a supper that may have been more meagre than that of his co-worker – yet this second man's social status was considerably higher. Although he might have been only a "location ticket holder," having

only conditional rights to occupy his lot prior to completing the settlement conditions that would allow him to patent it, he was commonly
viewed as eligible to vote, as a budding yeoman farmer.

How would this man describe himself? He would most probably
report his occupation as "farmer" even when he might have had to earn
his subsistence by clearing another farmer's land or go further afield to
find wage labour to sustain himself and his family. A common jibe at
pioneer farmers was that they were too easily led astray from clearing
their own land by the prospect of wages working in the lumber camps
during the winter or the ease of keeping a tavern on a country road.[7] The
expectation of most literate Upper Canadians was that pioneers should
focus all their energy on making their own farm as the surest way to
secure the social and economic position to which they aspired. However,
the need to provide subsistence to their family, and possibly also some
of the "conveniences" of life, frequently led pioneer farmers (and others
much longer on the land) to seek out what we might call parallel occupations to supplement what the farm itself could provide.

It was not uncommon in rural areas to find farmers who had craft
skills. These artisans, such as shoemakers, wheelwrights, or weavers,[8]
had found it both socially and economically rewarding to begin a farm
while following their craft. As farmers they enjoyed a higher social status
than as mechanics or artisans. Also in rural areas there might not have
been enough demand for their output (at least in the early period of
settlement) to make a living. A farm allowed them to at least partially
feed themselves as well as develop a capital asset that could later be sold.

For Canadian historiography, much more problematic than artisanal
work has been the category of *regular* (not occasional) off-farm work by
farmers as unskilled migratory or seasonal workers. Several Quebec historians have used the "agro-forestier" model to describe what they see
as lumber companies exploiting French Canadians' desire to have farms,
using marginal farmers' *need* for an off-farm income to create a dependent and underpaid labour force in the forests and lumber mills.[9] It is
argued that lumber companies encouraged French-Canadian families to
take up farming on land that would never provide adequate subsistence
for their families. Moreover, the families' work on their marginal land,
by providing for *part* of their subsistence needs, enabled the lumber
companies to pay less than a living wage to those they hired. Implicit in
the agro-forestier critique is an assumption that a family farm *ought* to
be able to become reasonably independent once it was fully developed.
For those wishing to become farmers, to be *compelled* to seek regular

off-farm employment lowered their social status, compounding the impact of their below-market wages.

In other regions, farmers may have had regular employment in a number of non-farm roles in fisheries, fish-processing plants, and various aspects of the forest industry. Where the size of the farm and the quality of its soil limited its output, as in many cases in the Maritimes and parts of British Columbia, non-farm occupations may have been necessary for the family's prosperity or even survival.[10] How should we classify "farmers" who spent most of their time off the farm? Were they migrant unskilled workers whose families lived on small holdings? Multi-occupational workers who were no more farmers than they were fish-plant workers? Farmers with alternative seasonal employments? Likely the last would have been the favoured description by most such persons in the nineteenth century, not necessarily because they believed that they were on their way to becoming fully independent farmers but because they recognized that – out of the array of identities to which their various employments entitled them – that of farmer held the highest social status.

The three labels of peasant, pioneer, and profit maximizer,[11] in the language of Max Weber, can be read as signifying three ideal types of farmer.[12] On occasion, historians have confused the ideal type with reality, *assuming* the reality of the ideal type and letting such unarticulated assumptions stand in for actual evidence. Moreover, they have endowed these ideal types with a certain moral authority. They have become implicit norms of how a group of farmers ought to be farming; those who appeared to deviate from the assumed norm have been implicitly or explicitly scolded for their inconsistency. It is important to separate out of past usage the ideal, or pure type, and then ask to what extent the behaviour of those previously described as *being* (say) peasants has actually fit the ideal.

The peasant farm family's goal was to achieve the highest possible degree of autonomy from external circumstances, in order to avoid starvation and make provision for the next generation. The usual means of attaining this autonomy was through the highest possible degree of self-sufficiency. In terms of neo-classical microeconomics, then, the peasant family household economy was geared not to profit maximization but to risk avoidance. The motive for increasing output or assets (such as cleared land) was to ensure that, whatever the circumstances (e.g., general crop failure), this peasant family would never starve. The peasant mode of production was centred on the farm family. While all family members did not have the same economic roles – these were divided according to gender – all contributed to the household economy.

The peasant household could have regularly participated in local produce and labour-exchange markets, but distant markets dealing in money were marginal to it. A bumper crop coinciding with high prices offered by local merchants could have led to the peasant selling what was surplus to family needs. In this way, at irregular intervals, he would have acquired some cash to pay for essential needs that could not be met from the farm household itself or the local community market of labour and produce exchange. Farm debts, thus, might be routinely accumulated over long periods, to be paid off when a bumper crop and high prices made that feasible.[13] There is some evidence from eighteenth-century Lower Canada that the most prosperous peasant households acquired land beyond even the long-term needs of their progeny as an investment outlet for the surplus their farms produced over their subsistence needs.[14]

For the pioneer farmer, the immediate goal was to *create* a farm (where the peasant already had a farm) large enough to support the family, either by provision of subsistence or by off-farm sales. The usual means for attaining this goal was to "break" "wild" land, either by forest clearing in central and eastern Canada or sod busting on the prairies. The intention was to create a productive asset, sometimes for sale (to realize a capital gain), but more often to support a family by its production. The pioneer mode of production was thus a mixture of production for market and production for subsistence, whichever was most feasible, to sustain the family through the period of creating a viable farm.[15]

The pioneer farm family, like the peasant farm family, was highly structured by gender roles. Fathers and older sons devoted most of their time to forest clearing. Ideally this work would have been done on their own farm, but if the farm was not yet self-sufficient, they might have had to earn their subsistence by clearing the land of a more established farm that already generated a surplus over and above its own immediate needs. Women's labour was confined to the kitchen garden, the dairy, henhouse, barn, pigpen, sheepfold, and the house. Depending on their social status, background, and the degree of need, women might also join in harvesting crops on their own farmland and even help in some land clearing operations that were particularly labour intensive.[16] Mrs Agnes Turnbull, whose family took up land on the River St Clair, described this common pattern in a letter to a friend: "Since we came up here [my husband] has been obliged to hire out a good deal and by a little industry and perseverance we are now able to pay [for] our land[;] provisions of all kinds are very high. Owing to my husband's being hired out I was obliged to be farmeress in the bush. I planted eight bushels [of potatoes], and from that we had a produce of eighty."[17]

The pioneer farm, if it was oriented toward becoming a commercial farm, was related to two markets – the local one, largely based on barter, and the distant one, based on money and credit. The intermediate goal for such a pioneer was to be free of the constraint of having to exchange labour for subsistence on the local market, while increasing his dependence on distant markets by the successful production and sale of cash crops. His ultimate goal was to be a cash purchaser in the local market – hiring labour to speed further clearing, purchasing not only the necessaries but also the conveniences of life locally, financed by the sale of cash crops to local or external markets. One example of such a successful transition would have been considered the pioneer family's ability to purchase cloth or clothing at local stores rather than relying on domestically produced cloth.[18]

Whether pioneers were profit or subsistence oriented, their land needs were defined by three criteria. First, to begin the clearing process, they had to have enough land to eventually support a family. In Upper Canada, the fifty-acre "pauper lots" had this function.[19] Second, they wanted to have sufficient additional land to maintain clearing when a viable farm had been created (if not by them, then their heirs). Third, they needed the prospect of an ample supply of land (almost always wild lands) to set up their sons or sons-in-law with the beginning of farms of their own. There is abundant evidence that pioneers aiming at commercially oriented farms eagerly sought to acquire wild lands as a speculation. They counted on their own success in building a farm to substantially raise the value of the wild land in their immediate vicinity. Their land speculations seem to have been geared to more immediate prospects of profit than those of peasant households, but this might well have been only a matter of degree or opportunity. In terms of neo-classical microeconomics, the pioneer was in a phase of asset accumulation in which his stock of wealth increased even though his off-farm cash income could have been small and irregular.

For the third ideal type, the commercial farmer or profit maximizer, the goal was to have a high and stable cash income, no easy task in a world where both harvests and prices could fluctuate greatly from year to year.[20] The usual means for attaining this goal was the efficient production of one or more cash crops in high demand. The motive for increasing output was to achieve the optimum scale of production, to yield the highest possible income from the resources available. As Clarence Danhof has pointed out, this type of farming could not be carried on in any systematic way until farmers had a means of accounting that took both costs and revenues into account.[21]

The profit-maximizing farmer's mode of production was that of an independent commodity producer. (The *locus classicus* of this was the mid-twentieth-century prairie wheat farmer who drove to town to buy a loaf of bread.) The farm family's labour needed to play only a marginal economic role, most evident, and closest to being essential, at harvest. Otherwise farm household production could have been so marginal that it was possible by the height of Prairie settlement for the first time to conceive of a bachelor farmer.[22] In fact Paul Voisey in his study of the district of Vulcan found an enduring population of bachelor farmers in southern Alberta both before and after the First World War.[23]

The commercial farmer's land acquisitions were dictated by what he considered the necessary scale of operations for profitable production. He readily entered into land speculation, not only in rural property but also in urban property where there was an opportunity. Voisey found that in the early settlement of southern Alberta, farming was often incidental to the expected gains from sale of the land.[24]

In terms of neo-classical microeconomics, the profit maximizer responds rapidly and efficiently to the market's price signals. He is ready to shift from one crop to another, and even from one type of farming to another, depending on the demands of the market. If wheat demand falls and demand for dairy products is strong, he converts his farm from wheat to dairy cattle. He is quick to take up whatever new mechanical innovation promises to increase efficiency, output, or both. To make the necessary purchases of capital equipment, he is prepared to borrow substantial sums where he believes the increased profits will more than cover the costs of the debt. If all feasible forms of farming become less rewarding than another occupation, he will be prepared to move his capital out of farming altogether, to pursue a more profitable enterprise in another industry.

The peasant ideal type, as defined above, obviously lies closest to the pole of pure subsistence farming. As V.C. Fowke has argued, it would have been almost impossible for a European immigrant to have operated a purely subsistence farm.[25] However, the peasant would likely not have been a single, fixed point on the continuum of market participation but rather would reflect a range from minimal to maximal participation. No matter how highly a family farm household might have prized its independence, if unusually favourable circumstances yielded a bumper crop – one able to supply far more than the family's subsistence for the foreseeable future – and, at the same time, high prices were being offered in the neighbourhood for that surplus, any peasant would have made the sale in a given year. This did not mark an erosion of family independence or an aberration in *mentalité*, just an opportunity to gain more for the family at no significant cost. If successive good crop years combined with continued high prices, the family could have continued the pattern of selling its surpluses without departing from its primary orientation. It can be argued that the market actually expanded the family's range of choices: the more it sold, the more it could buy, and therefore the less it would have to make for itself. Peasant households, like native peoples in the fur trade, realized they could reduce the most onerous part of their workload by buying what was most difficult to make. This hinged, however, on being able to sell enough to buy what was needed on an ongoing basis. But what if revenues fell (whether because of a poor crop or low prices, or both) below what was required to purchase what was needed? A family could try to revert back to making what it needed. However, this regression from the market depended upon the family still having the skills, equipment, and resources to again make what it had found easier to purchase. Thus many households faced the issue of borrowing money to purchase desired consumer goods in the hopes of paying off the debt at the next bumper crop. In this way an increasing dependence on the market could lead a family to a further dependence on credit. This is quite a different matter from borrowing to increase a farm's productive capacity. The debt borrowed for the acquisition of production goods (more land, machinery, livestock) could be paid off from the increased productivity of the farm, due to the acquisition of the new resources. However, consumption debts had to rely on future *above-average* earnings to wipe the slate clean. Some at the time clearly saw debt – at least of a certain type – as undermining the farm family's independence.[26]

As the peasant ideal type lies closest to the pole of pure subsistence, so the profit-maximizer ideal type is closest to the pure commercial farmer. As noted, in the nineteenth century almost every type of farming in British North America continued to have a subsistence side. Indeed, in all of North America, only Southern plantation owners could afford to debate whether it was more economical to feed their slaves by

homegrown produce or more profitable to devote the plantation solely
to a cash crop and buy the necessary subsistence.[27]

To an even greater degree than with the peasant ideal type, the profit-
maximizer ideal type represents not a fixed point on the spectrum but a
range of values. Where market access was very limited, even an avow-
edly commercial farmer may have had to raise nearly everything that
was consumed on the farm. His market participation might amount
to an annual trip to town, carrying only high-value goods like potash,
staves, and wheat. An older, more settled area offered far more opportunities for market participation, to the extent of weekly or even daily
market exchanges.

Clearly the pioneer ideal type does not appear at any one point on the
spectrum – or, rather, can appear at almost *any* point. The family taking up a tract of forest to farm could have come with almost no resources or with a complete complement of food, furniture, livestock, and
other possessions. (Pioneers were not just found in the distant back-
woods; as late as 1840, a process of in-filling was still going on in lakeside townships in Upper Canada.[28]) These variables meant that pioneer
farmers sometimes were virtually pure subsistence farmers (if we take
their initial endowment of goods out of account) – too far from any market to sell or purchase anything, at least in their first years on the land.
At the other extreme, they may have been regularly selling their labour
to purchase subsistence by clearing a neighbour's land and devoting such
of their own land as they had cleared exclusively to wheat, in order to
sell it to purchase foodstuffs that could not yet be raised as readily on
their clearing.

TYPES OF MARKETS

Markets, like farmers, have been described as ideal types. In the first type
are local, often reciprocal, networks of exchange, goods, and labour.
These were valued primarily for their use value rather than their potential to facilitate future exchange, i.e., exchange value. The second type
are external or regional markets, which featured impersonal dealings
based on exchange value. In these local merchants became part of the
scene and matters become conceptually more complex. Store accounts
of local clients were often kept in money terms, farmers being credited
with money sums when they brought their produce for sale, and deb-
ited when they took away goods, with never a coin in sight. As M.L.
Magill commented on the businesses of William Allan, a leading Toronto

businessman, "except for the official class hardly anyone in the community handled five shillings in cash in six months."[29]

The extent to which farmers were integrated into markets beyond their local community can be thought of in two senses. First, what proportion of the farm's produce was disposed of off-farm? Second, to what extent were local merchants integrated with regional or international markets? Price convergence between local and international markets is considered to be strong evidence that the second type was going on; to the extent that local merchants actively sought to gather local surpluses by offering higher prices, they sped the integration of farms with larger markets.[30] For purposes of determining whether or not a farm was primarily subsistence oriented, the first sense of market integration would be more important.

Farmers' relationships with markets are best seen as a continuum, from pure subsistence farming at one extreme to pure commercial farming at the other. Four issues arise with such a spectrum of relationships: model linearity as implying an ideal of progress, the perils of bipolar typologies, the role of staples, and farming as an exclusive or non-exclusive occupation.

The models that both left and right apply to the question of farmers' relationships to markets reflect a strong linear or teleological presumption of progress. Marxists believe that they know how history is unfolding. For them, the farmers of the nineteenth century, by definition, must have been in the midst of a "transition to capitalism."[31] However, at that time the only self-evident "transition" was forest into farmland. (Neither had that transition begun with European settlement, since Native peoples had been clearing forests for centuries before the arrival of the newcomers.[32]) New Economic History, which introduced neo-classical microeconomics into the study of history, similarly foresees the inevitable triumph of the market over tradition. In this presumption, economics mirrors an image common to several social sciences, which understand time as a two-stage process: a traditional past and modernity.[33] Before modernity, there existed only timeless tradition, within which no significant change ever took place. The only meaningful change was that of modernization, in which tradition gave way to modernity.[34]

There is no intent here to mount a defence of the ideal of progress. With Ranke, I hold that "every epoch is immediate to God."[35] Nineteenth-century farm families should be understood in terms of what they actually were, instead of what someone thinks they were inevitably to become. Rather than assume that over time farmers *must* become more and more integrated with markets, whether local, regional, or international, we must ask to what extent farmers in a given time and place did participate in whatever markets were available to them.

However, when we turn our backs on the ideal of progress, we should not lose sight of another sense of the term. The European settlement of the New World created a situation for which contemporary Europe provided few examples: expansion onto an open land frontier.[36] There was a dynamic in the settlement of new, fertile land that had long since disappeared in Europe, except on its furthest margins. Thus, as lands were being continuously put under cultivation where relatively few had been cultivated before, there was a "material progress" in the sense of new resources being constantly added to the agriculture of the Americas. To capture this dynamic, we need a category of farming not to be found in seventeenth- or eighteenth-century Europe. The commonest term for this novelty has been "pioneer."

It is possible to define a bipolar model to represent the full range of possibilities for farmers' participation in markets that does not imply inevitable movement from one pole to the other. Such a model can be found in neo-classical microeconomics, which describes all possible market structures initially on the basis of the sole criteria of the number of firms in the market. If there is only one seller, the market is called a monopoly (if only one *buyer*, a monopsony). If there are many firms – so many that no one firm's decisions can have any effect on the market as a whole – then the market is called a perfectly competitive one. However, for a market to qualify fully as perfect competition, supplementary criteria are required: perfect knowledge, perfect mobility of the factors of production, freedom of entry and exit, homogenous product, and no government interference. All other market structures fall within these two extremes. For example, if there are many firms but their products are not homogenous, then that variation might give one a slight degree of monopoly power because its product can be differentiated from that of other firms. Economists call this imperfect competition. Similarly, if there are only a few firms, the market structure is called an oligopoly.

A similarly bipolar pair of logical categories can also define the two extremes that could exist in the relationships between farm families and markets. At the one end there could be a farm where the family wholly consumed all that was cultivated, and moreover, the family could not expect to consume anything they did not produce. At the other extreme would be the farm on which everything grown was for sale in a market. As with the extremes of the microeconomics continuum of market structures, whether there are *any* examples of each – perfect competition and pure monopoly, the purely subsistence farmer and the purely commercial farmer – does not matter to the usefulness of the two categories. While we may be able to observe some cases that lie close to each extreme, that is not the utility of the model. Rather, as with market structures and the number of firms, the value of the continuum lies in allowing us to see what *degree* of market participation there was and to ask what factors *influenced* that degree of participation.

The degrees of market participation can be explored in terms of the proportion of farm production that goes to market and, correspondingly, the proportion of family consumption found off the farm. Clarence Danhof proposed just such a spectrum.[37] Closest to the pole of pure subsistence in nineteenth-century North America were many farm households that kept off-farm consumption to an absolute minimum of essentials (mainly metal goods) and sold only the "accidental" surplus produced by an outstandingly good crop year: "Although no farm was wholly self-sufficient, there were many that produced little more than the products necessary to the family's subsistence requirements for food, fuel, and shelter. The objective of such operations was to produce as wide a range of products as the family required for consumption and a surplus of some commodities in excess of family needs to be sold or exchanged for items that could not be produced. Such farms differed significantly in objectives and in management from farms that viewed the production of family requirements as incidental to maximizing the production of products to be marketed for a money income."[38] While Danhof recognized that in terms of the proportion of production, one type of farm "shaded into the other," he proposed a rough rule of thumb to mark a transition phase on the continuum: "We define as a subsistence operation any farm that devoted 60 per cent or more of its net product to on-the-farm family consumption." Clearly, a farm where the family routinely buys goods like cotton cloth or tea and just as regularly sells some farm products to pay for its purchases is a very different farm from the pure subsistence model. Yet another distinct stage is reached when the farm begins to allocate some resources specifically to produce something for sale. Only in the modern era do we encounter the totally commercial farm.

Another of Danhof's important contributions is his observation that the complete profit maximizer could only emerge once a farmer had adopted a system of accounting sufficiently sophisticated to show what profit each part of the farm operation could make. As long as farm accounts were only lists of debits to be paid (and possibly produce sold), a farmer could not actually calculate profit and loss on a given activity such as livestock or tobacco production. To know if an activity were profitable, all costs (including the farmer's own labour input and farm-produced inputs such as feed grains) needed to be taken into consideration, not just cash outlays and cash receipts.[39]

Numerous factors could be at work to influence why an individual family farm or a farm community participated in the market to the degree that they did. For example, a farm household might have been able to produce some textiles, such as wool and linen, with great effort but may have preferred others, such as cotton, that could be readily purchased for something more easily produced on the farm, such as chickens. By producing for the market, the family farm household could have expanded the range of consumer choices available to it and lessened its workload.[40]

Throughout the nineteenth century in British North America (and in much of the northern United States as well), most farm families expected to supply most of their own needs from within the farm. When we speak of a given farm family's goals, it is necessary to distinguish between the gender-defined roles within that family. The responsibility for subsistence fell largely to the women in the household and the children working under their direction. The wife and older daughters produced and processed the food to feed the family and the textiles to clothe them. The latter activity might have entailed production of raw materials such as flax and wool.[41] The role of the adult males was largely defined in terms of capital accumulation (land clearing), production of crops, construction, off-farm labour (for wages directly or to earn part of the family's subsistence), and a variety of on-farm processing and manufacturing pursuits. An example of the latter would have been men breaking flax to prepare the fibre for further processing. Some production, such as potash and barrel staves, was intended for off-farm sale. The spectrum proposed, from pure subsistence to pure commercial operation, thus applies to the *total* operation of the farm, recognizing that within even the most commercial of nineteenth-century farms, women continued to devote their considerable labours almost wholly toward providing for the family's subsistence.

In several debates over peasants – whether Canadiens, Scottish crofters, or Ukrainians – it has been argued by some that they were so bound by tradition that they failed to act rationally. Against that criticism, others argue for the integrity of culture over economics. There is more to life than mere instrumental reason, calculating maximum utility. Indeed, economists, who speak of "bounded rationality" and "rational ignorance," have recognized this. People, even when striving to make rational decisions, can only make those choices within the bounds of what is available to them. Moreover, few will be able to canvas *every* possible option before making a decision. This is because for many situations the effort required to gain the information necessary would not be compensated for even by the most favourable outcome. Thus, economists understand that because acquiring information entails costs, many people will rationally choose not to seek information whose benefit could not or would probably not compensate for those costs. Some of those bounds within which rationality works may be cultural, especially linguistic boundaries. Thus to posit a bounded rationality does not necessarily mean that one has entirely discounted cultural factors in the choices of economic actors.[42]

For much of the twentieth century the prevailing model for explaining Canada's economic history was the staples thesis developed by W.A. MacIntosh and expounded by Harold Innis. A common criticism has been that it focused too exclusively on the export of a few staple products. In the case of agriculture, it was wheat. But there is more to the economy than production; there is more to life that producing. The founder of modern economic theory, Adam Smith, wrote that "Consumption is the sole end and purpose of production; and the interest of the producer ought to be attended to only so far as it may be necessary for promoting that of the consumer."[43] Even Innis, in setting forth his version of the famous staples thesis, clearly saw the production of staples for export as a process driven by the settlers' consumption needs, not by a need to produce or a need to export: "The migrant is not in a position immediately to supply all his needs and to maintain the same standard of living as that to which he has been accustomed. If those needs are to be supplied he will be forced to rely on goods which are obtainable from the mother country." While many immigrants brought with them a stock of goods they hoped would enable them to flourish in the New World, they had significant, ongoing consumption needs that could not be met directly with the resources of the new continent: "Goods were produced as rapidly as possible to be sold at the most advantageous price in the home market in order to purchase other goods essential to the maintenance and improvement of the current standard of living."[44]

Where Innis appears to have erred is in mistaking a part of the colonial economy for the whole. He focused on production for export and thus omitted from his field of vision all other sorts of production, such as production for subsistence and production for local or internal markets. In the era of New France (especially in the eighteenth century), this skewed vision resulted in a picture in which the majority of the population had little or nothing to do with the part of the economy on which Innis focused most attention: fur exports. He missed a large part not only of the agricultural economy but also of the forest industries of the nineteenth century. Douglas McCalla has shown that almost half the forest products produced in Upper Canada went to internal markets (at least internal to British North America) rather than to transatlantic exports.[45]

Not yet clear is the relationship between local markets and the international or export market. Winnifred Rothenberg has suggested the existence of relationships between local and regional markets and international markets in eighteenth- and nineteenth-century New England for important farm outputs. First, there is evidence of price convergence over time. While both local and international prices fluctuated, there is a long-run pattern (1750–1850) in which the range of local prices came more and more within the range of the international prices. Individual farmers engaged in the necessary arbitrage to effect this result by being prepared to haul their produce to ever more distant markets. Second, there is evidence of the parallel movement of local and international prices: when international prices rose, so did local ones; when international prices fell, so did local ones.[46]

Can one find a wholly internal drive amongst farmers that compelled them to resort to markets, whether local or international? Daniel Vickers has suggested that farmers' concern to establish their sons on farms of their own led to more intense competition between farmers for new lands, as good land became scarcer or as the open land frontier became more distant. This competition drove up land prices, which compelled farmers to produce for sale in markets in order to raise the money they needed to buy land.[47] In this ingenious scenario, farmers are the source of increased market participation, not because they wanted particular manufactured commodities from the market but in order to compete successfully in the local land market.

Settlers were unlikely to attempt to sell produce off-farm where they had little interest in consuming things from off-farm (here, "things" may include local land resources). To describe staple production as export-led growth is not to imply that farmers were helpless victims of an impersonal process. After all, it was the decision of immigrants to settle in the New World that had summoned the transatlantic trade into existence.

THE DEBATES

In the long-running debates over the nature of the early nineteenth-century agricultural crisis in Lower Canada, Fernand Ouellet has taken the position that habitant farmers were peasants, pretty much according to the ideal type. As such, he argued that after 1802 they were less and less able to respond to auspicious market signals because the supply of new good land was exhausted. Ultimately most were forced to retreat into as complete a degree of self-sufficiency as possible.

When Ouellet makes a strong case for a distinctive *ancienne regime mentalité*, he seems to argue for seeing the habitants as purely peasants. Yet it is also part of his argument that many habitants responded to favourable market signals at the end of the eighteenth century, expanding their holdings of cleared land, which led to the successively higher cyclical peaks of wheat and flour exports between 1770 and 1802. High wheat prices due to strong long-term demand from Britain, he believed, led many to expand wheat production. In his view, they did this by clearing land more rapidly and devoting more of their best land to wheat. However, when new good land became more and more scarce at the beginning of the nineteenth century, Ouellet saw many habitants as failing to adapt to this new market situation. In part he considers their adherence to a given set of agricultural practices to have resulted from a cultural conservatism at least in part due to their presumed *mentalité*, which stopped them from responding to the continuing strong demand from Britain. As newly cleared land became a smaller and smaller proportion of the total cultivated acreage, as the new land cleared was of less and less natural fertility, and as wheat yields began to fall on land repeatedly cropped with wheat, Ouellet saw many habitants who were unable to maintain an annual surplus above family needs turning away from the market not by choice but by consequence of their inability to innovate, to adopt new agricultural techniques that presumably could have kept yields high.[48]

Ouellet's critics often portray his argument in an over-simplified form.[49] It must be said that sometimes his own general presentations of his work give the critics ammunition.[50] These polemical exchanges, however, miss his more nuanced presentation of the variety of habitant responses to the growing crisis, brought on by the increasing shortage of good virgin land after the turn of the nineteenth century. In his study of Quebec District, he showed that *all* habitants did not react in the same way to the onset of the agricultural crisis. Some opted to remain with wheat as a crop despite declining yields, even at the expense of denying some of their children a share in the family estate. Others followed the classic pattern of subdividing land holdings amongst their children, who had to turn the smaller farms more and more toward subsistence crops.[51]

Allan Greer has argued that the fundamental orientation of habitant farming was always subsistence. In his view, most (but not all) of the lower Richelieu Valley habitants were peasants near the ideal type whose surpluses were appropriated not directly by the market but by traditional elites. While the larger-scale habitant producers sold surpluses in good crop years, he believes that most did not normally grow crops for market or sell directly to markets. Habitants had both seigneurial dues and church tithes to pay, and thus their surpluses went not directly to market but to seigneurs and priests who marketed grain on a regular basis. Some larger-scale habitant producers did deal directly with markets, at least on occasion, but even this group consumed most of their produce and supplied most of the farm family's needs by the labour and resources of the farm family household.[52]

Local studies of individual seigneuries that have focused on the habitants (as distinct from those written from the seigneurial perspective), such as those by Thomas Wien and Christian Dessureault, have shown that eighteenth- and early nineteenth-century habitants did not form a community of equals. (This is also evident in Greer's study, although he does not focus on it.) A substantial minority – call them the "landed poor"– lacked even the basic stock of farm equipment and animals. But there emerged an elite whose accumulation of wild land, cleared land, livestock, and an ever-fuller array of farm equipment, livestock, and even artisanal tools was clearly above the average. Wien argued that this "peasant accumulation" at least in part reflected the lack of other outlets or uses for the surpluses being produced on the largest and best-stocked farms in the late eighteenth century.[53]

Normand Séguin, from his work on the Saguenay region, has described "le systèm agro-forestier" in which the farmer who could not make a living for the family on the farm of necessity had to work in the forest industry as well. The ideal type of the independent peasant enters his model implicitly as the norm against which the agro-forestier deviation is measured. Séguin and his followers clearly see this form of combined farm and forest economy as bad, a system of employers exploiting marginal farmers by offering wages below subsistence level. Only by combining the produce of the inadequate farm with the below-subsistence wage of the forestry job could these families survive. In Séguin's view, for a farmer to work in the forest was implicitly bad because it undermined the goal of autonomy, the true goal of every farmer.[54]

The moralizing content of this view becomes explicit in Guy Boisclaire's criticism of J.I. Little for suggesting that Eastern Township farmers on marginal land might have deliberately sought out other economic activities to complement their farming occupation. Little was also faulted for suggesting that French-Canadian elites, not just the evil anglo-Canadian businessmen, had sought to foster such a strategy of settlement and development.[55] Also implicit in Boisclaire's criticism is the idea that Canadiens ought to be farmers who did nothing but farm – they *ought* to be peasants, pursuing economic autonomy rather than market opportunity, especially where the pursuit of such opportunity might lead them into becoming dependent upon *les anglais* in any way. In contrast to Séguin, yet drawing originally from the same region, Gérard Bouchard offered an alternative model of co-integration. He saw the farm families as active agents pursuing their own goals in opening new farms as well as working off-farm, rather than passive victims of large forestry companies.[56]

When we turn from Quebec to Ontario, the presumed dominant ideal type switches from that of peasant to that of profit-maximizing commercial farmer. Perhaps no one has been so unguarded in stating this assumption as John McCallum: "In terms of its contribution to cash income, wheat was more important to the Ontario farmer of the 1850s than to the Saskatchewan farmer of today [1980]; in the 1850s wheat made up about three-quarters of the cash sales of Ontario farmers, and in earlier years the proportion would have been no lower."[57] Something like that orientation perhaps lay behind Marvin McInnis's reaction to his own findings from studying the 1861 Agricultural Census for Canada West. McInnis allowed that he was surprised to find the very low level of off-farm sales reported.[58] The presumed stark contrast between the self-sufficient Quebec peasant and the market-oriented Ontario commercial farmer turns out to be in part a contrast of ideal types rather than contrasting historical realities. At the middle of the nineteenth century, Ontario farms, like Quebec farms, consumed most of what they produced and produced most of what they consumed.

However, this similarity between farm types in the two Canadas should not be overemphasized. The distribution of wealth and income on Ontario farms reflected a pattern that was clearly above all but the most affluent of Quebec farms. And the key to this difference turns on sales of wheat to external markets – shades of Innis! Those Ontario counties that grew the least wheat looked most like the median farm counties of

Quebec.[59] But we are not driven all the way back to the staples thesis, which erred in mistaking a part of Canadian farming (wheat grown for export) for the whole of Canadian farming. Our much greater knowledge today of the detailed output of Canadian farms at mid-century allows us to put that one part into proper context.

Douglas McCalla's work on the application of the wheat staple thesis to Upper Canada's history has been confounded in another way by the attempt to take ideal types as norms beginning with the ideal type of the profit-maximizing commercial farmer. McCalla then argued that the staples thesis could not explain the *rate* of economic growth in Upper Canada, because the waves of settlement had little or nothing to do with trends in the prices for wheat.[60] In his more recent work, McCalla noted that settlers did not become wheat exporters the moment they received their location tickets;[61] building a farm (for whatever sort of farming) was the work of a lifetime. The Upper Canadian pioneer farmer's primary orientation was less his wheat crop (if he had one) than the clearing of his land. The rationale of the long-term strategy of farm-making, according to McCalla, was to establish an independent family farm that would include growing a commercial crop. If wheat was the province's main cash crop, then it could have a staple role, even if its price from year to year bore little relation to the rate of settlement. Like Little on the Eastern Townships, McCalla established that the Upper Canadian farm family household was a diverse centre of economic activity, not uniquely or exclusively tied to farming. In his work on the development of local markets and the on-farm production of forest products, he pointed to a diversified family economy that had a range of products to take to market for either sale or exchange.

This latter point has been taken up by Marjorie Cohen, who made a compelling argument that farm families pursued multiple strategies structured by gender. While in the earliest pioneer phase all or almost all production could be consumed on the farm, the men's longer-term strategy was to create (by land clearing) a productive asset and increasingly to grow a commercial crop. Thus Cohen presents two ideal types combined in a single farm family household, with women working largely in peasant mode while the men worked successively in pioneer mode and then either household production or profit-maximizing mode.[62]

Moving west from central Canada to the Canadian prairies at mid-century, we find the ideal types applied in different ways to the mixed-blood peoples of the Red River. An older historiography, shot through with a fairly explicit racism, saw the French and Catholic Métis as unruly nomadic hunters whose agricultural efforts were beneath mention. Civilization was equated with farming, while hunting and fur-trading were considered the activities of a primitive people.[63] The English-speaking Protestant mixed bloods were seen as farmers, the progressive element in the population. However, in reappraisals of Métis life and culture, which have attempted to leave racial stereotypes behind, the ideal types of farming have been applied instead. Douglas Sprague, in order to legitimate Métis claims to Aboriginal land title, has argued that the Métis (or at least some substantial proportion of them) had developed a stable agriculture at Red River, giving up their old nomadic ways.[64] Thus the movement of the Métis out of the new province of Manitoba after 1870 was seen by Sprague and his followers as "dispossession" by English Protestant bigots – mainly from Ontario – which could be compared to the civil war in "bleeding Kansas" prior to the American Civil War.[65]

Sprague and others took the Métis "strip farms" along the riverfront to be the transplantation of Quebec's rural culture into western Canada (though more probably it was an adaptation of the Scottish in-field/outfield system).[66] The notion seems to be implicit that the Métis were on their way, progressing from the status of hunters and traders to that of peasant farmers. However, Gerhardt Ens argued that this equating of farming with progress did not match the reality of Métis life at the Red River at mid-century.[67] Ens contended that many Métis were much more migratory than Sprague allows. A substantial part of the population had already begun to shift further west, away from the Red River, before the crisis of annexation. Ens asserted that by examining Métis movement only after 1870, Sprague had overestimated the impact of ethnic conflict in the new province. In Ens's view the Métis hunters were following a rational economic course in devoting ever more time to the buffalo hunt because of the high prices that could be had for hides. In his view it is the hunters who were increasingly integrated into the capitalist market, which is taken as a measure of progress, in contrast to those who stayed in Red River and clung to a subsistence agriculture.

In fact Métis agriculture at Red River deserves a closer look. Given the extreme variability of the weather, devoting all one's efforts to farming for subsistence at the Red River was hazardous. Crops could be frozen, eaten by insects, or beaten flat by hail, leaving the family without resources to face an extremely severe winter with little or no prospect of drawing resources from elsewhere. The combinations of farming, fishing, hunting, fur-trading, and shipping represented comprehensive strategies for balancing risks to ensure survival in an unforgiving land.

With only the supply of the fur trade as a possible market, Red River farming was unlikely to focus on an exclusively commercial orientation. As well, before the development of dry-land farming, almost all European cultivation would be limited to the bottom land of the river valleys.[68] All of these factors militated against focusing exclusively on farming as a way of life.

From the 1870s to the 1890s, newcomers to the West strove to find the methods necessary to farm the prairie lands. While old problems like clearing the hardwood forest had been left behind in the East, new ones emerged, especially the shorter growing season and the recurring problems of drought. Anthony Ward argued that the series of successive implementations – the drill seed press, the chilled steel plow, the binder – made extensive farming of low-yield prairie soils profitable. Before the 1890s the first arrivals sought by trial and error to find the best way to farm the new region. Some sought locations near wood and water that might enable them to approximate the pioneer subsistence model of Eastern Canada. Within two decades, however, the pioneers learned the advantages of moving away from labour-intensive tree clearing to capital-intensive sod busting. Where their eastern counterparts faced a lifetime of labour to create a viable farm out of forest, prairie pioneers could have one of much larger size in a few years. The promise of much higher returns to scale led most prairie pioneers from the 1890s on to go into substantial debt in order to practise a more extensive capital-intensive farming. Especially with the mechanization of the harvest, the prairie farm could operate on a much greater scale in a much shorter time than had been possible in the East. The price of such debt, however, was a wholehearted commitment to production of a major cash crop whose revenue could service that debt.[69] To the uncertainties of the short growing season and rainfall, prairie farmers added that of dependence on cash crops and long-term debt.[70]

Paul Voisey and others have noted the prevailing official orthodoxy that mixed farming was more secure than one-crop monoculture.[71] While some farmers devoted considerable energies to activities that did not generate off-farm sales (more than Voisey's argument allowed), his conclusion that wheat prevailed holds for much of the prairie grasslands and even much of the parkland as well. Capital-intensive farming required a substantial cash income every year to support the debt that had made the high productivity possible.

Some European ethnic and religious groups sought to re-establish aspects of peasant farming on the Canadian Prairies before the First

World War.[72] However within a few decades it became apparent that peasant farming was either impractical or impossible. In the face of drought, the short-grass prairie would not even yield enough to support a family, ruling out any retreat into subsistence farming. Where peasant immigrants had picked the parkland areas in which subsistence farming might be possible, the returns from capital-intensive farming eventually lured almost all of them away from traditional methods and expectations.

More tragically, in the late 1880s officials in the Indian Affairs Branch imposed peasant farming on treaty Indians. Reserves were supposed to yield no more than subsistence. In spite of several early successful native efforts at commercial farming and ranching, Indian agents, under the new approach, prevented natives from leaving the reserves to sell grain or livestock or from borrowing to purchase farm equipment or live-stock that might compete with local white farmers. The effect of the new regime in the Prairie climate forced treaty Indians into the very depend-ence the policy was supposed to prevent. Denied access to credit, farm equipment, and markets, they could not farm more than large gardens whose output in the uncertain Prairie climate could not guarantee even enough food to feed reserve populations already decimated by disease and, in some cases, starvation.[73]

It was on the Canadian Prairies that the ideal type of the profit maxi-mizer came closest to reality, especially in the drier short-grass region. There, the pioneer phase was much shorter than in the East for most who could afford the necessary equipment to break the prairie sod. The rapid development of farm equipment both reduced farmers' dependence on off-farm labour and increased their dependence on a cash crop to pay the ongoing cost of mechanization. There was limited scope for any form of peasant farming, even in the parklands.[74] The severe drought of the 1930s would strikingly illustrate the difficulty and sometimes even the impossibility of any retreat into self-sufficiency in Prairie farming.

Most immigrants came to British North America in the nineteenth cen-tury looking for land of their own. In the context of Europe's great land rush, John Weaver places Canada (with the brief exception of southern Alberta) in the "small holder/politically influential speculator" portion of the land allocation spectrum.[75] Land holding and granting systems var-ied between regions and over time. Quebec's seigneurial regime offered effectively free grants under feudal obligations with heavy taxes on sales intended to discourage land speculation that applied both to seigneurs and *censitaires*. While in the Eastern Townships, Upper Canada, and the Prairies land was held under English tenure, methods of granting varied.

Until 1826 Upper Canada offered free grants that stipulated settlement conditions.[76] After 1826, the Crown sold its lands, as had always been the case in the Eastern Townships.[77] On the Prairies the federal government simultaneously offered free homesteads and land for sale.[78] Outcomes for individual and corporate speculators varied enormously. Col. Thomas Talbot in Upper Canada amassed an estate of 65,000 acres. But none of it survived his death.[79] The Hudson's Bay Company as a land company on the Prairies was spectacularly successful – far more so than its better-known roles as fur trade company and chain of retail department stores.[80]

It was the prospect of land ownership that drew settlers to North America in the nineteenth century. Many, perhaps most, of those born on farms in British North America in that same century had that same ambition. Broadly speaking they pursued one of three goals that distinguished three types of farmers: those who sought to create a farm, those who sought to maintain a family's autonomy on a farm, and those who sought to have a prosperous farm. The first group, where successful, might join the second or the third. The second was risk averse, where the third would undertake some risk if the profit incentive was great enough. Farmers faced two types of market. In the local community face-to-face exchange was often done by barter and co-operative labour. Then there was the local merchant who was tied by credit and supply to the larger impersonal regional and international markets. The first and second types of farmer could readily participate in local markets, but had to limit their contacts with the wider markets. The pioneer had a very limited ability to carry debt. The peasant had a positive aversion to any long-term debt as a threat to the family's autonomy. Intermediaries might take the peasants' produce to market (seigneurs and priests in Quebec), but most would limit their own direct participation, outside years of bumper harvests. The profit maximizer looked to the larger market for signals, hoping to catch the crest of a wave where a good crop year in North America combined with a poor one in Europe, and peace, allowed uninterrupted shipping across the Atlantic. Each type of farming had its own rewards.

Pioneer, peasant, and profit maximizer: ideal types can be valuable tools. They can establish bases of comparison. But the key to the successful use of an ideal type is not to mistake it for a description of real life. An ideal type has a heuristic function in guiding research: it is not a substitute for research. A given population may have behaviours that fit one aspect of a given ideal type. Consequently it makes sense to concentrate investigation on whether other behaviours fit other aspects of the type. Unfortunately, there has sometimes been a tendency to assume that if some behaviours – which we can readily document – fit, then other behaviours that are not so easily documented will also follow the pattern of the type. A heuristic device cannot hot wire the hard work of research. These definitions and concepts – of farmers and markets – are offered as an aid to the following analysis of the debates over Canadian agriculture in the nineteenth century.

Quebec: An Agricultural Crisis
and Its Critics

Agriculture has been integral to the self-understanding of Quebec. It has been intimately tied to French Canada's sense of its own identity from the Conquest to the mid-twentieth century. Even after most Quebecois lived in urban centres, rural values prevailed until the Quiet Revolution of the 1960s.

Since Fernand Ouellet's controversial thesis of an agricultural crisis beginning in the first decade of the nineteenth century has been central to the major debates over Quebec's rural history for half a century, we begin with a brief overview of that thesis. Ouellet and Jean Hamelin first systematically presented it in an article in 1962.[1] While the agricultural crisis is by no means the whole of Ouellet's analysis of the Lower Canadian economy from 1760 to 1850, his interpretation of that crisis – and his argument for its commencement before the War of 1812 – has attracted more criticism than any other aspect of his work.

Ouellet described New France as having a dual economy of agriculture and the fur trade, with little linkage between these two principle sectors. According to Ouellet, France succeeded in establishing a feudal form of agriculture along the St Lawrence. Royal grants to seigneurs not only gave them substantial territory to administer but also the right to exact significant revenues from those who settled on the land, the *censitaires*. The latter usually cleared enough land to assure themselves a comfortable subsistence, and once that limit was reached, did little ongoing clearing.[2] While wheat composed between 65 per cent and 73 per cent of the harvest between 1706 and 1740, the yields were low, between 6.7 and 4.1 minots per arpent.[3] Ouellet attributed the relatively low yield to the fact that not much new land was being cleared on established farms.[4]

The seigneur and curé took their feudal appropriations in kind (such as the wheat tithe), in labour (the *corvée*), or in cash. To obtain the latter, as well as to purchase essential imports, Ouellet argued, the *censitaires* were regularly obliged to sell wheat when a good harvest provided more than the farm family needed or to find some off-farm employment. Depending upon their location, they found this in the fur trade, fishing, lumber, or the various projects of the French crown such as the St Maurice ironworks.[5] The farms could not supply all the food the fur trade required, but they did provide a substantial portion of its seasonal labour.[6]

While the seigneurial system established and reinforced a feudal mentality in New France, the fur trade represented a commercial system of values. Ouellet considers that these latter values did not have a large impact on New France. The commerce in furs was always a dependent and external trade, reliant on France not only for trade goods and part of its food but also for transatlantic transportation and credit facilities.

In the 1950s the Montreal school of Maurice Séguin and Michel Brunet proposed a "decapitation thesis" to explain the impact of the Conquest. They held that New France's thriving bourgeoisie had been cut off by the British, replaced by English merchants first in the fur trade and then in all subsequent business leadership.[7] Given Ouellet's view of the dominant values in the colony and the dependence of its fur trade, it naturally followed that he would not accept the concept of decapitation. Ouellet emphasized that some Canadiens found British suppliers and creditors and continued to carry on their business as before. There had always been English competition in the eighteenth-century fur trade, from Hudson Bay in the north and Albany in the south. Now some of that competition was located in Montreal. However, Ouellet repeatedly emphasized that twenty years after the Conquest, three-quarters of Montreal's fur traders were still Canadiens.

Ouellet saw the economic impact of the Conquest as positive for the development of agriculture. Within the British Empire, habitants eventually found a more ready market for surpluses of crops such as wheat. An early boom occurred in the years just prior to the American Revolution. However, the Revolution – including the invasion of Quebec – caused disruption, followed by one of the era's worst harvests in 1779. It was only *after* the Revolution that change in the colony began to move more briskly.

Ouellet's sources for this picture of expanding wheat production are the export figures from Quebec City. While his graph is entitled "Production of Wheat," the figures in fact were drawn from wheat and flour exports from the port of Quebec, with adjustments made for Ontario and

American wheat shipped through Quebec.[8] The export records show a rising trend from the early 1770s to a peak in 1802. From his analysis of exports and wheat prices, Ouellet concluded that habitants responded to strong if occasionally uneven demand within the British Empire through expansion of their productive capacity by clearing more land.

Oullet's projection of a subsequent declining trend in *exports* beginning in the first decade of the nineteenth century into a declining trend in *production* is supported by other, more conventional evidence. Various observers at the end of the eighteenth century reported average wheat yields of 10 to 12 *minot* per arpent. By 1822 observers were reporting wheat yields of around 6 *minots* per arpent. The bumper crop of 1831 showed an average of only 7.7 *minots* of wheat per arpent in the 1831 census.[9] Ouellet turned to other sources for confirmation of a trend of falling wheat yields after 1802. The most important of these was the tithe or *dîme*, as reported by the *curés* to their bishop. Despite problems with how tithes were calculated and collected, Ouellet believed these reports provided direct evidence of declining wheat production.[10]

Ouellet's anecdotal sources – letters, travellers' accounts, testimony from committees of the legislature – while pointing up trends similar to those he has found in the quantitative data, sometimes give the reader pause. In numerous cases his specific criticisms of habitant farming practices, for example, are found in the context of a litany of complaint that seems shot through with ethnocentric bias. Such contexts – for instance, describing habitants as litigious dancing drunks – might undermine one's confidence in the impartiality of the criticisms directed at agricultural practice.[11] Ouellet sought to balance these with the testimonies given "without animosity," for example, before the 1816 Lower Canadian legislative assembly inquiry.[12]

Even though habitants were responding to market signals before 1800, Ouellet's view was that most did this primarily by accelerating the clearing of their lands rather than by any improvement in their farming techniques or practices.[13] As Christian Dessureault documented from wealthy habitant inventories, there is no indication that even these became fully commercial farmers: most of their production continued to be consumed on the farm, or at least on their neighbours' farms.[14]

With the rise of the Nor'westers, the only role in the fur trade in which the Canadiens predominated was as the voyageurs who paddled someone else's canoe. This became a major source of off-farm income for the young men of some seigneuries near Montreal.[15] The closing of the Old North West beginning in 1783 coincided with a boom in Quebec agriculture. The twenty years following saw a long-term trend of expansion in wheat exported from the port of Quebec. First peace in North America and then war in Europe and a long string of poor British harvests successively stimulated British demand and restricted competing European wheat producers. A rising trend in prices encouraged Canadiens to clear more and more land.[16] Incomes rose, amongst not only habitants but all social groups linked to agriculture: seigneurs, clergy, and grain merchants. New and more substantial manor houses, new churches, and new merchant houses all reflected the spread of new agrarian wealth through the colony.

The North West Company prospered over three decades. However, the final merger in 1821 meant the end of the Montreal-based fur trade. That closed off the prime commercial outlet of Montreal businessmen, but also ended a major source of what had become lucrative seasonal employment for many young habitants.

However, parallel to the fur trade's decline in the first two decades of the nineteenth century, the Napoleonic Wars gave rise to a third major economic sector: the lumber trade. Called into existence largely by a temporary wartime program in 1806, Canada's lumber trade underwent a transition from a wartime business with an uncertain peacetime future into a more permanent peacetime venture when the imperial Parliament extended colonial preferences in 1815. The new trade provided far more employment than had the fur trade. However, like the post-1783 fur trade, it attracted investment or risk capital mainly from the English-speaking. As well, at Quebec City a substantial shipbuilding industry developed from the colony's lumber resources.

Against that backdrop of shifting commercial opportunities, Quebec agriculture went from prosperity to crisis. While Lower Canada continued to export wheat in substantial quantities up to the War of 1812, Ouellet argued that a longer-term trend of declining production set in after the bumper harvest of 1801–02. This affected the oldest settled areas near Quebec City first, even before the end of the eighteenth century. He saw that decline stemming from a combination of factors whose impact varied across the colony.

The long period of agricultural expansion (1783–1803) had encouraged rapid clearing. Until near the end of the period there was good land for the asking, which ensured that the habitant's children could readily set up farms of their own, if not adjacent to their parents', at least in the same area on lands at least as good as those of their parents. The demographic pendulum swung first west and then east. "New parishes were, it is true, founded in all districts, to absorb for some time the overflow of the old parishes; but the search for land proceeded from one district to another."[17] As the best lands in the Quebec District had all been taken up, toward the close of the eighteenth century new generations migrated to the Montreal District. When even marginal lands grew scarce in the Montreal District, the pendulum swung east to take up the marginal lands in the Trois-Rivières and Quebec districts after 1831.[18] However, around the turn of the century the demographic pressures generated by large habitant families met the territorial limits of both the seigneur-ial system and the fertile lands in the St Lawrence Valley. Less and less frequently were new fertile lands freely available to be granted. There is some debate whether land was being withheld by seigneurs seeking to enforce payment of higher feudal duties or speculating in lumber, or whether arable land was genuinely no longer available within the sei-gneuries.[19] Increasingly the new generation had to either see the sub-division of their parents' land or be forced onto less fertile (and more distant) lands as colonists. In either case – on small farms already too frequently cropped for years or on new farms cut from marginal lands – the habitants practised the traditional techniques of extensive cultiva-tion that now produced falling yields.

Part of Ouellet's account of the agricultural crisis was a criticism of most habitants for not responding to the demographic and land pres-sures by a change in farming techniques. "An enlightened and active elite had succeeded in adapting itself to new demands and techniques but it was only a minority."[20] Implicit in this criticism is an idea that some form of farm modernization would have been a more appropriate method of response than either land fragmentation and reversion to sub-sistence or continued wheat production at the expense of putting one's children off the land.

The good practices Ouellet believed habitants should have used are the common creed of eighteenth-century agrarian reformers. The soil needed to be adequately drained, harrowed thoroughly before planting, and kept clear of weeds when in fallow. Crops should have been rotated, using forage crops to vary the demands made on the soil's capacities and enhancing those capacities where possible. Herds of livestock should have been expanded and improved by careful breeding and attentive feeding with the forage crops. Finally, the manure of the animals should have been regularly returned to the soil to enhance its fertility. Each of these processes called for farm equipment beyond the rude tools of clear-ing, planting, and harvesting.

Ouellet has been criticized for writing as if there was some monolithic average habitant. While he sometimes used generalizations in a summary way to speak of what most habitants were doing,[21] the careful reader will also find a more nuanced understanding. An example of this is Ouellet's distinction between the common practice of most habitants and the elite who did adopt new farming practices and consequently could maintain a higher level of output than their neighbours.[22] However, Ouellet noted, while "the large landowners reaped large oat harvests even in the poorer crop years and sold their surpluses relatively well to offset their losses on wheat ... [in] localities where the soil was rich and land ownership stable were the most successful at resisting the decline in production, but these pockets of resistance gradually disappeared and Lower Canada became a major importer of wheat and flour."[23]

Much debate has focused on whether farmers passively followed the law of inheritance or actively used it for their own ends. The Custom of Paris specified that all children should receive an equal share of their parents' estate. During the expansion phase of settlement, the spirit of the law could be met by the *censitaire* securing grants of new lands for most of his children, while leaving the home farm to one or two heirs. When the limits of good land began to be reached within a given seigneury or region, *censitaires* had to look further afield for such compensating grants. The further away the new lands were, the more expensive it became for the aging parents to sustain their adult children through their first years of settlement. While the combination of demographic pressure and increasing shortages of good land was felt across the colony, how individual families and particular communities responded could vary. In 1966 Ouellet said, "Once the good lands had been granted, an increase in population was possible only through the expansion of the cultivated area, within each lot and through the subdivision of the properties. But as soon as the soil became exhausted, a decline in population was observed."[24] Thus he concluded the fragmentation did not necessarily lead to ever-increasing population densities. However, he saw such fragmentation as a cause for falling productivity on farms.[25] In a 1972 article he showed how habitants in the Quebec District followed diverse strategies to avoid or accommodate the population pressures on land within (or by going around) the requirements of the Custom. Some habitants sought to evade the spirit and the letter of the civil law by finding ways to grant the whole of their home farm to one of their children. There are cases where this appears to have been the result of a family council, with land portioned out to several (if not all) children, then exchanged with one particular heir for some consideration, to substantially reassemble the home farm. In other cases, the parents "gave themselves" to one of their children: in return for the gift of the home farm. The favoured heir undertook to support his parents for the rest of their lives. In this case, upon the parents' death the remaining estate could be distributed equally amongst the children, but the principle asset was no longer part of the estate.[26] By 1820 it is generally agreed that there was no longer good land to be had within the seigneurial system.[27]

Given that most habitant families, even when exports were at their peak, still produced most of what they consumed, what did it mean to revert to a greater degree of subsistence? For Ouellet it means the replacement of wheat by some other dominant crop, perhaps even the total abandonment of wheat. He noted that potatoes replaced wheat for most habitants by 1827–31: 46 per cent of the harvest was the *patate*. Other secondary crops were oats and peas. Ouellet rejected W.H. Parker's assumption that habitants had simply planted less wheat in order to plant more oats in the 1820s. Ouellet inferred that the same number of arpents produced less wheat. By 1831, 17 per cent of the harvest was oats; by 1844 it was 33 per cent.[28] As well, the habitants expanded and changed the composition of their livestock holdings. From 1765 to 1831 horses replaced oxen as the principal draft animal. While the average household increased its pigs and cattle, the number of sheep rose most dramatically, from an average of three to ten.[29] Ouellet was aware that this development could be seen as production for off-farm sales. But he argued that the poor quality of the animals and the low yield of wool were proof that this expansion of livestock holding was meant to increase the family's autonomy from the market, not its participation in that market.[30]

Ouellet linked the strategy of maintaining the home farm largely intact to a specific wheat farming orientation. He noted in passing that the strategy's effect was to increase the social cleavage within the habitant community, since larger farms could only be maintained by putting other heirs off the land. Some were tilling smaller and smaller farms with each generation, while a fortunate few managed to maintain much larger-scale farms. The least fortunate were the landless habitants, who became a migratory unskilled labour force. By 1831, in over half of all parishes, 30 per cent of the rural population owned no real estate. Ouellet added that these figures "were only provisional assessments subject to revision through more thorough inquiries within each locality."[31]

From the scarce and sometimes faulty census records of the time, Ouellet drew evidence of rapid population growth and an increasing general subdivision of habitant farms. All three of these sources – wheat exports, church tithes, and the surviving census rolls – have been the subject of disputes with other historians. According to Ouellet, the impact of these general trends varied from one region to another. The longest settled and longest tilled parishes lay in the District of Quebec. It was there that demographic pressures first appeared, sending an increasing proportion of the district's children in search of new lands in the colonization parishes of the Montreal District. However, after 1806 the flourishing lumber trade provided both regular and seasonal employment to the landless and those whose inherited lands could not fully support them: "The timber industry seems to have helped to create a sizable number of new jobs." But while "this industry helped to raise the standard of living of a large section of the population," Ouellet noted that "unfortunately" much of the expanded domestic market was fed from American imports.[32] In later debates the extent to which habitants could find markets in the non-agricultural parts of the economy became a major issue. Except for secondary industries such as shipbuilding, most of the jobs created were seasonal or part-time. By contrast, when the best lands of the Montreal District had all been ceded, there were no new lands of such quality to be had, nor a thriving lumber trade at hand to employ the surplus population. Thus the increasing demographic pressure after 1820 lacked sufficient outlets of colonization or substantial off-farm employment, factors that had softened the first impact of the demographic crisis around Quebec City.

Much subsequent debate would hinge on exactly when the agricultural crisis began. Ouellet argued in 1966 that the fall in wheat and flour exports after 1802 did not represent either merely a fall from an unprecedentedly high peak or a cyclical decline in harvests. He held that British demand, reflected in high prices, remained very strong. The lower average levels of exports up to 1812 were, for him, a "symptom" that a long-term decline in agricultural productivity in Lower Canada had begun.[33] He saw no emerging internal market that could account for a drop in exports on such a scale; "unless, of course, the local market had experienced an abrupt revolution, one could in all certainty lay the blame on problems of production."[34] The fact that Ontario as well as the United States continued to ship wheat to the British market through the port of Quebec raised the question of why Quebec's share of the wheat export trade was declining.

Linked to that analysis of agriculture in Quebec was Ouellet's view of the origins of Canadien nationalism. He has argued that before 1960 several scholars had established the existence of an agricultural crisis and so this issue itself was not controversial. Instead he maintained that the controversy was inspired by his connection of that crisis to the rise of Canadien nationalism. In his view, the rising Canadien liberal professional class harnessed the distress caused by the agricultural crisis for their own class ends. Ouellet identified the initial impact of the crisis in the Quebec District with Pierre Bédard's struggles to defeat Judge De Bonne to win a seat in the legislative assembly. The agitation of the Parti canadien in the Assembly grew from that first use of a nationalist appeal.[35] Similarly, Ouellet saw the rise of Louis Papineau's Parti patriote as in part due to the onset of a general crisis in the colony's agriculture felt most acutely in the Montreal District.[36] A politically ambitious class of liberal professionals deflected the habitants away from directly addressing their farming problems into a political avenue that came to a dead end in the 1837–38 Insurrections.

In the aftermath of 1838, Roman Catholic clergy played a leading role recasting nationalism into a clerical form that would dominate Quebec for a century. A key element in the nation's newly articulated religious mission was its agricultural vocation. In an address to clergy in the nineteenth century Bishop Laflèche declared: "I do not hesitate to say, gentlemen, that agriculture is the normal state of man here, and that which calls to the mass of humanity. It is also that which is the most favourable to the development of the physical, moral, and intellectual faculties, and above all that which puts one the most directly in touch with God."[37] In the twentieth century, Abbé Groulx carried on that perspective: "The family domain, since it was inherited as a bequest from one's ancestors ... was a living thing incorporated into the very character and history of the family; it was like some relative of one's fathers and forefathers who, through long proximity, had acquired some of their features; it was a religious reliquary, gathering and preserving the results of their labours."[38] From the 1940s on, this clerical agrarianism came increasingly under attack from rising neo-nationalists such as Michel Brunet. He mocked the politicians' attempt to equate agriculture and nationalism: "Georges-Etienne Cartier, who made his fortune as the lawyer for railway companies [said to farmers] that if they abandoned the soil 'that day will finish our nationality.'"[39] While Ouellet, seen as part of the Quebec school in the 1950s, crossed swords with Brunet as spokesman for the Montreal school, his economic history in the mid-1960s drew fire from a new quarter.

The earliest and most persistent critics of Ouellet's economic history of Quebec have been J.-P. Wallot and Gilles Paquet. From 1967 to 1972 they published a rapid succession of articles challenging Ouellet's sources, methods, and conclusions.[40] The first decade of this debate produced an exchange after which T.J.A Le Goff tried to assess both positions.

Wallot and Paquet did not merely argue the detail of Ouellet's case: they wished to propose an alternative large interpretive framework. They viewed Quebec as part of an Atlantic world tied together by ever-expanding markets that worked to more tightly integrate all the local or regional markets. Through several articles they developed their explanation for the nineteenth-century economy and politics of Lower Canada in its first two decades, in which their criticisms of Ouellet were usually tangential. But in 1972 they offered a direct and sustained critique of Ouellet's thesis of an agricultural crisis.

Wallot and Paquet offered a schematic analysis of Ouellet's thesis, which is useful for making clear at least their perceptions of the formal steps to his argument.[41]

1 General postulate: Agriculture was the colony's "prime mover."
2 Specific assumptions:
   a) Habitant farmers were conservative.
   b) Overseas (UK) wheat demand was high and stable.
3 Mechanisms:
   a) Overpopulation within the seigneuries and land scarcity
   b) Poor agricultural techniques and low wheat productivity
4 Presumed effects:
   a) Habitant living standards fell.
   b) Rural discontent fed political activity.

As to what they term Ouellet's "general postulate," Wallot and Paquet repeatedly tag his views as those of the "Labrousse syndrome," referring to the French pioneer of serial history, whom they see as wrongly giving priority to production for subsistence over the market economy.[42] They regard commerce in general and forestry in particular as the real prime mover of the Quebec economy. Their argument is that, while the great majority of the population were engaged in agriculture, the most dynamic element in the economy (at least after 1806) was commerce, which was responsible for the modernization of the province.

The bulk of their 1972 critique centred on what they called Ouellet's first specific assumption: the role of external demand for wheat as against the domestic demand. They needed to proceed carefully here, as their argument was somewhat complex. On the one hand, their own thesis argued that Lower Canada's first two decades saw it rapidly drawn into the international market, with market forces penetrating the colony and spurring it on to a modernizing restructuring. On the other hand, they have to explain the apparent drop in the trend of wheat and flour exports after 1802. The rising trend of wheat exports from the early 1770s to the turn of the century seems to argue for an increasing market connection between habitant farmers and the international market. Does the falling trend in exports after 1802 mean that habitants were abandoning the market and the modernity it represented for peasant self-sufficient autonomy?

Their case depended upon giving an appropriately "modernizing" explanation for this apparent retreat from the market. Wallot and Paquet applied a model developed by R.E. Caves with the intention of demonstrating that the patterns of price and quantity fluctuations between 1791 and 1812 revealed that the instability of exports was not due to any failures on the part of production, but rather to the erratic nature of demand. Their data intended to show demand dominant in eleven of nineteen time periods; but even taking the data at face value, it is not clear that it supports their argument in more than seven of those eleven cases.[43] There was also no specification of the conditions under which Caves's model could be expected to hold. Does it, for example, rely upon such fictions (beloved of economists) as perfect competition, perfect knowledge, and an absence of any government intervention? They repeatedly stressed that this exercise is only "a first measure of the plausibility" or "a rough view of the general plausibility" of Ouellet's thesis.[44] They did not share with the reader the reasons for their tentativeness about the model's application.

Their criticism of the second "specific assumption" of habitant conservatism was grounded more in logic than evidence. They read the attribution of traditionalism and conservatism to the habitant as a denial that habitants were capable of acting in their own rational self-interest. They argued that Ouellet had implicitly assumed an extreme model of rationality that ignores that people always act under the constraints of circumstance. Their case was that the habitants made rational choices within the constraints that they faced. Capital was scarce and extremely hard for them to come by, which limited most innovations in farm techniques. Moreover, in the face of an uncertain foreign demand, habitants may have rationally chosen to sell only to the local market where uncertainty was presumably less. Wallot and Paquet argued that after 1850, habitants adapted their farming to the demands of the newly opened American markets, thus demonstrating their sensitivity to market signals. One would have thought a more powerful and more relevant argument would have been the habitants' response to market signals after 1770, when for three decades wheat production mounted to successively higher heights in response to sustained demand from the British Isles.

Wallot and Paquet conceded none of the "mechanisms" that they had identified as linking the assumed causes (failure to supply the British market) to the presumed effect (nationalism). While they acknowledged there was rapid and remarkable demographic growth from 1780 to 1820, they chose to emphasize that this could be a positive aspect of the economy. The larger population meant that there was a larger domestic market to supply. It also meant that there was a larger workforce. Implicit in this presentation is the notion that population growth alone was not necessarily a bad thing. It was a question of whether the resources are available for that extra labour to feed that extra market.

In denying Ouellet's second mechanism – land scarcity – they offered their most damning, yet least-documented, criticism. They argue that only 20 per cent of "the fertile land in the seigneurial zone" had been granted by 1784, of which only 5 per cent had been cleared.[45] The critical element of course is what should count as fertile. This may not be as straightforward as it first appears. The land that counts is that which could be used for specific purposes by turn-of-the-century habitants with the technology then available. Since wheat was the principal cash crop, how much land could have been tilled with the ox-drawn wooden plows predominant in 1765, or the horse-drawn plows more common by 1831?[46] Certainly one cannot just assume that *all* lands in the seigneurial zone were fertile (or equally fertile), as Wallot and Paquet appear to do when they offer the figure of 6.5 million arpents as the arable land available.[47] Nor can one turn to the later extent of cleared lands as a measure of what would have been available in 1800. While land clearing was still going on in late nineteenth century in Quebec, the structure of the province's agriculture had greatly changed: much of the new clearing was to create pasture, not to grow wheat. Nor are modern soil surveys without their problems. Soils that rate highly today, because they give high yields when tilled with a tractor-pulled steel plow, would have been simply impenetrable with nineteenth-century farm technology.

In failing to recognize the differences in soil quality, Wallot and Paquet miss an important part of the case being made for falling wheat productivity. First, there is the issue of good soil, which when newly cleared will give high yields, but which eventually loses that productivity. The second, less-recognized aspect, is that as good soil became harder to come by, habitants had to turn to more marginal soils, where the initial fertility was not nearly so high, and was more quickly exhausted.

Wallot and Paquet attack the idea of falling wheat productivity or yield in two ways. First, they dispute that there is a strong, direct, empirical case that wheat yields fell. The anecdotal evidence offered by Ouellet and Hamelin in 1962 for an early nineteenth-century fall can be offset by other anecdotal evidence. We simply lack precise statements of how many *minots* to the arpent were grown.[48]

However, the authors have a further and more powerful case. They grant that the initial fertility of newly cleared land was soon exhausted. But what evidence is there that this suddenly became a general phenomenon in the whole colony after 1802? Their defence of habitant farming techniques followed directly from their earlier argument about rational choice in contrast to one's environment. They point out that the methods so often criticized by visitors to the province were those common to the North American frontier. That is because every owner/operator in the forest west of the Mississippi-Great Lakes faced the same constraints: a lack of labour and capital, and an abundance of land. However, Wallot and Paquet offer this astonishing caveat to their defence of this "rational agrarian regime": "It was growing harder and would become even, disastrous, when the landholdings became rare and fragmented, the population numerous, and the markets more diversified and more exacting."[49]

Having denied the postulates and mechanisms, they also denied what they saw as the presumed effects of the crisis: falling habitant living standards and consequent political discontent. The former provided the other major empirical part of their critique. They constructed agricultural price indices from a variety of sources as well as drawing on church and seigneurial records to make the negative case that there is no evidence of an agricultural crisis or a general economic crisis before 1812. Their reading of the results of the indices of agricultural prices showed that in the Quebec District, habitants' standards of living rose substantially, while there was a less clear-cut rise in the Montreal District. Examining records for six parishes, they found a similar trend: those near

Quebec City seemed more generous in their donations to the church (which is assumed to be a sign of greater wealth). Looking at land revenues for an assortment of seigneuries, they calculated those in the Quebec District were higher. Finally they looked at peasant indebtedness and found very little that could not be accounted for by a strategy of habitants' deferring payments to the seigneur as a form of savings.

They also briefly introduced data on other occupations to demonstrate that there was no generalized economic crisis. Rather, day-labourers, professionals, and even civil servants enjoyed a rising standard of living (if not so great, in the ease of the latter). Given this picture of rural prosperity (or at least, an absence of crisis) and rapid commercial growth, they argued that the rise of French-Canadian nationalism cannot be explained in any such simple "economism" as that proposed by Ouellet.

Wallot and Paquet saw Lower Canada's first two decades as the point at which the colony entered fully into the world of international commerce. Prior to 1800 the colony's commerce apart from wheat had been dominated by fur, which had little connection to the rest of the colonial economy. Agriculture only sporadically produced a wheat surplus to connect it to any market. What transformed the economy was its international sector, above all the rapid development of the lumber industry, which radiated a dynamic impulse of commercialization through the whole society. They trace the impact of the lumber trade in several ways, through the rapid increase in the tonnage of exports from the port of Quebec, and the rising value of exports.

Of the 661 ships that left the port of Quebec in 1810, their research shows, 500 were carrying lumber. Moreover, there were not merely *more* ships at Quebec, but also *larger* ones, which meant lower per-unit shipping costs. The rapid growth in lumber exports compelled changes in the domestic sector. Unlike fur or fish, lumber required both substantial agricultural inputs and a larger labour force, drawn from the agricultural sector as either seasonal or permanent labour. Lumber spurred the expansion of other industries, especially shipbuilding. In 1806–08, between five and seven ships were built. In 1811, thirty-seven were built.[50]

The consequence of this stimulus, according to Wallot and Paquet, was a general rise in living standards throughout the colony. While they noted that the labour drawn from the agricultural sector was creating prosperity closely linked to both lumber and shipbuilding in the Quebec District, the Montreal District appeared less prosperous as it was still largely dependent on agriculture.[51]

Wallot and Paquet were convinced that lumber exports dominated Lower Canada's first two decades and that this rapid growth in the domestic sector drew inhabitants away from the wheat export market by offering higher prices and more reliable demand. The market had more diverse demands than simply for wheat, and therefore the habitants began to diversify away from wheat in response to the stronger domestic market price signals. Thus Wallot and Paquet explained Ouellet's primary evidence for an agricultural crisis – falling wheat exports – as a consequence of modernization, growth, and prosperity.

In 1974, T.J.A. Le Goff, a European social historian, offered his "review of a controversy." Calling the recent exchanges between Ouellet and Wallot and Paquet "a rather bitter polemic," he sought to bring some clarity to the debate, to arrive at a conclusion as to "what was really taking place" in Lower Canadian agriculture. He considered that Wallot and Paquet accepted Ouellet's view that habitants had only been able to increase their production up to 1802 by increased clearing of new lands. Thus such increased production could be only temporary, as the available good lands would eventually run out. However, he considered that they agreed on little else. He saw the issues in terms of four factors: external demand, domestic demand, shipping, and, more broadly, economic structures.

Ouellet assumed that British demand for wheat was consistently high. Wallot and Paquet used two arguments against that assumption. First, as noted previously, they offered an application of R.E. Caves's model to demonstrate that price and quantity fluctuations originated on the British demand side, not the Quebec supply side. Second, they quoted several grain dealers and other businessmen in the colony to the effect that there was great uncertainty over what price would prevail in Britain once the grain arrived there. Le Goff pointed out that these two "cannot stand together."[52] If no one could know what price would be paid in Britain until after the crop had been harvested and shipped, then price fluctuations in one year could have no effect on the quantity shipped in that year.

Le Goff considered that neither side had provided enough evidence to know whether domestic demand could have been great enough after 1803 to explain the fall in the amount of wheat exported. He considered both as "going on faith here."[53] What was needed was an examination of population growth and the potential for growth in agricultural production. On the supply side, he assumed that Ouellet was in agreement with Wallot and Paquet that "there was no real lack of land in the seigneurial settlements before 1812, if not before 1820."[54] Given this view of Ouellet's position on land availability, he understandably faulted Ouellet for not being able to explain why wheat production should have begun a downward trend after 1802. Yet Wallot and Paquet had not explained why it would have been a rational choice for the habitants not to expand production when they decided to supply the domestic market.

When Le Goff turned to the problem of economic structures, he faulted both sides for not producing a national accounting model of the colonial economy, before pointing out that one is not possible due to the limitations of early nineteenth-century statistics. Everyone (including Le Goff) was trying to find measures to approximate the data available in modern economies. Specifically, Le Goff agreed with Wallot and Paquet in criticizing Ouellet for offering "serial history" in place of proper "analytical history," in which the data are given appropriate weights (or "valences") according to their significance in the overall economy. On the other hand, he considered that Wallot and Paquet had not carefully examined the relations between that international market, the domestic market, and price fluctuations.

Le Goff was not impressed by Wallot and Paquet's attempt to create price indices to estimate standards of living. Since each index was made up of agricultural prices, and sometimes the same prices in each index, it was small wonder that the results came out close to unity. When Le Goff turned to their other evidence for rising standards of living, he was similarly unimpressed. The various parish and seigneurial records are fragmentary: how can it be established whether they are truly representative of the colony as a whole? Moreover, the revenues could have grown due to factors other than productivity. Where the dues were paid in grain, rising prices would increase the value of grain paid even if the amount of grain stayed the same or declined at rates less than the proportionate price rise. As well there may have simply been more people in the parish, or seigneury: we need to know the yield per person.

Le Goff attempts not only to assess the arguments about evidence on both sides but also to offer some work of his own on the questions at hand. As for the fragmentary data offered by Wallot and Paquet to show a rising standard of living, he introduced birth and death rates, commenting that they do not seem "to signal any drastic betterment of the lot of the rural people."[55]

He also offered a reworking of export data from Quebec in comparison to wheat exports from Philadelphia. Since Britain imported anywhere from three to ten times as much wheat from the United States as from all of British North America, Quebec appeared as a relatively minor subsidiary supplier. From this perspective, it was clear to Le Goff that British purchasers were willing "to buy unlimited quantities of wheat at a given price."[56] "This demand, as far as Lower Canada was concerned, was virtually unlimited."[57] He asked, then, why the province did not continue to supply that insatiable demand. The answer is the price: "Quebec wheat cost too much."[58] He then examined reasons why the Quebec domestic price moved above that at which it could successfully compete internationally after 1805. He ran through three models, using the Wallot and Paquet assumptions, for estimating the domestic consumption and production. His conclusion was that wheat production "stagnated after [1801–02] near its earlier levels while population continued to rise, steadily and inexorably."[59] He concluded that the fall in exports before the War of 1812 need not be attributed to an actual fall in wheat productivity, but to the levelling off of the available wheat surplus in the face of a rapidly growing population. The combination of stable productivity and population growth yielded higher domestic prices for wheat, which not only prevented large-scale exports of wheat, but also encouraged imports of wheat into Quebec from Ontario and the United States.

Somewhat gloomily, he concluded that the lack of precise, reliable, and comprehensive statistics, may mean that the debate had reached "a dead end."[60] On a more positive note he suggested that "local studies of social structure and economic change within small well defined regions" might offer more convincing evidence than province-wide generalizations.[61]

However, Wallot and Paquet were not prepared to leave the debate at a dead end. They replied to Le Goff (and he in turn replied to them). In their view, Le Goff had imposed a false dichotomy in which Ouellet argued for agricultural crisis and they argued for agricultural prosperity. Thus they rejected his argument, from birth and death rates, that there was no great improvement in rural Lower Canada. Rather they held that it was Ouellet who must marshal an argument for "a thoroughgoing disaster." "If such a disaster did not appear to exist, then this certainly confirms our view that there was no agricultural crisis *in the sense of Ouellet*."[62] We will return to that pregnant phrase later.

Wallot and Paquet argue that Le Goff made too much of their "crude test of plausibility" derived from the application of Caves's model.[63] However, they tried to defend their use of it. They conceded that "while it is true that demand does not affect supply in the same year in the same way as supply affects demand, even the well-known lag between price changes and farmers' response to it must be felt as sharply in the market place: even if production does not change supply may change."[64] A high price might both bring onto the market more wheat in the year that price prevailed (as farmers decide to sell more than they had intended, replacing their own subsistence stocks with other foodstuffs) and cause more wheat to be planted the following year. But again their case was supported by testimonies to *merchants'* reluctance, rather than habitants', to enter the grain trade.

Their more "elaborate test" of plausibility consisted of a family of independent indicators. While these indicators point in the same direction, all had many problems. None of them, in Wallot and Paquet's view, invalidate the conclusions. For example, they defend their use of parish revenues by arguing that they had selected parishes with relatively stable populations precisely to avoid the danger that worried Le Goff, of population growth alone raising revenues. They both qualified claims made for their indices – "nothing but a crude approximation" – and offered a more broadly based index to support their claim.[65] Their conclusion reiterates the view that every point of Ouellet's argument has been met and refuted.

They then turned to Le Goff's rival hypothesis. As throughout their reply, they insist that Le Goff shares either their assumptions or those of Ouellet. In constructing his own model, Le Goff has accepted Ouellet's belief in land scarcity (which he erroneously thought that they shared) and in the unlimited nature of export demand. They insist that the assumptions underlying Le Goff's three models did not favour their view. On the contrary he overestimated domestic consumption and underestimated production. In a footnote, they dismissed his comparison of Quebec and Philadelphia wheat prices, saying that he has not been able to grasp how the rapid expansion of the domestic market had forced up prices in spite of strong agricultural production. They concluded by reviewing their own alternative of a modernizing restructuring of the Lower Canadian economy in which agriculture shared in the prosperity. As a harbinger of the debate's future direction, they also mentioned the use of the notarial document known as "inventory after death," or postmortem inventory, to provide a more direct measure of habitant wealth. From their preliminary examination of this new source, they agree with Le Goff that the "average habitant" was a myth, since there were considerable differences amongst habitants according to their wealth.

In his brief reply, Le Goff reiterated that he considered the economists' model of export price relations to be meaningless; that they had still not made a case for sufficient domestic demand to account for the fall in exports; that the scarcity of *good* land had to be addressed, not just any sort of unallocated land; and that the indices used in their standard-of-living argument remained defective. He chided them for not paying attention to problems of supply (as well as demand). He concluded that Lower Canada had experienced a "structural crisis" – the onset of a long-term decline in the productivity of Quebec agriculture – rather than a "sharp, sudden crisis," which Wallot and Paquet seemed to think Ouellet had identified.[66]

In their criticism of how Le Goff had constructed his models of domestic consumption and production, Wallot and Paquet hammered Ouellet's use of parish tithe data as unrepresentative. It came from only "a few parishes" (later specified as nine), they said, so no reliance could be put on "this vaporous data" representing only a "haphazard selection of observations." However, I would note in passing that their own "*crise agricole*" article had used four parishes they identified as "typical" and "important" without offering the reader any reason for the use of those adjectives. This issue of the real representativeness of data from a source would recur throughout subsequent rounds of this debate.

Ouellet's immediate and direct reply came in a francophone journal, *Recherches sociographiques*. Unsurprisingly, he rejected the dichotomy of habitant images presented by Wallot and Paquet. He denied ever describing the habitant as a "moribund conservative," against which they set their own description of "an habitant sensitive to the market."[67] His own analysis relied upon habitants reacting positively to market signals in the British imperial market from the 1770s on. He saw their inability to continue supplying that market after 1802 as arising from the increasing scarcity of new good land to clear and their unwillingness or inability to change their farming practices. He also rejected as oversimplified their claim that he attributed the rise of Canadien nationalism solely to the agricultural crisis.

Ouellet pointed to several faults in Wallot and Paquet's attempt to apply an abstract model to Lower Canadian export volumes and prices. Firstly, they only dealt with the relatively short term. Their work with grain buyers' records led them to think that merchants' seasonal anxieties over prices could also be attributed to habitants themselves. Wallot and Paquet proposed an alternative hypothesis to explain falling exports: perhaps the habitants abandoned the imperial (or "Atlantic") export market because its sales fluctuations made it seem too risky. Nonetheless, Ouellet noted, American and Ontario farmers – at greater distances – continued to sell along the St Lawrence route to the British market.

Secondly, Wallot and Paquet had habitants turn away from the uncertain export market because there was a more reliable domestic market at hand in the growing cities of Montreal and Quebec and the burgeoning lumber trade after 1806. Ouellet agreed that the rapid expansion of the latter did stimulate the Quebec economy. However, according to him, there was no growing *domestic* demand for agricultural produce of *sufficient* size to explain the sharp decline in exports. He offered census data on Quebec City's population as its region gained most from the boom in the timber trade, estimating that by 1819 the city had about 15,000 people. In the first thirty years of the nineteenth century, Quebec grew increasingly rural, as its urban population actually shrank in relative terms. Not only was there not the non-farm population to consume all the non-exported grain, but customs records show that Quebec and Montreal were drawing part of their foodstuffs and other agricultural supplies from the United States. As to population pressure, Ouellet noted that the very politicians Wallot and Paquet cite as agents of modernization were quite aware that good farmland was scarce within the seigneurial zone.

Ouellet then offered data from fifty-three parishes comparing 1790 to 1822 in terms of out-migration. Of these parishes, 62 per cent already experienced out-migration.[68] Furthermore, Ouellet rejected the use of parish and seigneurial revenues as indicators of habitant prosperity. Where habitants paid in kind rather than cash, inflation would create the appearance of greater revenues even when the same quantity of goods changed hands. He was unimpressed by a display of price indices since there was not a corresponding study of consumption. That is, until we know how important a given good was to people, we have no idea how to weigh its price. A sharp fall in the price of a good when few people consumed it or only a low quantity was sold would not represent a general betterment in living standards. Finally, Ouellet pointed to his new source (first published in 1972) of tithe records to show the pattern of declining wheat production at the beginning of the nineteenth century.

One must note that Ouellet's method of presenting his wheat export data leaves him open to a ready objection, which his many critics have not been slow to take up. In his contribution to the Wallot and Paquet–Le Goff exchange, for example, he once again offered a comparison of wheat export volumes between the periods of 1793–1802 and 1803–12, which shows a fall from 4 million *minots* to 2.8 million *minots*, a decline of over 30 per cent. However, the extraordinary year of 1802 saw exports of 1.15 million *minots*. Therefore, if one simply moves that year into the

Graph 2.1:   Trend line in wheat exports, 1770–1850.

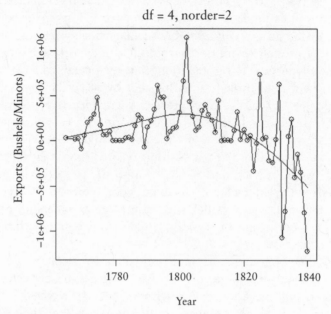

Wheat Exports vs. Year with connecting Spline

df = 4, norder=2

Source: Ouellet, *Economic and Social History of Quebec*, 668.

second time period, instead of a decline of wheat exports there is a rate of 14.8 per cent growth. If we follow the procedure suggested by Wallot and Paquet and just eliminate the exceptional year of 1802, then the fall in wheat exports was almost 21 per cent.[69] In fact, the trend line in wheat exports from 1770 to 1850 (see Graph 2.1) more clearly indicates the long-term pattern in wheat exports from Quebec, which began their decline shortly after the turn of the century.[70]

As Ouellet moved on to tithe records in the early 1970s for more direct evidence of falling wheat production and soil productivity, so Wallot and Paquet in the second half of the 1970s and through the 1980s used their new source of the post-mortem inventory to underpin their earlier arguments. They seemed initially to see the inventories as primarily a means to show that habitants were not impoverished but rather had a rising standard of living registered by the increase of goods in the household. However, they came to believe that the inventories also gave substantial testimony about habitants' landholdings.

The price indices published by Wallot and Paquet in the early 1970s had suffered from the uncertainty over what weight to give to each price. Thus in their first article Wallot and Paquet searched for "a discourse of production and consumption."[71] They hoped that the quantitative analysis of the inventories would reveal consumption patterns that would enable them to calculate a properly weighted consumer price index. Since that first article, however, their interest has turned much more to direct measures of end-of-life wealth and standard of living rather than more carefully constructed consumer price indices.

For new sources in the agricultural crisis debate, Wallot and Paquet turned to the notarial archives of Quebec, starting with those held at the Montreal branch of the National Archives of Quebec. There they found a rich deposit of many sorts of legal documents recording sales, leases, mortgages and other forms of debts and credit, marriage contracts, and individual bankruptcies. However, their attention focused on what they considered the richest single source: the post-mortem inventory.[72] The inventory was meant to be a list of all goods in the family household, its real property (such has buildings and land), and all outstanding debts owed or credits due. While strictly speaking not required by law in every case, the inventory was drawn up before a notary to mark the dissolution of the community of property between husband and wife at the death of either spouse. If an inventory was not drawn up within three months, then the heirs were assumed by law to have accepted the estate. One motive for heirs to insist on an inventory was the need to determine if the debts of the estate exceeded the value of its assets. If there was a net debt to be paid, the heirs could refuse to accept the estate, since under the Custom of Paris debts need not be inherited. However, the main motive for the drafting of the inventory seems to have been the need to protect the property of the heirs of a first marriage when the surviving spouse remarried. Wallot and Paquet regarded the post-mortem inventory as a kind of "micro-census" taken at the end of a family's life cycle.

They were well aware that its use as a historical source posed several problems.[73] Notaries drew up inventories according to their own lights and possibly those of the family concerned. There was no standard format nor any agreed procedures for the description of a household's property. Some were highly precise, at least for some sorts of goods. Thus, for example, one might merely enter on the inventory that the household had a bag of coins, while another would not only identify the coins in the bag but also offer comments on how well worn each coin was (thus refining the statement of value for coins of intrinsic worth). Some notaries recorded the quantity of grain stocks held by a habitant and noted how much was for payment of the tithe, how much for seed, how much for the family's subsistence, and how much was intended for sale (and might even offer a value for that surplus). Other notaries simply noted a quantity of grain as part of the estate, while yet others neglected to mention any grain. Even as individuals, notaries were not consistent in how they recorded data. Of special importance for the purposes of Wallot and Paquet, the same maddening imprecision was carried over into descriptions of landholdings. Some of the most precise not only give the dimensions, location, and condition of the land (e.g., whether cleared) but also placed a value on the land. At the other extreme, land is described in terms that, while evidently clear to contemporaries, are almost meaningless today (e.g., "from the house to the trees"). Some inventories stated the occupation of the head of the household; in other cases the occupation must be inferred from the contents of the household. In a few cases, some ambiguities can be resolved by resort to other notarial documents. For example, a record of sale might provide a precise description of land sold and its price, when the inventory offered neither description nor estimate of value.

A more serious and much less tractable problem is that inventories were often drawn up much longer than three months after the spouse's death. Yves Morin's study of post-mortem inventories from a parish in the town of Quebec showed only 45 per cent of all inventories were written less than three months after the death in question. Over a third were drawn up more than a year later.[74] While such late inventories might be reasonably expected to still catch the household's principal real estate holdings, they could not be relied upon to precisely state mobile wealth or even debt/credit balances as they stood at the time of death.

Wallot and Paquet expected that by dealing with aggregated data, these problems with individual post-mortem inventories would be surmounted. That is, the particular oddities of one inventory or those of one notary would be counterbalanced by taking an average of all inventories for a given occupational group, in a given period, in a given geographical area. Their initial study took a selection of post-mortem inventories from the Montreal area, with a smaller sample from the District of Quebec. They checked the registers of forty-eight notaries known to have been active in the District of Quebec in their chosen time period. Other notaries from outside the district may well have drawn up inventories for people living in the district. Wallot and Paquet were aware of forty-seven other notaries active in the Montreal area whose records were not held in the Montreal office of the National Archives of Quebec. They found that the registers needed careful checking as not every document listed as an inventory actually was the document they wanted; other inventories were found in the notarial archives which had not been noted in the register as such. As a result of their first sifting, they concentrated on forty-three notaries who between them had 2,905 inventories in the relevant period, which they estimated to have been about half of all the surviving inventories in the district.[75]

Given the large number of inventories and the complexity of each, Wallot and Paquet decided to take a sample of the total number they had located. On their first examination they chose a one-eighth (12.5 per cent) sample, structured by four time periods (within 1792–1812), three sub-regions of the Montreal area, and five occupations. For each time period, sub-region, and occupation, if there were less than five inventories, all were included. Thus, for example, for the city of Montreal and its suburbs, there were less than five habitant inventories, so all were included in the sample. If there were between five and ten inventories, they selected five. If there were more than ten, they took at least half. In this way they drew out 431 post-mortem inventories, not all of which, upon close examination, proved to be useable.

Since Wallot and Paquet were seeking to compare households' property holdings at the end of their life cycle, it was necessary to select only those inventories representing the final or peak holdings of a family. Those households where a spouse had died young were not counted as being at the end of their *complete* (or potential) life cycle. By this rule they hoped to be comparing like with like, "completed" households in one time period with those in another time period.

Each of the selected post-mortem inventories was then analyzed, its reported goods being sorted into ten broad categories (such as livestock, means of transportation, etc.). These ten, in turn, could be grouped into four even more general headings. In their initial 1976 article, Wallot and Paquet compared eighty-five households from 1792–96 with ninety-six from 1807–12. The global picture that emerged was one of burgeoning wealth. Average net mobile wealth rose by 350 per cent, far outstripping inflation variously estimated at from 40 per cent to 60 per cent in those years. Unsurprisingly, the greatest increases in mobile wealth were found amongst the merchants of Montreal.

The authors expanded this very partial view of the post-mortem inventory resources in subsequent publications. For the Montreal area they ultimately took a 15 per cent sample made up of 133 to 180 inventories

available for the periods 1792–96 and 1807–12. For the North and
South Shore in the Quebec City area, they also took a larger sample.
They contended that a careful analysis showed that these successive generations had not experienced an erosion of their end of life standard of
living as measured by possessions in the household. More striking were
the summaries of the median average landholdings and the changes over
time revealed by the inventories.

By looking at the median, the range, and its changes in direction
over time, we can compare the contrasting experience of habitants in
the Quebec and Montreal districts. In the Quebec District the median
farm size remained in the 90–149 arpent category throughout the period
1792–1835. The proportion of landless habitants over the period rose
(from 4.2 per cent to 10.4 per cent. That of small holders (1–49 arpents)
fell and then rose (from 8.3 per cent to 18.7 per cent). The proportion
of smaller medium-sized farms (50–89 arpents) fell from its highest to
its lowest value (22 per to 14.6 per cent). Larger medium-sized farms
(90–149 arpents) declined from 30.2 per cent and then rose to 37.7 per
cent. The large farms (150–189 arpents) rose then fell back to their lowest level The very large farms (over 200 arpents) continuously increased
their proportion of the total (from 6.5 per cent to 16.7 per cent). By
contrast, in the Montreal District, the median size rose from 50 to 89
arpents, to match that of Quebec. The proportion of habitants with no
land rose to 11.4 per cent and then fell to 7.5 per cent. The proportion of
small holders increased to its peak (from 4.1 per cent to 12.5 per cent).
That of smaller medium-sized farms fell over time (from 30.6 per cent to
20 per cent). The larger medium-sized farms increased their proportion
(from 26.5 per cent to 30.6 per cent). The proportion of large farms fell
(from 20.8 per cent to 11.4 per cent), while that of the very large farms
was mainly stable (between 9.4 per cent and 10.9 per cent).

The shift in distribution of habitant landholdings between 1792–96
and 1807–12 appears to confirm the authors' contention that this period
saw a general expansion in habitant landholdings rather than the subdivision and fragmentation of holdings often associated with Ouellet's
agricultural crisis. However, in the succeeding periods (at least for those
habitants who made out inventories that have survived), the apparent
improvement of the earlier period was largely lost by 1835. Still, none of
these results conforms to common notions of a relentless fragmentation
of landholdings as a universal phenomenon amongst rural Canadiens.

Both the changes in the distribution of landholdings over time and the
median averages for habitant holdings for different areas made it clear

that the Canadiens were not always helpless victims in the face of the Custom of Paris. Evidently some families at least were making choices that enabled them to retain or even augment their landholdings over time. However, Wallot and Paquet noted from the inventories a substantial increase in indebtedness amongst habitants in all regions. They also found evidence of an increased variation in habitants' holdings: that is, the gap between the largest and smallest holdings had increased over the forty-year period. They clearly consider this evidence the *coup de main* to all arguments that habitants' holdings were fragmented due to over-population.

But I would suggest that there are a number of reasons for reluctance in following their reading of this data. The question of representativeness arises on two levels. First, how representative is the sample of post-mortem inventories of the total of all surviving habitant post-mortem inventories? Second, how representative are the surviving habitant inventories of the tens of thousands of habitant households that existed in 1792–1835? Several of the numerous local studies done for this period manage to avoid the first problem by using all of the surviving inventories. The second problem is the more intractable.

There are several difficult aspects to the question of how representative these inventories are of habitants in general. One procedure for estimating representativeness is to compare the frequency of certain variables in the general population to the frequency with which they occurred amongst those persons for whom inventories survive. Yves Morin used this procedure to test the demographic characteristics of households for which inventories survive against those of the geographic area in which those households were located. Morin checked the inventories for a parish in Quebec City to see how well they reflected certain characteristics of the population at large: age, religion, socio-professional status, place of residence, and civil state (i.e., whether or not married).

Wallot and Paquet commonly cited Morin to uphold their claim to the representative character of the inventories.[76] However, Morin prefaced his discussion of how representative the inventories can be by explicit reference to their work: "Their presentation of the inventories' nature seemed pertinent, but their affirmation of the inventories' representativeness needs to be nuanced if not corrected."[77] In three instances he challenged Wallot and Paquet. When Morin compared the ages of the deceased with the general age profile of Quebec City, he found that the inventory was not, as Wallot and Paquet had thought, a document more common for the elderly than any other group of the population. He also found that Protestants were more likely to resort to inventories than Wallot and Paquet had assumed. This was related to his third correction, that mixed marriages were often treated as having a community of goods according to French civil law. One of Morin's findings of which Wallot and Paquet seem to take no account is that whether an individual left a (surviving) inventory varied greatly according to his occupation. Another was his argument that isolated years could give a severe bias to any results, as neither deaths nor inventories were evenly distributed over time.

Given that it is habitants who are the focus of rural history, more relevant than Morin's urban study is the work of Christian Dessureault on the rural seigneury of St Hyacinthe. There, he found that 40 per cent of all adult deaths produced a post-mortem inventory.[78] However, he found the average landholdings shown in contemporary inventories were 20 arpents larger than in the 1831 census. Poor peasants (less than 90 arpents) were under-represented, comprising 64 per cent of all farms in 1831 but only 48 per cent of all post-mortem inventories in 1825–34. By contrast, rich peasants holding 300 or more arpents were over-represented: 2.5 per cent in the census but 7.1 per cent of all post-mortem inventories in that period.[79]

If across the colony as a whole the "abundant" habitants' inventories turn out to be in the order of a few thousand for the entire period (1792–1835), then it is clear that records for the vast majority of habitants (if they were ever made) did not survive. The use of the inventories to infer characteristics of a larger population must then be prefaced with some consideration of why this relatively small proportion survived (or were ever drafted). Given the indications of *growing* disparities amongst the habitants over the period under review (which Wallot and Paquet themselves have noted on occasion), the greater the variance within the occupation of farmer, the less likely that the surviving material will record the full variety of habitants' estates at death.[80] To selectively sample a population (that is, all surviving inventories) that has already been greatly reduced by unknown factors would be a hazardous enterprise.

In spite of Ouellet showing in his article on the Quebec District the diversity of ways in which some habitants could get around the civil code's inheritance provisions, his critics see him propounding a view of inevitable fragmentation of landholdings. A major purpose of Wallot and Paquet's analysis of post-mortem inventories was to show that for many habitants, this was not the case. Yet the law of inheritance did produce an increasing fragmentation of another sort over time. Wallot and Paquet, in their study of patterns of landholding derived from post-mortem inventories, found that most of those who managed to maintain the *scale* of the family farm over the generations held that land in an ever-increasing number of separate parcels. For example, in 1792–96, 52 per cent of farms covered on Montreal's South Shore held a single piece of land. By 1830–35 only 17 per cent did, while over 20 per cent held their land in five or more parcels.[81] Even the tactics used to mitigate the civil law's pressure to fragment ownership could not always prevent the fragmentation of lands even when held by one person. This multiplication of separate holdings made for less efficient farming, since the owner had to expend time on moving livestock and equipment from one holding to another.

For Wallot and Paquet it was important to show habitants responding to domestic markets in ways that sustained or increased their standard of living; thus they looked for evidence that there was more money in circulation, such as increased use of credit and debt as well as the emergence of a land market. They produced two articles on the habitants' rising debts and, along with Jean Lefleur, another four on land markets in the County of Assomption. Several other authors have contributed studies of rural merchants and habitant debt, towns as markets for the countryside (especially Montreal and its surroundings), and land markets. In addition, articles on the rapid growth of villages and the rise of rural industries made the case that there was sufficient domestic demand to explain the disappearing exports, and indirectly account for the increasing number of those children of habitants who found themselves landless in a rural society, where population growth had outrun the supply of good agricultural land within the seigneuries.

In 1987 Louis Michel offered an insightful analysis of habitant debts, indebtedness, and their varieties. Habitants typically had three types of debt: from purchases of land, purchases of consumer goods, or dues owed to the seigneur or *curé*. They resorted to purchase as land in a locality became scarce and seigneurial grants in favourable locations could no longer be had. The purchase of a productive asset represented no long-term problem unless its cost was beyond the borrower's ability to pay or the land's ability to produce. Payments to the seigneur and *curé* were often episodic. Michel was not sure such amounts owing really qualified as debts. Similarly merchants, especially in rural areas, allowed running accounts to regular customers over the course of a year or more. Only if the habitant were unable to pay at "reckoning-up time" did the merchant commonly treat the sum as a debt, on which interest might be charged and for which a mortgage might eventually be necessary. Here, debt grew into indebtedness. Other types of debt emerged during inheritance settlements where the principal heir or heirs could be obliged to make payments to siblings. Michel regarded debt as an essential element especially in starting a farm of one's own. Chronic debt could become a problem, preventing a farm from expanding and sometimes even resulting in the loss of the land.[82]

Wallot and Paquet applied Michel's categories to their sample of postmortem inventories for the Montreal District. They noted that the seigneurial debts were most likely to be paid off not necessarily in a good crop year but when the *censitaire* wanted something from the seigneur. They found debts to the *curé* to be insignificant, at an average of 4 per cent of all debt. While there was little land debt in the 1790s, thereafter it was usually the largest portion of all indebtedness. The average merchant debt was 7.4 per cent but varied markedly by region. On the island of Montreal it was always very low, with a range of 0.4 per cent to 1.9 per cent (although its lowest numbers match the peaks of cash loans). The North Shore was the most stable at 6.1 per cent, while the South Shore had the highest average – 13.8 per cent – and the least stability, ranging from 6.3 per cent to 28.3 per cent. Over time, the debt per arpent increased steadily, more than tripling across the whole period (1792–1835); there were ever fewer inventories that showed no debt.[83] Wallot and Paquet wanted to read this rise in debt as a sign of greater market integration and increasing prosperity. That is, the scale of the debt increased with the scale of the farm. However, ever-increasing debt loads over time can also be read as an indication of growing poverty.

Wallot and Paquet also offered a study of habitant debt in the Quebec District and comparisons with patterns in the Montreal area. They identified access to credit as a major cause of the increasing social polarization within agriculture. The Quebec District had more credit available in the earlier two periods before the War of 1812, while Montreal had more after the war. There was again a radical reduction in the inventories without debt. For example, on Quebec City's South Shore, the proportion dropped from 34.4 per cent to 5.2 per cent without debts. There was also a steady rise in debt per arpent. As in the Montreal area, the amount tripled over the whole period (1792–1835). They were left with the apparent paradox of net enrichment (of those habitants whose inventories were included), while the level of debt grew dramatically in the Quebec District in the first three periods.[84] They conjectured that debts grew around the acquiring or re-assembling of family lands, which accounted for over 50 per cent of all debts. Thus debt was one way habitants avoided the fragmentation of their lands in attempting to provide for most if not all their children (or at least their sons).

In their examination of the land market in the County of Assomption, Wallot and his colleagues set out to refute an aspect of what they called the traditional view of the habitants. Specifically, they held that an active local land market would disprove that habitants were growing poorer in the first third of the nineteenth century, that land had become scarce, and that most rural families lived in a primarily subsistence economy largely isolated from commerce. However, in my view their research could not sustain all three critiques. Their case that habitants' economic position improved was based on evidence of rising land prices. In fact, like the study of Butler County, Ohio, that they had earlier cited, almost the whole of the increased wealth arose from higher land prices (estimated to have doubled over the whole period of 1792–1835). While that section of the habitants represented by inventories largely retained the same farm area as their ancestors (though not always the same land), the land market data showed a huge increase in very small holdings, of 2–3 arpents, by other habitants. Before 1820 such small lots accounted for only 5 per cent of all landholdings; after that, 88 per cent.[85]

Overall, the sales of plots over 80 arpents fell from 32.6 per cent to 9.5 per cent, while the average area declined from 57.6 arpents to 34.6 arpents.[86] While some habitants retained farms of traditional size and thus benefited from the rising prices, many more were forced out of the role of owner-operator, living in proto-villages trying to raise some of their own subsistence needs in what amounted to large-scale gardening, at the same time seeking employment to earn the balance needed to sustain their families. As Wallot and Paquet are driven to concede, while rising land prices made some habitant families appear more wealthy (at the cost of rising levels of debt), many others had been forced off the land or onto marginal holdings.

Why were land prices rising? Here the authors' first thesis defeated their second. Scarcity of land compared to demand was the cause of land prices rising. Over time, the best lands in the best locations had all been filled. Many in subsequent generations had to take up lands of lesser quality in less advantageous locations for which they had to agree to pay higher seigneurial dues.[87] More clearly than in their previous work, Wallot and Paquet concede that in Assomption, good lands had all been taken up before the War of 1812, forcing people onto poorer

lands whose meagre returns were further reduced by higher transportation costs and heavier feudal burdens.

Their third contention, that the existence of a land market disproved a
habitant decline into greater subsistence, does not fare much better. First,
they assume that because contracts were drawn up in money terms,
cash was changing hands – cash that only engagement with commercial markets could have made available. In actual fact, it was common
to have money used as a unit of account when it was seldom a medium
of exchange. This is most clearly the case in rural merchants' account
books.[88] Jean Lafleur's study of St Sulpice parish within the County of
Assomption showed a land market predominantly driven by the transmission of land between generations within families. Succession rights
made up 55 per cent of all sales (versus 19.6 per cent for Assomption
as a whole), while "donations" for lands were two to three times larger
in area than sales. For the county as a whole there was more activity
related to the development of villages (not found in St Sulpice) and fill-
ing out the remote parts of the seigneury. Forced sales of land to cover
merchant debt only appeared in the 1820s – hardly a sign of rising habitant living standards.[89] But merchants seldom sought to hold agricultural land (as distinct from wild lands, obtainable at negligible cost as a
long-term speculation).[90]

Lise Saint-Georges's earlier study of the parish of Pointe-aux-Trembles
on the island of Montreal (1821–61), rather surprisingly, resembles St
Sulpice more than the County of Assomption. With a stable population of about 100 *censitaires*, in forty years the parish averaged only
eight to nine land transactions per year. Most of these were family transactions (58.8 per cent). The most common forms of family transfer were
by donation (38.8 per cent) or at no charge (32.5 per cent). Almost all
sales took place within the parish. Even with Montreal only a few miles
to the west, urban buyers were involved in only 3 per cent of all sales,
while habitants from neighbouring parishes accounted for 5 per cent.
Although prices rose over time, that seemed to have little effect except in
the 1840s. In that decade donations and no-charge inheritance dropped
from over 70 per cent to 41 per cent and sales jumped to 29 per cent
(from 15.1 per cent).[91] However, in the following decade the older pattern resumed (no charge plus donations equalled 80 per cent).[92] The land
market was largely governed by transactions between generations.

Even the role of the market in the inheritance process needs close
examination. Sales linked to inheritance in Assomption cost more than
the going rate, from 5 per cent to 66 per cent higher. In part, this could

arise from inherited lands being more cleared than other lands, especially in remote areas where lands cost one-third to one-half those of older parishes. Over the whole period, the costs of inheritance rose. Family settlements grew more complex over time with heirs buying out siblings at higher prices, but payments were often delayed. In the county, such sales were 19 per cent to 27 per cent of all sales (depending on which sub-period is chosen).[93] While Wallot and Paquet dismissed Sylvie Depatie's finding for the mid-eighteenth century that many sales were cancelled, in view of the long delays shown in Assomption her assertion seems more probable.[94]

To sustain their thesis of habitants' rising level of wealth, Wallot and his associates have had to concede that land scarcity in Assomption was what drove up land prices. The very existence of a market for land does less damage to the idea of a growing trend to subsistence than they allow. Contracts in money terms are not in themselves evidence of cash transactions. The increasing cost, complexity, and uncertainty of settlements are no evidence for rising living standards. Neither is the appearance in the 1820s of forced land sales to cover merchant debts. Finally, they themselves concede that increasing numbers of habitants' children were forced into impoverished villages where they worked as day labourers, while eking out part of their subsistence on a couple of arpents. To confront that reality of polarization in rural society is to admit that many habitants were becoming impoverished, even as a minority managed to maintain at least something like the scale on which their ancestors had farmed.

For several years Ouellet did not offer any systematic critique of Wallot and Paquet's new source and their methodology for exploiting it. Instead, in the work of both sides, there were mainly series of lengthy, ill-tempered footnotes that primarily demonstrate that what Le Goff in 1974 called "a rather bitter polemic" did not grow more genteel with time. In his 1984 review of Quebec historiography, Ouellet used a footnote to dismiss the new work of Wallot and Paquet: "In our opinion it is the methodology of these articles which is at fault. The sample used does not seem to have been rigorously constructed with sufficient attention to the representative character of the results obtained."[95] He faulted Wallot and Paquet for choosing to compare a depressed period with a prosperous one. Moreover, he also considered that their readings of the inventories had apparently produced striking aberrations relating to both landholdings and livestock, of which he gave a couple of examples. Wallot and Paquet unfortunately replied in kind: "If this detractor had taken the pains of *reading* our articles ..."[96] In a footnote to their 1986 article, they accused Ouellet of wilfully misreading their results for land and livestock holdings. They welcomed what they took to be his retreat from arguing for a "brutal rupture" in 1802, now realizing that it was a much more short-term turning point and "also less deterministic" of later Quebec history. In their contributions to the Quebec-France colloquia, they referred to Ouellet as "the traditional historiography" or just "the historiography." In passing they argued that "the averages constructed from the census do not inevitably measure the same reality as that obtained in the inventories, which only deal with concrete communities and well-identified individual farms."[97]

Somewhat belatedly, in his book on francophone agriculture inside and outside of Quebec published in 2005, Ouellet engaged Wallot and Paquet in his text. He noted Dessureault's observation that the poorest habitants were the least likely to have a post-mortem inventory. Moreover, Wallot and Paquet's sample was heavily urban biased: only 13 per cent of the population lived in towns but accounted for 39 per cent of their inventories. While the population had tripled over time, they had only doubled their sample size. Dessureault had used every habitant inventory he could locate but found one for every fourteen habitants in the first period and only one for every forty-three in the last period.[98] To Ouellet this decisively undermined any claim that the inventories could be taken to represent the habitants of Lower Canada.

There is the problem of comparing the representativeness of inventories as against other sources, especially the census. By virtue of their function, the inventories most commonly recorded an individual's wealth at the end of their working life cycle. The inventories can be viewed as a valuable source because they tend to capture the maximum stock of wealth that an individual may have been able to accumulate in a life cycle. But such a severely selective source cannot be directly compared to another source that sets out to inform us of a whole community, all its members at their varying stages of the life cycle. The nineteenth-century censuses had their drawbacks, as we shall have occasion to note subsequently. But whatever their faults, they were intended to do something quite different from the inventory.

The inventories do document a social reality, but it may be that this reality was not as universal as first thought. They may be disproportionately recording the success of the successful, the achievements of the wealthier habitants and their heirs in maintaining and even expanding their landed patrimonies. But rural Quebec contained another reality:

the increasing numbers of landless children of the poorer habitants, some working part-time as farm labourers, in the forests, or at trades, others renting land in the hopes of regaining their old independent status. To see the whole reality of rural Lower Canada, we need to see both realities.

These conflicting accounts of Quebec's agriculture in the first half of the nineteenth century have drawn in other scholars who have further broadened the debate. They have often brought with them the perspectives of other academic disciplines. In 1985 Serge Gagnon published a survey of Quebec and its historians in the twentieth century from the stance of the sociology of knowledge. He devoted half his book to assessing Ouellet's work, especially the agricultural crisis. He not only reviewed the critiques of others, he offered his own critique, which includes some original research. He situated his project in terms of the debates over the role of subjective bias and objective methodologies in modern historiography. He saw Ouellet, in order to gain an audience for his views, making claims to objective, scientific methods that are in fact highly subjective.

In the first part of his critique, Gagnon used an analysis of language and grammar usage to show what he considered to be Ouellet's bias. However, I consider that Gagnon's own choice of words shows a tendency to prefer speculative alternative hypotheses to the arguments (whether well or poorly made) by Ouellet. In response to the question of whether or not the liberal professions were overcrowded before 1840, Gagnon opines, "Closer study would *probably* have revealed that the overcrowding was *perhaps* not as pronounced as Ouellet implied."[99] Later we are told, "Demographic pressures resulting in a rural exodus *probably* occurred far later than Ouellet supposed."[100] In response to Ouellet's argument for falling wheat productivity, Gagnon says, "*Possibly* this was another exaggeration"[101] Of his own argument that merchant debt had become a greater problem to habitants than Old Regime dues, he says, "The hypothesis mentioned here *may* one day be proved."[102] That style of dispute could only really work if Ouellet had based his case for an agricultural crisis on the argument that *no other hypothesis existed* that could explain the evidence. Ouellet nowhere makes such an argument.

Much of Gagnon's reaction is clearly attributable to his dislike of Ouellet's characterization of various social groups, which Gagnon considers to be wholly subjective: "The problem with Ouellet's use of serial, quantitative methods was his profuse accompaniment of psycho-ethical discussion, particularly his moral portrait of the rural population."[103] However, his substantive argument is with Ouellet's use of statistics to build and support a case: "The spread and refinement of quantitative methods now make it possible to appreciate the unsubstantiated nature of Ouellet's statistics. He had to rely mainly on arbitrary samplings from very incomplete series of data, and all too rarely advised the reader of their undependability."[104] Gagnon charged that Ouellet's use of data did not fairly warn the reader of its limitations: "When Ouellet illustrated a point with statistics relating to a single parish, seigneury, riding, or significant region, how was the reader to know whether there was consensus on whether certain criteria defined any one area as representative? He gave no indication of whether the figures reflected widespread or merely marginal activity in the community as a whole."[105] These methodological suspicions were applied to both Ouellet's use of census materials to argue for overpopulation and his use of tithe records to argue for a fall in agricultural productivity.

In his attack on Ouellet's use of census data, Gagnon drew on Serge Courville's studies of shifting parish boundaries and concludes, "As the pioneers of quantitative history have taught us, statistical sources must be thoroughly checked with the usual methods of historical criticism, just as qualitative sources must."[106] Beyond citing Courville, Gagnon offered his own attempts to reconstruct Ouellet's figures. For Kamouraska he pointed out what seems to be a transcription error. But his most developed critique is of a parish in the St Eustache area, where he argued that Ouellet was mistaken to count the 1842 parish population as if the parish had the same boundaries as in 1790. He noted that in the English-language version of *Bas-Canada*, Ouellet added the qualification, "despite much subdivision,"[107] but clearly he was not satisfied with such a non-specific qualification.

Gagnon's other major attack is upon Ouellet's use of parish records to directly estimate wheat production. Focusing on a voluntary church collection known as the *quête*, Gagnon's argument hinges on the problems of interpreting a free will contribution. He argues that habitants' givings might well have increased as they felt in greater need of God's help in hard times. This would mean that the level of givings should be read inversely as an indication of agricultural productivity. However, it may be that Gagnon did not intend this argument to be taken too seriously. If his above argument held, then at least part of his own earlier case – that some parishes had *higher* donations later in the crisis – would support Ouellet's argument.

On tithe records Gagnon mounted an altogether more serious assault. There seem to be several serious problems with the tithe records that have survived. First, they are a problem as the source for a time series, because of the subdivision of parishes. However, as revenue did not necessarily split when the parish did (the same rector receiving the benefit), this is not as serious a difficulty as with census comparability. Second, Gagnon objected that there are "too many gaps in time and space" for the tithes to be as accurate as the census (a somewhat surprising parallel, given his earlier criticism of the census).[108] Third, since these reports were prepared for the bishop's visit, they only covered a limited area for any given year. Fourth, the law on tithes and especially the law's application, Gagnon argued, were much more complex than Ouellet allows. The growth of villages in the 1820s and 1830s would have meant the ratio of tithe would have fallen merely due to the growth of proto-urban proportion in the rural population. Gagnon further cited evidence that different priests followed very different methods in trying to collect the tithe, from the diplomatic to the severe. He pointed out that as the tithe was not collected in the field (as in parts of France), the priest took the habitant's word as to his total wheat crop. He noted that habitants could and sometimes did pay part of their tithe in crops not covered by the tithe (e.g., peas). Finally, there were legal limits on collecting the tithe: the clergy had to collect it within one year or their claim lapsed. Gagnon concluded his lengthy critique of tithe records, "Until such time as these questions have been carefully researched, however, the reasonable assumption is that tithe records are not the most useful basis for writing a history of agriculture."[109] Is that conclusion justified?

Gagnon quoted Ouellet's own caveat on the use of tithes, asserting that "he nevertheless proceeded to use the tithe data as though it were an accurate reflection of production fluctuations."[110] Yet the question remains whether the objections Gagnon marshalled do indeed invalidate Ouellet's use of the tithe. Did all the factors producing variations work equally at all times? Did they cancel each other out *or* regularly over- or under-report? The tithe could still give a good general indication of crop yield trends, unless a systematic bias could be demonstrated in how it was collected.[111] Indeed Ouellet's caveat warns us that the unwillingness to pay was most severe in times of crop *shortage*. Thus the tithe may overstate declines in crop yield. In this instance, he has warned the reader against a major problem of the tithe as a *trend* indicator, which is different from an accurate annual crop yield measure.

Gagnon summarized his critique of Ouellet's subjective bias and misuse of what should have been objective methodology: "Ouellet's polemical temperament and his tendency to dramatize were well illustrated by his style of quantitative analysis, in which he *overestimated* 'demographic pressures' on the basis of parish census records, and placed *too much emphasis* on a drop in wheat production and yields, relying on a variety of secondary sources. A little less emotional involvement would have given us a work commensurate with his talent."[112] However, it is not clear whether Gagnon thought completely objective history is possible or desirable. He explicitly acknowledges that his own work was highly selective, covering only what he decided to be important or influential work. He stated that, with Ouellet, Hamelin, and Dechêne, "I have not limited myself exclusively to their value judgements, but have also tried to show the scientific merit of their work." As an assessor of "science," he at times conceded that he was perhaps counselling perfection. In the midst of demanding more detail of how Ouellet had derived his price series, he noted he was making "a stringent requirement – and perhaps I am being overly strict."[113]

Gagnon demanded that Ouellet be impartial since he presented statistical data leading to what are supposed to be objective conclusions. Certainly Ouellet has been drawn into polemic exchanges, but his occasionally intemperate remarks do not by themselves subvert his quantitative analysis. When Gagnon tried to investigate the data, he came up with only one possible error. His criticism runs largely on speculation, tossing out possible or hypothetical alternatives. For someone concerned about bias, his own relentlessly hostile perspective is self-refuting.

Was there in fact an agricultural crisis in Lower Canada that began just after the turn of the century? Ouellet strenuously argued there was, because he read the decline in wheat exports as a fall in wheat productivity. He drew on tithe records in a number of parishes. Since the tithe was based on 1/26th of the wheat crop, it provided a direct measure of wheat production. The decline in the tithes collected reflected the decline in wheat produced.[114] He saw the consequences of the crisis as increasing rural poverty, aggravated by overpopulation within the seigneurial zone, leading to migration out of the seigneuries and eventually out of the province.

Wallot and Paquet have argued an alternative account of a restructuring of the Quebec economy driven by its integration into the Atlantic market. They want to focus on the burgeoning timber industry, which they considered provided a more stable domestic demand that consumed wheat formerly sent to the unstable British market. But was there a large enough domestic demand to compensate for the fall in exports?

From a new source, the post-mortem inventory, they drew evidence of some farmers maintaining the extent of their lands, rather than fragmenting it, over the generations However, this success entailed rising indebtedness and the exclusion of most children from an equal share in the family's patrimony. Moreover, Wallot and Paquet's research also showed many other farmers reduced to small holdings as, in effect, landless habitants. For the latter there was unquestionably an agricultural crisis. The major work of the historical geographer Serge Courville has identified the rapid growth of a host of villages that never gained official standing due to the lack of municipal legislation in the period between 1815 and 1835. These burgeoning rural villages can fit into the Wallot-Paquet paradigm. Were they part of that modernization Wallot and Paquet count on to create the domestic market as an alternative to exports, thriving centres of proto-industrialization that attracted people away from agriculture by offering greater economic opportunities?[115] Or were they mainly clusters of rural poverty where essentially landless habitants sought to eke out a living by large-scale gardening and seasonal labour at harvest time or in the forest? The surprising number of "villagers" who identified themselves as farmers and the absence of full-time non-agricultural jobs tell against the proto-industrialization thesis.[116] Ouellet observed, "As Quebec society was becoming ever more rural and less urban in those years ... it is difficult to see how this explanation could be correct."[117] If the rapid rise in villages in 1815–35 was supposed to account for falling exports (creating a larger domestic demand) and to demonstrate greater market engagement by habitants purchasing locally produced goods, what are we to make of the collapse of the village populations at mid-century? Courville, with two younger colleagues, sought to correct the impression of his earlier work that rural industries stagnated from 1831 to 1851 by applying a new definition for "unit of production" to the 1851 individual census schedules. While this procedure more than doubled the number of rural units, it did not, as the authors hoped, "contradict the earlier impressions of sluggish growth, or of a decline in the number of rural industries" since the same procedure to inflate the number of units was not applied to the 1831 census.[118] The after-1850 migration out of the seigneuries to the Eastern Townships and out of the province to the United States suggests those villages had been primarily pools of landless habitants holding on to local ties in hopes of getting some land rather than enterprising artisans entering a commercial economy.

Louise Duchêne, a social historian, sought to dispel the idea of a decline in Quebec agriculture in the first two decades of the nineteenth century by pointing to bugs and bad weather.[119] The Hessian fly and wheat fly did affect wheat crops in some areas for a number of years around the time of the War of 1812. However, the insect pests were not sufficiently widespread or lasting to explain a long-term trend. Similarly, the global "reversal of seasons" in 1816–17, characterized by unusually cold spring and summer temperatures, included Quebec, which experienced ice and snow in June. Yet agriculture bounced back in 1818 and 1819 in Europe and United States – but not in Quebec.[120] Duchêne dismissed the use of province-wide generalizations, insisting that statistical data need to be interpreted by scholars with local knowledge (a sweeping generalization in itself that would discredit Wallot and Paquet as well as Ouellet).

We now turn to the studies of specific localities in the seigneurial zone to see whether they bear out the thesis of an agricultural crisis. Four local studies cover the late eighteenth into the nineteenth century using all available records, including the post-mortem inventories: Christian Dessureault's master's thesis on the seigneury of Lac des Deux-Montagnes (from the 1790s to the 1820s) and his doctoral dissertation on St Hyacinthe (1760–1815); Allan Greer's doctoral dissertation on the lower Richelieu Valley (1740–1840); and J.-S. Piché's master's thesis on Soulanges (from the 1760s to the mid-nineteenth century).[121] These four areas are not representative of the whole of Quebec, being all concentrated in the lower portion of the Montreal District. However, they give a comprehensive array of data from which to assess the debates over the existence of any agricultural crisis, its timing, and its character on the Montreal plain where the Rebellion of 1837 was concentrated.

The three central issues of the agricultural crisis debate have been those of agricultural productivity, demographic pressure on available land, and the related issue of production for the farm household's self-sufficiency as against production for the market. Ouellet's argument has been that falling wheat exports meant falling agricultural productivity. He has pointed to rapid population growth and the increasing shortage of good farmland to match that population growth. Finally, both Ouellet and Wallot and Paquet have raised the issue of whether or when all or most habitants became oriented either to the market or to self-sufficiency.

All four of the local studies referred to above see a shift away from wheat as the primary crop from the end of the nineteenth century to the 1820s. All report that habitants instead relied on other crops. For example, Dessureault found that in Lac des Deux-Montagnes, wheat fell until it accounted for less than half of saleable value of farm crops (outranked by higher-yielding potatoes and peas). For St Hyacinthe, Dessureault noted that wheat declined from accounting for 75 per cent of the value of all agricultural produce in inventories recorded from 1795 to 1804 to about 60 per cent of all such value in inventories drawn up between 1805 and 1815. He notes that farmers were switching away from wheat to vegetables, tobacco, flax, and potatoes.[122] However, potatoes were adopted much more slowly around St Hyacinthe than elsewhere. Greer's data for three seigneuries in the lower Richelieu Valley show similar trends (wheat fell, potatoes rose), with some local variations (wheat never completely dominated in sandy Sorel).[123] While Piché does not give comparably detailed figures, he confirms that wheat was the dominant crop around 1784, but by the 1830s had been replaced by oats and potatoes.[124] Each study draws the conclusion that the decline in wheat was due to farmers' decisions to rely on other crops. Did the switch away from wheat indicate (as Ouellet assumed) a declining fertility of the soil?

Few writers have worried over this precise question as much as Greer.[125] What was the yield per arpent (or acre) as compared to the quantity of seed sown? If one had to sow twice as much seed in 1830 as in 1762 just to get the same harvest, then soil productivity would have fallen by half. However, Greer noted, we have no such precise comparisons in the records. Consequently for him, "it is simply impossible to answer" the question of changing levels of productivity.[126] If one follows Greer, is it impossible to tell whether soil exhaustion was causing falling soil fertility? Ouellet's response was to ask, "How can one explain why peasants gave up a successful system in favour of eventual emphasis on the potato, a product of no great value which enjoyed no external markets? The phenomenon itself should be beyond question, as the evidence is clear."[127]

At the end of the eighteenth century or shortly thereafter, when habitants switched away from wheat, mainly to potatoes, oats, and, to a lesser extent, peas, their choices give us a clue to their motivations. The most popular substitute was the humble potato. Only in the closest proximity to urban centres could this be regarded as a commercial crop. In fact, it was the subsistence crop par excellence, not just in Lower Canada but, most famously and disastrously, in Ireland. Dessureault noted that the cluster of subsistence-oriented crops fell during 1772–94 when wheat exports rose, then rose when wheat fell 15 per cent between 1794–1804 and 1805–14. He observed that the one sort of livestock enjoying continuous growth in numbers was sheep. Yet flocks still remained small, suggesting that most if not all of the wool was destined not for the market but for domestic use.[128] This perception is reinforced when the inventories show more habitant households in the third period with the tools necessary for the manufacture of both linen and woollen cloth.[129]

In all four of the local areas studied, there was substantial population pressure on available land resources. However, the most common response to such pressure did not seem to be the process of land fragmentation that Ouellet found in Laprairie, but rather the creative avoidance he discovered in the Quebec District. While Greer did not find convincing evidence of a crisis in agricultural production, he did consider there to have been a long-term demographic crisis: "Given the limited supply of land and the requirements of the grain trade, the reproduction and multiplication of farm households could not keep pace with the burgeoning population and the result was long-distance emigration and the growth of a landless proletariat."[130] He disagreed with historians who held that the habitants were "so foolish as to destroy the basis of their way of life by subdividing their land excessively."[131] However, he found clear evidence of even wealthy habitants struggling to provide at least their male children with the resources necessary to start their own farm. Population pressure interacted with a variety of other factors to produce different outcomes in different settings. The availability of wage labour in Sorel before 1821 allowed land fragmentation because the families were not wholly dependent on having a viable farm. In St Denis, habitants strove to keep their farms intact, with the result of emigration out of the seigneury. For seigneuries adjacent to the Eastern Townships, a short-distance migration could be achieved by squatting, if it was necessary to have the benefit of family support, without the immediate cost of either feudal dues (as on seigneurial lands) or payment to a distant absentee landowner.[132]

From his study of Lac des Deux-Montagnes, Dessureault argued that the appearance of land fragmentation was most acute at the moment of inheritance. One needed to follow through the entire sequence of inheritance. While the heirs initially appear to receive small parcels of land, these are frequently redistributed amongst family members to create viable farms, though not of the same extent as the parents' end-of-life holding.[133] In St Hyacinthe he found a more complex long-term picture: the proportion of medium-sized farms declined from 1795–1804 to 1805–15, while that of the largest farms grew. The proportion of habitants farming 60–89 arpents jumped from 20 per cent to 30 per cent. The proportion of the holders of the next largest category fell from 46 per cent to 34 per cent of all habitants, while their holdings fell from 40 per cent of all land to less than 20 per cent.[134]

In his two parishes of St Joseph and St Ignace in Soulanges, Piché found that population grew at an average of 6 per cent per year from 1784 to 1831, while the extent of land ceded grew at an average of only 3 per cent per year. While the average landholding declined from 104 arpents in 1777–81 to 79 arpents in 1831, the demographic pressure had not led to a general fragmentation of landholdings.[135] He explained that "the land seemed to have resisted demographic growth at the price of excluding from the region a great part of its population."[136] As Greer found in the Richelieu Valley, the cost of retaining viable farms (often smaller than in the eighteenth century and often split into many small parcels) in Soulanges was out-migration, frequently into the role of landless labourer.[137]

The degree of market participation turns on the issue of the hierarchy within the habitant class. At the bottom were the landed poor, who owned neither plow nor draft animals.[138] They were necessarily dependent on their wealthy neighbours for the means to till their lands and could only pay with their labour. At the top were the most wealthy families, who commonly had more than one plow, several teams of draft animals, and often several different sets of artisan's tools. The diversity of the tools indicated not specialization but a kind of cautionary investment. Already in the eighteenth century, as Thomas Wien has pointed out, a farm's scale and the quality of its land had much to do with its potential and capacity to participate in any market that might come available. Some could ride out nearly any storm, while others, especially those who farmed inferior land, were vulnerable even to a slight harvest shortfall; some had a surplus to sell when prices were at their peak, while others purchased or borrowed when conditions favoured them the least.[139] Dessureault began his doctoral dissertation arguing that inequality amongst habitants was neither the product of an agricultural crisis (versus Ouellet) nor of a modernizing market (versus Wallot and Paquet), but an inherent condition of the eighteenth-century seigneurial system.[140] Greer argued that for the habitants of the lower Richelieu Valley in the century he studied, the primary goal of all farm family households was to secure their livelihood from their own land. Where land was poor, as in Sorel, young men might have to take up wage labour to compensate for their farms' inability to support their families. Where land was good, as in St Denis, the opportunity to sell a surplus "tended to keep the minimum viable farm size relatively large."[141] But even in St Denis the first function of the farm was to feed the family. What would be sold was the surplus over and above the primary requirement of subsistence. Ouellet chided Greer for "hiding" the evidence of habitant market participation in a footnote: in the 1770s there were forty-eight sellers with commercial surpluses averaging 208 *minots*.[142]

Dessureault concluded his study of St Hyacinthe with a strong stress on the role of the market in accentuating economic stratification amongst the habitants. "The strong growth of moveable and immoveable wealth amongst the upper rank of the peasantry reveals an agriculture more and more concentrated on production of marketable surpluses. In the medium term, the dynamic of the market carried along the development and the concentration of productive riches in 'maskoutaine' agriculture."[143] Yet there was little evidence in 1815 of farms specializing in livestock or grain production. Rather, the largest farms produced surpluses of all types. Larger farms had larger than average livestock holdings, yet they also had more land and more artisanal tools. Piché concludes his study of Soulanges with the comment: "Only a part of the peasantry reached the point of engaging in the process of modernisation, being the middling proprietors and the large-scale ones. Those alone reached the point of long-term intensification of their cultivation and of improving their equipment. That fringe of the peasantry which remained in the agricultural sector in so far as proprietor producers saw its condition improve in a considerable fashion."[144] By contrast he noted that, "inversely, the most archaic practices often persisted in the farms of less extent."[145]

Did a falling trend in wheat exports after 1802 signal a falling trend in wheat production? I believe that we can return to the debates of the 1970s and conclude that wheat production did fall. It was not diverted from export markets to a thriving domestic market. Was the choice to grow less wheat and more of other crops a response to domestic market's demands? This seems unlikely, since the crops to which habitants turned were largely those of a subsistence orientation, such as the potato. Moreover, in the early years of declining wheat production and exports, the proportion of urban population was actually declining. Did demographic pressure and limited land resources within the seigneurial system lead to the fragmentation of landed patrimonies? In some areas this does seem to have happened. For example, in Sorel where wage labour had been available, farms were subdivided because they were not the family's sole support. Elsewhere, responses were much more complex. Successful farm families sought to accumulate substantial amounts of real estate in order to set up their children with at least as great a potential to succeed as the parents had enjoyed – but not with holdings on the scale of the parents. This process worked as an upper limit on the process of land accumulation of the most successful.[146] With each successive generation the largest holdings were reduced – not back to the level of the majority of habitants, necessarily, but below the level of the parents' end-of-life accumulation. For middle-rank habitants, once local land resources were exhausted, the home farm had to be conserved as a unit to support one heir while the remaining children emigrated to find land elsewhere. This complex process often involved the legal dismembering of the home farm, which then had to be reassembled (more or less) as the "favoured" heir bought back the pieces formally ceded to his siblings in return for his support of their re-establishment elsewhere. The poorer the soil and the scarcer the land over time, the less attractive and even less possible became emigration to new lands. Increasingly, some of the sons of even well-established habitants found themselves left to earn their bread by their labour. This fate was near universal for the children of the poorest habitants. The height of the parents' ambition may well have become not establishing each of their children on land of their own but conserving intact the small farm their labour had created. The demographic crisis did not produce an immediate and universal fragmentation of the habitants' land base. Yet just as wheat exports did accurately signal a turn away from growing wheat, so the demographic crisis signalled a severe tension within habitant society, to which a variety of responses were possible.

Just as wheat production and population growth had to be refracted through the lens of economic stratification amongst the habitants, so the question of market participation needs to be seen in the context of that community. Even the most enthusiastic proponent of modernizing agriculture acknowledges that only a minority could be considered as moving toward becoming commercial farmers before the 1830s. Moreover, it is that group of farmers who succeeded best in maximizing the use of traditional equipment and using new techniques and new mechanical tools to respond favourably to market signals. As to average and smaller farmers, they followed the modernization movement only when the process was well underway on the large farms.[147]

While he acknowledges some inequalities amongst the habitants, Greer insists that, "insofar as there was exploitation *within* the peasantry, it was more a matter of generations than of classes."[148] Wien and Dessureault are much more emphatic that while there were significant generational cleavages, there were also definite class divisions amongst the habitants. Wien concluded that "even under the French regime, the disparities among the Canadian peasantry reflected more than merely the evolution of family size, or the temporary poverty of the first years of land-clearance."[149] Dessureault noted of the large-scale producers around St Hyacinthe that "they truly accumulated the advantages of self-sufficiency and those of the market in reducing to a minimum their buying needs outside the farm and in selling the largest possible surplus in one or another commercial production."[150] These were not specializing commercial farmers but large-scale farms that sought to be as self-sufficient as possible, ready to sell onto the market whatever they had in excess of their own needs. It was these well-to-do habitants that Dessureault found over-represented in the post-mortem inventories in St Hyacinthe, and that may also be looming large in the aggregate samples of Wallot and Paquet.

Habitant participation in the market turns out to be dependent not only on factors such as favourable weather in a given year or soil at the peak of its fertility to give an abundant crop, but also on a particular habitant's position in the hierarchy of rural society. Even a mediocre year might yield more than enough to meet family needs on the large-scale farm. At the other end of that hierarchy, the plowless habitant had to annually pay with his own labour or do without even basic spring plowing. Comparisons with farmers in other parts of Canada need to bear in mind that the habitant was not a monolithic unity but a broad spectrum from the most wealthy to the landed poor.

So, was there in fact an agricultural crisis in Lower Canada that began just after the turn of the century? Ouellet has strenuously argued there was, because he read the decline in wheat exports as a fall in wheat productivity. He drew on tithe records in a number of parishes, which directly showed a decline in wheat production. He sees the consequences of the crisis as increasing rural poverty, aggravated by overpopulation within the seigneurial zone. The four local studies from the Montreal District provide a measure of support for his analysis. Wallot and Paquet have argued an alternative account of a restructuring of the Quebec economy driven by its integration into the Atlantic market. They want to focus on the burgeoning timber industry, which they considered provided a more stable domestic demand that consumed wheat formerly sent to the unstable British market. But was there a large enough domestic demand to compensate for the fall in exports? The increasingly rural proportion of Quebec's population in the first three decades of the nineteenth century tells against the assumption of a domestic demand large enough to account for the "disappeared" exports.

From the post-mortem inventory, Wallot and Paquet concluded that some farmers maintained the extent of their lands. But this success entailed rising indebtedness and the exclusion of most children from the family's patrimony.[151] Many other farmers had been reduced to mere landless habitants. For such families there was unquestionably an agricultural crisis.

Part of the dynamism of this debate lies in its ability to draw in more scholars even from different disciplines, offering other perspectives on rural Quebec. Thus the discussion over agriculture has become part of the much larger controversy over whether, or to what extent, Quebecois society is unique in North America. Within the Canadian context, the most immediate point of comparison has been between Quebec and Ontario.

3

Comparisons of Agriculture in Nineteenth-Century Quebec and Ontario

When leading scholars since the Second World War have made explicit comparisons of nineteenth-century Quebec and Ontario farming, the common starting point has been Ontario's presumed superiority and Quebec's corresponding need to catch up. All assumed that there were significant differences in farming in the two provinces and sought ways to explain them.

From the older literature, especially from Robert Jones, came a picture of Quebec in agricultural decline from the beginning of the nineteenth century, with gradual reversal by a turn from grain to livestock, especially dairy, around mid-century. Ontario in this view began the nineteenth century in the pioneer phase, reaching maturity as a commercial grain producer in the 1840s and 1850s. After a short, sharp crisis of collapsing wheat and land prices, the older settled areas of Ontario began to shift to livestock production (beef, dairy, pork) as well as to regional specialty crops such as tobacco and fruit. Scholars from the 1970s on began from that picture, varying significantly in the extent to which they accepted or challenged it.

To a greater extent than later scholars, Paul Phillips largely accepted the older view and sought to explain differences in terms of different landholding systems. He set agriculture in the larger frame of staples theory, which sought to understand the economy in terms of linkages between sectors. In his view, the "dependent-paternalistic organization of resources" in Quebec formed a barrier to economic development, because the seigneurs did not invest in capital goods.[1] Phillips sees the abolition of seigneurial tenure in 1854 as a necessary but not sufficient condition for the economic development of the province.[2] The limited growth in agriculture's final demand restricted positive linkages to industrial growth.

For Phillips, farming's relatively poor performance in New France and later Quebec was due not to poor resources or peasant *mentalité* but to the seigneurial system that separated the habitant – whom he described as "unfree" labour – and the landowner. Priests and seigneurs deprived the habitant of a substantial part of his surplus beyond immediate family needs, which left him with the primary goal of self-sufficiency. Receiving so little of the fruit of his labours, the unfree habitant lacked the incentive as well as the means to be other than a peasant. I think that habitants would have laughed at the notion that they were unfree labour. Phillips's contention that "an abundance of cheap or free land relative to labour supply encourages "unfree (paternalistic or feudal) labour institutions" is itself laughable.[3] That very abundance prevailed across the northern half of North America. While the frontier thesis has been overdone at times, there is no question that the abundance of cheap land drew millions of Europeans because of its promise of economic independence as the basis for personal freedom.

Phillips recognized that the Conquest removed what check there had been on seigneurial power. That and the decision not to create more seigneuries after 1784 meant that population growth would greatly increase seigneurial power to claim more of the diminishing supply of land within the seigneurial zone. However, while he cited the work of Fernand Ouellet, he seemed to take no account of the great expansion of wheat exports from the 1770s to the turn of the century.[4] He was aware of a production crisis in the early nineteenth century, which he considered to be only in part due directly to the seigneurial system. He pointed to the lack of improved agricultural techniques, which he attributed in turn to the lack of investment resulting from low habitant incomes, which also limited the extension of cultivation to new lands beyond the seigneurial zone. But he then argued that the "real" cause of exports' decline was the wheat fly. He characterizes the years between 1823 and 1832 as three deficit years with eight years of mediocre surpluses, before wheat's final collapse after 1831.[5]

In contrast, as loyalist refugees, Ontario farmers were encouraged from the start to produce grain surpluses, with British garrisons as their earliest markets. Assured of bourgeois property rights, without a civil law tending to fragment family landholdings, the Ontario farmer got the full value of his crop, providing the incentive and the means to re-invest in his farm's productive capacity. Such prosperous farms selling a variety of products created backward linkages (e.g., farm implement manufacture) and forward linkages (e.g., flour milling) that sparked Ontario's early industrialization.

Like Phillips, John Isbister, accepted the traditional picture of Quebec
and Ontario agriculture. He too focused on the links between sectors,
contrasting Ontario's balanced growth in agriculture and manufacturing with a view that most Quebec farms were not connected to markets in any significant way, except possibly in the sense of the rural
exodus feeding the urban demand for cheap labour. Isbister's distinctive contribution came in trying to compare the relative productivity
of farms in the two provinces by converting the great variety of agricultural outputs into calories. Compared to Quebec, Ontario farms
were on average two and a half times more productive – sufficient "to
support from one to two non-farm families."[6] Isbister accepts Jones's
view of francophone farmers as largely self-sufficient. While he noted
Quebec's parallel turn to livestock in the second half of the nineteenth
century, "the contrast is that, while Ontario dairy products and meat
were added to a substantial base of field crops, in Quebec dairy products substituted for a level of crop production which was inadequate
for domestic needs."[7] He attributes the lag "largely to cultural differences" rather than soil or climate. Yet by the twentieth century, Quebec farms produced a surplus that came within 20 per cent of Ontario
farm productivity.[8]

While John McCallum's study of Quebec and Ontario began from the
same staples frame of reference as Phillips's and Isbister's with its concern for linkages, he widened the scope of his comparisons to include
early New England. In contrast to Isbister (and Phillips to some extent),
he placed much greater emphasis on soil, climate, and the timing of
settlement than on cultural differences such as the civil law or the seigneurial system. By looking at the advance of agriculture across the continent from the St Lawrence and Atlantic to the Great Plains, McCallum
set the Upper and Lower Canadian experiences into an informatively
larger context. The farmers of the seventeenth- and eighteenth-century
northern colonies found wheat to be the most reliable earner in the
transatlantic market. However, as the virgin soil's initial fertility faded
with repeated cropping, farmers began to move further west onto new
lands to keep up the high yields that could feed a family and provide
some surplus to sell. By the mid-eighteenth century, many New Englanders had moved into upper New York and even western Pennsylvania. In
Quebec, habitants moved from the older seigneuries along the St Lawrence around Quebec City to the fertile Montreal plain. But as the best
lands were taken up by the end of the century, francophone farmers did
not continue the westward migration to find more good land. Instead

they (and the next generation) moved onto increasingly more marginal lands within the seigneurial zone.

In spite of his declared intent to stay away from cultural explanations, McCallum allowed that for Canadiens, "social factors must form an important part of the explanation ... American farmers could never have suffered as the habitants did, for they would have moved west long before that point was reached."[9] While 25 per cent of those born in New England left the region during every decade from 1800 to 1850, francophones hung on to an increasingly subsistence-oriented agriculture until the 1840s.[10] By contrast, McCallum presented a picture of Ontario farmers as almost a caricature of the staples model: "More specialized in wheat production than the farmers of present-day Saskatchewan, Ontario farmers of the mid-nineteenth century exported at least four-fifths of their marketable surplus."[11] However, this rosy picture suddenly dimmed in the later 1850s due to the conjuncture of a variety of factors, short term as well as long. Just as farmers in Quebec had begun to encounter the limits to the supply of good land at the turn of the century, the more rapidly expanding Ontario farm frontier – fed by high levels of immigration as well as a high rate of natural increase – hit the southern edge of the Canadian Shield just after mid-century. The initial impact was to drive up land prices. The end of the Crimean War resulted in a worldwide wheat glut that drove wheat prices down sharply in 1857. Disappointing wheat crops compounded the impact on the province. However, the short-term crisis coincided with the arrival of railways and the Reciprocity Treaty's opening of the American market after 1854, a new market that seemed even more inviting with the outbreak of the American Civil War.

McCallum noted that by then the average wheat *yields* in Ontario had already begun their inexorable decline. Average yields in the 1820s of twenty-five to thirty-five bushels per acre in the best years had fallen to sixteen bushels per acre by 1851. Only three of forty-two counties had averages above twenty bushels.[12] Ontario farmers began to switch away from wheat – to barley in some areas, to regional specializations like tobacco or fruit in others, as well as to increased holdings of livestock and greater outputs of animal products. Ontario's transition could be much more rapid than Quebec's because Ontario's abrupt crisis occurred when many of its farms were at or near their peak in terms of having more than enough land cleared to support a family. Despite some severe cash-flow problems arising from heavy mortgage charges owing to recently purchased overpriced land, low wheat yields, and low

wheat prices, the financial problems could be resolved by financial solutions. Meanwhile the farm family was left in possession of a substantial
land base, most of it (the core region) cleared, with ample livestock and
implement holdings. The farm's real assets (as distinct from its financial
condition) enabled farm families to seize opportunities presented by new
transportation facilities and newly opened markets.

McCallum stressed not only the strong linkages from prosperous
agriculture to local industries but also Ontario's ability to control the
gains from such linkages. Through their financial, transportation, and
manufacturing institutions, Montreal merchants had hoped to capture
an "empire of the St Lawrence," but Ontario's railways and trade ties
to the United States enabled it to retain a major share of the profits.
Montreal's initial dominance was overcome because "the economic
advantage of larger local markets, more abundant capital, and possibly
more advanced technology ... confer[red] cost advantages on the better
endowed region."[13]

Marvin McInnis and Frank Lewis compared the relative productivity of francophone versus anglophone farmers in Quebec. They found
an anglophone productivity edge in the range of 7.6 per cent to 15.7
per cent. "That difference is much less than a long tradition of historical
writing has implied."[14]

Marvin McInnis went on to offer a direct quantitative comparison
of Ontario with Quebec from the 1851 census. He identified wheat as
the major explanation of why Ontario's net output per farm and net
output per improved acre were substantially higher. However, he went
beyond provincial averages to look at the range of variation in each
province. In each province there was a wide range between the poorest and richest counties; the poorer Eastern District of Ontario matched
Quebec's average performance. Moreover, Quebec's most productive
francophone county exceeded all but nine of Ontario's counties. When
McInnis looked at the distribution of counties by average level of net
output per farm, the two provinces overlapped: Quebec's largest concentration lay below the mid-point, while Ontario's straddled it, with a
significantly greater concentration at the upper end – representing the
province's wheat belt.[15]

McInnis noted that Quebec farms produced more "miscellaneous"
output (such as maple sugar), but dismissed it as not significant. He also
pointed out that Quebec farms had 4 per cent *less* livestock per acre than
Ontario farms, but did not draw attention to the fact that Quebec produced 1.9 per cent *more* in animal products per improved acre.[16] Both

topics deserve greater examination because they point to a profound difference that appears to be forgotten in statistical comparisons of the two provinces.

While he elsewhere alludes to debates over relative soil fertility over long periods of cultivation, McInnis does not dwell on his own calculations that show the newer province had the higher average cleared acreage per farm.[17] Given that parts of the St Lawrence had been farmed continuously over 150 years, why did the older province have a smaller average clearing? The enormous rush of settlers into Upper Canada in the early 1830s and 1840s would have meant very large numbers of small clearings by 1851. Yet they were apparently more than counterbalanced by the steady long-term clearing in the oldest Lake Ontario front townships, which by 1851 had between one-third and one-half of all lands cleared (and some over 50 per cent).[18] The oldest of Upper Canada's clearings, begun in the 1780s, coincided with the expansion of francophones' cultivation across the Montreal plain.

Two processes had been at work to bring down the average cleared acreage in Quebec. Despite family strategies to the contrary, some degree of fragmentation of landholdings had occurred in some parts of the province: the oldest farms' large clearings allowed the creation of two or more farms with sufficient area to support a family. The other process was the ongoing pioneering into the least-favoured recesses of the seigneurial zone and the beginning of movement beyond it into the Eastern Townships and the Saguenay region. The smaller farm that was already cleared needed a higher earning output than wheat, since extensive farming increasingly gave way to more intensive farming. Hence, the significance of the more efficient utilization of livestock (producing 1.9 per cent *more* with 4 per cent *less*) and development of diverse products such as maple sugar (also characteristic of some older farms in Upper Canada).[19]

The debates begun by Phillips, Isbister, McCallum, McInnis, and Lewis comparing Quebec and Ontario farming have drawn in four further interventions from five other historians. First came Donald Kerr and W.J. Smyth, who disputed Isbister's assumptions and methodology. They insisted, like McCallum, that Ontario had a clearly superior resource endowment for agriculture. They pointed to its more southerly, milder climate and consequent longer growing season. Their appeal to modern soil classification is less compelling. Some of the very factors that make certain soil types highly desirable in an era of high-powered machinery would have severely limited their cultivation in an era that relied wholly on muscle power.

Much more striking is Kerr and Smyth's table showing changes in improved land in the two provinces from 1871 to 1971. It reveals that Quebec's improved acreage steadily expanded to 1891. In the following decade, more than a million acres were taken out of production. The province's all-time peak was 9 million acres in 1921. But from 1911 to 1951 the total repeatedly fluctuated between 8 and 9 million before beginning a long-term decline. The fact that hundreds of thousands of acres fluctuated in and out of production is striking evidence of those soils' marginality.[20]

By contrast, Ontario reached its all-time peak in 1891 at 14 million acres. For the ensuing five decades, the total hovered at or above 13 million. The next two decades saw a further gradual decline, followed by a sharper drop after 1961. While Ontario undoubtedly had cultivated much marginal land, the proportion was not so great as to substantially influence the province's totals from decade to decade.

Kerr and Smyth dismissed Isbister's stereotypic picture of the failed subsistence farm that could not even feed the farm family. They pointed to the growth through the later nineteenth century of animal husbandry, especially dairying, "the most logical entry into commercial farming."[21] By the end of the century, on a smaller land base with smaller herds, Quebec's dairy industry was producing proportionately more than Ontario's. They mounted several criticisms of Isbister's attempt to estimate calorie production. Some of these criticisms focused on problems in the census data with which he worked: many of the minor crops characteristic of longer settled farms are either omitted altogether or consistently under-reported. For example, in 1891 the census commissioner estimated that unreported maple sugar amounted to $391,000 for Ontario and $1,356,000 for Quebec.[22] Kerr and Smyth concluded that "the census data offer only a very crude source for the derivation of calorie tables."[23]

The second contribution to these debates, from J.I. Little, has been much more far-reaching. In his response to Isbister, he joins Kerr and Smyth in questioning the use of calories as a basis for comparisons of agricultural productivity. He contended that calorie-based tests tend to favour grain production over livestock. Further, he agreed with Kerr and Smyth in dismissing Isbister's characterization of Quebec agriculture as being at "only subsistence level of production; it was poor and commercially isolated." As he pointed out, "If Quebec farms had truly been indifferent to the marketplace and concerned only with self-sufficiency, an increasing specialization in dairy products would have been a strange option to choose ... Grain-growing was the most efficient option in terms of calorie per acre" – but food is not sold by the calorie.[24]

Little saw the work of McInnis and Lewis comparing French and English farmers in Quebec as generally the "more accurate."[25] For McInnis and Lewis, "efficiency" meant "profitability." However, on several grounds Little faulted their attempts to compare the two ethnic groups within Quebec. First, he noted that their samples consist of *all* areas of English-dominant farming, but only a *selection* of areas of French-dominant farming. Second, when they assert that actual crop yields amongst francophones in the seigneuries were comparable to those of anglophones in the townships, they compared level arable lands like the Montreal plain with the steep and rocky hillsides of the townships. "Calculations of capital input should be expanded beyond the cost of the livestock to include differences in the value of cleared acreage as well."[26] Little also raised questions about the amount of planted acreage that was, in fact, hay. "Pasture" in the seigneuries would be fallow lands, not rocky hillsides on which only grazing, not cultivation, was possible. Hence, the seigneurial lands such as the Montreal plain would have had a much higher sale value than the rugged lands of the townships.

While Little's contribution to these debates was published before McInnis's explicit comparison of Quebec and Ontario, it has a bearing on that work as well. As McInnis and Lewis had compared Quebec's francophone and anglophone farmers in 1851 without considering their different types of farming (grain versus livestock), so McInnis in 1992 sought to compare Ontario with Quebec through the later nineteenth century, not considering the different types of farming that came to predominate in each. Isbister had asserted that Ontario *added* dairy and meat to its field crops, where Quebec largely *replaced* field crops with dairy and meat. Indeed, he noted that Quebec's grain production declined to the point where it could not always meet domestic needs. Little pointed out that while reported meat production per average Quebec farm remained constant, dairy production expanded almost sixfold between 1851 and 1901, when it finally equalled that of Ontario. Quebec's farms were highly diverse, from the potato patch of the agro-forestier (Scots as well as French in the Eastern Townships) to the prosperous dairy farms on the island of Montreal. "Even the poorest Quebec farmer could ... grow enough food for his family's dietary needs, leaving at least some of his butter and cheese as revenue for other purposes."[27]

The third contribution came from Robert Armstrong, who criticized McInnis and Lewis for not defending the assumptions that underlay the use of the Cobb-Douglas production function: constant returns to scale, equal rates of return on land and capital, equal factor marginal prices, equality of factor prices, a high degree of substitution between factors of production, and the absence of risk. The last two are especially troubling. Capital was clearly not a ready substitute for the labour of habitants. Risk was a crucial factor in Quebec farming. A consequence of subsistence farming is that starvation is always just one crop failure away. Armstrong took up the rationality argument of Wallot and Paquet: "the rational subsistence producer may have been reluctant to shift from the traditional technology and a diversified crop pattern to new technologies and a more specialized crop mix for sale to the market because of the potentially high costs of failure. Risk-averting producers may prefer a pattern of output involving low 'mean' incomes with low variance to alternative configurations promising higher 'mean' incomes with greater variance."[28]

Finally, Morris Altman revisited the 1851 census, also challenging the assumptions of McInnis and Lewis that francophones and anglophones had the same dairy output and identical weights and quality of livestock. He recognized that those assumptions went "directly against the Ouellet hypothesis."[29] Similarly the assumption that small holders had no horses gave a high estimate of surplus horses when "the horse surplus was critical" to showing a high level of Canadien farm output. Altman concluded that, overall, Ouellet's picture of less productive Canadien farming was confirmed. However, decisive regional variations told against Ouellet: Montreal's strong local Canadien response of more intensive land utilization countered fewer resources to produce the highest farm incomes in the province.

The most recent comparison of nineteenth-century farming in Quebec and Ontario has come from a very different perspective than the four already considered. Fernand Ouellet compared the economic standing of Canadiens in Quebec with those outside Quebec and with other ethnic groups within Ontario. Since Canadiens were the most rural ethnic group in Ontario, most of Ouellet's attention focused on agriculture and those regions with the highest francophone concentrations. This concern with ethnic groups and regions led him to criticize McInnis for seeing too quick a transition from wheat to dairy. He also criticized Gordon Darroch and Lee Soltow for their focus on central Ontario,[30] seeing them, like David Gagan, as choosing an ethnically homogeneous area that would not point up differences in divergent ethnic groups.

In comparing the two provinces, Ouellet opposed the wheat mono-culture image of the extreme staples view with the assertion that mixed farming was the norm for all regions at most times. In neither of these two regions was wheat ever the predominant crop. Ontario's mixed farming developed a wheat orientation in the 1840s that had largely passed by the 1860s. The Maritimes always had mixed farming; after Confederation its proportion of "other crops" (meaning "other than wheat, oats, and potatoes") rose from 14 per cent to 29 per cent. From 1844 to 1871, Quebec had 18 per cent to 20 per cent in "other crops"; after 1881, that rose to 25 per cent. Ontario's wheat declined from 16 per cent (1881) to 10 per cent (1901), while its "other crops" rose from 24.5 per cent to 49.5 per cent.[31] Nonetheless, Ouellet wanted to stress that even when wheat's proportion of the field crop fell, Ontario's wheat belt to the end of the century still produced more than all the rest of Canada combined.

Ouellet compared Quebec's agricultural production to that of Ontario after Confederation. From a high of 60 per cent of Ontario's output in wheat, oats, and potatoes in 1871, Quebec steadily declined to 37.6 per cent in 1911.[32] While livestock holdings grew in both provinces, there was no such clear trend, although Ontario was consistently ahead. Sheep in Quebec went into permanent decline as women turned from domestic production of wool to purchase cheap cotton.[33] Ouellet insisted that too many scholars have assumed a ready transition from wheat to dairy production. Rather there was a prolonged transition (especially long in Quebec) as subsistence-oriented mixed farming sought some marketable surplus. Both provinces had falling domestic cheese output as it moved to industrial production. By 1901 Quebec had 1,992 cheese factories to Ontario's 1,336 (but Ontario's were larger with higher output).[34]

Ouellet also pointed to the regional disparities in agricultural productivity within both provinces (as did McInnis).[35] Quebecers who moved to Ontario went to its least-productive regions, the east and the north. They often began by trying to combine farming with forestry as was common in Quebec's marginal regions. Farms in eastern Ontario in 1861 had a substantially lower average value than farms in the Montreal district.[36] Yet on the good soils of Essex, the long-established Canadien farming community raised corn and hogs like their neighbours and did as well or better than the county's other groups. Even on the poor soils of Prescott, late-arriving Quebecers – first growing oats and potatoes, then switching to dairy farming – had, within two generations, improved their economic standing beyond that of most of their counterparts in their native province.

Against the findings of Darroch and Soltow, Ouellet found that the timing of an ethnic group's arrival in a specific area had a substantial and lasting impact on that group's degree of success in farming.[37] In Essex, where Canadiens were the first Europeans to farm, they gained a predominant place in the eighteenth century, which carried forward into the next century. In the Essex townships of Sandwich and Malden, according to the 1871 census, Canadiens made up 56 per cent of the farmer-operators, owning 51 per cent of all improved acreage and 52 per cent of all land occupied.[38] Later-arriving British settlers obtained marginally larger farms – 89 acres to Canadiens' 72 acres – but the Canadiens were more productive per acre (producing 97 per cent of British output with only 80 per cent of their acreage). However, Ouellet noted that ethnic groups were not economically homogeneous: 73 per cent of Canadiens owned less than 100 acres (compared to 86 per cent of all black farmers, the most recent group to enter the area).[39]

Those Quebecers who moved to eastern Ontario were significantly disadvantaged by their late arrival. Along the western shore of the Ottawa River, the British arrived first to take up farms, followed by the Irish, and lastly the Quebecers. By 1871, whereas 76 per cent of Canadiens in Essex were born in Ontario, in Prescott County's townships of Hawkesbury and Alfred, 85 per cent of francophones had been born in Quebec.[40] They occupied 45 per cent of the farms and 40 per cent of the occupied land, but only 29 per cent of the cleared acreage. Canadiens arrived very poor as well as late, with an idea of subsistence farming combined with forest labour. They possessed little in the way of capital, farm implements, or livestock. The gradual advance of the lumber frontier to the Upper Ottawa meant that English farmers lost their immediate market for oats and hay, while the Irish and French Canadians found their principal source of seasonal employment ever more distant. The British and Irish began to leave the region or to adapt their farms, while the Canadiens turned their attention to fully exploiting their farms. From 1871 to 1891 francophone farmers in Prescott moved to dairy production at a faster rate than those in Quebec (except in the Montreal district).[41]

Ouellet's third area of interest, Simcoe County, lay within the central Ontario region of interest to Darroch and Soltow. Canadiens were never even locally in a majority in the county, although half of the region's francophone population lived there.[42] Their farms out-produced those in Quebec or the Maritimes in 1881, 1901, and 1911, although they produced less per acre than their English neighbours.[43] Over time, the

francophones lost ground as an ethnic group because they lacked sufficient numbers to sustain their separate cultural identity.

The move into Simcoe was part of a general northern advance of
farming, following the lumber camps or railways. On poorer soil with a
shorter growing season, almost everyone concentrated on oats and potatoes with few livestock. By 1901 Canadiens constituted 32 per cent of
the farmers in Algoma East-Nipissing and out-produced their English
neighbours.[44]

Ouellet's major conclusion about both provinces was that a longer gap
in time between wheat production and dairy existed than other scholars
have so far concluded.[45] First, he contended that farmers in every region
began with mixed farming, not wheat monoculture. In the first three
decades of the nineteenth century, even Quebec moved out of wheat.
In Quebec's case, it is obvious that there was a very long delay before
dairy emerged as a new focus for a mixed farm's off-farm sales. Ouellet
insisted that there was a similar, if not quite so lengthy, delay in Ontario.
In that transition phase Ontario's farmers, like those of Quebec, turned
to a wide variety of alternatives derived from the mixed-farming base,
whether it was oats, peas, potatoes, barley, sheep, pigs, or various sorts
of cattle, in addition to such regional specializations as fruit and tobacco.

The five scholars who have undertaken systematic comparisons of
nineteenth-century agriculture in Quebec and Ontario have all referenced
(though not necessarily believed in) the same assumptions of Ontario's
superiority and that superiority being rooted in cultural differences, as
well as the same staples approach. Phillips and Isbister have accepted the
notion of difference, and they have largely accepted the staples theory.
McCallum and McInnis had challenged some of these assumptions, while
McInnis has gone on to question the staples approach itself. Ouellet's
focus on Canadiens offered comparisons not only between Quebec and
Ontario but also between Canadiens and other farmers within Ontario.

Phillips, although he conceded some role for differing resource endowments, insisted that the key difference between the provinces was the
seigneurial system, read as social relations of production. However,
his perverse notion that an abundance of land tends to create unfree
labour undermines his credibility. Isbister explicitly rules out questions
of resource endowment to stress even more than Phillips the cultural factor in Quebec's low level of agricultural output. Isbister's main contribution to the debate came in trying to measure output by calories. From
that perspective it appeared that the average Quebec farm was not even
self-supporting. According to Isbister, one outcome of that subsistence

failure was widespread malnutrition. Kerr and Smyth, against Isbister, stressed Ontario's soil and climate advantages for agriculture. Even Ontario's marginal lands were a much smaller proportion of the province's arable land base. They challenged his picture of a failed subsistence agriculture completely disconnected from markets. In fact the turn to dairy was itself a product of market logic. J.I. Little went further: like Kerr and Smyth, he noted that a dairy specialization would have been a "strange option" for farm families failing to feed themselves. He rejected the calorie approach to productivity: calorie counting cannot be applied uniformly to diverse types of farming such as grain versus livestock.

McCallum's analysis more directly embraced the staples model shared by Phillips and Isbister, but he placed differing resource endowments at the centre of his argument. He also considerably widened the geographic scope by examining the ecological succession of pioneer wheat frontiers across northeastern North America from the seventeenth to the nineteenth centuries. Yet, having begun his analysis by discounting culture, McCallum was nonetheless compelled to concede that it was cultural factors that held Canadiens in the seigneurial zone decades after New Englanders would have abandoned such worn or marginal lands.

Unlike Phillips, Isbister, or McCallum, McInnis challenged the staple model and questioned the idea of Ontario's general superiority in farming. His detailed examination of Ontario farm outputs showed that the commercial farms were far fewer than the literature had assumed and that their net outputs for markets were much smaller. The key to Ontario's edge in provincial averages of farm output came from a minority of farms and counties that produced substantial surpluses in wheat. While wheat may not have been the be-all and end-all imagined by Harold Innis (and McCallum), it still played a key role in the provincial economy. Consequently McInnis ended up not so much with a rejection of the staple thesis as a better sense of its limits, as well as its pertinence.

By concentrating on a single ethnic group and the regions where it clustered, Ouellet brought a different perspective to the comparative study of Quebec and Ontario. His regional studies showed that *when* an ethnic group took up farming had significant and enduring impacts on its degree of economic success. While Ouellet never made the point explicitly, the relative success of francophones in Ontario tells against the old stereotypes of writers like Jones about Canadiens' lack of capacity for farming. Ouellet concluded that Canadiens did better in Ontario than most of those who remained in Quebec. Sometimes early arrival gave them an edge in finding good soil. But even when they came late onto poorer soils, in the long run, they did better than most in Quebec. Ouellet also pointed out that wheat was never the predominant (exclusive) crop in either Ontario or Quebec.

Shifting through these debates, I believe several conclusions can be drawn about the mid-nineteenth century. Canadiens were not inherently incapable farmers. They succeeded where they had opportunities, not only in the high-performing regions in Quebec but also in several Ontario counties. Culture is a significant factor in economic success: it cannot simply be wished away by appeals to rational economic man. Canadiens strove to stay on the land, where others chose to move on. The great majority of farmers in both provinces consumed most of what they produced and sold a surplus when they had one. A minority in both provinces regularly produced large-scale surpluses, which were not limited to wheat. For example, in 1861 Ontario had five counties that produced more than 100,000 pounds of cheese on the farm (not that cheese was the only thing that those farms produced for sale).[46] Ontario had a greater resource endowment than Quebec. Consequently, it had a larger minority of these surplus producers. The agriculture of the two provinces, then, was strikingly similar in structure; the essential difference lay in the size of that highly productive minority.

These comparisons between the two provinces clearly show that the debates over the staples thesis are integral to understanding the historiography of Canadian farming. The next chapter explores that thesis in its application to Ontario agriculture.

The Staples Thesis Expounded, Critiqued, and Modified

The debates over Ontario's agriculture have not been as central to understanding the province's history as those in Quebec. The reason is obvious: the state of Quebec's agriculture has been the focus of the debate over the origins and character of Canadien nationalism. But to understand the contrasting nationalisms of the two provinces and the particular roles those nationalisms played in the Confederation era and subsequent decades, we need to understand the provinces' different agrarian experiences. Moreover, while Ontario's agriculture has seldom been linked to that province's aggressive determination to dominate the Prairie West, that link certainly exists.

The historiographic debates over Ontario's agriculture have also been smaller in every sense than those over Quebec, most significantly in terms of both the numbers of participants involved and the issues thought to be at stake. The thesis of a mid-century agricultural crisis in Ontario came later in the discussion and (when discussed at all in the existing literature) has been looked at in the context of the debates over wheat as an export. An examination of farms as family enterprises leads us to significantly modify the view of wheat as a staple, partially retrieving its role as a driver in Ontario's rural economy.

As far back as Adam Shortt (1859–1931), Canada's economic history has been described as the development of a few natural commodities – fish (cod), fur (beaver), lumber (white pine), and minerals (such as nickel and copper) – for export to a metropolitan centre. While W.A. Mackintosh is generally credited with the first formulation of a staples thesis, Harold Innis, as both teacher and writer, made it the predominant interpretation in Canadian economic history.[1] Innis considered that each staple evoked its own settlement pattern and transportation system. From his various writings a coherent, if somewhat cursory, view emerges of how Ontario's agriculture developed from earliest white settlement to the post-Confederation era.

Innis saw the earliest settlers – loyalists and late loyalists – as bringing to the new colony of Upper Canada the techniques of pioneer farming developed in the southern colonies. However, even his passing comments make clear that he did not see a wheat monoculture geared to export springing instantaneously into existence with those early pioneers. He noted that farmers' first markets were local ones, provided by the fur trade, the military, and then new incoming settlers, at least in periods of peak migration such as the early 1830s. Contemporary accounts mentioned quantities of wheat and flour being brought to market as early as 1790–1800, showing that when farmers could produce an off-farm surplus, it would most likely have been wheat.[2] There is obviously a very strong parallel here with Fernand Ouellet's focus on wheat and exports from Lower Canada.

With his great concern for the influence of transportation and other export staples, Innis noted links between pioneer agriculture and the fur trade and, later, the timber trade. Both activities provided immediate markets for the first wheat surpluses.[3] He speculated that the timber trade also contributed to accelerating the settlement process, since returning timber ships provided much cheaper passage for immigrants to British North America.[4] Innis viewed the canal building along the St Lawrence–Great Lakes route from the late 1820s to the 1840s as showing the determination to extend the water transport system developed for the timber export trade into one for wheat as the emerging staple: "The rapid increase in the importance of agricultural produce and especially wheat precipitated the problem of the upper St Lawrence."[5] It was the volume of wheat to be shipped that pushed canal development forward.

Innis was aware that British demand was neither constant nor assured in every year before 1846. The Corn Laws offered a limited preference to colonial wheat and flour, but their primary goal was to protect British agriculture from overseas competition, not to foster colonial development.[6] Thus Canadian wheat at times faced barriers in the British market. Farmers were committed to a staple that did not have assured access to the metropolitan market for which it was grown. Innis noted that there was also a domestic market, "to meet the demands of incoming settlers."[7]

Innis frequently described Ontario farming *before* 1850 as based largely on wheat, but he never explicitly gives a date or even a period when he considers that circumstance to have come into existence.[8]

However, his usual distinction or cleavage focused on the 1850s, when he saw a combination of factors forcing Ontario farmers away from a concentration on wheat to other forms of farming. The first factor was the decline in wheat yields (and so also farm incomes) due to soil exhaustion brought on by continuous cropping. The second factor was that "unoccupied fertile land" had largely disappeared in southern Ontario.[9] He considered that there were two immediate responses to this situation: Ontario emigration to the western American states where virgin soil was still available for wheat farming, and a shift to livestock, which he dated from the decade after 1855.

Innis's perceptions of early Ontario agriculture were not wholly monolithic. For example, he considered that the Ottawa Valley had its own pattern of agriculture, geared to the needs of the lumber industry. Hay there sold for $15 to $20 a ton. Farmers also found a winter cash income in the lumber shanties upriver.[10]

While not denying that many farmers kept cattle for dairying, Innis saw their output as being consumed almost wholly on the farm or in the immediate neighbourhood. Before 1850, the concentration on clearing had led farmers to value oxen over dairy or beef cattle, since what they needed were draft animals (also in demand in the timber trade). However, the burgeoning American market, newly opened by the 1854 Reciprocity Treaty, created a demand for beef cattle as Ontario farmers imported American Shorthorns and greatly expanded their livestock holdings. This shift in turn favoured a variety of forage crops that grew well where wheat no longer did. By 1860 Ontario had changed from a livestock-importing to a livestock-exporting region.

The end of reciprocity in 1866 restricted entry into the American market. However, the introduction of new labour-saving farm machinery from the United States freed the labour necessary for the transition from land-extensive wheat and livestock farming to dairying. The existence of large herds of cattle, many of them dual-purpose beef and dairy, eased the transition to labour-intensive dairy farming. From New York came techniques of cheese making, which combined with the great transportation revolution wrought by steam to once again open a British market for Ontario's agricultural output.[11] Yet even in his essay on the development of the dairy industry, Innis did not suggest that dairy products replaced wheat as an export staple. Rather, dairy became, at best, first amongst equals. The passing of the wheat monoculture saw the emergence of different regional agricultures in Ontario built around fruit growing, barley, tobacco, beef, and pork as well as dairying. Ontario's livestock industry was expected by many at the time to receive a further boost from the 1878 British ban on American cattle. However, as the transportation revolution proceeded worldwide, Argentina, Australia, and New Zealand became effective competitors, squeezing Ontario's dairy produce share of the British market. And while urban growth in central Canada created an alternative domestic market for dairy products, since the end of the nineteenth century, Ontario dairy farmers have had to rely on protective tariffs to hold their place in their own home market against overseas competitors.[12]

Innis's ideas were developed by his followers, with Vernon Fowke preeminent among them, especially in regard to farming in Ontario. His approach began from the perspective of public policy toward agriculture, which he considered had been the product of the interests (sometimes conflicting) of urban business elites, not of farmers. Before 1850, Canadian colonial governments – like the business leaders who dominated them – had been primarily concerned to perfect the St Lawrence transportation system, first by canals and then railways, in order to capture the American Midwestern trade. Neither government nor business took much notice of the commercial opportunities offered by the much smaller agricultural base within British North America. However, during the 1850s, the end of Ontario's expanding agricultural frontier sharpened the awareness of some businessmen as to how much they had profited from supplying transportation, provisions, and equipment to new immigrant settlers. The agricultural frontier came to be seen as a potential investment opportunity that could vitalize the whole economy.

Fowke attempted some precision in the application of the term "staple" to wheat in Ontario. Like Innis, he distinguished between wheat grown as part of a general "provisioning trade" for local or regional markets and wheat grown as a specialized export product.[13] The gradual increase in wheat shipped before 1850 was primarily part of a provisions trade rather than a staple trade. While saying that "definition is difficult and unnecessary," Fowke nonetheless offered the following rule of thumb: "The distinction seems to rest on the relative importance of wheat in the export cargo. If wheat, or wheat and flour, comprised simply one element in the assorted provisions cargo ... wheat then would be thought of as a *provision*. But when wheat came to be exported customarily in such quantities as to move in one-commodity cargoes, then wheat came to be thought of as a *staple*."[14] One reason that Fowke considered precise definition unnecessary was that "whether at a particular time wheat was a provision or a staple altered only the degree of interest in its production."[15] However, he clearly gave himself latitude in how to classify wheat by the emphasis he put on the *degree* of difference between the staples and the provisions trades: "Before 1850, perhaps much earlier, Upper Canadian farms were supplying surplus wheat in sufficient quantities to warrant the suggestion that Canadian agriculture was now the basis for a new staple trade."[16]

In time, Fowke's emphasis shifted from the idea of a wheat staple replacing the fur staple and complementing the timber staple to the idea that the settlement process itself was the "vitalizing" force, not the pioneers' first crops: "The exchange activities of the Canadian frontier settler in eastern Canada were far from negligible and ... his integration into the price system did not await or depend upon his production of a staple agricultural export."[17] Fowke felt that from the absence of a single predominant agricultural staple in the early years of settlement in Ontario, some writers had wrongly inferred that the farmers of that era must have been self-sufficient. But he argued, "The frontier farmer might have no single staple product and still sell a great variety of produce in substantial quantities."[18] He pointed to the potash and pearl ash trade of the newly settled pioneer farmer, followed by meat, butter, and wool, as well as wheat.

If we take Fowke as the expositor of the classical staples thesis of Innis as applied to wheat, then it is apparent that he did not argue that wheat exports were the sole engine that drove the rural Ontario economy. In his stress on the "investment opportunities" in the "capital-creation processes" at work on the agricultural frontier, he sounded remarkably like Douglas McCalla.[19] Where the two perhaps differ most is that Fowke considered that government policy, which had been geared largely to commercial interests, was suspect: "The willingness of the lumber interests to have farmers establish themselves in situations with no long-term prospects for survival may not be surprising, but the willingness of government to conspire towards that end under the guise of 'aid to agriculture' is."[20] From Fowke's writings we do not get a picture of a wheat monoculture in Ontario, certainly not before 1850. He portrayed farmers who consumed most of what they produced and produced most of what they consumed. Their off-farm output was diversified. Their major collective impact on the rest of the provincial economy was not always what they had to sell but the process by which their farms were established, in the investment opportunities it opened to others.

For Ontario and wheat, the staples thesis reached its apogee in three texts published between 1980 and 1991, aimed at retelling Canadian

history with the economy in centre stage William L. Marr and Donald
Paterson, Richard Pomfret, and Kenneth Norrie and Douglas Owram.
Written by economists and economic historians, the texts bring the disci-
pline's tools of analysis to bear on the topic.[21]

Marr and Paterson considered that nineteenth-century agriculture
in Canada had three possible roles: acting as the centre of export-led
growth, supplying the local needs of the export sector (e.g., food for the
fur trade), or providing subsistence (on the level of the individual farm
or of a region as a whole, thus implying the existence and importance
of local markets). They viewed these three roles as successive stages of
Ontario farming in the nineteenth century: "The widespread development of mixed farming for general markets, which changed the focus of
central Canadian agriculture, occurred only after 1846."[22] After 1860,
Ontario moved away from wheat to livestock and dairying, since wheat
blight had compounded the longer-term problems of soil exhaustion and
competition from ever-cheaper wheat from the American Midwest.

Before 1860, for Marr and Paterson, wheat was Ontario's central
export, and Britain was the definitive market: "Between [1794 and
1846] the staple export of wheat emerged as the dynamic element in
agriculture based almost entirely upon entry to the British market ...
The wheat-import policies of both Great Britain and the United States
greatly influenced the prosperity of Upper Canada."[23] However, as they
developed their argument about entry into the UK market, a curious gap
emerged. On the one hand, they provide a reasonably clear exposition
of the British Corn Law and its operation from 1800 to 1846: "Basic-
ally [the Corn Law] prohibited imports of grain and flour when British prices were very low, but permitted them when prices were high."[24]
Under the 1815 Corn Law, "no wheat was permitted to enter Great Britain at prices below 67 shillings per quarter."[25] The first hint of inconsistency appears when the authors moved to describing the actual effect
of the law. In 1820 "good British harvests" drove down the UK wheat
price, invoking "the high Corn Law duty," which had the result of "forcing British North American exports down."[26] "The climax, in a sense,
of this staple dependence took place from about 1832 to 1840 when
Great Britain experienced excellent harvests ... which ... reduced exports.
Note the relatively low wheat prices ... from 1832 to 1838 and the correspondingly small amounts of British North American exports to Great
Britain."[27] However, intermingled with the above was an apparently different account of Ontario's access to the UK market. In general terms we
are told, "During this period, 1794–1846, the demand forces were the

essential ones, and they, in turn, were related to the degree of preference which Great Britain showed Canada."[28] The next sentence is critical: "Preferential access to the British market was ensured under the provisions of the Corn Laws which were designed to protect British home agriculture." Note that "access" was not "ensured," only the preference. This nuance seemed to have been unintentional, although accurate. "Access to the British market guaranteed a market for British North American grain and flour; however there was an associated cost." That "cost" was "a high variance in income." When the UK market effectively closed due to low domestic wheat prices, British North American prices fell sharply. "Not surprisingly, Upper Canadian farmers resented the income-instability imparted by the Corn Laws even though they were the guarantee of entry to the British market." It would appear that "unstable farm income" was the authors' way of saying that Ontario wheat was effectively excluded from the market to which the Corn Laws "guaranteed" it access.

However, the burden of Marr and Paterson's overall argument fell not on that "instability" but on that strangely unreliable "guarantee": "Nevertheless, the British Corn Laws were the instrument which encouraged specialized agricultural production on the frontier of Upper Canada ... It was the protection of the Corn Laws which gave Upper Canada the impetus to develop its agricultural sector through the creation of an export staple."[29] Given their own insistence on an unqualified classical model of supply and demand, their stress on the power of the British market to draw forth a specialized wheat staple from the province was especially inappropriate. If "the demand forces were the essential ones," then why was there no exodus *out* of farming during the prolonged periods when that demand lapsed – 1820–24 and 1832–38? Something better than such a simple and uncritical application of a classical model is necessary to explain the relationship between the British market, wheat prices, and the pace of settlement in Ontario.

By contrast, Richard Pomfret's compact treatment of Canadian economic history gave almost no attention to Ontario agriculture. He described the colony, already a net wheat exporter in 1794, as not escaping dearth through poor harvests until mid-century. "The important point is not that Upper Canada had found a new staple export, but rather that she was more self-sufficient in food than the rest of British North America."[30] Norrie and Owram, at greater length, gave a much more rounded account of the province, its slowly evolving wheat staple, and the linkages between economic sectors. Unlike Pomfret, they saw the colony as a wheat-export region by 1820, though hampered by the vagaries of the Corn Law.[31] While they carefully incorporated arguments critical of staples, their text, as Douglas McCalla observed, was organized around and reinforced the staples thesis.[32]

Given that there was *not* a guaranteed or ensured UK market constantly drawing Ontario farmers into wheat specialization, we need a rather different picture of how the pioneer clearing progressed toward commercial farming. In terms of the development of farming in the province, two related debates emerged amongst those who largely accepted the staples thesis. One was over the degree of farmers' self-sufficiency and the role of export markets. The other was over the relationship between Innis's thesis and Marxist theory, especially notions of economic dependence. Staple-thesis critics in both debates have argued for the rejection of single-factor determinism in favour of a more balanced and nuanced understanding of Ontario agriculture and the Ontario economy in general.

Fowke argued fifty years ago that the self-sufficient pioneer farm was a myth and that, from its earliest years, the pioneer farm was oriented to the production of wheat for an export market. More recently, Leo Johnson has argued that Fowke posed a false dichotomy between self-sufficient and commercial farming. Marvin McInnis's work with a sample of farms from the 1861 census appears to reinforce Johnson's view of a continuum from the largely self-sufficient to the commercial farm that regularly produced and sold an off-farm surplus.

In fact the self-sufficiency debate was merely an argument over ideal types. No one denies either that farmers produced *some* off-farm surplus or that farmers consumed *much* of what they produced and produced *much* of what they consumed.[33] Fowke was plainly aware that no serious historian before him had maintained that pioneer farmers were entirely self-sufficient: "Contexts nevertheless reveal the basic assumption that the commercial life of the pioneer was negligible and without significance for other segments of the national economy."[34] Seeking to engage A.W. Currie's "more cautious" description of pioneer agriculture, Fowke was reduced to admitting, "With staple production thus held to be compatible with self-sufficiency, there remains only a question of more or less,"[35] and "the typical frontier farmer could never be regarded as indifferent to conditions in the market-place."[36] To that end, he recounted the costs of immigration, the need for some capital (whether brought from the Old World or acquired through credit or labour) to commence a farm, and the continuous need for off-farm articles such as salt and iron.

"The migrants were thrust initially and continuously into reliance on an exchange and monetary economy."[37] He argued convincingly that lack of coin or currency and the consequent resort to barter were *not* indications of self-sufficiency. The fact that pioneers frequently worked for someone else to gain their necessities, however, does not readily demonstrate, in my view, a desire for dependence on others, but rather a struggle to get away from it.

Fowke believed his strongest argument was pioneer farmers' resort to credit, most commonly from the country merchants' stores: "Credit would be wholly incompatible with self-sufficiency; yet credit is a familiar, almost indispensible, element in frontier agricultural economies."[38] While his primary sources repeatedly point out merchants' folly in extending credit to farmers who could not earn enough from their marketable surpluses to pay the debt, he considered "the pioneer's firmly rooted propensity to incur debt" as the "final and convincing demonstration of the unreality of the concept of agricultural self-sufficiency."[39]

Leo Johnson's retort to Fowke focused on the explicit message of the market's importance, rather than the subtler subtext. He began with the dichotomy and noted that Fowke was aware that no one had made a case for absolute self-sufficiency. Observing that Currie especially spoke of a continuum from subsistence to staple production, Johnson saw this continuum as spanning both time (a gradual shift from primarily subsistence farming to ever-larger off-farm sales) and space at a given time (some pioneer farms could market little surplus, while others could both produce and market a substantial surplus). He regarded Fowke as deliberately creating a false dichotomy to attack the interventionist left liberalism of the Rowell-Sirois Report in favour of a non-interventionist classical liberalism of free markets.[40]

According to Johnson, classical liberal economics has always had problems with any producers whose products are not included in commercial exchange. How can the all-powerful market operate upon them? He cited Samir Amin on the existence of rival modes of production as well as the traditional Marxist view of rival socio-economic classes. The tension between these modes commonly arises from one of them being dominant. He noted that, at first, hunter-gatherer (and migrant farming) native societies also had little connection to the European market. Johnson offered use-value from Marxist theory as an alternative to exchange value as found in neo-classical economic theory.

Pioneer concerns with roads and other means of transport reflected their relative inability to get their produce to market and their desire to market crops as well as purchase essential supplies. Johnson weighed the farmer's time to get to market with his crop against the opportunity cost of a tradesman's wage, to show the very poor return a farmer could have expected from the attempt to market a farm surplus from the edge of frontier settlement. Not everyone could afford the luxury of waiting for winter to make the trip to market.

Johnson also noted the problems of gristmills (too scarce, too seldom in working order) and the unstable British demand for wheat and flour (as in the negative 1820 operation of the 1815 Corn Law). In the 1820s and 1830s, it was an unwise farmer who thought of the market as any more than a *possible* destination for a surplus not needed on his own farm or in his own community. The failure of the 1815–25 agricultural improvement societies showed that most farmers knew that more effort to produce an off-farm surplus would be largely wasted because markets were inaccessible due to both trade barriers and lack of transportation. This reality changed in the 1840s and 1850s when the completion of the canal system, gravel roads, and finally railways provided much-improved access to markets. At the same time, access to both markets (British free trade in 1846 and reciprocity with the United States in 1854) and credit became more secure.

It seems to me that the transition of at least part of the wheat crop from use-value to exchange-value would have been complex. At first, the farmer might well have seen all his grain as use-value. But part (one-tenth or one-twelfth), which he paid to the miller to obtain flour, would have entered the market as either flour or whiskey. To the miller, the wheat gained by barter had only (or largely) exchange-value. While the commercial farmer needed a good price just to survive, the more self-sufficient subsistence-oriented farmer – looking to dispose of an unneeded surplus – was less likely to be vitally interested in the price or price fluctuations, since his survival did not depend upon the price. That observation may help explain Douglas McCalla's findings (noted subsequently) that grain exports showed little relationship to price.

Johnson argued that the importance of use-value "natural production" had consequences for pioneer farming. The first was the tendency before 1850 for farmers to subdivide their holdings. An orientation to use-value favoured a small, highly diversified farm, while "independent commodity production" favoured larger, more specialized and more efficient farms: "Although the size of the original grants ranged from 200 acres to 5,000 acres, by 1850 the size and distribution of farms in the longest settled areas was indistinguishable from that in newly settled

Table 4.1: Number of Ontario townships by category of population density, 1820–51.

Urban population	(%)	Township categories		
		Pioneer	Transitional	Mature
1820	3.4	158	20	1
1830	3.6	186	34	7
1840	6.7	189*	84	23
1851	13.4	142**	110	110***

* These pioneer townships contained 32% of the colony's total population.
** These pioneer townships contained only 12.6% of the colony's total population.
*** These mature townships contained 60% of the colony's total population.

Source: Johnson, "New Thoughts on an Old Problem," 21.

areas where grants and sales were in the 50 acre to 100 acre range."[41] After 1850 Johnson noted that the predominant trend was to consolidate and enlarge landholdings. He also cited the rise of towns and villages in rural areas after 1840 as evidence of a change to exchange-value, which favoured off-farm specialization. As evidence for the timing of that change, he offered a useful system for classifying townships by population density. Table 4.1 shows Ontario's townships by population density. "Mature" townships were those with forty to fifty persons per square mile, while "pioneer" townships held less than twenty.

The clash of debate ought not to obscure the fundamental consensus shared by the protagonists. Fowke strove to debunk a myth (of his own making) that pioneer farmers were so completely self-sufficient as to be indifferent to any markets. However, in making a case for the importance of the market, he missed the important distinction between a local "internal" market (to which his own sources testified) and an external staple market. Johnson offered a valuable corrective in stressing the continuum (already alluded to by Currie) between production for on-farm subsistence or personal use-value and the evolving off-farm market with its tendency toward exchange-value.

A second debate, involving many more participants, arose over the relation between the staple thesis and attempts to apply Marxism to the study of Canadian society and history. In 1963 Mel Watkins wrote the clearest early restatement of Innis's staple thesis as a theory of economic growth.[42] As he moved to the left in Canadian politics, Watkins took Innis and his version of a staple theory with him. In 1977 he reviewed the staples debate, culminating in its Marxist adaptation. Left-leaning academics had begun adapting Innis's dependency reading of staples to explain the evolution of social and economic classes. Watkins considered that a generation of economists had sought to ignore or downplay the radical side of Innis and that side had now been rescued: "It is scholars working out of the Marxist paradigm who are now predominant in the literature on the staples approach."[43] Two years later C.B. Macpherson described Innis as a kind of proto-Marxist: "The further he went on his own, the closer ... he moved towards a Marxian analysis. If his life had not been cut short so early, this might have become more apparent."[44]

In 1986 David McNally published a stringent critique of what he called "Left Innisianism" and its pretensions to being Marxist. He accused the new fans of Innis of accepting a technological determinist conception of Canadian capitalism, and of Canadian economic and social history.[45] As a result of following Innis, he maintained, would-be Marxists had lost their conceptions of social class, in the abstraction of labour as a factor of production rather than a self-conscious force that could shape the production process to serve itself.

The attempt to re-work Innis's staple thesis into a universal theory of economic development and the response of Marxist theory to that attempt together raise some very old issues about the nature of theory in the social sciences. Part of the nineteenth-century methods war between Carl Menger and Gustav Schmoller was a conflict between the universal claims made by the new microeconomics and those of the emerging Historical school of economists, who focused on particular historical experience as the critical factor in understanding economic behaviour.[46] The new economic history of the 1960s and 1970s can be seen as a renewed methods war, as the tools of microeconomic analysis were applied to the traditional subject matter of its old rival, the Historical school.

The critical responses of Robin Neill and Hugh Aitken to Watkins's interpretation of Innis's thesis as a theory of economic development can be understood as following in the tradition of Schmoller, insisting on the historical particularity of any given situation against those who want to stress universal claims or the more universal elements. Neill set Innis's work against the claims of Watkins, seeing the first as a historical thesis and the second as a theoretical model. In fact Neill had a better argument to make. He wanted to argue that Innis advanced his thesis as a historically specific explanation of the pattern that could be discerned in the succession of predominant export trades. He wanted to find Innis putting even his own thesis aside when he considered it did not (as in the Yukon) "fit the facts." Not only could a specifically Canadian pattern *not* be applied universally to other countries, but in some particular cases, it would not help to explain events even in Canada.[47]

Aitken, on the other hand, described the staples thesis as a "myth" that had "the power to engage the imagination, the power to energize the often dull and tedious work of scholarly research and convert it into an exciting enterprise." Myths "give meaning, significance, and purpose to [our] lives ... and cultures are formed as much by myths as by artefacts."[48] Aitken appeared to consider Innis's thesis as the predominant paradigm for Canadian economic history. He argued that no one can directly test a myth, only theories or hypotheses derived from it. Thus, Innis's myth can be neither true nor false "in the positivistic sense," since it is not subject to "empirical verifiability" (as Edward Vickery has tried to undertake).[49]

We now turn from the general formulation of the thesis and its proponents' use of Ontario in the nineteenth century to develop it, to the critiques that argue that it was a fundamental misreading of the role of wheat in Ontario agriculture and, more broadly, in the province's economic development. Both Douglas McCalla and Marvin McInnis have offered substantial empirical evidence against the primacy given to wheat as the export staple that drove Ontario's economy. Both have also given comprehensive analyses of agriculture's role in the provincial economy. After examining their critiques of wheat as a staple, we will turn to specific applications that seek to test or apply the staples approach on particular issues.

McCalla attacked Innis's staples determinism as lacking both internal logical consistency and supporting evidence. The external demand for staples, and the stress on geography and the technological imperatives that arise from a given staple, do not serve to explain either the timing or the rate of economic development. In particular, neither wheat nor timber can be shown to have been central to the provincial economy. McCalla proposed an alternative approach, stressing measurement of overall economic activity allowing the measurement of each sector's relative contribution on the one hand and the strength of the linkages between sectors on the other hand. McCalla explicitly faulted Innis's description of the relationship of export staples and transportation networks. According to McCalla, Innis's reading of the relationship between wheat and railways was derived from the experience of the Prairies and then projected back onto the economy of Ontario. Innis believed that "particular commodities had relatively consistent implications for development."[50] But on the Prairies the construction of the railway largely preceded the development of wheat production for export. However, in Ontario the railway boom came *after* wheat had established itself as a major export commodity:

"The 1840s expansion of wheat exports [came] before even the canals were completed on the St Lawrence and well before railways were built."[51] Moreover, McCalla maintained there was no evidence to support Innis's speculation that the timber ships' unused capacity encouraged immigration to British North America: "The westward movement of emigrants actually correlated only quite imperfectly with eastbound timber shipping volumes, suggesting a weak relationship at best between migration and the physical movement of timber ... Costs of passage by various types of vessels must have been only a small factor in any migration decision. Thus, cheap rates to Quebec were no more than a necessary, not a sufficient condition for provincial development."[52] Even if cheap rates attracted emigrants to a particular North American port, there was no guarantee that they would settle where they landed. If returning timber ships really attracted immigrants, why did New Brunswick's proportionally larger return capacity not seem to raise its population? Moreover, Innis had considered that "the rapid increase in the importance of agricultural produce and especially wheat precipitated the [transportation] problem of the upper St Lawrence."[53] By contrast, McCalla showed that the construction of new canals and the expansion of existing ones had more to do with politics than Upper Canadian wheat exports. In fact, "At no time was the [Welland] canal physically taxed by the volume of ships seeking passage. The decision to expand evidently resulted from a desire to accommodate larger sailing vessels which now served the American side of the upper lakes and some steam-powered vessels."[54] That is, the technological imperative that affected canal construction did not arise out of the nature of wheat as an export commodity or even the volume of wheat being shipped; instead, "Canadians built canals to carry ships rather than, as on the Erie [canal], boats; thus the minimum scale for physical reasons was massively excessive in terms of the volume of Upper Canada's interregional and international trades."[55]

McCalla further examined the *volume* of wheat exports and the *price* of wheat compared to the *rate* of economic development (measured largely by population growth, increase in cleared land, and credit expansion) in Ontario as a test of the staple theory's explanatory power. He found no obvious link between surges of immigration and either the volume or the price of wheat exports: "The decline in emigration after 1819 can be associated with the continuing downward slide in wheat prices, and the 1831–32 peak in emigration followed the peak in prices in 1829 and in earnings from wheat exports in 1830–31. After 1832, however,

such a direct relationship between colonial wheat prices and British emigration seems less likely."[56] The most he conceded was that the 1830–31
boom stimulated interest in or expectations about the province's longer-
term profitability. The collapse of the British wheat market and the fall
in prices in the mid-1830s did not seem to drag down the Ontario economy. In part this may have been because the multiplier effect of rising
wheat prices had a greater impact than that of falling prices. However,
as his argument developed, he saw that a direct relation between wheat
prices or export volumes and volume of emigration was perhaps not as
probable as he first thought: "Emigration was an investment process,
driven primarily by longer-term thinking, though influenced by short-
term considerations. On the other hand, variations in the rate of migration do not appear all that clearly in province-wide rates of increase
in population and land under culture, which were much steadier."[57] He
noted that farmers, once on the land, had little choice but to continue.
"It may still be that many people had thought of the economy as a wheat
economy all along, or at least as a wheat economy in the making, but
that is not the same as arguing that it was actual wheat production and
its linkages that drove the economy forward."[58] Why, then, did local merchants and their suppliers still allow credit to finance that longer term?

McCalla posed an investment theory to explain colonial economic
growth. The abundance of natural resources was a *constant*, as are several other factors commonly offered to "explain." But what we need to
do, he maintained, was to focus on what produced *change* – not just
demand for exports but changes in land grant or tariff policy, business
cycle, and financial institutions. However, he warned, "This is by no
means to argue that investment was a purely independent variable, but
rather to suggest it is logical to begin an inquiry with it as the first stage
in a sequence of processes that expanded real productive resources and
real output."[59]

Before turning to examine McCalla's investment thesis, we need to
look at his understanding of how the forestry industry interacted with
farming. In McCalla's eyes, if wheat fails to live up to the staple role,
timber fares worse. Both in Ontario and elsewhere, left-wing critics considered the lumber trade to show the shortcomings of staple-based economic development. Especially amongst the left Innisians, the stress has
fallen on dependence, external control, and exaggerated vulnerability
to trade cycles in the international economy. But McCalla argued that
much of the southern Ontario timber frontier developed autonomously.
Again he faulted the logic of those using the staple thesis that assumed

British North America had a comparative advantage in geography, enhanced by appropriate technology, in producing certain key natural resources such as lumber. However, McCalla argued, the conventional timber trade story of a moment of "creation" in 1806 – when the British cabinet offered a bounty for colonial timber – suggests not comparative advantage but the central role of government policy decisions.

What was the role of the lumber trade in Ontario's economic development? What linkages to the rest of the economy can be *shown*? McCalla started with 1823, the beginning of the record for timber exports, and ended in 1846, to avoid the complexity of free trade and the growth of sawn-lumber exports to the United States. In this period, serial data are sufficient to give an idea of the relative orders of magnitude between internal and export markets and among different sectors. After reviewing the many problems in getting reliable data that apply directly to Ontario (such as how to distinguish Ontario from American lumber on the St Lawrence River, or how to distinguish Ontario from Quebec lumber on the Ottawa River), he concluded there is enough evidence to question the central role given to the Ottawa Valley as the most important aspect of Ontario's forest industry.

For every year up to the early 1840s, McCalla pointed out, the St Lawrence River above Montreal carried more wood products than the Ottawa River. The leading item by value was potash and pearl ash. Squared oak and oak staves showed a continuously rising volume with some short-term fluctuations. Previous historians have assumed that farmers created these items merely as by-products in clearing their land. McCalla countered this: "But the high total value of such products; the fact that volumes fluctuated in a period when assessment data indicate a relatively steady rate of land-clearing, and evidence of localization and specialized production and marketing all suggest that these were products in their own right."[60] The export of ashes from eastern Ontario remained high long after settlement was complete but fell west of Niagara in the 1830s even as clearing was accelerating there. Staves were another forest-derived product that farmers could produce during the slow winter months to augment their cash income. "The proximity of forest and farm (indeed most farms included much forest) sustained a local economy of some complexity, offering numerous choices, to those with and without land, and helping local economies to make the fullest use of their land and labour."[61]

On the lands along the St Lawrence and Great Lakes, there was a substantial integration of farming and lumber, with farmers making a small

Table 4.2: Value of exports from Upper Canada, selected years: 1831–39. Peak years only for each of wheat and wood products shipped via the St Lawrence River, and wood products shipped via the Ottawa River.

| | St Lawrence River | | Ottawa River |
	Wheat (£ 000's)	Wood products (£ 000's)	Wood products (£ 000's)
1831	256	179	63
1836	238	210	115
1837	102	270	113
1839	191	265	123

Source: McCalla, *Planting the Province: The Economic History of Upper Canada, 1784–1870*, 260.

annual cash income, although some larger operations were evident. This trade also heavily supported the lake fleet, a transportation system available to other activities such as bringing in imports and immigrants. On the lower Ottawa, a similar combination of farming and forestry was at work, with lumber being dominant. Only on the upper Ottawa could the full-time logger be found, cutting in winter, shipping in summer. Here the large specialized operations were predominant. But McCalla insisted that their workforce could have been as low as 1,500, against the older claims (based largely on the arguments of the timber lobby) of 7,000 to 8,000 full-time workers (or the equivalent number of part-time workers).

Starting from that lower estimate of the upper Ottawa labour force, McCalla argued that the linkages to the rest of the provincial economy must have been much less than commonly assumed. The principal linkages were pork, flour, and government revenues. For the period 1835–39 these direct links accounted for only about £25,000 a year, and even less before then.[62] By contrast, McCalla offered "lower bounded estimates" to show that lumber produced across Ontario for the local market was greater than the much-reported lumber exports. Moreover, the local lumber market equalled in value the wheat exported from the colony. Even a low estimate of the output from hundreds of local sawmills outside the Ottawa Valley shown in Table 4.2 indicates a higher volume than wheat exports, the supposed motor of the Ontario economy.[63]

To put wheat export volumes and values into the larger context of the province's economy, McCalla offered a series of estimates for the various sectors of that economy. Wood products exported via the St Lawrence on occasion totalled more than the much-touted staples of wheat and Ottawa lumber combined. Even from low estimates of output for sawmills outside the Ottawa Valley, it is clear that those mills produced more lumber than was exported down the Ottawa. Firewood consumption is estimated at 1 million cords a year in 1831 and 2 million cords by 1841. If even 20 per cent of this wood had been sold (to steamships, for example, as well as in urban centres), it would have generated £60,000 in 1831. McCalla portrayed farmers as selling timber to local sawmills and producing potash (or even selling just the ash to a merchant with a potashery), as well as making deals (fir or pine boards cut to standard dimensions) and staves during the winter. The sums earned in each of these activities was probably small: of sixty-eight individuals delivering staves to a merchant in Napanee in 1847, only eleven earned more than £5 and only one earned more than £10.[64] Even so, "In terms of the typically small marketable surpluses produced by most farmers, the data might seem to suggest that whether paid directly or indirectly, forest income represented the indispensible margin between success and failure for the provincial economy."[65] He added a qualification: "But while forest-generated income was essential for some farmers, the evidence can be read differently, as indicating that the rural economy was broadly based and could have allocated scarce time and resources in other ways had markets made that more appropriate."[66] The importance of the forest industry for farming in Ontario was not the supply of Ottawa shanties with pork, hay, horses, or labour but the on-farm production of forest products across the province that sold in local markets.

In agriculture itself, McCalla was determined to show that wheat grown for export was not the central focus of production. While the high prices of 1800–03 called forth increased wheat exports, on the basis of several reasonable assumptions even that boom would have produced no more than an annual average of $16.80 per household in 1803. At their pre-1812 peak, wheat exports could only have been grown on 34,000 of the province's 180,000 cleared acres.[67] From 1815 to 1839, except for the outstanding crop year of 1831, Upper Canadians were consuming more wheat than they exported.[68] Even after the wheat boom of the 1840s, wheat exports accounted for no more than 21 per cent of the total provincial income.[69]

McCalla also rounded out our picture of the province's economy by looking at transportation and manufacturing. The Ontario lake and river fleet grew to hundreds of sailing ships and dozens of steamers by the end of the 1840s. These vessels represented a major capital investment. The value of the sailing ships was £160,000 and that of the less numerous but more expensive steamboats, between £100,000 and £230,000.[70] To operate the steamers in 1849 would have cost about £40,000 in wages to sailors. Investment and employment on this scale was seldom found in manufacturing before 1851, when most production was still done by artisans in their shops rather than in factories. The 1851 census showed 40,000 artisans (of whom no more than 10 per cent worked in factories) as compared to 86,000 farmers.[71] Given the highly erratic way in which census-takers reported (or failed to report) workshops and factories, McCalla cannot give figures comparable to those for shipping. He can only proceed from isolated evidence. For example, smaller sawmills that could be built for as little as £500 numbered in the hundreds. At various times census-takers enumerated 1,000 potash works, 147 distilleries, 239 carding mills, 74 woollen mills, 152 tanneries, 692 gristmills, 1,584 sawmills, and 99 breweries.[72] Many of these were located in rural areas (breweries being an exception) and depended on purchases of local farm products such as wool, hides, barley, timber, ashes, or wheat. Provincial growth was thus "a balanced process, in which the local economy provided many of its own needs and grew with a momentum not closely tied to a particular export. If women's work was fully quantified and included, our sense of the scale of local production and consumption would be further enlarged."[73]

While McCalla was determined to dethrone the staples thesis as the sovereign explanation of Ontario's economic history, the results of his efforts at measurement and estimation, rather than giving a totally different picture of the colony, add nuances to some aspects and much-needed precision to others. In concluding his research agenda in the mid-1980s, he asked, "Does the commonly depicted single, general transition in Ontario agriculture from wheat to mixed farming, coming after, say, 1860, properly describe what happened, or could farming rather be seen as mixed farming with a wheat orientation all along?"[74] From a study of a dozen farm records, he concluded, "Actual total sales and wheat's share of them ... reveal a pattern of continuing reliance on wheat, with, indeed, total farm income tending to fluctuate with the value of wheat sales."[75] However, these records show that other products also produced cash income, and over the longer term, farmers shifted their patterns of production. As a result, he concluded that Ontario's mid-century transition from wheat to other crops was "less absolute than has traditionally been argued."[76]

In the culmination of his work on the Upper Canadian economy, McCalla delivered a similarly grudging acknowledgement of wheat's importance, and even the importance of wheat exports. In part he wanted to suggest the subjective nature of wheat exports' influence on people's economic expectations. Contemporaries saw wheat as the most likely saleable crop. He said, "We may therefore wish to see wheat as having a strategic, or at least talismanic, role in inducing and sustaining settlement and the investment process it entailed."[77] After looking at the influence of international prices in 1800–03 on local Ontario markets, he conceded, "Such brief peaks probably stimulated an enduring increase in provincial wheat output, as farmers responded by increasing production and new settlers were attracted to the economy. Intervening periods of low prices do not appear to have stopped immigration, however, or the continued expansion of the rural economy."[78] But why should only *high* wheat export prices and volumes affect pioneer farmers, and not *low* ones?

In part McCalla tried to explain the uneven influence of export volumes and prices by looking at the interplay of local and international markets: "If peaks in wheat and flour exports were followed by increased immigration, domestic consumption might initially rise faster than production; that would tend to reduce exports, even though production continued to rise."[79] But more fundamentally, he recognized that "emigration was an investment process, driven primarily by longer-term thinking," and not by year-to-year wheat export prices or volumes.[80] The *expectation* that farmers would be able to produce an off-farm cash crop was the foundation of both the emigration process and the willingness of merchants to extend credit that enabled emigrant pioneer farmers to create farms out of the forest.[81] While the *actual* rates of emigration, settlement, and land clearing do not seem to correlate with fluctuations in wheat export prices or volumes, McCalla admitted that "the economy may have needed the idea of wheat as a staple to justify farmers' and others' faith in the system."[82]

Parallel to McCalla's work has run that of economic historian R.M. McInnis. While both sought to dethrone wheat from its role as a staple, McInnis offered different evidence and a different line of argument. Like McCalla, he developed his own picture of what Ontario agriculture looked like, based on his analyses of the 1851 and 1861 censuses. He offered comprehensive indicators for estimating net farm output, by township and county across the province.

McInnis began his critique with his own restatement of the wheat staple thesis: that everyone grew wheat to meet the endless open demand of the British market. That was the force that drove forward the agricultural frontier, and consequently frontier farmers (above all others) grew wheat. But what is wheat supposed to explain: the level of per capita material well-being, the reason labour and capital migrated (thus serving as a theory of factor mobility), or the shape of all other institutions due to its economic predominance? Through his work with the 1861 census, McInnis looked at a series of aspects – geography, farm size, length of settlement – and at the British-Canada price linkage. He concluded that his evidence weighs against the wheat staple thesis.

McInnis was able to show that the greatest amount of wheat was grown in some of the longest settled townships, where production centred on a concentrated group of wheat specialists. He took this as evidence against his own version of the predominance of wheat on the frontier. But, of course, the total wheat production would have been highest in the longest settled areas, because that is where the most cleared land was to be found (and also, by 1861, land that was often more favoured by good soil and climate than the increasingly marginal frontier areas). On the frontier, pioneer farms had less land cleared, so could not rival the very extensive areas planted in older areas. Yet their relatively low wheat acreage need not mean that wheat was not central to the individual pioneer farmer.

McInnis sought to make the same point in his study of the 1851 census returns: "The main areas of wheat concentration were favourably located, long-settled districts with large farms," which had both higher wheat yields and higher proportions of cleared land in wheat than "frontier districts."[83] However, his examples (the township of Dover compared to Adolphustown and Fredericksburg) actually show low wheat yields in the older areas, and larger proportions of cleared land in wheat in frontier townships. It is possible that those older townships specializing in wheat (at least relative to other crops) produced most of all the province's wheat, yet frontier areas produced higher yields and had a higher proportion of cleared land devoted to wheat. While the largest farms (in the older areas) grew the greatest quantity of wheat, they may well have devoted a lesser portion of their land to it than the pioneer. Thus wheat was a larger proportion of each pioneer's farm output, even though all pioneers together did not produce as much wheat as all the larger farms combined. With substantially larger amounts of cleared land, the older farm, even with a relatively lower proportion in wheat, would still have had more total acres in wheat than a pioneer farm with only a small acreage cleared.

When he came to measure wheat production according to farm size, using the 1861 census, McInnis needed to make a number of important distinctions. First, 92 per cent of all farms in his sample grew wheat;

it was ubiquitous. The proportion of cultivated land devoted to wheat declined as farm *size* increased. Farm size in cultivated acres was largely dependent on the farmers' length of settlement: in general, larger farms were older farms. This inverse relation between farm size and proportion of wheat grown on cleared land, then, could be read as evidence that wheat mattered more to pioneer than to longer-established farmers.

However, McInnis had an important distinction to make between fall and spring wheat. Almost everyone planted wheat in the spring (90 per cent), and harvested it in the fall. But they could only plant as much as they could harvest in the limited time available in the fall before winter set in. For a farmer with one or two sons, 10 acres was the norm. Matters were otherwise with wheat planted in the fall. Where climate allowed, the seed could remain dormant over the winter and sprout in the spring. This gave the farmer the option of putting in a larger wheat crop since he had more time to do the harvesting. Those large farms that planted in the fall planted almost twice as much wheat as did medium-sized farms. But half of the large farms did not plant fall wheat at all, presumably due to climate. Thus the largest amount of wheat produced per farm in the province was grown by a particular group of large-scale farms that planted both spring and fall wheat.[84]

The relationship between farm size and proportion of various crops grown leaves a number of important unanswered questions. The larger the farm (i.e., as it ceased to be a pioneer clearing), generally the smaller the proportion of wheat grown. Consequently, larger farms were more diversified. Did they always have a choice? Had years of "wheat mining" – planting repeatedly in the same field – left much of their "cultivated" land fit only for pasture or hay? Did a relative shortage of labour (compared to the total cleared land) on large farms also compel some diversification to a less demanding crop, say, hay rather than wheat?

McInnis measured the age of the individual farm by the length of time that its township had been settled.[85] But what about the "new" farm in an "old" township? In his more recent work on the 1851 census, he noted that his map showing cleared land might overstate the northern extent of settlement, "since within counties there would have been a general north-south gradient to the actual density of settlement."[86]

McInnis found from the 1861 census that farms in more recently settled areas tended to plant more spring wheat (9 acres), than those in the oldest settled townships (just over 7 acres), and that the former's yields were slightly higher. Given that some areas could not grow fall wheat, we need to know whether this (presumably) climatic restriction

limited the appearance of fall wheat in newer and more northern townships. In the few new townships where farms grew fall wheat, the yield
was substantially higher and the amount sown was not much affected
by farm size. Yet McInnis returned to his earlier conclusion that wheat
was not a factor on the frontier! He denied "the impetus to settlement
and agricultural expansion comes from the desire to exploit wheat
markets."[87]

Turning to the relation between British North American prices and
those in Britain, his hypothesis was that "the staple commodity ... is one
that has a readily available market internationally."[88] The price of wheat
in Canada "was set in Britain."[89] "If wheat were an export staple ... its
price in Canada should be determined in Britain and the Canadian price
should be approximately the same as the export threshold price" (i.e.,
taking into account shipping and other costs such as the British tariff).
Could Canadian wheat always be sold at a profit in Britain? McInnis
acknowledged the great problems involved in getting comprehensive,
continuous, and reliable time series (and had some passing criticisms to
make of Ouellet's series, even while using them). But most of the time he
found the Canadian (i.e., Montreal) price set locally, not by the British
(i.e., international) market. The reason, of course, was that Canadian
wheat did not have free access to the British market in the early 1830s;
only after the mid-1840s could it routinely enter.

McInnis's new data from the 1861 census were not revolutionary,
more a matter of interpretation rather than evidence. But he went on
to say that *evidence* hitherto has been made to fit the interpretation
that "development was motivated by the wheat staple."[90] He was convinced (in spite of his own earlier statement) that the weight of *evidence*
is against the staples interpretation. In fact, his own new evidence shows
the critical importance of spring wheat to the pioneer farmer as a cash
crop (if not *the* cash crop). He further had shown that fall wheat was
the major cash crop of half the larger farms in his sample. Like McCalla,
McInnis – while striving to rein in the uncritical acceptance of wheat as
rural Ontario's sole staple – was providing evidence for qualification
rather than refutation.

As in his work with Frank Lewis on Quebec, McInnis sought to give
an overview of Ontario's agriculture as a context for both description
and analysis. From the 1851 census, he calculated and plotted the proportion of cleared land in each of 324 townships. The results highlight
more precisely the regional character of farming patterns in the province at mid-century. Eastern Ontario (except for the long-settled parts

bordering the Bay of Quinte) was underdeveloped, while west of London very substantial amounts of occupied land remained to be cleared.

Rather less straightforward were his attempts to create "the synthetic net output calculation" to estimate the township and county averages of farm productivity. He reviewed the difficulties in reading early census reports and his means of overcoming these. He was also aware of the limitations of a single snapshot of a society in a given moment: "Caution is called for in interpreting the results of a calculation of net farm output based on only one census year."[91] Using market prices in Toronto, he put a money value on the output of farms reported in the census: "One fixed set of prices is used in the calculation where in fact farm gate prices would have been lower in townships more distant from the main market centre."[92] At times it is difficult to know just what he had selected, and thus it can become difficult to know how seriously to take his figures: "There are components of output that are omitted from the calculation. The provincial average [of cleared land] ... would represent less than the full amount available to the farm family. It is impossible to say precisely how much less but a considerable guess would be probably as much as one-third."[93] Later he stated, "These estimates are not fully comprehensive and leave out some important but unmeasurable components of farm output. Those excluded components probably varied less across counties than the measured items."[94]

McInnis's data showed in 1861 a provincial average net farm output of $198 with the largest category of farms ($100–$149) being below that average. Older settled areas had higher output, with exceptions. For example, in Essex County some newly settled townships had very high net output (which he noted may be overstated) due to growing tobacco, a very high yield-per-acre crop. Another example was east of Kingston: despite long settlement in some areas, not a single township was above the provincial median for net farm output.

McInnis found that net farm output was determined largely by the amount of land *cleared*, while amount of land *occupied* had little relevance. In fact, most farms fell into the category of 90 to 115 acres occupied. Most townships in 1851 had farms that, on average, had just under 40 per cent of their land cleared. The longer-settled townships had more than the average: for example, Adolphustown with 64 per cent and Fredericksburg with 52 per cent cleared.[95]

In 1851 the average farm had 8.8 acres planted to wheat, or just under 25 per cent of its cleared land. While wheat was grown nearly everywhere, there was clearly a wheat belt from just east of Toronto around the head of Lake Ontario where most of the province's wheat was grown. However, the level of output was not exactly the same thing as the extent of cleared land planted to wheat. Pioneer Hay Township devoted 37 per cent of cleared land to wheat, versus less than 10 per cent in long-settled Fredericksburg. But as noted, McInnis was most insistent that many older townships also had large proportions of their cleared land devoted to wheat. His example is Niagara, where 27 per cent of the cleared land was planted to wheat.

The prominence of wheat in the 1851 census led McInnis to reflect on the relation between his own critique of the staples thesis and his new data. "Farm prosperity was commonly related to wheat production in mid-nineteenth century Ontario," he says, "a familiar story" – but "rather different from the story that is usually told."[96] Nonetheless, as previously noted, his township examples do not seem to support his argument that wheat-oriented older townships had higher wheat yields and larger proportions of cleared land in wheat than frontier townships. He conceded that "relatively high proportions of improved land in wheat are found in at least some of the newly settled frontier counties of western Ontario."[97] Moreover, some frontier areas that devoted little attention to wheat, such as Renfrew and Lanark counties, may have been at a disadvantage due to soil or climate. Indeed one of the two counties with the highest proportion of wheat on cleared land was Victoria at 33 per cent, in central (not western) Ontario. Certainly "the largest amount of wheat production" came from the "well-established, well-situated farming districts," just because they had the most land cleared. What is not obvious is that one would find there "the greatest concentration of farm effort on wheat" as compared to on "the frontier."[98]

Although both McCalla and McInnis began their studies with fundamental critiques of the staples thesis as applied to wheat in Ontario, the time-focus of their work was rather different. McCalla, in writing an economic history of Upper Canada, consequently deals with agriculture from earliest white settlement until after Confederation. McInnis concentrated on what the censuses of 1851 and 1861 can tell us about Ontario's agriculture at mid-century. McCalla estimated the province's total output, covering all sectors, to show wheat exports were only one element in the total economy and not always the largest one. He stressed the importance of local markets as against export markets for lumber, wheat, and other farm produce. However, he concluded that for most farmers (except in certain regions, such as the Ottawa Valley), wheat was usually their main off-farm surplus.

Unlike McInnis, McCalla considered wheat to be "a pioneer's crop, of course."[99] However, McInnis's reading of the staple thesis as implying that most of Ontario's wheat was produced by pioneers is not to be found in the literature produced by the founders of the staple thesis. McInnis effectively demonstrates that most wheat produced in 1851 came mainly from older rather than frontier areas. But wheat, at least where it could be grown, was *also* the pioneer's preferred crop, whether for subsistence or off-farm sale. Both of these powerful critiques have added an enormous amount to what we know about Ontario agriculture. Our view of its central features is now far more detailed and more highly nuanced. Nevertheless, the role of wheat, while set into a much more sophisticated context, still remains an issue, even if its export now appears less critical.

The staples thesis also figures prominently in five debates that have taken up particular issues in Ontario's rural history. These discussions have dealt with (1) whether large farms were more staple oriented than smaller ones, (2) whether tenants mined the soil by repeatedly planting wheat because of their presumed short-term interest, (3) whether land acquisition could be linked to wheat prices, (4) whether mechanization went with wheat specialization, and (5) whether (more precisely, when) the farmers of southern Ontario shifted toward various sorts of livestock. What these debates cumulatively point up is the assumption of wheat monoculture.

In the first of these debates both McInnis and William Marr have studied the differing outputs of differing sizes of farms. Marr took a sample from the 1851 census of nine counties split into three classes: older, newly settled, and intermediate. He divided farms into four groups: tiny, small, medium, and large. Like McInnis, he found for 1851 and 1861 that an overwhelming proportion of farms of all sizes in all areas grew wheat, some 88.3 per cent.[100] While older areas put more acres into wheat (13.3 acres versus 7.8), because of the different mix of farm sizes between different areas, both older and newer areas allocated about 24 per cent of their cleared acreage to wheat. Table 4.3 shows the marketable surplus by farm size. Surprisingly, older areas had annual average yields of 243.8 bushels per farm, compared to 170.9 for intermediate and 146.4 for newly settled areas.[101] Given largely constant domestic needs of 32 bushels, large farms had much greater saleable surpluses.

Thus wheat surpluses were produced across all regions and all farm sizes. The average surplus for all regions and farm sizes was 115 bushels, enough to feed 3.5 other families (versus McInnis's 4.3 families in 1861).

Table 4.3: Marketable surplus wheat in bushels by farm size at different stages of agricultural development, 1851.

	Farm size (acres)			
Agricultural development	Tiny (10–31)	Small (32–69)	Medium (70–169)	Large (over 170)
Developed	20	72	164	356
Intermediate	2	50	98	182
Underdeveloped	4	20	84	172

Source: Marr, "Allocation of Land to Agricultural Uses in Canada West, 1851," 196.

As one would expect from Marr's strong commitment to the staples thesis, against McInnis, he stressed "the extent to which wheat farms relied on wheat as an economic pursuit."[102]

In his work on the size structure of Ontario farms from 1861, McInnis emphasized how little wheat was grown – one-quarter of the land actually under crop. "For a region that was supposed to be specialized in wheat that appears to be surprisingly low."[103] However, when he came to examine what farms grew for sale, he sounds not unlike Marr: "Wheat was the preeminent marketable commodity ... a much larger component of the marketable surplus of agriculture than it was of net agricultural production."[104] Wheat accounted for 70 per cent of the total surplus. While larger farms (in occupied area, not improved acres) produced larger surpluses, these were not proportionally larger. Larger farms in older areas produced the greater surpluses, although McInnis included livestock and livestock products and Marr does not.[105] McInnis noted that, "In any locality only a few farms had become substantially specialized producers for the market."[106] Most farms produced largely for their own subsistence, selling their small surplus to local markets. By focusing attention on how few farms – the larger farms in the oldest settled areas – produced a substantial wheat surplus, McInnis tried to diminish the significance of wheat as an export staple.

In the second type of debate, Marr also looked at the relationship between wheat production and tenant farmers. From the 1871 census, he found that the rates of tenant farming varied across the province from less than 2 per cent to nearly 30 per cent, with the highest proportions usually in the longest-settled counties near larger urban centres. In one of the highest areas of tenant farming, York County, the tenant farmers were usually younger and more likely to be foreign born than owners. Tenant farmers had less to work with in terms of livestock or

equipment and usually produced slightly less of everything, except potatoes. They grew slightly less wheat than owners, with lower yields. However, although they had fewer cattle, they produced more cheese per cow,
suggesting they were more focused on dairy production. Owners and
tenants of the same age had farms of about the same size, but owners
over the age of forty-one had larger farms. "Any differences between
owners and tenants became more pronounced for older age groups,"[107]
Marr noted. His subsequent study of the distribution of tenants for all of
Ontario in 1871 confirmed these general conclusions. The proportion of
tenant farmers was highest in the longest-settled areas, the most highly
urbanized, with the best agricultural land.[108]

Extending his analysis to the 1881 and 1891 censuses, Marr found
confirmation for the "agricultural ladder" view of tenancy as the first
step up for the young or foreign-born would-be farmer. Wheat was more
prone to risk that livestock farming, hence, landowners and tenants
would spread that risk by their type of rental contract.[109] Once again,
the proportion of tenants correlated with an area's wheat focus. From
this Marr concluded that the decline in wheat's prominence was a major
factor in the decline in the rate of tenancy over time.[110]

Where Marr assumed a co-relation between tenancy and wheat production, a more recent study of tenant farming before Confederation by
Catherine Anne Wilson demonstrated that in at least one township, a
specific sort of tenant grew wheat. Wilson used the 1842 and 1848 censuses and focused on a long-settled lakeside township east of Toronto,
allowing her to link the census records to other sources such as property tax assessments. That data enables a longer-term study of individual tenant farmers and their families over several decades. Like Marr
for the later period, she found the highest rates of tenancy in "parts
of the province where land was good, wheat production greatest, net
farm output high, urban markets and immigration ports most active,
and the population at its densest."[111] While Marr speculated how different types of tenancy might relate to different economic conditions,
Wilson, by her local study, was able to identify three types of tenants
and their characteristic approaches to farming. One type, tenants who
rented on shares, had younger, smaller families; had little livestock; and
focused mainly on grain operations. Of all tenants, these had the smallest, most highly developed farms, averaging 87.9 acres of which 64.3 per
cent had been cleared (against township averages of 116 acres and 39.3
per cent). They grew mainly oats, buckwheat, and potatoes for both subsistence and sale (most likely to town merchants for the timber trade).

By contrast the second type, cash renters, tended to be older, more often foreign born, with larger families. Wilson considered that they wanted to run their own farm and get the risk premium (rather than share it, and the crop, with the landowner). Their crops were more diversified (since they had larger families to feed), with more livestock, in particular hogs and sheep. She found the third type, leaseholders, showed much more long-term interest in crop rotation. With the lowest rent, they were the most willing to risk growing wheat, as well as oats. They had far more uncleared land, which they sought to bring into production (to capture the capital gain, since the landowner had to pay for the improvements they made) or clear for grazing some livestock. Their larger families produced more diversified outputs such as cloth and maple sugar. Wilson repeatedly stressed how similar leaseholders were to titleholders in their practices, landholdings, and even their social status as church and local government leaders.

In her local longitudinal study Wilson could actually measure whether the agricultural ladder worked in practice. Following 97 tenant families over several decades, she found 27.8 per cent moved up to land ownership. These farmers were older, disproportionately Canadian or European born, with medium to large farms (an average of 110.9 acres with more improved acres, 45.7 per cent compared to 26.2 per cent who did not move up to ownership). They had both more livestock and more grain production (wheat and oats). Almost the same proportion left the township. Those who left were poorer, younger, had less property, and had spent less time in the township. But landowners who matched that age and property profile were also prone to leave the township. Some 33 per cent of all tenants stayed in the township and remained tenant farmers, behaviour that Wilson insisted cannot be read as failure: leaseholders especially saw their "property as a commodity, a form of wealth that could be exchanged in the marketplace."[112] Five tenants went "sideways" into occupations other than agriculture, while only three went down to become labourers. Clearly, for more than a quarter of tenant farmers the ladder worked. Wilson's argument that remaining a tenant should not be read as failure, especially for leaseholders, challenges the assumptions on which the ladder concept rests.

The third type of debate has focused on land acquisition and the process of settlement that have been the particular concerns of historical geographers who are concerned with spatial developments over time. While the historians usually cite the end of good land in the mid-1850s, historical geographers point more precisely to the late 1840s, when arable lands could no longer be had on such free grants as were still available (i.e., settlement road grants in northern areas). However, good land could still be purchased from private owners.[113]

Some thirty-five years ago Kenneth Kelly described pioneer farmers, in terms of the staples thesis, as raising wheat for subsistence, then moving to mixed farming with more attention to livestock. He maintained that on newly cleared lands, wheat may have been alternated with naked fallow to control weeds and the regrowth of forest. Once weeds had been beaten down, wheat was supplemented with peas, clover, and timothy to allow more systematic livestock feed (as against leaving animals to forage for themselves in the bush). Kelly noted the debates over whether there were serious long-term declines in wheat yields, maintaining that in the short run, weather and insect pests had greater effect than soil depletion, which could be countered by improvement in the types of wheat grown.[114]

Much more recently David Wood has sought more empirical grounding for analysis of the early pioneer stage by examining five farm diaries he described as both "a remarkable record" and also "representative."[115] All five farms grew wheat as their main crop. The diaries revealed that the longer the settler was on his land (ten to fifteen years), the more diversified his output both in livestock holdings and in adding oats and rye to his cereal production. Wood saw a regional pattern emerging by 1848, as some farmers turned away from wheat to other crops, while some areas specialized in wheat. He saw a wheat belt that extended from the Bay of Quinte to London. Other crop concentrations were tobacco in the extreme southwest, wool west of Lake Ontario, flax in the Niagara Peninsula, and oats and livestock east of Kingston.[116] However, we should remember that McInnis's work cautions us to see these specializations as variations of a general mixed farming model, where most of what was produced on the farm was consumed on the farm, just as most of what the farm family consumed had been produced on the farm (or at least in the neighbourhood of their farm).

John Clarke's thirty years' labour pursued a project narrower in both geographic scope and focus of interest. He concentrated on Essex County, the extreme southwestern limit of Ontario (although he also made comparisons with the Huron Tract, the Grand River Reserve, and the regime of Colonel Thomas Talbot). His main interest has been land speculation and land acquisition rather than the process of settlement.[117] In attempting to assess the extent to which early land speculators were able to make good their gamble, he has inevitably been drawn into consideration of squatters. He attempted to paint the squatter as the sometime ally of the speculator, where the squatters occupied native reserve lands, forcing them onto the market where the speculator could buy them. However, in almost all cases the squatter was the rival of the speculator for capturing the increased value of vacant lands. As the authorities usually upheld the deserving squatters' claims to be paid for their improvements, the speculator had difficulty in collecting even the price of uncleared land.[118] Some speculators, in an attempt to hold on to at least the land title while waiting for land prices to rise, tried to get squatters to take up long-term low-cost leases, but these strategies did not prove popular (any more than they did in the Eastern Townships).[119] In the long run, did the large-scale speculators get rich? While Clarke attempted to estimate speculators' net profits, he had to concede that "they made money when they sold, though the full amount is not known because of imprecise data on 'carrying charges.'"[120]

Relevant here is that, in a way similar to McCalla, Clarke attempted to relate the rate of land acquisition to changes in the price of wheat. Like McCalla, he found that there was no positive link either short or long term. In fact the long-term trends moved in opposite directions, with wheat prices falling while land prices rose.[121] Clarke pointed out that a host of local factors influencing land prices did not affect wheat prices, which were set outside the colony. More importantly, he found that in Essex, a mixed farming region, farmers grew less wheat than corn, as well as growing tobacco.[122] While historical geographers have often begun their work assuming that wheat was Upper Canada's staple, their empirical findings do not bear out such a universal (as distinct from a regional) role.

The fourth debate focuses on farm mechanization. Economic historian Richard Pomfret, using the data of the 1871 census, sought to measure the rate of mechanization of reaping. However, his effort is largely defeated by his unstated assumption of wheat as Ontario's staple crop, which led him to over-read the census data. The census gives only one number for both reapers and mowers, which Pomfret decided to take as the upper limit for the actual number of reapers.[123] He ignored the fact that the two implements represented two sorts of farming: the reaper for cereal crops and the mower for forage crops. To the extent that Ontario was moving from wheat to livestock, his calculations of the costs of wheat harvesting are irrelevant. The increased numbers could just as well have been more mowers adopted by farmers who wanted to enlarge their forage supply to raise more livestock.

The flaw of assuming that "reapers and mowers" can simply be read to mean the former is shared with Marr's study of York County in 1871. Marr found that, as their size increased, farms grew more hay but only slightly increased wheat yields (which he finds higher on larger farms). Yet large-scale farmers who had a reaper (or mower, we must add) planted a smaller percentage of wheat (17 per cent versus 25 per cent).[124] If one assumes it is reapers that are in question, it is possible to suggest that low-yield soils could be harvested with less effort by a reaper. Alternately, the higher hay output might have meant that it was mowers rather than reapers that were more numerous. Both Pomfret and Marr made a critical mistake because of their assumption of wheat as Ontario's staple product.

The fifth and most widely debated issue in the application of the staple thesis to Ontario agriculture has been the question of a transition from the assumed dominance of wheat to a new staple: dairy. The debate has moved from the assumption of the necessity of a staple product to a more nuanced application of shifting emphasis within the surplus of a rural economy that was always mixed farming. The three issues throughout have been what happened, when, and why.

D.A. Lawr in 1972 argued that a shift from wheat to dairy took place around 1900. He speculated that Ontario farmers chose the greater price and output stability of dairy farming over the greater income potential of wheat with its greater uncertainty of price and output (for example, the weather in a given year could double wheat yield).[125] In 1981 Marr sought to use an econometric model to measure how readily farmers switched away from wheat and when. He assumed the same shift from wheat to dairy but concentrated on shifts between wheat and other field crops (barley, oats, and hay) rather than any direct comparison with livestock or their products. He found that the shift away from wheat had happened during the 1880s and 1890s, much earlier than Lawr assumed. Marr stressed that the motive was falling profitability of wheat compared to other field crops, rather than considering any evidence of dairy prices.[126] The next year Robert Ankli and Wendy Millar published an article with the provocative subtitle "Wheat to Cheese." However, their actual argument was focused on the change from the late 1870s mini wheat boom to a greater emphasis on dairy products, in particular cheese, in the 1880s. Similar to Lawr, they showed that wheat prices fell 21 per cent from 1882 to 1900, while the price of cheese declined only 5 per cent. Demonstrating as well that wheat prices had much greater variance that did dairy prices,[127] they consequently contended that farmers switched because dairy products offered more stability and increasingly better incomes.

That same year McInnis published a study of Canadian farming that devoted much of its space to Ontario. It challenged several assumptions on which previous studies had rested. However, perhaps most radically, he argued that the switch away from any concentration on wheat had begun in the late 1850s and was largely completed by the time of Confederation. In 1870–72, dairy products (17.8 per cent) already outweighed wheat (16 per cent), while meat nearly doubled (33.6 per cent), to equal both in total value of agricultural output. The late 1870s saw wheat briefly rebound to 20.6 per cent, but dairy products still accounted for 21 per cent and meat (in spite of losing its American export market) for 24.6 per cent in the total value of agricultural output. In subsequent decades (1889–92, 1899–1902), wheat dropped to 19.6 per cent and then 13.9 per cent, while meat and dairy held first and second place in Canadian agricultural output. Moreover, McInnis challenged the idea that cheese was an agricultural staple that replaced wheat. While no one denies that cheese was developed for the export market – more than 80 per cent of Canadian production was shipped abroad, mostly to Britain – it never contributed as much as 10 per cent to total agricultural production.[128] There is also the obvious point that cheese does not fit the staple description of a natural resource exported in raw or semi-processed form.

McCalla followed McInnis in seeing Ontario farming as essentially mixed from its pioneer origins. He argued that the average farm family's labour resources could not produce more than 10 acres of wheat. Thus, as farms grew bigger in improved acreage, their wheat acreage did not expand proportionately; rather, such farms tended to produce more of other products in crops or livestock. By 1860, while the average-sized farms almost all grew spring wheat (89 per cent) and only 36 per cent grew fall wheat, neither variety was grown on as much as 9 acres. On larger farms, not only was spring wheat also ubiquitous (91 per cent) and fall wheat more common (47 per cent) but also both were grown on somewhat larger areas (10.9 versus 15.4 acres).[129] In their analyses of the 1871 census data for Canada and Ontario, John McCallum, Marvin McInnis, and Malcolm Urquhart all agree that wheat accounted for around 14–16 per cent of agricultural output. However, McCalla considered that McCallum seriously underestimated animals and animal products at 32 per cent of total agricultural output, preferring the higher 55–60 per cent estimates of Urquhart and McInnis. Consequently,

McCalla considered there was not a transition from a wheat staple to some other agricultural staple but a shift in the balance within a near-universal mixed farming, from a wheat orientation to greater emphasis on livestock, not only dairy produce but also beef and pork.[130]

However, a more recent study of economic growth and the standard of living in nineteenth-century Ontario brings the staples thesis back to the centre of the discussion. Lewis and Urquhart's starting point seemed to draw straight from Innis: "Wheat flour was a staple from the beginning."[131] They stated that 40 per cent of the wheat crop was exported by 1851, accounting for 35 per cent of farm income. Taking note of the critiques offered by McInnis and McCalla, they added, "The case for wheat is certainly weaker in the earlier years."[132] Farmers then depended more on livestock products. Yet Lewis and Urquhart speculated that beef exports were "probably not large" and concluded that consequently "the early settlers enjoyed rates of consumption not seen again until the twentieth century."[133] But apart from having a lot of red meat in their diet, Ontario farm families did not seem to have done particularly well. "Per capita farm income was about equal in 1826 and 1851; moreover, living standards might have been as high in early Upper Canada as in Canada as a whole shortly after Confederation."[134] Despite a nod in the direction of McInnis and McCalla, Lewis and Urquhart asserted, "Upper Canada was fortunate in having two staple products that generated large export proceeds: forest products and wheat sold mainly in the form of flour."[135] Yet the fact that the relatively substantial cattle holdings did not show up in market statistics hints not so much at any necessary failings in data reporting as the shortcomings of the staples thesis itself in concentrating on the money economy and exports.

No less devoted to the idea of wheat as the province's staple is John McCallum's comparative study of agriculture in nineteenth-century Ontario and Quebec, published in the same year as Marr and Paterson's general text. Wheat for McCallum "bore all the hallmarks of a staple product, a commodity that was the driving force of the provincial economy ... A more classic case of a staple product would be difficult to imagine."[136] However, behind such bald statements lurked a more nuanced understanding of Upper Canadian agriculture. Unlike Marr and Paterson, McCallum took the closures of the British market seriously. "The effects of the exclusion of colonial wheat from the British market in late 1820 were dramatic."[137] "Canadian produce could almost always be sold at some price, since British brokers were normally prepared to buy bonded wheat as a speculation."[138] West of Lake Ontario, poor prices continued to about 1827. McCallum did attempt to estimate the available local markets such as incoming immigrants and the lumber trade, especially in the Ottawa Valley. By implication, he saw the pioneer as becoming self-sufficient in food and reverting to a great degree of self-sufficiency – rather than seeking another saleable commodity such as livestock – when the British market closed and wheat prices plummeted. Nonetheless, he concluded, "In the absence of a reliable home market, most Ontario farmers depended for their prosperity on external wheat markets."[139] His grounds for this claim were that wheat was the pre-eminent off-farm commodity, and that only an external market could possibly buy all that farms produced and offered for sale. However, he was bothered by the very low average wheat export per farm. New land was commonly said to yield 30–40 bushels per acre. In the 1820s *average* yields were 25–35 bushels per acre, yet between 1817 and 1825 the average wheat exported per farm was only 13 bushels per acre. By 1830 it had risen as high as 30 bushels. "Perhaps the most striking characteristic of these figures," McCallum admitted, "is their small size."[140] Behind these averages lie even greater variations, since some farmers would have been producing nothing for the market. Although he does not make it explicit, one clear implication is that off-farm sales of wheat for export must have been a small part of most farms' output. Even though he was aware that wheat was not the whole of the farm's production, he felt, "Nevertheless, the most important point is that wheat was the only significant *cash* crop."[141]

Between 1830 and 1833, immigrants doubled the province's population, but no sooner were they on the land than wheat prices dropped below the assumed cost of production, down to 35 cents a bushel in 1835 – even lower than the previous low of 50 cents in 1822. McCallum insisted that farmers felt these price movements "immediately." Aware of the conflict between the rapid rate of settlement in the early 1830s and the low prices and uncertain markets facing the newcomers, he attempted to reconcile the problem by pointing to evidence for rising levels of farm indebtedness: "Clearly the farmers of the day were tied to the cash economy, and a low price for the only cash crop brought steadily mounting debt and the threat of financial ruin."[142] During these years, he presumed, farmers tried to keep their new debts to a minimum by being as self-sufficient as possible and carried on clearing land, in the hopes of better prices and better access to markets (both in the sense of improved transportation and more favourable tariffs in Britain, the United States, or both). When large-scale wheat exports resumed in the

1840s, he noted, the previous decade had made possible much higher average off-farm sales that previously: "Much of the settlement of the 1830s constituted an increase in productive capacity which added to actual production [meaning actual exports] only under the more favourable conditions of the next decade."[143] Farmers had gone on clearing land during the mid- and late 1830s when there was little hope of an immediate cash return from wheat. When British crop failures of the "hungry forties" opened that market and prices rose, Ontario farmers chose to respond by changing their crop mix. "There was a close positive relation between the price of wheat and the volume of exports ... This suggests that variations in production resulted not only from fluctuations in yields caused by changing weather conditions but also from planned variations in acreage in response to price conditions."[144] From the 1830 average of 30 bushels per farm, exports increased to 45 bushels per farm by 1845. By 1850 that average reached 80 bushels. From 1850 to 1856, exports almost doubled in volume and tripled in value. It is clear in McCallum's account that Ontario's wheat boom was an episode in its economic history, not a pattern that could be extrapolated back to the end of the eighteenth century.

McCallum was equally clear about the end of that temporary wheat boom. The 1860s saw the peak and decline of Ontario wheat production. In 1861 it reached its highest export volume (to that date) and highest average number of bushels per farm exported (135). While the total output was soaring, average yields were falling: in 1851 they had dropped to 16 bushels per acre. Of forty-two counties only three had average yields above 20 bushels. By the 1861 census there was a clear "shift in wheat production from counties along the shores of Lake Ontario to the more recently settled counties further inland."[145] Fall wheat was replaced by barley in those older-settled counties. While McCallum largely accepted as true the critical descriptions commonly given of pioneer wheat farmers, he denied there was an economically feasible alternative to soil mining (planting wheat repeatedly in the same field). He pointed to the lack of profitable alternative crops to enable rotation. The costs of more expensive methods of soil-conserving crop rotation could not be recovered if wheat was the cash crop, since cheaper wheat was increasingly available from further west. The outbreak of the American Civil War at first seemed to promise some relief from western competition, but US wheat production rose between 1859 and 1863 by 50 million bushels, with some American wheat actually being imported into Ontario.[146]

At the close of his study, McCallum offered "a modified staples approach." He argued that Ontario's wheat boom (1840–57) played a major part in preparing the provincial economy for an industrialization that would overtake that of Quebec and specifically that of Montreal. Small banks channelled farmers' swelling savings into an investment pool from which emerged import-substitution manufacturing (initially supplying the wealthy rural market with items such as farm machinery). "Ontario's industrial growth, then, was inextricably bound up in an organic process of wheat-based economic growth."[147] He argued that Ontario's economy could break free from Montreal's dominance by gaining control of a major share of the profits arising from its linkages (finance, transportation, manufacturing) to the ultimate external market. "Other things being equal, linkages from a new staple will tend to flow to the region with the greater initial endowment."[148] At the start of Ontario's wheat boom, Montreal had a clear advantage over any and all of its Ontario competitors in its entrepreneurial class, its financial and productive capacity, and its place in the transportation network. However, McCallum insisted that the economists' principle of comparative advantage be taken as dynamic: the new region's development can create a domestic market in that region. "If the characteristics of the staple are such that region B [Ontario] receives the larger part of the linkages, then the endowment of region B will rise over time relative to the endowment of region A [Quebec]."[149]

While critical of some readings of the staples thesis, McCallum himself at times fell into Innis's error of reading the later experience of the Prairies back into Ontario's history. "More specialized in wheat production than the farmers of present-day Saskatchewan, Ontario farmers of the mid-nineteenth century exported at least four-fifths of the marketable surplus. Close to three-quarters of the cash income of Ontario farmers was derived from wheat and wheat and flour made up well over half of all exports from Ontario until the early 1860s."[150] McCalla and McInnis have shown how misleading this picture is. McCalla's figures demonstrate that less than half the cleared acreage in the province would have been needed to produce the wheat exported from it. McInnis's review of the census data from 1851 and 1861 made clear that even during the peak of the wheat boom, wheat represented less than half of most farms' net output. Both McCalla and McInnis pointed out that marketable surplus often went to domestic markets rather than export markets.

A much more thoroughgoing modification of the staples thesis comes from Marjorie Griffin Cohen, who drew on the conclusions of staples thesis critics, and also offered a feminist perspective of her own. Cohen combineed the work done on the subsistence orientation of most farms (from Greer and McInnis), the roles of local as against export markets (from McCalla), and patterns of farm inheritance and migration (from Gagan) to the original insight of Innis on the role of wheat during a certain period, as a *cash* crop, with a feminist analysis of changing gender divisions in the workplace and of power relations inside the farm household, to provide the most sophisticated and comprehensive restatement of the staples thesis yet to appear.

Cohen questioned both the universality that is often assumed of the UK model of industrialization and the primacy of market relations, an assumption as dear to the new economic historians as to Marxists. Instead, she argued that in nineteenth-century Ontario the family was the primary production unit. In the province's early days, the pattern of dispersed settlement and the absence of transportation networks severely limited market opportunities: "The underdeveloped nature of the economy, the limited supply of labour, and the primary orientation of market activity toward the export market tended to produce a much sharper division of labour in the household economy between production for the market and that for household consumption."[151] Men's labour was directed primarily (almost exclusively) toward capital formation and the production of cash crops. In the first instance, the capital formation in question was clearing land, to turn forest into farmland. Women's labour was directed primarily (but not exclusively) toward providing the subsistence necessary for the family's physical survival, especially food and clothing. "The farmer's labour was directed toward the market; the extent that he could be freed from providing for his family's immediate needs would determine the rate at which he could accumulate capital in the form of cleared lands, farm buildings, and livestock."[152]

Cohen explained why farms were able to produce for an export staple market that was often uncertain: "By starting with the family, rather than the market, we may learn about the various strategies families adopted in order to survive in the face of extremely unstable market conditions."[153] "The imperatives of a pioneer economy, characterized by poor transportation, underdeveloped local markets, and an unstable staple-exporting market, made women's subsistence-oriented labour crucial to the success of the agricultural unit."[154] Like Allan Greer, Cohen considers that "the bulk of productive activity in the pre-industrial period operated outside a market system."[155] But in her view, Greer saw capital accumulation too narrowly, as arising only from market activities:

The process of capital accumulation in countries on the periphery of capitalist development is highly dependent on the existence of subsistence production in agriculture ... its primary importance for the capitalist sector is in supplying and maintaining a labour force at prices which permit capital accumulation in this sector ... This is particularly important in a staple-exporting economy where labour shortages tend to drive up wage rates. In Canada the capitalist staple-extracting sector relied on the subsistence sector for its labour supply, but even more important, the subsistence sector, by its very existence was able to supply this labour relatively cheaply ... The key to the availability of labour at prices which encouraged capital accumulation was a division of labour by gender such that women's primary economic activities were associated with non-wage, non-market work in subsistence production.[156]

Subsistence production was the foundation for producing a cash crop that could be sold to an export market: "The limited nature of colonial manufacturing meant that substantial amounts of goods for consumption and production could not be obtained except through foreign markets. For these transactions, cash was needed, and to the extent that agricultural markets could not provide the necessary income some members of the family might be forced to engage in work for wages."[157] Until local markets were sufficiently developed to enable pioneer farmers to earn cash by their labour or sell agricultural produce for cash, the sale of wheat was essential.

Cohen pointed out that male and female spheres of labour on the family farm were not wholly separate. Some tasks could be performed by men or women, such as carrying water, milking, chopping firewood, caring for the livestock or the garden, and some types of butchering. And while the contemporary literature, derived largely from the literate women of the gentry, gives the impression that field labour for women was a new and unexpected role, European peasant women had always worked in the fields, especially at harvest.[158] However, with the exception of a few "Amazonian choppers," clearing the forest was largely a male domain. Cohen did not denigrate that work: "Without the concerted effort of male labour ... it was difficult for any farm to advance beyond the subsistence level of production."[159] She stressed that while women might at times move into the male domain, working in the fields, the reverse did not happen. "Males rarely performed duties regarded as women's work"[160] – child-rearing, cooking, and cleaning – no matter

Table 4.4: Domestic textile production, 1842–81.

	Linen (yards)	Woollen cloth and flannel (yards)
1842	166,881	1,160,813
1848	71,715	1,923,143
1852	14,711	1,727,589
1861	37,055	2,093,034
1871	25,502	1,775,320
1881	13,641	1,426,558

Source: Cohen, *Women's Work, Markets, and Economic Development in Nineteenth-Century Ontario*, 82.

how difficult that work might be: "Adult males ventured into the realm of the household only under the most exceptional circumstances, such as when the wife was totally incapacitated or dead."[161]

A key part of the subsistence that women provided was clothing. Women produced both linen and woollen cloth. "Both processes were very labour-intensive and, since various stages of production could be performed outside the household, the usual practice was to attempt to reduce farm-women's labour in this area."[162] Men broke the flax after it had been harvested, while the women spun, dyed, and wove it. Weaving a yard of linen cloth was reckoned at a day's labour, valued at about 6 shillings. Cohen considered (incorrectly) that while little linen or woollen cloth was sold, it played an important part in conserving the household's small cash income for other things. Women did the wool spinning, while men usually did the weaving in her view. There was a sufficiently large rural textile manufacture that farmers' daughters could earn money hiring out as spinners. Similarly, itinerant weavers travelled the countryside, where some homes had looms that were worked seasonally. Table 4.4 indicates domestic textile production. The significant scale of this domestic manufacture is often forgotten.[163]

Cohen made telling use of the well-known failure of hemp production, despite all the government subsidies offered. Household labour was almost wholly occupied with the demands of subsistence: "Unless a family had a great many children or was sufficiently well off to hire servants, the ordinary tasks of providing for the family's daily needs consumed most of the farm-women's time. Because so much had to be provided by the farm itself, there was precious little time for production of commodities for the market."[164]

As more and more of Ontario moved out of the pioneer phase, local markets developed that profoundly changed the productive patterns of the farm family. "With a more integrated local economy women were able to provide for their families' needs more efficiently by producing agricultural goods for the market."[165] Specifically, she thought that farm households began to purchase cloth rather than make it, because the labour needed for household textile production could produce other goods (such as poultry and dairy products) of more value than home-spun. "Certain forms of production which had occurred within the household were gradually replaced by goods produced in artisan shops or factories, but this did not reduce women's work in the household economy."[166] Instead of reduction, women's work switched from a con-centration on production for family use to production more oriented to the market, such as dairying, poultry raising, fruit growing, and market gardening. All of these were extensions of women's traditional domestic work. The products of all could have been (and were) used for domestic consumption. However, Cohen thought, unlike the production of home-spun, all these other activities also had the potential of surpluses that could be sold. "Certainly the manufactured goods that women were able to purchase reduced the amount of time they needed to spend in areas which were the least remunerative and most time-consuming, while ris-ing markets created new outlets for their farm products."[167]

As Cohen noted, domestic textile production was often a neighbour-hood, rather than a household, affair. But textile production could expand as farms became more prosperous. Once rural communities were well established, carding and fulling mills took over much of the most arduous labour in transforming raw wool into cloth.[168] Coun-try merchants sold factory-made cotton warp that farm women wove with varying ratios of wool into homespun.[169] However, Cohen seems to have been mistaken about the weavers' gender.[170] Many households both bought cotton cloth, for their own inner wear, from local mer-chants and sold homespun to them, which was in demand as outerwear for lumber men and fishermen.[171] Consequently there is no simple uni-versal equation between the production of homespun and a quest for self-sufficiency.

Cohen devoted particular attention to dairying as the pre-eminent of the new specializations and the one that best exemplifies the limits on the market activities that were open to women.[172] The completion of the province's canal network and the construction of both mainline and branch line railways as well as the denser settlement of rural areas allowed the increasingly profitable production of dairy products, includ-ing cheese, but above all, butter, as shown in Table 4.5.

Table 4.5: Domestic butter and cheese production, 1851–91: Quebec and Ontario.

| | Production (millions of pounds) | | | |
| | Ontario | | Quebec | |
	Butter	Cheese	Butter	Cheese
1851	16.1	3.4	9.6	0.8
1861	25.8	2.7	15.9	0.7
1871	37.6	3.4	24.3	0.5
1881	54.9	1.7	30.6	0.6
1891	55.6	1.1	30.1	4.3

Source: Cohen, *Women's Work, Markets, and Economic Development in Nineteenth-Century Ontario*, 104.

In the 1860s, low prices in the United States and the beginning of larger-scale American exports to the United Kingdom caused some Ontario farms to switch to dairy. From 1865 to 1870 Canadian exports of butter to the UK rose from £7 million to £15.5 million. Americans not only supplied a ready market for dairy products but also a source of technology for the production of those products. The growth of factory cheese making, in particular, saw Ontario follow closely the lead of New York: "The specialization of farms in the production of milk to supply cheese factories meant males increasingly became involved in the production process. As large dairy herds developed, dairying ceased to be the part-time occupation of women and more and more became the major work of males on the farm."[173] Cohen was surprisingly reticent about the reasons for the male takeover. On the one hand, "Because production methods in early cheese factories were similar to those used in domestic production and because the factories themselves were often located on the farm, it was not unnatural for the makers of farm dairy cheese to participate in factory work. But even from the beginning it was recognized that factory production would eventually eliminate women from cheese-making."[174] On the other hand, "the forces which restricted women's access to capital and their labour to work in the farm household were powerful deterrents to women's participation in capitalist development."[175] For the people of that era, "a more capital-intensive industry outside the home was rightly the sphere of males." The key factor that worked to exclude women from dairying was thus the need to gain access to working capital, in the form of an expanded herd, purebred dairy stock, and the necessary buildings and equipment for a modern dairy.[176] Governments, which had never shown any interest in dairying when it was women's work, began to appoint factory inspectors, make grants to dairymen's associations, and even establish model dairies where men could learn how to become efficient butter and cheese makers.[177]

Cohen, again with surprisingly little comment, noted in passing the awareness that contemporaries had that dairying was becoming a male preserve. A farm publication observed that "women would no longer have to do this heavy and difficult work."[178] "A woman might have naturally greater patience and more innate kindness and a higher ideal of cleanliness than a man."[179] However, men entering into the dairy industry were making it more "scientific" in order to break into export markets. Almost all of the various dairy schools established had male staffs to teach other men the new and scientific way to handle milk to make butter and cheese. Despite the pious thought about the relative "cleanliness" of women versus men, the new scientific milking was explicitly described as superior to the old (female) ways because it produced a purer product. Rather than provide better training and equipment for women, governments, like most farmers, decided to have dairying handled by men. Cohen showed some awareness of what was happening: "Whatever success women achieved was seen as having less to do with learning the trade well or acquiring skill through practice than through some haphazard approach associated with women's nature."[180]

There is evidence that women themselves sought to play a collective part in this transformation. "Home-makers clubs and Women's Institutes had become interested in providing information to farm women on dairying techniques, but the focus of these organizations regarding dairying was less on organization and distribution than on production techniques on the farms themselves."[181] Another way of reading that evidence is that even organized women's groups largely accepted that the central issue was one of scientific management rather than who controlled the farm's dairy operation.

More recent and more detailed examinations of the dairy transition draw attention to the differences between cheese and butter. Heather Menzies saw gender division on the farm as less sharp did than Cohen: the dairy was one of the areas of overlap, where men often did some of the tasks, such as churning. Menzies drew on McInnis's and McCalla's work, showing most farms as largely self-supporting with a small minority specializing in commercial production. Only sixteen counties produced over 50,000 pounds of cheese in 1860, of which two produced over 200,000 pounds – with one of those, Oxford County, producing

457,348 pounds. Menzies confirmed that there, cheese was not just produced at subsistence level by many farmers but was a commercial activity of a few large-scale producers. Seventy farms (out of some 4,000) produced over 1,000 pounds of cheese per year. Most of these were the larger farms that tended to produce a surplus of several products, such as wheat, peas, and wool as well as cheese. Only forty-three farms produced over a ton of cheese, and of those, only twenty-six produced over two tons. Even the largest of these specialists had just ninety cattle, indicating that this farm had to regularly buy milk from others.[182] Male help was hired to assist the farm wife in her dairy work. All this was done by refined craft methods that could produce large amounts of cheese and large cheeses before 1864, when New York factory technology was first introduced. An industrial approach to innovation has led historians to both undervalue what craftsmanship could accomplish and to overestimate the importance of imported innovations.

Margaret Derry faulted Cohen for oversimplification in running the stories of cheese and butter together. Like McInnis, Derry stressed that butter was produced primarily for the domestic market rather than export.[183] Unlike cheese, butter was widely produced and often in quantities geared for home or local consumption rather than sale abroad. While cheese production moved to factories in the decade following Confederation, butter production remained with women on farms. The push toward factory production came in the 1890s when the federal and provincial governments decided to promote butter in export markets. The result was again an attack on women's competence in the name of "scientific production," which could only take place in factories, which employed men. Men even began to replace women in milking cattle, although this was accompanied by the introduction of milking machines.[184] In contrast to Menzies, Derry saw the displacement of women from milk production and butter making as a deliberate move to downgrade farm women's productive capacity, to restrict their sphere to the privatized household.[185]

Cohen's modified version of the staples thesis succeeds in incorporating the evidence of its principal critics while retaining the original insights of Innis. Both McCalla and McInnis have demonstrated, in different ways, that the wheat exported from Ontario accounted for only a small portion of the total farm output. McCalla used data on wheat exports, land cleared, and probable yields per acre to show that at no time could the province's wheat exports have used most of the available agricultural land. McInnis's analysis of the 1851 and 1861 census data confirmed this picture, even at the peak of the wheat export boom. Like McInnis, McCalla's critique also pointed to the uncertain demand emanating from Britain after 1815, culminating in the brief closures of that market to Canadian wheat, as an argument that the colony's agriculture cannot be explained solely in terms of the production of wheat as an export staple. What did people do when the UK market was closed to them? Cohen has an answer. Her model of two farm economies, one geared to subsistence and the other to a cash income, not only explains what farm families were doing with most of their farms' resources but also how those families survived periods of little or no export demand. Like McCalla, she stressed the role of local markets and the diversity of production on farms. However, she retained a firmer grip on the essential insight of Innis: farms needed cash incomes (as well as barter and labour exchange) to survive, and wheat answered that demand more effectively than any other crop for most farmers. McCalla's merchants extended credit to farmers in the expectations that eventually they would get something in exchange that would pay their own bills in Britain. Staves and potash could provide valuable supplements, but in the long run wheat was the pre-eminent means of paying those bills.

McCalla concluded his study of the Upper Canadian economy by arguing that while the staples thesis at one time had given some "clarity" to our understanding of that economy, it came at the cost of "an unreasonable level of abstraction." He preferred to place stress on continuity, seeing growth as cumulative, in a highly interdependent process: "Everywhere the rural economy involved wheat, cattle, and forest products; specialization was nuanced, not absolute. The essence of the rural economy was its balance, not its specialization. Constrained by climate and soil, and influenced by family values and expectations about markets, farm households had many choices to make in allocating time and resources."[186] Cohen was free to accept that entire conclusion. But, unlike McCalla, she is not at a loss to explain why merchants would extend credit to farmers who could only exchange labour or subsistence goods to pay for their purchases from overseas. The expectation of a cash crop for export and the occasional fulfilment of that expectation (at least before the 1840s) sustained that complex web of credit and debt on which McCalla was so intent, but whose foundation he left curiously under-specified.

From his study of the 1851 census, McInnis concluded, "A predominantly subsistence base founded on mixed farming and animal husbandry generated about the same level of output per acre in the two provinces."[187] The reason Ontario agriculture was better off than that of Quebec "boils down to whether wheat was or was not grown."[188] He was obviously somewhat ill at ease with a conclusion that is "pretty much in line with a conventional account."[189] For someone who began denouncing the idea that wheat was a staple, it was awkward, to say the least, to be concluding that wheat "was the leading product and principal, if not the only reason why farming in Ontario was more prosperous than farming in Quebec."[190] Cohen can both embrace that conclusion and feel at ease with it.

Innis, by an apparent exclusive focus on wheat as an export staple, mistook an important part of the colonial economy for the whole of it. Understanding the farm as a family enterprise sets wheat into its proper context. The first goal of every farm was provision of its own subsistence. What may or may not have been part of that farm's subsistence economy depended on the quantity and quality of its soil, location, working capital, and livestock. Where wheat was grown, depending on the abundance of a given year, there might be a surplus beyond the family's needs (including socio-economic obligations such as payments to seigneur and curé). For large-scale farmers (and those paid in wheat, such as curés), abundant harvests allowed sales for export. Smaller-scale farmers could participate in markets proportionately.

When wheat was not grown, or when wheat yields were poor or prices low, family farms relied on their domestic side. Women and children in the garden, orchard, pigpen, henhouse, dairy barn, sheepfold, or sugar bush or on the loom produced food and clothing for the family. Without the support of this subsistence-oriented domestic economy, the wheat staple would not have been possible. As farms matured, some of the originally subsistence products could be sold for supplemental income.

Both the staples thesis and the character of the family on the family farm are central to David Gagan's thesis of an agricultural crisis in Ontario on the eve of Confederation. Gagan saw rural Ontario as reshaped by the sudden fall of wheat prices and the ensuing collapse of land prices at the end of the 1850s. Amongst the responses to those "critical years," he counted a land-hungry Ontario nationalism that expressed itself in the demand to annex Rupert's Land as a potential new farm frontier and the consequent demand for Confederation as a means to that end. The extension of farming onto the Prairies will again raise the questions of staples and linkages. The next chapter examines the case for and against Gagan's thesis of another "agricultural crisis."

Gagan and the "Critical Years" in Canada West: A Second Agricultural Crisis?

David Gagan has suggested that rural Ontario suffered an agricultural crisis during the "critical years" of the mid-nineteenth century. While the crisis he identified for Ontario was much briefer that that posited by Ouellet for Quebec, the two accounts have features in common. Both saw an advancing ecological frontier stalled by reaching the limit of prime cultivation. Both understood that agriculture was pressed beyond those limits onto ever more marginal soils. Both saw the need for farm families to plant their sons on farms of their own as the force driving that expansion. Both historians have been criticized for overemphasizing the social and economic impacts of that stall. Their critics questioned the degree of land hunger in each rural society, arguing – at least implicitly – that any son who left the farm for town should no longer be counted amongst those seeking farms of their own.[1] Ouellet believed that a falling trend in wheat exports at the beginning of the nineteenth century meant falling agricultural productivity and a consequent fall in the living standards of most habitants, and that out of that rural discontent was fashioned a broad-based nationalist movement. Gagan saw rural Ontario reshaped by the sudden fall of wheat prices and the ensuing collapse of land prices at the end of the 1850s. Amongst the responses to those critical years, he counted a land-hungry Ontario nationalism that demanded the annexation of Rupert's Land as a new farm frontier. The movement for Confederation drew on that desire.

While the agricultural crises of the two Canadas are each linked to the names of these individuals, the relation of each person to their crisis is rather different. Fernand Ouellet's work has been that of a lifetime. While he has enjoyed the collaboration of some of his peers (most notably Jean Hamelin) and numerous graduate students, these links have most often been informal. David Gagan, by contrast, was engaged in a more formally structured collective relationship. That formal structure had both beginning (at the mid-point of his career) and an end. The Peel County History Project began in 1971, and a decade later its work was effectively completed with the publication of Gagan's *Hopeful Travellers*.

What became Ontario at the time of Confederation had been the poor man's country for over half a century.[2] While it attracted substantial numbers of middle class and "gentle" folk who hoped to maintain or restore their fortunes, it was advertised above all as the place where the landless could get land. In 1826 the Crown ended the "free" grants, consolidating all reserved crown lots into the Huron Tract, which was sold to the Canada Company in return for regular payment to support the colonial government. However, the Crown continued to give away land as pauper lots or for settlement roads. Through the 1830s the abundance of land on the market kept prices low and credit terms often easy for newcomers. For the experienced Canadian born of small means there was always squatting.[3] The eventual or ultimate owner had to either pay the squatter for improvements made or sell the land at the price of unimproved land. George Forbes's message to the rest of his family still in Scotland was emblematic: "the ground whereon we tread is our own and our children's after us[.] No danger of the leases expiring and the laird saying pay me so much more rent or bundle and go, for here we are laird ourselves."[4] For those who were born at the bottom end of the social and economic spectrum or who arrived at the bottom end from overseas, obtaining land held the promise of upward social mobility.

In 1973 Gagan and Herbert Mays set out their goal of a rural social history of Ontario that lay beyond "the limited worlds of the literate few":[5] "The experience of ordinary men, multiplied by the number of individuals with whom they shared it, represents the sum of human activity in a given place at a particular point in time."[6] The new social history demanded new sources, for these anonymous masses had created "historical records in spite of themselves."[7] Census records, land tax assessments, land registry records (including mortgages), wills, and obituaries "routinely generated more or less continuous documentation of the major 'events' in their own lives."[8] What emerged from these sources was the central place of the family as the fundamental unit of social organization. To give the family its due place, as Gagan explained, historical demography had begun "reconstituting the entire population of a given community at regular intervals across an historically unified time span."[9] The enormous cost of such population studies has meant that they must be "'microstudies,' intensive analyses of very restricted populations."[10]

For Ontario, the researchers sought the answers to a series of broad questions. How was a forested wilderness transformed into an established society? What were that society's broad characteristics at each stage in its development? How were they altered, from time to time, by the movement of people, or groups of people into or out of that society? Why did some families put down permanent roots, while for others rural Ontario offered a place to stand just long enough to catch their breath?

Gagan chose Peel County to represent the middle point of nineteenth-century Ontario, neither early nor lately settled. He considered it far enough from Toronto or other major urban centres to reflect essentially rural development. (Peel had the added benefit of being close to McMaster University in Hamilton where Gagan taught and the project would be based.)

Peel County's five townships at their closest point lay approximately twenty miles northwest of Toronto. Almost the whole of the county has good to excellent soil. While some settlement had begun before 1812, it received its main population after 1820. In that year there were 245 resident proprietors on the assessment roll. However, the roll also showed eight non-resident proprietors who collectively held over 27 per cent of the land. Combined with the crown and clergy reserves, these speculative holdings represented a major barrier to early settlement. By 1840 the number of large-scale non-resident landowners had risen to sixteen, while their proportion of the total amount of land had fallen to 10 per cent.[11] These large holdings were certainly not the frontier of cheap land that many immigrants had expected. As late as 1835, a quarter of all farmers were either tenants or squatters. Access to land, which Gagan saw as producing a crisis at mid-century, was never easy or automatic in Peel.

Gagan's project developed in the shadow of Michael Katz's larger, urban Hamilton Project, which sought to capture the social reality of the city's population at mid-century.[12] Two kinds of links connected the projects. The first were record linkage methods. Second, Katz's work, as the only other major study of population movement in nineteenth-century Ontario, offered both a basis for comparison and a model to emulate.

Gagan began by assuming a society divided into self-conscious classes, where the thing to be explained (or explained away) was the failure (as he saw it) of those at the bottom to challenge the social hierarchy. Geographic movement was read as a continuous search for upward *social* mobility: "High levels of mobility arose from the inequalities of limited social environments ... Geographic mobility was both an act of faith and an act of desperation. It reflected hope that the society in the next place the transient came to would be more fluid in response to his aspirations; but it was also a release from the social structural constraints on vertical mobility in the place he had just left."[13] The implicit, underlying assumption was that geographic mobility, especially leaving a community in the New World, meant that one had failed in that community.

Gagan could not get very far with that thesis. We can see him working himself out of his original assumptions. He began framing a hypothesis: "Can physical movement be construed as a desperate alternative ... or is there evidence ... that ... migration opened up avenues to socio-economic improvement?"[14] He had two problems. First of all, his micro-study could not follow those who left (nor tell much about where they had arrived *from*) to see if either generalization might hold. "What is possible, however, is to compare the experience of the migratory population with that of the persistent, or at least temporarily stable, minority in order to determine what, if anything, appears to distinguish one group from the other."[15] Gagan's second problem arose trying to identify social mobility with occupation: "Whatever occupational mobility transpired in this community was primarily in one direction, towards the status of rural operator."[16] But if everyone wished to be a farmer (that is, an owner-operator), the farmers did not seem to think other occupations beneath them. "The ability of rural operators to enter all other vocational ranks with more or less equal facility suggests that they may have had equally flexible perceptions of their vocations even after they had become farmers." Geographical mobility did offer a strong indication of restless search for social advancement because "ultimately everyone was on the move."[17] Under circumstances of general geographical mobility, the level of vocational opportunities in nineteen-century Ontario may have been considerably greater than we normally associate with agrarian societies, particularly if the occupational labels men wore tell us more about what they were doing in a particular place at a particular time than they tell us about their ultimate place in the scheme of things.[18]

Gagan laid out the Peel County History Project's substantive findings in 1978. Ontario's political elite perceived a rural crisis in the late 1850s and 1860s. They worried about the sharp fall in property values in 1857–58, the rise in agrarian indebtedness, and the out-migration of young men and young families. For Gagan, Peel County offered "an acceptable surrogate" for rural Canada West, in which that crisis could

Table 5.1: Distribution of families by percentage of total land occupied, Peel County, 1851 and 1871.

	Land Occupied (in acres)				
	10 or less	11–50	51–100	101–200	200+
1851	10.4%	21.3%	52.4%	13.7%	2.2%
1871	13.8%	15.2%	45.4%	20.7%	4.7%

Source: David Gagan, "Land, Population, and Social Change," 296.

be more closely examined. The near-universal land hunger was the underlying force behind the crisis. From just under 100 occupied acres in 1851, the average farm size rose to almost 140 acres by 1871. However, in the second decade, that expansion had taken place at the expense of smaller farmers: the only farm size categories to increase their proportions of the total were for farms over 100 or under 10 acres.

The ratio of adult males per 100 acres of occupied land, after climbing steadily for three decades, declined sharply in the 1860s, "the greatest displacement taking place among men between the ages of thirty and sixty."[19] Table 5.1 indicates the distribution of families by the percentage of the total land occupied in Peel for 1851 and 1861. The number of males (aged fifteen to thirty) per 1,000 acres of available land, having risen from 29 to 41 between 1851 and 1861, fell back to 29 in the following decade.

The family farm household economy had been built upon the labour of all family members, including the children. In the past, the parents had rewarded their children (meaning, almost always, sons) by giving them a start on farms of their own, usually on the outer frontier of settlement. For the sons, this start consisted in land, almost always "wild land." Many of these families had numerous sons: "Among the farm population of Peel County between 1850 and 1870 a full quiver – a completed family – appears to have consisted of at least eight children."[20] When Peel no longer had arable unappropriated land, farmers' sons had to either compete for already appropriated land within the County or leave. In the 1860s approximately 20 per cent of the adult male population between the ages of fifteen and sixty had left Peel (and were not replaced).

The competition for land amongst those who remained drove up land prices in the longer term, a fact concealed by shorter-term fluctuations. However, for farmers striving to accumulate the patrimony they considered necessary to provide to their sons, the dramatic fluctuations threatened the stability of their investment. Since many had undertaken mortgages to their holdings, that instability was a source of acute anxiety. It became more and more clear that the traditional practice of endowing sons with land locally could not be continued. There was not enough land in the county to satisfy the demand at the prices that had previously prevailed. The costs and uncertainties of ever more intense competition for land deterred most farmers from buying or mortgaging their individual way out of the collective crisis.

Farm households could have responded to the crisis in a number of different ways. Two were relatively minor. The new technology of labour-saving farm machinery could reduce some of the labour demands (especially at harvest) of a farm devoted to field crops (wheat or the increasingly popular substitutes of barley and oats), thus making a smaller family economically feasible. The other longer-term factor was the diversification made possible by the growth of major urban centres (Toronto and Hamilton) and the improved transportation by railway. As farms converted from field crops to market gardening or dairying, the necessary man-land ratio changed as well, making smaller farms viable. However, the principal ways farm families responded were changed methods of inheritance (leading to substantial out-migration from the county) and changes in family structure.

The primary short-term response to the crisis was a change in the pattern of inheritance. Given the children that they already had, raised on the premises of at least each son receiving his patrimony, farmers sought to ensure the continuation of viable farms without altogether neglecting any of their children. An inevitable consequence of such inheritance practices was that most of the new generation would have to either leave farming or leave Peel. Thus a second pair of short-term responses grew out of the first: migration or occupational diversification. The longer-term response to the crisis affected the formation and structure of the farm family itself. Gagan argued that the availability of arable farmland in Peel influenced the decisions of when to start families and how large those families would be.

In mid-nineteenth-century English Canada, three possible methods of inheritance existed. The perfectly impartible method settled the entire inheritance on a single heir to the exclusion of all others. The perfectly partible method involved an approximately equitable division of the estate amongst all heirs. The third method, which A.R.M. Lower called the "Canadian" model, settled the estate (or the largest portion of it)

Table 5.2: Distribution of farmers' estates by method of inheritance, Peel County, 1845–90.

	Inheritance method (%)		
	Impartible	Partible	"Canadian"
1845–55	32.1	28.6	39.3
1856–65	17.3	11.5	71.2
1866–73	11.9	8.4	79.7
1874–90	18.2	6.5	75.3

Source: Gagan, Hopeful Travellers, 52.

upon a single heir, who was then required by the terms of the will to make specific provisions for the other heirs.[21] The latter "was adopted wholesale by testators in Peel County during the crisis years 1856–1865 [and] was only slightly less popular during the more optimistic years surrounding Confederation."[22] This form was most heavily favoured by farmers who had greater numbers of children and greater wealth to bequeath. Table 5.2 shows the distribution of farmers' estates by method of inheritance for Peel between 1845 and 1890.

Farmers caught midway in their life cycle sought to reconcile the need to keep the economic basis of the farm family household intact and the need to satisfy, as much as seemed possible, the claims of their children. "Continued economic stability had been purchased at the expense of the legitimate, and traditional, expectations of the majority of Peel's younger generation, many of whom would now join the army of migrants who passed through the county every year."[23]

Gagan's study of farmers' wills detected patterns of female inheritance, which Marjorie Griffin Cohen also found.[24] Not only were the inheriting sons left to police the morals of their sisters, some wills even provided the heir with control over whom his sister might marry. Widows were left dependent on their sons, sons-in-law, or executors. A substantial minority of farmers could not rest content with having controlled the life of a wife while alive. "Thus, more than 20 per cent of the deceased husbands who devised their estates according to the 'Canadian system' explicitly forbade their wives to remarry or cohabit as a condition of inheritance."[25] But while the labour of wives and daughters was essential for any farm's long-term viability, it was largely the sons whose maintenance worried fathers the most.

Gagan did not portray rural women as passive and hapless victims. In language that foreshadows Cohen's work, he argued that farm women made a vital contribution to the farm family's survival: "What these

Table 5.3: Marital fertility of farm wives, showing number of children under 10 years of age per 1,000 married women by age group, Peel County, 1851, 1861, and 1871.

	Age group of farm wives		
	15–19 years	20–24 years	25–29 years
1851	1,585	1,879	2,492
1861	500	1,405	2,558
1871	452	1,124	2,222

Source: Gagan, Hopeful Travellers, 74.

women did in their roles and functions as wives, mothers, and mistresses of their households was quite inseparable, in terms of the economy of the farm family, from the equally specialized functions of other members of the family whose well-being was determined by its collective productivity."[26] The domestic hearth and motherhood were not "preoccupations" but "occupations on which the survival of the family depended in a world made more secure by the strength of its dependent relationships."[27]

The real long-term challenge was to solve the problem of those overpopulated rural households that had once depended for their standard of living on the labour of many children but could no longer compensate them adequately for their contribution and even victimized them in the interests of social security and stability.[28] This specific crisis began the longer-term decline in farm family size that continued throughout the rest of the nineteenth century.[29]

Family size was reduced largely by the delay of marriage, which meant that farm wives started their families later: "The youngest group of married women in the community in 1871 experienced a significant change in the timing of their first conceptions compared with a similar group of women starting their families in the late forties."[30] Table 5.3 shows the marital fertility of farm wives in terms of the children under 10 years of age per 1,000 married women by age group in Peel from 1851 to 1871.

The changed behaviour of the youngest wives was the primary factor in producing smaller families: "Delaying conception in the years of highest fertility results in a disproportionately large decrease in completed family size." The relative delay in women marrying is all the more striking as it occurred just when the sex ratio was shifting from the long-run male surplus characteristic of the frontier of European settlement to a small surplus of females. Table 5.4 indicates the number of males per 1,000 females by age cohort in Peel from 1850 to 1870. Indeed, the out-

Table 5.4: Number of males per 1,000 females, by age cohort, Peel County, 1851, 1861, and 1871.

	Male age cohort		
	10–15 years	*16–20 years*	*21–30 years*
1851	1,090	1,102	1,216
1861	1,081	957	1,160
1871	913	984	1,072

Source: Gagan, *Hopeful Travellers,* 78.

migration of younger males may have played a large part in that shift. "Marital fertility, family size, and youthful independence ... were functions of the age at which marriage was permissible or possible."[31]

The crisis in the farm family household economy that began in earnest in the late 1850s had been largely surmounted by the 1870s. By means of a dramatic shift in customary patterns of inheritance and consequently the displacement of surplus population, through the exercise of social controls over the formation of new farm families, and by limiting the offspring of new partnerships, the community had taken steps to protect the integrity of the traditional economic space from which the farm family derived its security, and to maintain the standard of living – the rewards of its labour – historically associated with rural prosperity.[32]

The losers in this adaptation were the other (usually younger) siblings. The sons found themselves getting something other than the landed patrimony enjoyed by their father's generation. Granted, in most cases they would not be left wholly without provision, but the compensation would more often be cash or promises of continued subsistence rather than land to start a new farm. In contrast with Lower Canadian habitant children of small estates, these sons began their independent life with some sort of stake, whether they sought cheap land elsewhere or went into business as shopkeepers or artisans. The daughters' potential marriage partners – abundant in their mothers' day – had become suddenly scarce. Marriage, their only hope of an independent existence, was to be delayed. For a small but increasing minority, marriage would have to be forgone. The security and stability of the new order were not to be shared out any more equally than the land.

Herbert Mays focused on a single (and singular) township within Peel, Toronto Gore, which offers the opportunity to follow the trends and themes into the lives of a single township's inhabitants. Mays's especial interest was in permanence in the midst of the seemingly endemic geographic mobility. He defined permanence "as a kin relationship to a settler who entered the township during its formative years between 1820 and 1850."[33] In trying to identify the reasons for the success (within the confines of the township) of some settlers, the key was early arrival: "For most, the time at which they took up residence in the township was the most important factor in determining the size of their farms ... The length of time they had been on the land had a direct bearing on their worth ... The earlier they settled, the longer this process had been at work."[34] Of the township's first nine settlers who persevered beyond the first years of clearing, all but one founded permanent families and became amongst the wealthiest in their community. That same pattern of persistence leading to success was apparent in Emily Township. The twenty families out of the first pioneer cohort that stayed, twenty years later owned some of the best-developed farms in the area.[35] All of the families that would remain in the township had arrived and begun farming before 1850. Some, especially the Irish, commenced as tenants, but all of those whose families would subsequently remain, soon purchased land of their own.[36] This finding parallels that of Catherine A. Wilson, who found in Cramhé township that renting or leasing could be part of a family strategy to control and develop land resources either in the long term or as a means of gaining ownership.[37] However, after 1850 "there was little chance for the ambitious newcomer to acquire sufficient land ... Almost all would pull up stakes and move on."[38]

Before the onset of the crisis in the 1850s, Toronto Gore township's permanent families already possessed farms of, on average, 127 acres, twice the size of Peel's average.[39] "Early settlement enabled the first generation to acquire comparatively large farms ... Later, in the face of considerable economic stress, the adoption of particular practices of inheritance ensured that at least some of their children could not only acquire land, but also aspire realistically to the good life."[40]

Using Donald R. Leet's "Index of Economic Stress," Mays argued that by the 1850s Toronto Gore could only provide new farms for about half of its sons, and by the 1860s less than a quarter. "The farmer's *expectation* that his capital in the form of land would multiply was shaken in two ways ... Any investment in land was a risky business ... Even if ... land prices were moving upward ... those increases were relatively small."[41] In that uncertain context, the first generation of early settlers tried to pass their property to the second. Most of the places opened by transients went to tenant farmers. Even sons of the first settlers had to start (at least temporarily) as tenants: "Better than two-fifths (43.5 per cent) of the second and third generations began their independent economic life as tenants on the lands of their parents, relatives … or other absentee landowners."[42] But if tenancy was *not* temporary (i.e., if it lasted more than ten years), 90 per cent of the young men left the township. Some stayed, as "the aging of the permanent population ensured that more land would become available as time passed."[43]

What did change over time was *how* the land was transferred between generations. Direct sales to sons declined significantly between the 1840s and the 1880s. Instead of direct sales, sons who inherited land also inherited substantial responsibilities. "When a son was provided with early inheritance, he was required to assume obligations to care for his parents in their old age, as well as to furnish the capital that his brothers and sisters would need to establish their own independence."[44]

The end of the land frontier within Peel occurred shortly before the advance of settlement all across Ontario had met the southern edge of the Canadian Shield in the late 1850s. Farmers' sons leaving Peel might have been able to find available land in the nearby Bruce Peninsula (where some moved), but that limited supply was disappearing rapidly and its quality was increasingly marginal. In spite of the changes in inheritance and family structure, the pressure of surplus population in the province contributed significantly to a change in outlook, from the local to the national, soon embodied in the Dominion of Canada.

In more ways than one, the debates over Gagan's agricultural crisis thesis have been less central to Ontario history than those over Ouellet's *crise agricole* thesis. The issues involved have been regarded as less profound in relation to the province's history and the number of individuals involved has been correspondingly lower. Gagan's first substantial publication of the project's findings drew a very sharp reaction from other quantitatively oriented social scientists, focused largely on methodology. Subsequently, several other writers on the mid-nineteenth century have responded in various ways to Gagan's work.

In 1981 George Emery and José Igartua published a forceful critique of Gagan's work. They considered it founded on a series of dubious assumptions about the use of the county as a unit of study and the supposedly static character of rural culture. They saw Gagan's exposition as flawed by both imprecision and lack of congruence between the model he proposed and the data that he presented. Finally, not only did he present the specialized results in an erroneous way but also he did not understand the import of the numbers he cited in support of his argument. They considered that Gagan had used the county as a closed system. The scarcity of available farmland within a single county was not the whole context in which farm families would have been making decisions, when they had the whole of Ontario and the whole of the North American continent before them. Emery and Igartua also wanted Gagan to look at the different experiences of the five townships inside the county. By doing that, they expected that he would have found a spatial dynamic, especially with respect to the influence of Toronto. Secondly, they stressed the relatively recent settlement of Peel County against the assumption of a static rural culture to argue that first- or second-generation farmers would not have rigid ideas about how much land their sons ought to have had. Families that had uprooted themselves from Europe to venture onto a new continent should not be seen as bound by tradition (a view shared by Chief Justice John Beverley Robinson when it came to the customary rights of tenant farmers).[45] Emery and Igartua here agreed with the later criticism of Douglas McCalla, that while the household economy is often seen as traditional, that emphasis "downplays the implications of both transatlantic and shorter-distance migration, ignores the capital that had to be invested or created, neglects the multiplicity and complexity of choices that the farm household faced, and underestimates the knowledge that had to be acquired of successful farming in that region and even on that specific land."[46] Even though migrants felt they were pushed out of the Old World by the increasing difficulties of maintaining a family farm, that did not make them "simple traditionalists carrying on in timeless peasant old-world ways."[47] If custom had ceased to be a guide in so many things in the New World, why should it have had a determining influence on how much land a man needed to start a farm and family?

Emery and Igartua also criticized the three measures Gagan used for demographic pressure within the county. Against his use of the density of males over fifteen compared to occupied land, they thought he ought to have used either the total *farm* population or *only* rural males. (They did not make explicit the assumption in the latter alternative, that only young men living on farms ever wanted to be farmers.) This concern parallels the conflict between Ouellet and Courville as to whether Quebec's growing villages represented landless habitants or an emergent proto-industrialization. Emery and Igartua also disputed Gagan's use of land *occupied* rather than *cleared*, or even acres in *wheat*. They offered an alternative hypothesis: "Farmers found some relief from demographic pressure simply by putting a greater proportion (from 50.7 per cent in 1851 to 72.7 per cent in 1871) of occupied land to use."[48] If adult males are compared to improved acres, cropped acres, or acres planted to wheat, population pressure appeared to be falling. Furthermore they faulted the *logic* of Gagan's argument: given a fixed quantity of land, how could there be *both* larger farms (growth in farm size) and *more* farmers? This they describe as an "inconsistency."

They took issue with Gagan's land price series. Rising prices need not be taken to show increased competition for available land: "If Gagan cannot determine how much of the observed variation in land prices comes from currency fluctuation or other factors unrelated to demand, then the trend in prices cannot 'testify' [Gagan's term] to anything."[49] How many transactions per year did the aggregate numbers represent? What was the standard deviation from the mean price? Had he compared like to like – that is, did he compare the price of cleared land in one period with the price of cleared land in another and the price of wild land in one period with the price of wild land in another period? If any and all land sales in one period were compared to all those of another period, the rise in price might be solely due to more cleared land being offered for sale in the second period as against the first.

Could mortgages be used as evidence to show population pressure on the land? Gagan argued that farmers took out mortgages in a time of crisis to continue expansion of their land holdings (to provide land for their sons), and then retired the mortgages as the crisis eased. Emery and Igartua replied that farmers might just be retiring 1860 mortgages in 1870 as part of normal farm financing. Farm debt need not always mean crisis.[50]

Not only did they dispute his measures of demographic pressure (i.e., the cause) but they also argued that he erred in describing the farmers' response to the crisis (i.e., the effect). They held that he did not have conclusive evidence either that farm families limited their size or that a significant change in inheritance practices had taken place. They argued he had not isolated his explanatory variable in dealing with the changes in family size. There might be some *other* factor (than his supposed crisis) that could explain why families apparently had fewer children. In their view, the three census populations (1851, 1861, 1871) had to be "standardized" to eliminate any other possible cause for an apparent variation in family size. For example, "sex ratios were not constant from 1851 to 1871, and they might account for the rising age at first marriage of women, since fewer men meant a longer search for a spouse."[51] While Gagan argued that a pattern of rising age at first marriage reflected both short-term crisis and longer-term trends, his use of *moving* averages effectively deleted the former in order to see the latter. He needed a better measure to show *annual* variations compared to a longer-term trend. The short-term peaks were more frequent and coincided with *different* economic cycles (but they did not indicate which cycles they meant).

Emery and Igartua were similarly critical of the second reaction to the demographic crisis: changing inheritance patterns. *Variations* in the proportions of different sorts of wills were not necessarily due to recurrent crises. First, were the figures offered for types of wills actually percentages (as the totals varied from 106 to 91)? Second, did everyone make a will? How many wills were made in each period? They offered simpler ways to show the data, by a time series or a correlation statistic.

However, they had little confidence in Gagan's capacity to handle statistics, in particular Multiple Classification Analysis (MCA), a way to analyse variance, to determine whether mean values for a dependent variable vary more than randomly with data divided into categories by the independent variable (i.e., the predictor). He did not give enough information about how he used MCA to give them any confidence in his results. First of all, MCA requires a dependent variable on an interval scale (not a *nominal* scale).[52] Secondly, MCA only works if there are no strong interactions between independent variables. He *ought* to have explicitly stated that he had tested for such interaction and found none. Furthermore, they claimed that Gagan did not understand what a significance variable is in a null hypothesis: "A significance variable is simply a measure of the probability of a particular statistical relationship not having occurred by chance. It says nothing about the nature and strength of the relationship."[53] There is no question of more-or-less, of measuring degree with MCA: "Either a statistical relationship falls within the accepted level of risk and is significant, or it does not and is not."[54] They nominated beta-squared or the "eta" statistic as *true* measures of the *relative* importance of various independent variable on the dependent one. Finally, one of Gagan's key tables simply used the wrong MCA summary statistic: multiple-R instead of R-squared. The result of that error was to significantly overstate the strength of the relationship he had presented.

In conclusion, "his model rests on dubious assumptions and his use of data is inadequate for testing the model."[55] Emery and Igartua allowed that there was some room for argument over how well such data might be able to sustain the model (which itself might be refined), but "there can be no such room for accommodation concerning his mishandling of statistical methods."[56] The new social history could not break ground by capturing the experience of the common people with quantitative methods if those methods had not been properly handled.

Gagan replied that he considered that Emery and Igartua had both misstated and misinterpreted the scope, objectives, and conclusions of his article. He pointed out that his intention was to test three hypotheses, each arising from an extensive historiographic tradition. First of all, was there a social and economic crisis in rural Ontario in the years preceding Confederation? He sketched out the parameters of this crisis: "The high cost of acquiring land, the risk to debtors of financing land in unstable real estate and commodities markets, limited opportunities for new emigrants, an inheritance crisis among farmers' sons, and the uncertain future of the wheat staple in Canada West."[57] Second, what could inheritance patterns tell us about the society's character? In the 1850s the province was moving away from the sort of inheritance pattern one would expect from European studies toward more Canadian or perhaps North American practices of inheritance. Third, did the longer term of settlement lead to smaller families? He had elsewhere shown that the work of Richard Easterlin and Donald Leet had posed the question of the relation between land availability and aggregate farm family fertility.[58]

In contrast to these three historiographic streams, Gagan saw implicit in the critique a "metropolitan model" that held that Peel's proximity to Toronto ought to have had pride of place. He had previously examined that model and found it wanting.[59] Moreover, he cited Marvin McInnis's work on the 1861 Canada West farm sample in which McInnis had found the variable "distance from an urban centre" to be just another way of measuring length of settlement and availability of land (i.e., *all* recently settled land with lots of room to expand will be a long way from any sizable town). Thus distance from major urban centres and length of settlement could not be treated as independent variables. On the basis of McInnis's empirical findings and his own theoretical reflections on the metropolitan model, Gagan considered that he had good grounds for not seeking to test for metropolitan influence within Peel.

Gagan denied that he had taken Peel to be in any sense a closed system. For example, he had noted the movement of farmers' sons into the Bruce Peninsula. Moreover, he cited the work of Darrell Norris as an indication of the out-migration pattern one might find if it were possible to trace families beyond the county.[60] He rejected the suggestion that the township would be a more appropriate unit, because it would be too small a unit for a study of longer-term patterns of landholding.

Furthermore, Peel contained the county's most pertinent urban centre: Brampton.

Responding to Emery and Igartua's questioning of how such a recently settled area could have so soon acquired a static rural culture, Gagan pointed out that the incoming settlers had come to North America with their rural culture already in place. The immigrants had quite durable notions of how much land was "enough." In support of this, Gagan cited a range of studies from Richard Houston, James Lemon, Allan Brogue (on the United States), and Gérard Bouchard (on Quebec) and a study of twentieth-century rural Saskatchewan.[61] Land hunger had brought settlers to Ontario.[62] Their early experiences confirmed their hopes: enough land of their own to be independent.

He responded to their criticisms of mortgage activity as an indication of demographic pressure by pointing out that they offered no explanation of why farmers who had begun using mortgages in 1855–65 did not continue to do so after 1870. While Emery and Igartua said (somewhat gnomically) that "Gagan failed to consider the nature of mortgages," they did not say what they considered that "nature" to have been or how that "nature" might have invalidated Gagan's argument.

Gagan defended his land price series by saying that they *ought* to know that his sources (the abstracts or copy books of deeds) never specified the quality or condition of the land (i.e., whether cleared or wild). However, in saying this he appears to concede their criticism that he may not be comparing like to like (i.e., the price of cleared land with the price of cleared land).[63] If one cannot control for land's condition, the *rise* in price might reflect only the increased clearing on the land rather than more competition for it. On the other hand, it could be argued that if the land *offered* for sale was costing more, then the would-be buyer faced a higher land price, whether the land was wild or improved.

Gagan took more seriously the criticism made of his direct measure of the demographic pressure on land by the ratio of adult males to occupied acres. Not only farmers' sons wanted farms. However, he conceded a need for better measure of demographic pressure. He agreed that for age of first marriage, a weighted moving average had an arbitrary element, but the weighting he chose did fit one set of cycles. Emery and Igartua had not offered an alternative set of cycles in order to demonstrate that a better fit was possible.

In response to whether the wills cited covered the whole population, he said that his were a sample of all intergenerational transactions (others being covered by other forms of transfer such as sale to heirs).

Although he did not claim to be able to demonstrate this, the surviving wills could also be considered a sample of all wills ever extant.

In response to criticisms of his handling of MCA statistics, Gagan defended his presentation while conceding an error in one particular. Emery and Igartua had demanded that he make explicit his testing of various assumptions (e.g., that there was no interrelationship between independent variables). Gagan stated that he had not tested whether or not his independent variables would influence each other but that any study would *always* rest upon *some* untested assumptions. They had not asked that he test *every* assumption that he had made. He considered that it was for them to make a compelling case why a particular assumption ought to be explicitly tested. He had muddled multiple-R and R-squared and thus overstated the influence of his independent variables, for which he offered a correction. However, he rejected the broader criticism of his use of quantitative methods in the service of social history: "I am not convinced that the essence of good historical reporting is a lab report, or that quantitative history will win many converts among general readers when it uses 'statistics as a drunken man uses a lamp post – for support rather than for illumination.'"[64]

When his book appeared a year later, Gagan provided a further, indirect reply to the criticisms of Emery and Igartua. His argument remained the same, but several refinements in his use of statistics responded to their criticisms. As presaged in his direct rebuttal, he offered a new measure for demographic pressure on land. He did not accept that non-farm males ought not to be counted on the assumption that none of them wished to become farmers. Instead, he focused on a better measure for the availability of land.[65] His new measure of available land encompassed unimproved land not yet appropriated, as well as land made available by out-migration and mortality. He also dropped his earliest year (1838) of data, which had the unfortunate result of compressing the period of the rise, perhaps weakening his case for a longer-term upward trend. He compared all males over fifteen to available land; this showed a sharp rise from 1851 to 1861, followed by a drop in 1871.[66] These changes resulted in a more robust measure of demographic pressure on land in the county, as long as one accepted that non-farm males also sought to establish themselves as farmers (an assumption that Wallot and Paquet would not have allowed in the debates over Quebec's agricultural crisis).

On his use of MCA statistics, Gagan made a sharper break than one might have expected.[67] Rather than the rewording that he had offered in his 1981 rebuttal, he dropped the use of correlation measures altogether.[68] He dropped the significance *numbers* in favour of simple yes/no responses to the issue of statistical significance. While he took an alternative route (to the one his rebuttal offered), he was still accepting the substance of the Emery-Igartua critique of his initial reading of significance statistics.

A second, more technical critique of his record linkage methodology came from several of those working with Gérard Bouchard on his Saguenay Project. Raymond Roy, Christian Pouyez, and François Martin explained the problems in linking the name of the same individual from one source to another, whether from one census to another or one type of source to another, such as a tax assessment record to a census report. After outlining their own project's methods of coping with these problems, they specifically criticized Gagan's approach. He had only sought to link household heads, assumed to represent whole families, while ignoring single men (aged 18–25) on the assumption that the latter would balance out those who died between censuses. They could see no necessary connection between the number of unmarried males and the mortality rate to justify any idea of balance. Their project had tracked each individual rather than just household heads. They expressed concern that the "SOUNDEX" automated linkage system that he used matched only surnames of the heads of households. Gagan's second step was to compare the first names. These had to be exactly the same, or the automated match of surnames was rejected. In their Saguenay Project, they said, 17 per cent of men and 26 per cent of women who were correctly matched had first names that varied. They were also concerned that Gagan had allowed too little variation in matching ages. They concluded that these rigid rules had produced very few matches, leading Gagan (like Katz) to greatly underestimate population persistence in one place. If those rules had been applied to their project, they said, it would have excluded 23 per cent of their definite linkages.[69] Surprisingly little attention has been paid to their analysis, even though it indicates that both Katz and Gagan have seriously overstated mid-nineteenth-century geographic mobility and thus overstated social instability.

Most writers on nineteenth-century Ontario agriculture since Gagan's book have had to take it into account. In some cases they made use of his data (Cohen), and in other cases, they have used their own findings to reflect upon those of Gagan. In some cases, as with Lockwood and Akenson, their perspective is informed by their own microstudies done in other parts of Ontario. In other cases, Gagan's study of Peel has been put into a larger provincial context.

Part of Gagan's original rationale for choosing Peel as his county for study had been his belief that it was in some way representative of Ontario farming in the mid-nineteenth century. In fact what McInnis's analysis of the 1851 Agricultural Census for Canada West has shown is that Peel, far from being representative of the whole, was one of the most extreme cases in the province: "Peel, with 34.5 percent of its land in wheat was the heart of the wheat region and the quintessential wheat farming county of Ontario. It might be added that it continued as such right up to the end of the nineteenth century. Peel was one of the most prosperous farming areas of Ontario at mid-century. It may have been the only area where farmers specialized in wheat to the extent of having to buy other farm products, although that remains a debatable point. Elsewhere, wheat was produced over and above the variety of products needed for subsistence of the farm family."[70] While Peel was planting more wheat proportionately than any other county, its stocks of animals were about average.[71]

Gagan's choice of Peel, then, as a county to represent Ontario was seriously flawed. However, we can now see that his choice arose out of the prevailing view of the province as having an economy based on wheat as an export staple. Since the 1970s our understanding of the provincial economy has deepened greatly, thanks in part to the work of scholars like McInnis and McCalla, which allows the comparison of broad economic and social parameters. In light of that understanding, we would now read Gagan's microstudy as focused on one of the most heavily commercial farming areas in Ontario. Rather than mistaking it for the whole of the province, we now read it as a study of the wheat-growing belt as it neared its peak in the 1850s wheat boom.

Douglas McCalla, in his economic history of Ontario, found much of worth in Gagan's study. He cited Gagan approvingly on the diversity of the rural economy, where not everyone was a farmer.[72] He appreciated Gagan's stress on how quickly farmers adapted to the long-term shift from extensive to intensive growth.[73] Yet even while stressing that the fertility transition to which Gagan pointed "represented a cultural, economic, and biological transformation," McCalla wondered if we needed to call this a "crisis." In part, his reserve seemed to arise not over the profound nature of the change but over whether the motivations and mechanisms were quite as Gagan said they were. Nonetheless, McCalla considered that "in key aspects the main demographic changes Gagan discusses for his sample region characterized Upper Canada as a whole."[74]

McCalla also chose to stress Gagan's and May's contributions to our understanding of nineteenth-century transiency in a rural community: "Just 39 per cent of householders in 1851 remained in 1861, and just 31 per cent of the 1861 householders remained in 1871; of all the 10,000 households captured on one of the three census manuscripts, only a tenth were present on all three."[75] McCalla noted that comparably high rates appeared in Michael Katz's study of Hamilton. McCalla wanted to expand on the relationship Gagan had suggested between persistence and property ownership. Not only did property owners persist much more than non-owners, McCalla wanted to add, but property owners who arrived *early* were most likely to endure and succeed in farming. Not all commentators have been so favourably impressed by this correlation.[76]

Gordon Darroch and Lee Soltow, in the course of their study of property and inequality in Ontario according to the 1871 census, also asked from the longer-term perspective whether there was any rural crisis in those so-called critical years. They sought not to deny Gagan's findings for Peel County but to deny that they applied to the province as a whole: "By the end of the 1860s accessibility to farm land had become seriously constricted at least in some areas, fostering rural depopulation and the growth of a class of landless families."[77] But for the province as a whole, "there is no evidence to suggest a *sufficiently* dramatic change in access to land in Ontario between mid-century and the 1871 census.[78] "The notion of a genuine crisis in access to land probably overstates the case. In the end, the choice of terms may be a matter of emphasis, though it seems to go beyond mere nuance."[79] As in the debates between Ouellet and his many critics, the issue was not whether there was any land left that could be cultivated, but whether good farmland was running out. "On a provincial level no dramatic crisis in access to land had been experienced two decades after mid-century, though the term may be an appropriate description of the circumstances of a core of stable and aspiring farmers in a given locale, as Gagan has observed for Peel County."[80] However, a strong desire to possess land of their own kept many people focused on even the diminishing opportunities for anything more than subsistence in agriculture.   It is already clear that Peel did not represent much more than the wheat belt that wrapped around the western end of Lake Ontario. Glenn Lockwood and Donald Akenson studied townships in eastern Ontario and found Gagan's claims that Peel represented the province did not hold. Lockwood's comparison of Montague Township in eastern Ontario with Peel clearly showed that the pattern Gagan had found did not apply universally. Against Gagan's dismissal of ethnicity as a factor, Lockwood pointed to the tenacious persistence of Protestant and Catholic Irish on the unpromising soils of Montague. It was less clear whether persistence meant a rising standard of living, but at least their fields were steadily cleared and early shanties were replaced with wooden houses by 1881. Moreover, he found a similar fertility transition: "a norm of small families once the extraordinary task of clearing the land was accomplished."[81] At least in this township, the failure of wheat (through falling yields as well as the general price fall) led directly to dairying, which proved much more profitable.[82]

Donald Akenson's microstudy of Leeds and Lansdowne township, through which he pursued the role of the Irish in Canada, took issue with Gagan and others who put such emphasis on the transience of early migrants. Akenson's major disagreement is relegated to a lengthy footnote. He deprecated the "very fashionable topic in Upper Canadian social history" of focusing on transiency: "The degree to which Canadian historians were surprised to discover that there was a good deal of transience in nineteenth-century Ontario is in itself surprising. Can they really have thought that individuals who lived on a continent of frontiers and who often had travelled thousands of miles before even arriving in Upper Canada would simply plop down in one place and remain?"[83] Moreover, he maintained that the methodology adopted in geographically based microstudies is singularly ineffective in telling us anything about the transients. The data, by its nature, tells us about who stayed, and very little about who left. In order to study transients, one would need quite a different methodology, derived from genealogy and studies of family life course. However, "the excessive emphasis upon defining levels of transiency obscures the fact that continuity and stability in the patterns of social evolution characterized most communities despite the continual rotation of population."[84]

Akenson was not a censorious critic, but rather gave credit to others whenever he could. Even when he disagreed, the disagreement is cast in a good-natured form. On the utility of microstudies, he chided Gagan for "one of the few thuddingly wrong sentences in his fine study of Peel county" when Gagan attempted to argue that his was not "local history." Akenson found valuable insights that confirmed his own work. Inheritance under the Canadian system could place a heavy burden on what might be seen as the lucky child who inherited the home farm, since this child also had to undertake, with the inheritance, a series of sometimes-onerous responsibilities to compensate other would-be heirs who did not get land. These could amount to as much as three years' cash income from the farm.[85]

Bruce Elliot, in his *Irish Migrants in the Canadas*, also faulted the stress on transience. "Katz and Gagan suggested in the 1970s that the highly mobile society depicted was very different from the stable, rooted communities of families that were assumed to be the popular stereotype, and asserted that many of Canada's nineteenth-century inhabitants were rootless wanderers."[86] Elliot's own work, like that of Gordon Darroch, has focused on the extent to which the transience that undoubtedly existed need not have been morally reprehensible individualism, but in fact often reflected the purposeful search by families for their place in the New World.[87] In some sense as an ethnic historian focusing on the Irish, like Lockwood and Akenson, Elliot may here be somewhat *parti pris*: one of the slanders directed at the Irish in the nineteenth century was that they were not only lazy but shiftless, constantly drifting from one community to the next. One common concern of those new social historians of ethnicity whose particular province is the Irish diaspora has been to demonstrate that the Irish were no more feckless and changeable than members of any other ethnic group.[88]

As in the debates over Ouellet's *crise agricol* thesis, so in the smaller debate over Gagan's crisis: much turns on matters of timing and causation. As McCalla has noted, there was a long-term underlying change in the province's economy from extensive growth – characterized by ever-larger numbers of farms but relatively stable levels of per farm output and man-to-land ratios – to intensive growth, in which output per farm began to rise sharply and the male-heads-of-farm-families-to-land ratios fell. Gérard Bouchard has used the term "saturation" to describe the process of the settlement frontier reaching the physical limits of arable land in the Canadian Shield. One needs to distinguish carefully between not only the quality of the land available (relative to nineteenth-century technology) but also the differences in remaining ungranted land versus uncleared land. Farmers in both Ontario and Quebec were still clearing forest from their lands at the end of the century. However, for the dynamic of the farm family household, which relied upon its children's labour – labour traditionally rewarded with new land of its own – the relevant measure of available land was the extent of lands not yet ceded or granted. Settled long before Ontario was even created, Canadien society in the seigneurial zone hit the physical limits of its arable extent early in the nineteenth century. However, the large-scale migration into Ontario pushed its frontier forward much faster than Quebec's had ever gone. By the 1850s, ungranted lands still left were already those of lesser quality.

As Quebec's declining agricultural productivity can be shown from the long-term trend in declining wheat exports, so Ontario's long-term transition from extensive growth (which ended when it met the Shield) to intensive growth can be shown from the rising output per farm, the falling ratio of rural adult males to occupied land, and the fertility transition. Certainly, the early 1830s marked a severe worsening of Quebec's agriculture. Some historians want to reserve the word "crisis" for that, and thereby possibly limit its causes to bad weather and insects, without looking at other aspects of the province's agriculture. For Ontario, the hard question is: what is the relation between the long-term transition process and the short-term crisis caused by the fall of wheat and land prices in 1857–58? To what extent did the short-term crisis mark the beginning of the long-term changes from extensive to intensive growth; from mixed farming, with the largest farms oriented to wheat, to a more predominant emphasis on dairy farming; from large to small families? Earlier falls in wheat and land prices (as in 1819 or 1835) had not produced any major demographic transition. Rather, the immediate crisis in 1857 brought home more sharply the need for the longer-settled parts of this rural society to adjust to the new realities of limited land resources within the province and the implications of that for the organization and operation of farm families in future. Migrations to urban areas, to Michigan or Minnesota, and eventually to Manitoba as well as the rise of animal products in the agricultural surplus testify to the ways in which Ontario farm families strove to adapt.

The province's increasingly felt necessity, after 1850, to expand its frontiers was an important factor in the drive to Confederation. Gagan, who had already written a study of "Canada First," considered that the Ontario reaction to the resistance led by Louis Riel at Red River produced what was, by any name, an armed invasion of the West, fired by the rhetoric of nationalism but fed by the thwarted imperialism of Ontario.[89] The rush of young men to settle in the new province of Manitoba reflected the pressure that had been building up in counties like Peel for over a decade.

The end of Ontario's open land frontier led to migration in three directions. First, rural population pressure found a political outlet in Confederation, as a result of the re-valuation and subsequent demand for the appropriation of Rupert's Land. The discovery, or perhaps even the invention, of a fertile belt available for farm settlement became one of

Map 5.1: Density of Canadian settlement in the American Upper Midwest.

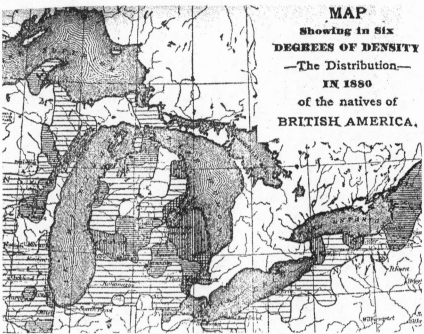

MAP
Showing in Six
DEGREES OF DENSITY
—The Distribution—
IN 1880
of the natives of
BRITISH AMERICA.

The darker the shading, the more numerous the Canadians, with the darkest indicating more than 20 Canadians per square mile, the lightest indicating up to 2 Canadians per square mile.

Source: Abstract of the Tenth Census: 1880, Government Printing Office, Washington, 1884, vol. 1, 492.

the forces that drove forward both Confederation and the annexation of Rupert's Land.

However, many farmers' sons could not wait upon political developments and availed themselves of the American open land frontier, especially after the passage of the American Homestead Act (1863). The 1880 report of the United States tenth census included a map showing the areas with concentrations of British American population. Apart from French-Canadian settlement in New England, the heaviest concentration was closest to Lake Huron along Ontario's western boundary, gradually thinning westward across the state of Michigan toward Wisconsin and Minnesota.[90] (See Map 5.1) In the 1850s about 22,000 Canadians moved to Michigan, a number that jumped to over 50,000 in the 1860s and 1870s, then fell back to 36,000 in the 1880s. The census report also included a special section on Canada as the United States' single largest source of immigrants.[91] Table 5.5 shows the number of British North

Table 5.5: British North American/Canadian settlers in the American Midwest, 1850, 1860, 1870, 1880, and 1890.

	Michigan	Wisconsin	Minnesota	Illinois	Iowa
1850	14,008	8,277	1,417	10,699	1,736
1860	36,482	18,146	8,023	20,132	8,313
1870	87,481	22,767	13,751	29,919	16,431
1880	145,968	25,682	25,288	32,131	19,451
1890	181,416	33,163	43,580	39,525	17,465

Source: Census of the United States: 1850, 1860, 1870, 1880, 1890.

American (or Canadian) settlers in the American Midwest from 1850 to 1890. The 1890 US census for the first time broke down Canadians by language as well as occupation: 91,787 English speakers were classified as agricultural (compared to 23,367 French speakers).[92]

The third direction in which the displaced rural population could go was toward the growing urban centres where industrialization had begun: "Between 1851 and 1871 the number of people living in places of 1,000 or more almost tripled, a more rapid rate of growth of urban population than in any subsequent pair of decades before the Second World War."[93] Whereas Quebec's demographic crisis reached its peak at a time when that province's urban centres were stagnant or in decline, Ontario had a dynamic urban frontier of opportunity that could absorb a displaced rural population, especially those who had some capital to bring with them. The growth of Brampton in Peel, like that of Gananoque in Leeds and of Lansdowne in eastern Ontario, reflected expanding urban opportunities even in smaller centres for a rural population on the move.[94]

The rapid growth of new urban centres should not be over-read as being the beginning of rural depopulation in Ontario. Some left-wing scholars, impatient to see the rapid emergence of industrialization predicted by Marx, tend to push rural depopulation much further back in time. Ian Drummond took Leo Johnson to task for his history of Ontario County: "Johnson tells us that small farmers were forced off the land by debt in periods of depression such as 1867–1869." Johnson "writes of a social crisis, complete with rural depopulation, in the decade of the 1870s."[95] Drummond pointed out that not only did Johnson offer no evidence to support his claim but the census also shows that 1871–81 saw an increase in the number of farms in the county from 4,837 to 5,386 (an 11.4 per cent increase). In fact both the number of farms and the absolute numbers of those living on farms in the province continually increased to the end of the nineteenth century.[96] In offering an overview of class and society in Victorian English Canada, Gagan betrayed the same anxiety to see the emergence of a two-class society in rural (as in Katz's urban) world: "In the 1860s, plummeting production values, market dislocation, blight, overpopulation and land shortage all combined to drive the least adaptable farmers west to the United States and then to Manitoba, to impel farm labourers and surplus children towards the factories, shops and universities of the cities, and to reduce marginal farmers to work for wages in town and county ... Marginalized smallholders and tenant farmers ... became the motive power behind the diffusion of industrialization throughout the towns and villages ... communities which swiftly became local social structural microcosms of the two-class model that had emerged in the larger metropolises."[97] The creation of 44,000 farms in the twenty years after 1871 showed that Ontario continued to offer the prospect of farming to its sons as well as immigrants, even though the land put into production was often increasingly marginal.[98]

For the new Dominion of Canada, those drives for urbanization and western expansion would become central forces shaping the second half of the nineteenth century. For many farmers' sons in the new province of Ontario, one of the necessary purposes of Confederation was the annexation of Rupert's Land to create a new farm frontier for them. This Ontario nationalism demanded that the land be cleared of all previous title in order to be available for prompt British (meaning anglo-Canadian as well as) settlement. It also called for the institutions of the new region to reflect not merely Ontario, but Ontario as Clear Grits wanted it to be, without Roman Catholic separate schools (a necessary, but regrettable, part of the Confederation agreement).[99] However, in the initial institutions the federal government created for the North West, Quebec nationalism would also have its impact. The resolution of the demands of those two land-hungry nationalisms would shape the Prairies for decades.

6

Land-Hungry Nationalisms
on the Prairies

To outsiders, Rupert's Land was a blank sheet on which to write their hopes of cultural dominance by fulfilling their people's quest for new lands. First, in the thirty years after Confederation, the land-hunger-driven nationalisms from Quebec and Ontario collided on the Prairies.[1] Quebec's representatives succeeded in establishing a bilingual and bicultural Manitoba.[2] However, in the race to populate the new province, the timing of Ontario's "crisis" gave it a decisive edge. The short sharp downturn in the late 1850s had alerted a rising generation of farm families that their sons would have to look elsewhere for new farmland. The earlier onset and long, drawn-out nature of Quebec's agricultural crisis meant that the province's land hunger slackened before Confederation as many of its landless habitants had already turned to the low-cost options of forestry or factory labour in the United States. Second, just when it seemed that conflict had been resolved in Ontario's favour – dominance in the region's institutions and enforcement of its language – land hunger brought new national groups from overseas to the region.[3] To varying degrees, they sought to preserve at least some of their own culture by seeking accommodation in public institutions such as schools. However, a further twenty years of conflict was also ultimately resolved in favour of Ontario's values and language. Thus we can see, running through the "usual suspects" used to explain Prairie history – ethnicity, language, and religion – the underlying current in agriculture: the need for land.

To those who lived in Rupert's Land, matters looked very different. The assessment of their actions and the reactions of the federal government have been complex. Ottawa's acquisition of the region together with its relations with the peoples of the region – especially those at Red River – has spawned a series of conflicting positions among Canadian historians. John Weaver concluded: "Partly from dumb luck, partly because of able civil servants, a sparsely settled colony successfully organized a vast territorial acquisition with relatively few murderous conflicts, no extended warfare, minimal pastoral landhunting, modest squatting, and sound land titles."[4]

From these outside and inside debates can be traced the interactions of farm families, land, and national identity: the consequences for the Prairies of the crises of central Canada. While A.S. Morton noted that "the Canadian Government acted with an undignified precipitancy. They entered into their new possession before it was theirs," the predominant voice in the oldest historiography saw the benevolent advance of civilization momentarily checked by an inferior people.[5] Canadian military historian, George Stanley said of the Métis, the largest group at Red River, "with few exceptions the French half-breeds were neither extensive nor successful farmers. Brought up in the open prairies they preferred the excitement of the chase to the monotony of cultivating the soil."[6] In the 1930s while Stanley published, French anthropologist Marcel Giraud did the field work for his book on the Métis: "It goes without saying that these nomads, essentially occupied with hunting, devoted too little time to the land to work it carefully, and were still influenced too directly by the attitudes of the native peoples to reach a state of mind favourable to agrarian occupations." Giraud did not restrict this characterization to the nineteenth century. "The Bois-Brulés [another name for the Métis] had too little time to go beyond this stage of creating rather primitive gardens, as many Métis families still do today in the western plains."[7] Writing in the 1950s, Manitoba historian W.L. Morton took issue with Giraud, contending that by the 1860s most of the Métis at Red River had seriously committed themselves to agriculture.[8]

In the context of the 1960s debates over bilingualism, Donald Creighton recast the earlier racial categories in terms of language and religion. He portrayed Louis Riel as seizing power at Red River, manipulating its assembly's bills of rights to force Ottawa into creating an unwanted bilingual province with separate schools. Without Riel, Creighton argued, there would have been no province of Manitoba (not even a "postage stamp size" one), no bilingual provincial government, and no equality between Protestant and Catholic schools or bilingual education.[9] Ralph Heintzman countered with an argument that both government and opposition of the day had agreed to a bicultural Manitoba in the "Spirit of Confederation."[10] Debate continued over whether the legislation represented a balance between Quebec and Ontario, perhaps in a "spirit of union," or whether the first voice heard from the West had played a part, large or small.

Part of the earliest historiography of Stanley and Girard had been a view of primitive hunters – Indians and Métis – in contrast to the civilized people – the Selkirk settlers who farmed at Red River.[11] W.L. Morton began the undermining of that simple dichotomy by showing that all parishes participated in hunting and farming, as well as working for the Hudson's Bay Company and fishing, to varying degrees.[12] To make the case for modern Métis land claims, Dennis Sprague strove to show both that the Métis were a farming people and that they were dispossessed by fraud and violence after the Canadian takeover.[13] The equation of farming with civilization, as market engagement, has been challenged by the work of Gerhard Ens. Agriculture at Red River was primarily oriented to family subsistence, a peasant agriculture, usually balanced with at least two other food sources. However, the rising buffalo-robe trade at mid-century involved much greater participation with the forces of emerging capitalism than with subsistence agriculture. To pursue the diminishing buffalo herds, Ens argued, Métis hunters had been leaving Red River for settlement further west long before Canada took control.

Ens's work on the Red River parishes of St Andrew and St Francis Xavier (1835–90) is complemented by Nicole St Onge's studies on Ste Agathe and St Laurent.[14] Both found emerging class divisions within their respective parishes. In all four there was a minority that farmed on a substantially larger scale, held more livestock, and often branched into lines of commerce (as merchants or millers), far beyond the parish's average inhabitant. The Métis, then, like the habitants on the St Lawrence, had a minority that prospered and expanded where others strove for subsistence. These economic factors played important roles in how the people of Red River responded to the attempted annexation by Canada in 1869 and to the political order of the new Manitoba that resulted in the 1870s.

Heintzman could argue for a spirit of Confederation over the causes and status of the bicultural aspects of Manitoba's constitution. However, in the 1880s there came a new generation, "a new pharaoh who knew not Joseph," which would expressly reject any attempt to appeal to the older ideal or spirit of Confederation. Men like D'Alton McCarthy amongst Conservatives and Clifford Sifton amongst Liberals would find common cause in seeking to replace the older unity in diversity with a new demand for a movement from diversity into unity, the uniformity of an Anglo-Protestant assimilating nationalism.

Table 6.1: Manitoba's population by place of birth, 1881 and 1891.

	Manitoba	Ontario	Quebec	Britain	USA	Total
1881	18,020	19,125	4,085	8,161	1,752	65,954
1891	50,648	46,620	7,555	28,014	3,061	152,506

Source: Census of Canada, 1880–1881, vol. 4, 14, and Census of Canada, 1890–1891, vol. 4, 390.

The proactive role of Louis Riel and his provisional government in 1869–70 allows room for scholars to debate whether the Manitoba Act's bicultural aspects might not have become law. However, the legislation that followed in the 1870s for the new North West Territories (NWT) was much more directly the creation of the government in Ottawa.[15] While the separate schools provision passed the Commons easily, the Senate gave the amendment intense scrutiny.[16] It was a major blow against Heintzman's "spirit of Confederation" that Senator George Brown – sounding very much like his old self as an Upper Canadian Grit – led the opposition, nearly defeating it (24–22). Even though federal legislation in the 1870s created a legal framework for biculturalism on the Canadian Prairies, it would ultimately perish when francophone and Catholic immigration failed to produce a population substantial enough to defend its legal rights. On the face of it, Quebec seemed the province that had stood in greater need of an agricultural frontier longer than Ontario and had more contact with the North West through its past links with the fur trade and its ongoing contacts through the Catholic clergy. In the second half of the nineteenth century, hundreds of thousands of Quebecois left their province. But, as Table 6.1 shows, Manitoba's population by place of birth registered less than 8,000 from Quebec by 1891. Why did so few go to the Prairies?

From the perspective and experience of the French-Catholic leadership in Western Canada arose a historiography that blamed Quebec's clerical and nationalist leaders for discouraging emigration from the province to the West.[17] This case has rested heavily on the qualifications that the Quebec Catholic hierarchy put on its official pronouncements in favour of western settlement and on individual bishops discouraging recruitment of settlers from entering their dioceses. In particular, western Catholics pointed to the work of Jean-Paul Tardivel, an ardent Catholic journalist who wrote for Conservative and Catholic newspapers in Quebec.[18] He constantly questioned both the feasibility and the desirability of western migration, even before French and Catholic legal standing came under attack in the West.[19] The assaults by Tardivel and others

on Bishop Taché's 1869 pamphlet on the prospects for western farming embroiled the bishop in controversy that did nothing to increase the
West's attractions for Quebec francophones.[20] Even the historic ties of
the fur trade and Catholic missions worked against recruiting settlers
in Quebec. Where Ontario immigration pamphlets could confidently
assume near-total ignorance in their readers, Canadiens had heard
repeated appeals from their clergy over the years to materially aid "*les
pauveres métis*" of Red River who had been hit by yet another grass-
hopper plague, drought, or early frost.[21]

In spite of all that, several thousand Canadien families did try their
luck in Manitoba.[22] One of the few enduring successes of Taché's efforts
established a francophone colony in the Rural Municipality of Montcalm
just west of the Red River above the 49th parallel.[23] It began with the
assisted migration in 1875–76 of several Quebec-born families who had
emigrated to New England. Although popular memory had them coming to one of Bishop Taché's colonization blocks, there was only a single
reserved section in the area. By 1891 those founders had been joined by
kin who came directly from Quebec, for a total of 988 settlers. The special 1885 census showed 115 Métis along the Red River. By 1901 these
had all but disappeared from the official record. Carl Dawson (of the
same stamp and era as Stanley and Giraud) saw what he took to be a
general pattern: "The entry of colonists with agricultural experience and
greater aptitude for community building caused the displacement of the
original French and half-breed settlers."[24] Even though the familiar pattern of chain migration seemed to break after 1891, by 1901 there were
1,891 francophones in the municipality. Nicole St Onge's work suggests
that the Métis disappearance may only have been on paper.[25]

The preference of Quebec's clerical and nationalist leaders was that
those Canadiens who had already left *la belle province* for the United
States should be the target of western recruiters.[26] Quebec pressure on
the federal government led to most of Canada's full-time immigration
agents working in New England where hundreds of thousands of Canadiens had gone to work in textile mills. The results – in comparison to
the extent of the target population and the need in the Prairies – had to
be discouraging. For the decade 1876–86 some 5,613 had been assisted
to Manitoba and the NWT (all but a few hundred being francophone).[27]
The massive scale of Quebec emigration to New England, however,
raises the question of whether the elites of Quebec were as influential as
the western Catholic historiography has long assumed. Those elites condemned the southern exodus year after year with little apparent effect.[28]

If the elites could not prevent a massive outflow, is it likely that they could have diverted it toward the West?

Why did the great majority of Canadiens from rural backgrounds prefer to go south to wage labour rather than west to homesteading? By 1870 generations of habitants had been forced off the land by demographic pressure. Initially they had clustered in ever-larger villages, eking out a living by local gardening and seasonal labour or in the forests. They lacked the means even to start a farm on the marginal lands in the province. After a generation or two off the land, they had neither the first-hand knowledge of farming skills nor the motivation, having been raised on stories of their grandparents' hard lives.

The relative cost of living and wages meant little to those who clung to their marginal farms in Quebec, since they lived largely outside the money economy.[29] To understand leaving the land as having given up a religious vocation makes it more than an economic calculation. Sometimes it is not all about the money. Both poverty and a sense of vocation tied them to their unproductive land.

The first group lived in the money economy but lacked the interest to return to their ancestors' way of life. The second lived on marginal farms too poor to enable the family to relocate on western lands.

Even before mid-century, the forest industries and shipyards of Quebec could not provide sufficient employment for a rapidly growing rural proletariat.[30] Midwestern lumbering and the rapid expansion of the New England textile factories in the 1860s and 1870s offered expanding opportunities for wage labour.[31] It was less seasonal than lumbering and within a few days' travel to Quebec on the newly expanded railway network.[32]

Compared to a Manitoba homestead, wage labour in the forests and factories of the eastern and Midwestern United States had several advantages. First, it required no capital beyond the fare for a few days' railway journey. The emerging model of grain farming on the Prairies required substantial sums that few marginal farmers or landless Quebecois could command. Second, a year or two of labour in the lumber shanties or textile factories did not require any definitive break from one's family or parish. Removal to Manitoba marked a far greater emotional and psychological break with one's past: the new farm was intended to be a permanent residence. Third, even where Canadiens began to accept that their long-term residence would be in the United States, they remained close enough to Quebec for frequent return trips and visits. Rail connections to Manitoba, by contrast, only came later. Ready rail service to the

West was not available until 1886, by which time the hanging of Riel had already begun to raise fears in Quebec that the new region was to be the exclusive domain of English Protestants.

While Quebec's prior contact and awareness of the North West might have tended to deter anyone from settling there, Ontario before Confederation had spawned an enthusiastic movement that had called for the annexation of Rupert's Land to provide young farmers with a new settlement frontier. That movement provoked not only the British Palliser Expedition to investigate the region's agricultural potential but also, more tellingly, the Hind Expedition from the Province of Canada on the same quest but with greater urgency, since the young expansionists worried that a British survey might not be sufficiently enthusiastic.[33] Most revealing of all, the young promoters began to distribute new maps to support their case before any of the new information was yet available.[34] By the Confederation era there were already groups promoting western settlement from Ontario, of which Canada First was the most prominent in the public eye. Within a decade of joining Canada, Manitoba had an English-speaking majority. That majority welcomed into the Anglo-Protestant flow many British immigrants, as well as Americans "of the right sort," including returning Canadians from the United States.[35] While the Anglo-Protestant flow into the North West had its ebbs and flows, the decennial censuses recorded its seemingly inexorable advance.[36]

The balance between Ontario's nationalism and that of Quebec influenced Ottawa's legislation for Rupert's Land. As the people of the North West found their own voice after 1870 in both provincial and territorial legislatures, they often came into conflict with legislation that reflected that federal balance. Ultimately, those voices would have a reciprocal effect on the 1896 federal election. As Ontario won the race to populate the new region, the Métis and Canadiens lost out, first in terms of local political power and then in local legislation. The primary focus of those rival nationalisms would be schools.

The old society at Red River in its several parishes underwent a painful transition through the 1870s. From 1870 to 1879 the distribution of seats for the Manitoba assembly was based not only on the older system of parishes but also on a notion of community representation. In the first assembly, seats for English-speaking and French-speaking parishes were roughly equal. In the second assembly, seats were added to accommodate the newly arrived English-speaking settlers, most of whom had come from Ontario. But in 1879 the old Ontario Grit cry of "representation by population" gave the English control.[37] There was no longer a majority in the Manitoba legislature drawn from the old society and loyal to its customs: only the law remained to safeguard the bicultural aspect of Manitoba's constitution. In an intolerant democracy, the law is a frail guardian.[38]

To what extent was the Manitoba Schools Question an extension of Ontario's chronic conflicts with Quebec and to what extent was it indigenous to Manitoba? An older historiography saw the beginning as D'Alton McCarthy's vehemently anti-French speech at Portage la Prairie on 5 August 1889.[39] McCarthy's speech now seems more of a consequence of the campaign's early start rather than its origin.[40] It was not McCarthy's campaign against the Jesuit Estates Act but the rising intolerance within Manitoba's Protestant majority whose government had decided to end publicly supported Catholic schools before McCarthy's arrival. In its momentous 1890 session, the Manitoba legislature eliminated French as an official language in the legislature and courts, created a new Department of Education, and ended public support for Catholic schools.[41] As the controversy evolved, Clifford Sifton, the new attorney general, emerged as the province's leading spokesman for secular, English-only education. After the Liberals' victory in the June 1896 federal election, the negotiations between Ottawa and Winnipeg quickly became a duet between Laurier and Sifton, with Manitoba Premier Greenway in the role of irritated bystander. By August the initial terms had taken shape: religious education allowed after 3:30 in the afternoon, Catholic teachers for schools with sixty or more Catholic pupils, and texts not offensive to anyone. Laurier's particular contribution was to ask that, where the parents of ten or more pupils requested it, instruction could be in French.[42] Sifton's response to Laurier's initiative struck once again at the notion that French had any special place in the new Manitoba: instead of a concession for French, he insisted it be for any language other than English.[43] His motive seems to have been wholly directed at denying any status to French as a founding language of either Canada or Manitoba. On the whole, Laurier had successfully appealed to Sifton's ambition to overcome his bigotry. At Sifton's recommendation, Manitoba accepted these terms, even as Sifton left provincial politics for the federal scene.

There had been attempts to carry at least some of the older fur trade society into the new settler society. Some proved ephemeral: John A. Macdonald's first plan for the western mounted police force intended to recruit half from amongst the Métis.[44] He tried to have Hudson's

Bay Company factor Richard Hardisty elected as a Conservative for the Alberta constituency. Frustrated by an independent Conservative candidate and his supporters who insisted on a white member of parliament, Macdonald appointed Hardisty to the Senate.[45] Other mixed-bloods did little better. The son and grandson of HBC factors, James MacKay attempted to win the Prince Albert constituency as a Conservative in 1896 but was undercut when local Liberals got Wilfrid Laurier to run, taking away the Métis vote on which MacKay had counted.[46] John Norquay's time as Manitoba's premier was dogged by attacks on his mixed-blood heritage. Likewise, the legal sanction for at least some of the old order's pluralism for the French language and Roman Catholicism fell before the Anglo-Protestant conformity of the new settler society.

In practice, bilingualism had meant very little in the NWT. It was never legally extended to schools. Lieutenant-Governor Joseph Royal in 1888 even refused to supply requested copies of the School Ordinance in French, since it would only provoke adverse English reaction. He gave his Throne Speech – in English only (although French-language copies were made available) and quietly dropped the printing of Legislative Assembly debates in French as well as English, a discreet action praised by territorial Premier Frederick Haultain.[47]

As territorial premier, Haultain, like Laurier and Sifton, assiduously avoided any mention of separate schools in his proposals for provincial autonomy between 1902 and 1905.[48] His declared intent was not to change the status of separate schools, although he did not believe they could be entrenched by the BNA Act's section 93(1), since he held that the territories had become part of Canada in 1870 without any previously legally established rights to be protected. During the 1905 debates, he made it clear that he wanted the new provinces to be entirely free to decide on their own school policies, like Manitoba in this limited regard, and unlike Ontario and Quebec.

Archbishop Langevin of St Boniface had never accepted the NWT School Ordinances of 1892 and 1901 limiting Catholic schools. Consequently he looked for the Laurier government to not only protect separate schools in the new provinces but also to restore their rights as granted in the NWT Act of 1875 and in the first School Ordinance of 1884.

While Laurier gave Sifton to believe that the government's goal was continuity, it became apparent that different parties intended to continue different things. Haultain intended that the 1901 School Ordinance would carry forward into the two new provinces but that each province would have complete autonomy as to its future schools legislation. Sifton may have shared that view in 1904, but in the crisis of 1905 he offered the compromise that the 1901 Ordinance would become constitutionally entrenched, beyond the control of the new provinces. Laurier argued that the continuity would be with the federal legislation of 1875 (which granted much broader scope for Catholic schools than they had come to enjoy by 1901). After months of often-acrimonious debate, following Sifton's resignation from the cabinet (and W.S. Fielding's threatened resignation), the Liberals held together to support Sifton's amendment. That gave permanent status only to Catholic education, leaving the language of instruction to each province's discretion.[49] By 1905 the Prairies had ceased to be a simple French-English conflict (with the occasional Mennonite German island), as a seeming host of new languages accompanied the hundreds of thousands of land-hungry Europeans seeking homesteads in the last best West.

The diversity of new ethnic minority groups entering the West around the turn of the century makes valid generalizations difficult. One cannot assume that every member of every group sought to preserve their ethnic distinctiveness, or even perceived themselves as ethnic group members.[50] The historical literature on the third force has tended not only to focus on the larger groups but also to emphasize those members of the group who sought most to preserve their ethnic identity.[51] For example, it has commonly been remarked that the German-speaking migrants to the Prairies settled in large groups by province, with Mennonites dominant in Manitoba, German Catholics in Saskatchewan, and German Lutherans in Alberta.[52] However, the 1931 census showed that less than half of Manitoba's German speakers were Mennonite and that Saskatchewan actually had more Mennonites than Manitoba. Most German Catholics in Saskatchewan lived outside of the well-known "colonies" of St Peter's and St Joseph's, while German Protestants nearly equalled the number of Catholics in the province.[53] In drawing material together for a picture of the Prairies as a whole, we will need to ask how representative those large groups and their best-known settlements were.

The famous "checkerboard" survey and land granting system tended to disperse early settlement.[54] The attendant random allocation of homesteads promoted the rapid assimilation of ethnic minorities by the putative Anglo-Protestant ethnic majority. However, a number of groups sought, in diverse ways, to create homogeneous settlement colonies. In the early decades of Prairie settlement the federal government was sometimes willing to allow groups of immigrants substantial blocks of land

for settlement. The best-known examples are the Mennonite and Icelandic settlements in the 1870s and the Doukhobors at the end of the
century.[55] Sometimes the group's leaders approached large-scale corporate landholders for special arrangements. Count Paul O. Esterhazy
persuaded the CPR to allow Hungarians to take up railway lands in
Assiniboia as homesteads in the mid-1880s.[56] Orr Card made similar
arrangements with the CPR in southern Alberta for Mormon settlers.[57] In
the 1890s, some groups purchased lands from individuals in a given area
to create their colony, as was the case with all of the Hutterites, as well
as some Mennonites in Saskatchewan, and all Doukhobors in Alberta.[58]

These groups, or at least some of their leaders, demonstrated their
determination not to be scattered but to sustain a cultural heritage and
distinctiveness usually associated with language and nationality. What
we need to ask is whether all members of ethnic minority groups shared
that intention and also whether any of them had the opportunity or
means to act on that intention if they had it. The *desire* to sustain a
group life usually depended on the ancestral culture (including religion) and their motives for migration. The *capacity* to sustain group life
depended greatly on the size and cohesion of the group's settlement area.

Depending on provincial legislation and the disposition of the federal
government, a cluster-size ethnic community might try to have their language and religion included in the local school. This, however, demanded
a high degree of consensus within the group as well as leeway from outside forces. The attitudes of different ethnic minorities toward education
owed much to their various origins. Some migrants came from highly
literate cultures that valued education. Nineteenth-century Iceland had
one of the world's highest literacy rates, even though it had little in the
way of a publicly funded school system. Icelandic immigrants assumed
they would continue to instill in their children not only literacy in their
own language but also a literary culture within the home, where it had
always been done. The public school was seen as offering an entrée into
a different language and culture that would be of great value for their
children's future. In many ethnic settlements there were extended and
often divisive debates about the value of the English-speaking public
school. Some settlers brought with them new nationalisms that came
into conflict with the newly established dominance of Ontario nationalism and, for some, conflict with the last bastion of Quebec nationalism
on the Prairies, the hierarchy of the Roman Catholic Church.

In Manitoba and (to a lesser extent) Saskatchewan, there was a period of time when the public school could offer some place for languages

of instruction other than English. Some ethnic minorities sought to seize these opportunities, while others did not. The latter may have lacked the means as well as motive. Only a substantial local majority with a high degree of consensus could form a school district in its own image or take over an existing school board.

Even the poorest Hungarian peasants arrived on the Prairies not only literate in Magyar (the Hungarian language) but also bringing books with them.[59] By contrast, other groups had little or no opportunity for literacy in their native language in their native land or had come to see attempts to impose literacy in another language as oppressive. Lacking literacy or possessing prejudice toward imposed literacy, these groups either resisted English-speaking schooling or (where possible) sought to capture the bilingual school to promote literacy in their own language as well as that of the new country.

Some ethnic minorities, often drawn disproportionately from a particular social class of their homeland, valued education more highly than did others.[60] Where education as such was not highly valued, parents were slow to agree to the organization of school districts (which meant higher local taxes) and even slower to send their children (who were a needed part of the on-farm labour force) to schools for any length of time. It is difficult to judge whether some part of this often-observed resistance may also have been due to a desire to preserve an ethnic culture based on family and local community, buttressed by an ethnic church.[61]

Just as the influx of European settlers challenged the recently attained Anglo-Protestant supremacy in public institutions, many of them also represented a different sort of challenge to the francophone supremacy in the hierarchy and clergy of the Roman Catholic Church. Prairie bishops often found themselves with an abundance of francophone clergy relative to the numbers of francophone settlers, yet with much larger Catholic populations of other ethnicities clamouring for clergy of their own nationality. Bishops sought stop-gaps, such as pressing their francophone clergy to acquire new language competencies to serve new language groups. Another expedient was to have itinerant ethnic clergy visit those groups that shared their language. Occasionally conflict came into the public eye, as with some Hungarian Catholics demanding priests (and even teachers) fluent in Magyar. However, the greatest conflict arose with the intense inter-denominational competition for the allegiance of the Ukrainians, the third largest linguistic minority on the Prairies. Like the state, the Roman Catholic Church found itself pressed by some groups for at least some accommodation for their native languages and cultures.[62]

A few of the new ethnic groups (and members of some ethnic groups) sought to limit or control their degree of accommodation by challenges the prevailing Anglo-Protestant norms. These people seldom sought to perpetuate their own culture to the exclusion of the new one, but sought some control over the process. Of the new ethnic groups to arrive in the 1890s, the most prominent in this regard were the Ukrainians. Their example in Manitoba sparked imitations by other groups such as Poles in Manitoba and Hungarians in Saskatchewan, and by fellow Ukrainians in Alberta.[63] The limited successes of these endeavours mark the extent to which the dominant Anglo-Protestant elites were willing to allow any exceptions in the culture of the new region.

Ukrainians more than any other non-communal ethnic group combined a determination to settle together in large, cohesive clusters with a determination to promote their own culture by control or influence over the public institutions of the new country. Like the first arrivals of any new ethnic group, to ease their transition to the new land, the earliest Ukrainian settlers sought out what was most familiar to them. In ethnic terms, this meant that early Ukrainian settlement gravitated to other ethnic settlements founded by peoples from eastern Europe: the Mennonite East Reserve in Manitoba and the Star/Edna area northeast of Edmonton in Alberta where a number of German-speaking families from Galicia had settled.[64] In geographic terms, Ukrainians strongly favoured the aspen parkland belt over the treeless prairies. The lands adjoining the East Reserve were both limited in extent and poor in potential for agricultural development; yet Ukrainians continued to settle in the area, despite its limitations, to be near either kin or at least fellow Ukrainians. The persistence in settling in some areas, such as near the Eastern Reserve or in Manitoba's Interlake region, indicates that social and cultural considerations sometimes took precedence over strictly economic concerns.[65]

The Ukrainians' poverty meant they could only settle on homestead lands. One short-term reason for preferring land with some trees was the possibility of earning income by cutting cordwood for sale. Ukrainians collectively played an active role in the location of their settlement not only in terms of being near kin in a parkland setting but also in the detail of individual locations.[66] When newcomers began clearing farms on forest reserve lands in Manitoba, to be near friends and family, the provincial government found them obdurate about moving. Eventually the boundaries of the forest reserve had to be redrawn to allow the determined Ukrainian settlers ownership of the lands they had occupied and farmed.[67]

The Ukrainian block settlements were never as homogeneous as the Anglo-Protestant elite feared. These were never group settlements in the same sense as some Mennonites, Doukhobors, or Hutterites. The geography of settlement within the largest Ukrainian block was influenced not only by the land granting system but also by other institutions, of which the most important were the railways. R.B. Bilash saw the integration of Ukrainian farmers into increasingly commercial operations as a parallel to the social and cultural disintegration of the older village formations, which declined with the advent of the new railway towns.[68] Initially Ukrainian pioneers farmed largely for subsistence, without means to take produce anywhere outside their local settlement. But the construction of railways through the Star/Edna block made wider markets available. As entry points for this access to markets, the railways created their own towns. These towns played a major role in undermining the Ukrainians' own network of communities. In a few cases the village cluster (school, post office, shops) migrated to the new location, as did Star/Edna, which became Lamont on the new Canadian Northern line. More often, the town became the district's service centre with businesses and services provided by an English-speaking business and professional class.

Undoubtedly the Ukrainians' most visible challenge to the dominant Anglo-Protestant establishment came over control of the school system. In each province Ukrainians sought to use the public school system to promote literacy in Ukrainian as well as English, to promote pride in being Ukrainian through stories and music as well as to learn about the new society. Each province dealt with these challenges differently, Manitoba taking pride of place in facing them first.

With the 1897 school compromise, Manitoba had unwittingly opened the door to language groups other than those of the country's two founding peoples to have their children educated on the bilingual system. Ukrainians, no doubt encouraged by the example of some of their Mennonite neighbours, began to organize their own school districts in rural areas where their numbers predominated and to demand teachers who could speak Ukrainian as well as English.

While initially the federal Conservatives (and some Liberal newspapers) had pilloried Sifton and the Liberal government for bringing in "the scum of Europe," the Manitoba provincial Conservative government

soon realized that a cohesive ethnic group could be a very useful political ally. In 1904 the Conservative government not only reversed its dis-
criminatory franchise legislation but also began financing a Ukrainian
newspaper in the run-up to the next election. Its successful capture of
at least an identifiable part of the new Ukrainian electorate led to the
creation in 1905 of a Ruthenian Training School in Winnipeg to license
Ukrainians as schoolteachers.[69] While the teacher training schools and
foreign language school inspectors were intensely partisan, a consequence was the founding of 114 Ukrainian schools over the next decade in rural areas with local Ukrainian majorities.[70] In Winnipeg itself,
the attempt at a Ukrainian bilingual school was limited by denominational rivalries amongst Ukrainians, since the Catholic archbishop was
its sponsor. Some Ukrainians saw the school (not without reason) as an
attempt to win converts to Catholicism.

On the eve of the First World War, Manitoba's politics saw the rise of a
series of reform movements, one aspect of which was a desire to see the
thoroughgoing and immediate assimilation of all other groups into an
English-speaking majority. While some Ukrainian politicians had hoped
that a judicious shift in political allegiance could save their schools, the
new T.C. Norris Liberal government that took office in 1915 had committed itself to not only ending the use of all other languages than English for instruction but also enforcing compulsory attendance at these
English-only schools. The foreign-language training schools were closed,
and all school districts required teachers who could and would teach in
English only.[71]

Several other ethnic groups sought to emulate the Ukrainians' success.[72] The Hungarian experience of trying to include their language in
the schools of Saskatchewan was considerably more complex. Unlike
most Polish and Ukrainian peasant immigrants, the Hungarian peasant
class was largely literate.. However, just before the First World War, a
number of Hungarian leaders sought to use Saskatchewan's openness to
other languages to have Magyar as well as English taught in predominantly Hungarian areas. Their effort's failure tells much about the limits
to accommodation available within public institutions, as well as offering a further insight into the problems of the Catholic Church in meeting
the needs of all its communicants.

The issue of schools for Hungarian children was bound up in the religious and political commitments of Hungarian pioneers. Indeed, the
involvement of the Liberal Party in the "Hungarian school question"
may have run deeper than contemporaries realized. The immediate cause

of controversy, however, was politics of a different sort. An attempt to forge a stronger Hungarian nationalist identity foundered on the religious divisions amongst Hungarians. In the spring of 1910 the internal Catholic debate over Hungarian nationalism became spectacularly public. The attempt to found a Magyar-language newspaper was defeated by the threat of excommunication of any Catholic who subscribed. The larger politics of the dispute remain controversial. One can argue that the archbishop chose to quarrel with the relatively few Hungarians in order to make a similar point to the much larger and potentially much more powerful Ukrainian community that his authority as archbishop came before any nationalist ambitions.[73]

As well as public institutions such as the land granting system and the school system, immigrants encountered pervasive private institutions such as railway companies and churches. The most extensive of the latter in the Prairie West was the Roman Catholic Church. While almost all public institutions of the Prairies were, by 1890, in the control of the English-speaking Anglo-Protestant elite, the Catholic Church remained the one major institution in which Quebec nationalism predominated. All of the bishops and most of the clergy were French-speaking, originating mainly in Quebec with a number drawn from Europe through several religious orders, the largest of which was the Oblate Order. The challenge for the Catholic Church lay in responding to the highly diverse needs of the new ethnic settlers with clergy whose focus had been (and often continued to be) ensuring the survival of French-Canadian culture as carrier and protector of the faith to francophones.[74] The francophone hierarchy faced another challenge from within: the English-speaking hierarchy in Ontario. By founding and funding the Catholic Church Extension Society, from 1908 on, the Irish bishops and priests of Ontario sought to ensure that new immigrants on the Prairies assimilated into the English-language majority. For example, they promoted the training of a new generation of Ukrainian Catholic priests whose second language would be English. After 1910, the francophone bishops were gradually displaced by the creation of new dioceses that included the majority of the region's Catholics under predominantly Irish bishops.[75]

The different ethnic groups provided a diversity of challenges to the church hierarchy. Initially least problematic were those groups that brought their own Catholic clergy with them, groups sufficiently numerous to support those priests. The premier examples were the German Catholic colonies that arrived with clergy, often leaders in the migration, who could immediately begin to minister in German.[76] Smaller ethnic groups – like more scattered clusters of German Catholics – looked to the western Catholic hierarchy for their spiritual needs. Lacking the population base to financially support resident clergy, most smaller Catholic settlements were served by travelling clergy, whom each settlement hoped to capture by attracting enough Catholic settlers to fund church, rectory, and salary. The bishops sought to supply clergy for ethnically diverse Catholic clusters through two main ways. The first was to adapt the existing force of francophone clergy to the new needs by promoting wider language acquisition. The other was to recruit priests from Europe or the United States who shared the ethnic origin of the new ethnic groups.

Each approach had its limitations. The rising tide of nationalism created tensions between francophone clergy and their ethnically conscious parishioners. We have already noted the conflict between the francophone clergy who served Hungarian Catholic settlements in Saskatchewan (which spilled into the public eye in the controversy over Hungarian schools). One example was Father Philip Roux, born and raised in German-occupied Lorraine, who spent two years in the Ukraine learning Ukrainian. He later changed his name to "Philip Ruh," apparently in the hope that a "German" Catholic priest would be more acceptable in Ukrainian Catholic communities than a francophone priest.[77]

The far more numerous Ukrainians posed far more complex problems for the Catholic hierarchy than any other new ethnic group. The complex ecclesiastical politics of eastern Europe were incompletely transferred onto the Canadian Prairies into a milieu where no one understood their complications.[78] In the sixteenth century, a large number of Ukrainian Greek Orthodox bishops, clergy, and laity joined the Roman Catholic Church, keeping their own liturgy as "Eastern rite" or Greek Catholics. The Catholic hierarchy on the Prairies pursued two strategies to win (or confirm the allegiance of) those Ukrainian Greek Catholics who settled on the Prairies. Archbishop Langevin initially assumed that they would accept the Latin Catholic Church as their natural home, provided the language barrier could be overcome. By 1906, he realized how deep the aversion to the Latin rite was amongst Ukrainian Catholics and began to seek Eastern rite priests. However, his model continued to be adapting resources to the problem: he sought Catholic priests who were willing to transfer to the Eastern rite.[79] Belgian Redemptorists and German Oblates set themselves to learn Ukrainian and adapt to the new rite. Bishop Pascal of Prince Albert and Bishop Legal of St Albert initiated a different strategy. They appealed directly to the leader of the Ukrainian

Catholic Church, Metropolitan Sheptytsky, to supply suitable clergy. This eventually produced Basilian monks, who founded a monastery at Mundare, Alberta, in order to minister to the large Ukrainian cluster northeast of Edmonton. Before and during the 1910 Eucharistic Congress in Montreal, Langevin carried this appeal to the Metropolitan, as the person next highest in the Roman Catholic hierarchy, who promised more priests and a Greek Catholic bishopIn 1912 Father Nykyta Budka became the first bishop of the "Ruthenian (i.e., Ukrainian) Greek Catholic Church" in Canada. The relative slowness of the Catholic hierarchy meant that while the great majority of Ukrainian families had come from provinces overwhelmingly Greek Catholic, only just over half in the first generation kept that affiliation.

Where members of an ethnic group had the will to sustain their culture and sufficient numbers for the capacity to achieve what they willed, the key to successfully resisting assimilation (or at least controlling its effects or its pace) was their relationship to land. Those groups that deliberately sought to prevent assimilation to maintain a distinctive way of life held their lands communally. They would find that the initial promise of the Canadian Prairies was illusory. Eventually the Community Doukhobors and Old Colony Mennonites had to leave the region or purchase land (rather than accept a land grant from government) in order to sustain their community ethos.[80] Independent Doukhobors and those Mennonites who remained had to adapt their religious beliefs to the Anglo-Protestant social order. The one communal religious group to successfully resist assimilation came last in point of time and received neither land grants (much less "reserved lands") nor guarantees for the education of their children. The Hutterites purchased land for their colonies and thus largely escaped government control over how they held their land. The essential element for sustaining their communities' ethnic survival has been communal land ownership. Without it, both Independent Doukhobors and most Mennonites became part of the same economic and cultural milieu, uniform in their land ownership and acceptably pluralistic in their religious beliefs.[81]

Between those groups in which most members appeared to have assimilated, willingly or not, and those groups that struggled not to assimilate, came those – pre-eminently the Ukrainians – who sought to qualify and control the terms of their assimilation into Canada. Most of the Canadian literature on ethnicity and assimilation has assumed that eventual assimilation is the inevitable fate of every ethnic group. However, such statistics mask important trends that show that language

Table 6.2: Ethnic language retention by percentage in Saskatchewan, 1941–51.*

	1941		1951	
Language(s)	Province	North central	Province	North central
French	75	97	65	79.7
German	73	103.3	58	91.1
Ukrainian	94	107.6	87	103.6
Scandinavian	59	78.4	40	47.9

Source: Alan B. Anderson, "Linguistic Trends among Saskatchewan Ethnic Groups," 63–86.

* The totals over 100 per cent show that people who gave their ethnic origin as "Ukrainian" or "German" were not the only ones who claimed to speak Ukrainian or German.

retention in local pre-eminently rural areas has been much greater, and has persisted far longer, than the global statistics suggest.[82]

Alan Anderson's study of Saskatchewan made these differences clear. The province-wide trend to declining use reflects heavily the urban experience.[83] By concentrating on the north-central region, which has the largest concentrations of French-Canadian, German, Ukrainian, and Russian settlers, Anderson focused where ethnic identity and language retention had the best chance of survival. While there is steady erosion for all the major languages over time at the provincial level, the trend is much less evident in the north-central area where ethnic populations are concentrated. By contrast, while the Scandinavian languages show relatively high retention in the region in 1941, a decade later the level had dropped to less than half both provincially and regionally. On farms the rates of retention were substantially higher than in urban areas. Table 6.2 indicates the rates of ethnic language retention in various parts of Saskatchewan in 1941 and 1951. Thus the province's rapid urbanization after the Second World War played a substantial part in the failing retention of ancestral languages. Those ethnic/religious groups who adhered most strongly to traditional ways in rural communities were those most likely to retain their language, not only due to a cohesive collective life but also by remaining rural. The final stage in assimilation for those who did not anchor their identity in a communal rural existence on the Canadian Prairies was urbanization.

The balance between the state of agriculture in Ontario and that in Quebec at mid-century largely determined which would predominate on the Prairies – and whoever won the first round, would have the edge on setting the terms for the newcomers in the second round. The sons of Ontario were primed to move. They had pent-up demand for farmland and the resources to make their demand effective. Moreover, they had

Map 6.1: Manitoba lands reserved for francophone settlement.

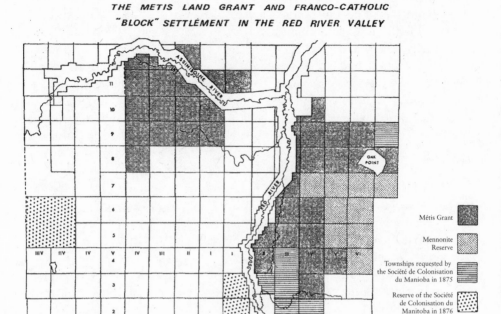

THE METIS LAND GRANT AND FRANCO-CATHOLIC
"BLOCK" SETTLEMENT IN THE RED RIVER VALLEY

Métis Grant

Mennonite
Reserve

Townships requested by
the Société de Colonisation
du Manioba in 1875

Reserve of the Société
de Colonisation du
Manitoba in 1876

Source: Robert Painchaud, "The Catholic Church and the Movement of Francophones to the Canadian Prairies, 1870-1915," doctoral dissertation, University of Ottawa, Ottawa, 1976, 470.

been fed for more than a decade on stories about the North West as the new Eden.

While Quebec's political and clerical leaders could exercise significant political power at the federal level it was not sufficient to hold even part of the Prairies. They secured a bicultural constitution for Manitoba. Bishop Taché's colonization societies held substantial land reserves in the 1870s (see Map 6.1). Federal immigration efforts focused largely on New England, striving to "repatriate" mill hands to become Prairie farmers. But it had all come too late for the great majority: generations had lived impoverished lives as the landed poor and then as landless habitants. When their families' experiences had been farms that could not even provide subsistence, it was almost impossible to persuade them to give agriculture another chance. Finally, Quebec's picture of the West was based on stories of missionaries' heroic ordeals in the wilderness and famine appeals for the Métis.

Ontario had only just established its primacy when new ethnic groups, some with vibrant nationalisms of their own, began to flood onto the Prairies. The Manitoba School Question's initial resolution on languages of instruction had unforeseeable consequences. Ukrainians, above all others, seized that opportunity to choose the terms of their own accommodation. Manitoba's example found echoes across the Prairies. But, as in Manitoba, all efforts to avoid English-language assimilation failed. The surge of population out of Europe at the end of the nineteenth century brought new land-hungry peoples to the Prairies, some of whom carried their own nationalisms. While the Prairies could accommodate the land hunger of most groups, their nationalisms could find no lasting home in public institutions, as Ontario's Anglo-Protestantism came to be even more rigidly enforced. Parallel to Ontario's cultural dominance was its economic dominance over the region's principal staple through control of its linkages.

At century's end, the Roman Catholic Church's hierarchy remained the last stronghold of Quebec nationalism. It was undermined from two directions: on the one hand, several new ethnic groups demanded clergy speaking their own language, while on the other hand, the Irish bishops in Ontario began to train new ethnic clergy who had English as their second language.

People were drawn to the Prairies by the promise of land. But often they sought it not as isolated individuals, but as communities that wished to enjoy their landed prosperity on their own cultural terms. Some sought to hold land communally to ensure that their religion and culture remained paramount in their lives. But most who sought to sustain their culture settled in cohesive groups as best they could under individual land ownership. By the First World War it was clear that in the public institutions there would be little or no scope for cultures other than the English speaking.[84]

The same drive that quashed Métis and French-Canadian hopes of a francophone future on the Prairies and that ultimately made cultural surrender the price of economic accommodation to all those European nationalities that came to the West, bore down earlier and much more heavily on the first peoples of Rupert's Land. On top of the long, steady drain of the fur trade came the more sudden collapse of the once-massive buffalo herds at mid-century. Increasingly faced by famine, many bands across the west began to shift their multi-source food strategies away from the hunt, especially the big-game hunt, toward varieties of farming, including gathering wild rice and planting potatoes. However, the advent of the Dominion of Canada's power – in purchasing the rights of the Hudson's Bay Company and then imposing massive land surrenders through the treaty system – overrode that gradual adaptation. Native peoples found themselves often forced by starvation to accept confinement to reserves accompanied by federal promises of assistance to take up sedentary farming as practised by Europeans. The outcome of that promise of reserve agriculture is the subject of a later chapter.

Railways and Homesteading on the Prairies: Sharing the Public Lands

The policies adopted toward public lands both on the Canadian Prairies and in the American West had the declared purpose of promoting the settlement on free land of those intending to farm and of providing railways to make that settlement possible in the short run and economically feasible in the long run. Whether the policies actually served those purposes, or to what degree or at what cost, have been the topics of extended historiographic debate in both countries. Because American policies were often the context and have since frequently been the measure of Canadian policies, the extent to which the two were intertwined also needs consideration. A further dimension to railways and settlement on the Prairies relates to the differing patterns of agriculture and transportation in Quebec and Ontario. Whereas the latter two always had the alternative of waterways as a check on railways, the Prairies from the beginning had to rely on the railway alone.[1]

Railway building in British North America sparked considerable deliberation in both the nineteenth and twentieth centuries. Should they be built and operated as public institutions? If railways were to be built by the private sector, what inducements should governments offer? Was Canada copying an American model at the very time the Americans were finding that model inadequate? That discussion continued long after the Canadian transcontinental railways were complete. By then several had gone bankrupt, been consolidated into a government-owned system, and then eventually sold back to the private sector.

While Joseph Howe in Nova Scotia made the argument that railways were essentially public works and thus belonged in the public domain, it was the repeated experience when trying to build and operate railways as public works that discredited that ideal.[2] The problems of political patronage scandals encountered by provinces, the federal experience with the Intercolonial Railway and the different parts of Alexander Mackenzie's "mixed medium" line of communication to British Columbia showed that even Clear Grit integrity could not overcome the political temptations of a "government road."[3] Railway construction by public authorities was synonymous with corruption by the end of the 1870s.

The use of land grants to promote private railway construction in Canada and the United States forms a pair of contrasts in time that has puzzled several commentators. The American federal and state governments had granted millions of acres for railways (as they had done earlier with canals and roads) from 1850 to 1872. The policy ended ignominiously when Congress listened to the voices of the West protesting the abuses of those land grants.[4] However, at almost exactly the same time, the Canadians began using what appeared to be a similar policy, only to reject it in another twenty years just as the Americans had done. Why did the Canadians not learn from the earlier American policy failure?

Chester Martin, in the earliest Canadian scholarly critique of railway policy, concluded that in the crucial period, 1869–71, when Canadian politicians and businessmen first formulated their plans for a Pacific railway, their impression was that the American railway land grant policy had been largely successful. Since the effective operation of the CPR was delayed for a decade by depression and Macdonald's political defeat, Martin referred to that railway's land grant as "the posthumous child of the preceding decade."[5]

The more recent reply to that criticism, from Lloyd Mercer, has been that the factors that led Americans to take up a generous railway land grant policy were the same ones that moved Canadians, and that those reasons were valid for Canadians at the time that they made their decision as they had earlier been for Americans when they had made their decisions. When it was largely empty in terms of white settlers, the West clamoured for construction of railways and accepted land grants as part of the necessary means to that desirable end. However, once the railways were completed, the now more settled and more politically powerful West opposed the railway land grants, which were seen to impede continued economic growth. Eastern Canadian taxpayers and capitalists were no more willing in the 1870s and 1880s to pay the full cost of a transcontinental railway than their American counterparts had been several decades earlier. The latent capital gains from land constituted an essential incentive to attract capital to large-scale projects in a mainly unsettled region.[6]

Table 7.1: Railway mileage and land grants by province.

Province	Miles (thousands)	Acres (millions)
Ontario	652	0
Manitoba	208	2.7
Saskatchewan	419	6.2
Alberta	336	9.8
British Columbia	268	0

Source: Chester Martin, "Dominion Lands" Policy, 74–5.

The potential for conflict between railway land grants and the settlers' desire for free homesteads could be reduced by the structure and operation of the land grant. When the lands were immediately adjacent to the railway line, the railway had a strong incentive to sell them to generate as much traffic as possible. The drive for a profitable railway company could thus incline it to sell at moderate prices. The railway could also speed up settlement of its own lands by offering credit purchase. In the United States these conditions were seldom met, by either the terms of the grant or the railway companies' administration of their land grants. In Canada, however, the largest railway almost always met these conditions. That outstanding example makes it all the more striking that several other, smaller Canadian railways emulated the worst of American railway land grant policies.[7]

The first obvious contrast of American policy with Canadian was the latter's uniformity. The initial grant to CPR, by far the largest land grant railway with over 80 per cent of all such lands, was twenty miles on either side of its main transcontinental line. There were several qualifications to that general model. First, British Columbia and Ontario owned their own crown lands, which meant that the public lands whose sale would pay for building the railway came entirely from the Prairies. This burden is most clearly seen in Table 7.1, which indicates the railway mileage and land grants by province.[8]

Second, the CPR received only every other section within its land grant. The alternate sections were designated primarily for homesteads, although some quarter sections were offered for sale, the moneys dedicated to education or paid to the HBC as part of its relinquishment of the charter to Rupert's Land. In addition, the CPR got what no American railway ever did: the right to decide whether to accept the lands within its grant or exchange them for "lands fairly fit for settlement." Thus the CPR also, for different reasons, came to have "indemnity" land claims.[9]

As in the United States, these claims tied up much larger areas of potential choice. As early as 1886 the federal government began opening some of those reserved lands for settlement. By 1908 it required all railways to locate such claims or lose them.

While the CPR land grant generally exemplified the most settler-friendly provisions, the land grants given to the ten settlement railways in Canada between 1884 and 1893 generally reflected, from the perspective of the settler, the worst aspects of American policy. In 1880, the federal government began by offering smaller colonization railways an option to purchase no more than 3,840 acres per mile of track laid at $1 per acre (raised to 6,400 acres in 1881). However, in 1885 Ottawa converted this option into a free grant on the basis of one railway's very specific circumstances. That exception then became the rule for subsequent colonization railways. Within a decade some 12 million acres had been granted – often nowhere near the actual line – giving the colonization railway little incentive to actually colonize. For example, the Manitoba and North West Colonization Railway was to have constructed 430 miles of track but only completed 225 miles. Of its 1.5 million acresof land, only 500,000 acres were located in Manitoba where the line ran. The other 1 million acres were in the province of Saskatchewan. The Great North West Central Railway only constructed 50 of the 450 miles it was supposed to build across Manitoba. Of its 320,000 acres of land, 98 per cent were located in Saskatchewan.[10] After 1894 the federal government made no further land grants to railways.

Most of these smaller railways sooner or later became part of either the CPR (as subsidiaries) or the Canadian Northern Railway. The consequences of the federal government's land granting policies turned out quite differently with each of these two companies. The CPR made a point of selling its lands rapidly, at moderate prices, often on reasonable or even generous credit terms. The Canadian Northern became known for its "fastidious standards" in choosing lands and its reluctance to sell except into a booming land market. As Chester Martin observed, "It is not by chance that the land grant acreage accumulated by the Canadian Northern has realized a higher average gross price per acre than any other category under the railway land grant system."[11]

Harold Innis argued that it was Ontario's wheat boom that called forth first canals and then railways to transport the new staple to the British metropolis. However, Douglas McCalla and others have dismissed that connection, since the St Lawrence and Great Lakes provided ample shipping capacity for both wheat and lumber exports up to the mid-century.

Rather, they contend, Innis had projected the Prairie experience backwards onto Ontario. Despite Mackenzie's notion of a "mixed medium" transcontinental transportation system in the 1870s and the appearance of steamboats on the North and South Saskatchewan in the 1880s, in actual practice only railways built well in advance of demand (i.e., settlement) could open the Prairies for substantial commercial farming.

Modern economic historians have sought to apply a different standard of judgment than past historians, who focused on settlement of the Prairies, to assess the efficiency of the railway land grant policies of Canada and the United States. The economic historians' attention concentrates on whether the land, interest-rate guarantees, and cash subsidies were necessary for the construction of the major railways and, if so, whether they were given in the right amounts or in the most useful form. This is a daunting task. Economics is oriented to assessing private sector costs rather than the social costs and externalities that arise from private sector actions. Much of the traditional economists' criticism is directed against any government intervention, on the assumption that the private capital markets alone know what is and can be feasible. However, the social returns to capital investments have to take into account. Some of these are factors that cannot be quantified, such as political unification and national defence. Those costs that can be calculated or estimated have to be weighed against other factors for which there is no possibility of a reasonable monetary estimate. Within these limits, one can ask whether the anticipated high social return could justify a subsidy when the anticipated private returns from a given railway project were expected to be low.[12] More importantly, one can ask whether land grants were the best type of subsidy for railway construction on a continental scale.

Economic historians have faulted government subsidies for the construction of the transcontinentals on several grounds. Some seek to demonstrate that these railways were built ahead of the demand for their services. Some have argued that subsidies caused railways to overbuild relative to demand.[13] All of the transcontinentals, starting with the Union Pacific, obviously were built ahead of demand, in the sense that they crossed the Great Plains and the Rocky Mountains before there was substantial settlement to provide traffic across those regions. The case for government intervention rested on a belief in the railways' social rate of return to the region or country rather than what private investors could then have expected as a private rate of return.[14] How can anyone calculate the social benefit of the Great Plains and Rocky Mountain states, which became populated almost entirely because of those railways? Certainly the fact that several American transcontinentals went bankrupt (and that the CPR narrowly averted that fate in the spring of 1885) suggests that these were high-risk private sector ventures. However, Albert Fishlow, who focused on the railway subsidies of the 1850s, argued that the first western railways (which went as far as the Mississippi) were not, in fact, built ahead of demand but passed through relatively high-density counties and were profitable from their start. He sees public subsidies as initially local and reactive.[15] However, looking at the railways subsidized both before and after the Civil War, Lloyd Mercer has concluded that Fishlow's conclusions do not stand up.[16]

Mercer made his own comparison of American transcontinentals with the CPR. He argued that it could not have been built when it was without government subsidies. His estimate, however, is that the amount of subsidy was about double the minimum necessary. Like other economic historians, he noted that land grants were not the most social or economically useful form of subsidy.[17] On the other hand, they were probably the most politically feasible at that time. Moreover, he pointed to the quick response to the Riel Rebellion of 1885 as the definitive social benefit of the CPR: Ottawa had troops on the Prairies in days instead of months, as in 1870. Ultimately national unity trumps economics.

The function of railways was not only to speed settlement but also to make it profitable. The promise of the homestead policy was free land to the actual farmer, which would lower start-up costs enough to give everyone a chance to create a commercial operation. To what extent did the federal government keep that promise? To what extent did those who took it up honour the promise's conditions? The first thorough scholarly study of Canadian homesteading was published by Chester Martin in 1938.[18] Homesteads had always been part of the federal plans for the Prairies. However, "'Land for the actual settler' may have been the most plausible of policies, but no system of land policy has ever been proof against fraudulent manipulation; and for many years whole districts in the vicinity of every frontier town and village were devastated rather than populated by the free-homestead system."[19] After this sweeping indictment, Martin was oddly specific as to time and place: after 1905, around Maple Creek, Gull Lake, and Shaunavon. While he described the "vicious process" of the "lurking speculator" with his "clutches," he was quite positive toward large-scale land companies, which he considered had a special "technique" that fostered rapid settlement of their own lands.[20] Yet he conceded that their technique amounted to nothing more than good timing: "Lands upon the frontier are usually sold 'when the selling is good' or not at all."[21] He condemned small-scale speculators for failing to sell their quarter sections at the opportune moment. In his view, perhaps the best that could happen to this acreage was that it fall into the hands of land companies equipped to dispose of it to actual settlers. The usual eventuality, however, was probably the worst: vast areas of land, uncultivated and weed-infested, were held by individual speculators for a rising market."[22]

Canadians did not have the American abundance of legislation that enabled the first arrivals to file multiple claims in a new area. But they also had to worry about speculators competing with genuine farmers.[23] Speculators filed homestead claims, and then made no attempt to "prove up" by completing the settlement conditions of plowing the minimum area and building even the minimum house in hopes of being paid to relinquish their claim.[24] But speculation is a grey area: what of the person who proved up, then sold as soon as a rising land market allowed? The main complaint of the time about speculators was that their land remained vacant after the area had been settled, which suggests that their hopes of a quick sale had failed.

A 1908 Conservative broadsheet condemned "Fake Homesteading" that resulted in land that remained vacant and uncultivated in the midst of settlement: "It is not from choice but from necessity that the Western pioneer travels through ten to fifty miles of largely unoccupied land to reach his home. He has settled in the back country because he could not get a homestead in the front." It quoted "the Liberal Organ" with approval that this was "a cold-blooded holdup" by town dwellers who entered for homesteads where they did not live.[25] The Conservative author of course went further, claiming that government favouritism prevented cancellations of speculative entries and that "government officials were holding homesteads for their sons who never lived on them." He claimed to quote from a 1905 Department of Interior report that showed some entries of more than six to twenty years standing that had not been cancelled. He then attempted what no subsequent scholar has tried: to calculate how much speculation there was (as of the 1905 report). His conclusions alleged 14,471 speculative entries for a total of over 2 million acres.[26]

In spite of extensive complaint and widespread speculative holdings, Martin treats the cancellations of homestead entries as if every one of them represented the failure of an "actual settler," with no thought of how many may have been speculative holdings. His choice of language is heavy with references to the Great War: "the man in the front-line trenches," "fell in no man's land," "deadly attrition."[27] To the extent that speculative holdings were cancelled, reading the total number of cancellations as failed homesteaders overstates the failure rate of homesteaders. Moreover, while he speaks of lands alienated by grant or sale but uncultivated in his own present, a good deal of those lands in the mid-1930s had been Western Canada's prosperous farms in the 1920s. This state of affairs in the late 1930s was evidence not of any very long-term speculation, but of the devastated state of Prairie agriculture in a severe drought.

Where Martin tried to assess homestead policy and outcomes for the Prairies as a whole, a much more recent study by Paul Voisey focused on the Vulcan district in southwest Alberta. He also devoted attention to speculators and the successes of homesteaders. His area lies just west of the Palliser Triangle, where the last rush of Prairie settlement ran down to the American border just as the First World War broke out. Voisey's perceptions of these last pioneers' motives is almost the inverse of Martin's: "Few pioneers in the Vulcan area developed an emotional attachment to their land ... Most came intending to sell out later, and did so."[28] In one township, before 1920, less than half the farmers remained as long as five years. "Intending to sell anyway, most Vulcan pioneers did so for a handsome profit."[29] These could not be considered tragic victims. Those who sold before 1920 realized capital gains from $1,000 to $10,000 per quarter section. "The real victims were those efficient, expanding farmers who failed to sell out before 1920 when falling grain prices and environmental difficulties that foreshadowed the catastrophe of the 1930s sparked a long-term fall in land values."[30]

Voisey does not concern himself overly much with the distinction between the person who filed a claim and then did nothing and the person who filed a claim and then did as little as possible. Many had other occupations that took their time and energy. Filing for a homestead was a low-cost investment. "If it did not prove too troublesome or too costly to earn title, it might be sold for a nice profit."[31] He dismisses the discussion over the costs of proving up. "The debate assumed that pioneers wanted to build a viable farm and that they complied with both the letter and the spirit of the regulations. Those unwilling to invest the necessary money and effort resorted to cheating. Most often they simply lied."[32] Speculators saw no reason to go to the expense of building a house since the buyer would already have one. Voisey glosses over this widespread fraud by noting the extensive official land speculation built into each Prairie township. Of the thirty-six sections, two were reserved for sale to support schools, one and three-quarters were for the Hudson's Bay Company (which had been given a right to one-twentieth of arable land), the remaining even-numbered sections were for homesteads, and the odd-numbered sections were for railway claims.

How representative of the whole of the Prairies is this local study of settlement? As part of the pre–First World War land rush, Vulcan represents the crest of a boom in which speculation can be expected to loom large, as it had done decades earlier, for example in the Manitoba boom of 1880–82. Southeastern Alberta corresponds with Martin's oddly specific examples of town-based speculation around Maple Creek, Gull Lake, and Shaunavon after 1905 – the Saskatchewan side of the same late boom, but located just inside the Palliser Triangle. Speculation was a factor in the settlement of the Prairies. There were land companies and colonization railways. There were a multitude of small-scale speculators in Prairie towns and villages, including localities that had hoped to become towns or at least villages but never did. It remains to be seen how much land ultimately went to each major player in Canadian Prairie settlement.

The Dominion acquired Rupert's Land primarily to keep its own Quebec and Ontario farmers' sons from going to the American frontier. As early as the Confederation debates, A.T. Galt pointed to the North West, lamenting that because Canada could not "assume possession and open it up to the youth of this country," many had gone south.[33] In the debate over the purchase of Rupert's Land, Georges-Étienne Cartier declared: "Within a few months we would be in possession of a prairie territory equal to that of the United States, and as the people of Ontario, Quebec, Nova Scotia, and New Brunswick were a population of producing people, their natural increase would rapidly fill up our western territory."[34] Speaking in opposition in 1878, Louis-François-Rodrigue Masson, the Conservative Member for Terrebonne, attacked the Liberal government for failing to stem emigration from Quebec by their delays in opening the West and failing to actively pursue repatriation of French Canadians back to Quebec or at least to Manitoba.[35] Canada needed to offer land on terms at least as favourable, if not more favourable, than those available in the Republic: hence the offer of 160 acres, to match the American homestead, rather than the 100 acres common in Ontario. Almost every commentator on the settlement of the Canadian Prairies has noted the close similarities between Canada's major instrument of public lands policy – the Dominion Lands Act of 1872 – and the American Homestead Act of 1862.[36] Those striking similarities are rightly taken to indicate the derivation of the former act from the latter. The Canadian leaders who framed the terms of the Dominion Lands Act had to answer the same set of questions as the American Congress in passing the Homestead Act: who would get how much land and on what conditions?

One important difference between the two acts was that Americans allowed single women to homestead in their own names. A significant number of single American women did enter for homesteads, although debate continues on how many took and farmed these lands independently rather than acting on behalf of a male relative.[37] The Dominion Lands Act of 1872 provided, like its American model, that "any person" over twenty-one years of age could file for a homestead. But in Canadian law, "person" did not include women until the famous ruling by the Judicial Committee of the Privy Council in 1929. However, in 1876 on the recommendation of Surveyor General J.S. Dennis, the act was amended to read "any person, male or female, who is sole head of a household or any male" over eighteen years.[38] While Canadian officials were almost always willing to allow female relatives to complete the homestead process for any deceased male relation, no matter how distant, they read their own legislation extremely narrowly, denying virtually all women the ability to file for homesteads in their own names. A study of nearly 360,000 homestead entries in Saskatchewan found six women. Local land office clerks apparently thought in each case the woman was head of a household (e.g., eldest of three sisters farming together). One relinquished her claim in favour of her brother. The government offered to sell one woman the lot she had homesteaded at a dollar an acre. Four got free homesteads, although all but one had to appeal to officials in Ottawa.[39] In most of these cases, the view from Ottawa held that the woman should never have been allowed to make a homestead entry, but once the mistake had been made, some leniency must be shown.

Both acts assumed very similar survey systems. Both offered 160-acre homesteads – in effect, a conditional grant of land – in return for a registration fee (of about $10–$15) and fulfillment of a series of settlement conditions. Canada required the settler to construct a dwelling of specified size on the property, live on the homestead for at least six months each year over three years (compared to five years for the American legislation), and cultivate at least 15 acres in that time. Each country allowed a person to homestead only once.

The common assumption of the two countries' survey and grant systems was a dispersed pattern of settlement, although the Dominion

Lands Act had a provision for rural villages, which was taken up at least for a time by Mennonites (1870s), Doukhobors (1890s), and some Jewish settlers (1902). "The communitarian agriculture of eastern European settlers was both more humane and economically rational before the construction of the railway and the local machinery of government."[40] Yet the members of each of these groups ultimately either came to hold their land as individual families or left the region in order to pursue a communitarian way of life. The railway brought the attractions of commercially oriented farming, which few groups could resist in the long run.

In both countries, the size of the grant reflected the assumption (usually unstated) that much the new western lands would prove to be at least as fertile and well watered as lands east of the Great Lakes in Canada or the Mississippi-Missouri in the United States. The pioneering experiences in the East had been governed by the perception that the quality of the soil could be judged by its tree cover. For pioneers from the Atlantic to Great Lakes and the Mississippi, the best lands were associated with hardwood trees, while softwoods, especially pines, were commonly associated with poorer soils. Where no trees grew, the soil was highly suspect. In Canada, the pre-Confederation expeditions by the British under Captain John Palliser and by Canadians under S.J. Dawson and H.Y. Hind had identified two separate regions on the southern prairies, a fertile belt running from the Red River along the Assiniboine and Qu'Appelle rivers to the North Saskatchewan River and an arid region along the forty-ninth parallel. Both expeditions considered the latter region to be the northern limit of the "Great American Desert." However, both their reports stressed the presumed fertility of the parkland that skirted the northern edge of that plains area. Reflecting contemporary opinion, they stressed that its open spaces were the result of fires set by natives, while the soil (and some local oral history) indicated that it had been covered with trees.

Hind and Palliser generally reflected the same assessment of the arid region. Hind observed, "There can be little doubt that the aridity and barrenness of the Great Prairie between the Qu'Appelle and the 49th parallel is owing to the small quantity of dew and rain, and the occurrence of [prairie] fires."[41] However Hind also suggested that it was the fires rather than rainfall that were the critical element in making these plains "sterile": "There can be no doubt that, if the annual fires which devastate these prairies were to cease, trees would rapidly cover them in most places. Everywhere young aspen and willows show themselves in groves where 'fire' has not 'run' for two or three seasons. A few years of repose would convert vast wastes, now treeless and barren, into beautiful and fertile areas. East and north of this dry prairie region there is a large expanse of cultivatable land."[42] This is the most striking example of Professor Hind's general tendency to see the Prairie region in more positive terms than the members of Palliser's expedition. However, both reports agreed that Canada possessed what the Americans did not: a habitable region across its West that could provide the necessary traffic to make a transcontinental railway a commercial feasibility.[43]

To draw settlers into this newly identified fertile region, the federal government needed to offer free land on terms at least as generous as its larger and longer-established competitor to the south. The similarity of the American Homestead Act of 1862 and the Canadian Dominion Lands Act of 1872, however, did not mean that the public lands *policies* of the two countries were similar. On the Canadian Prairies the Dominion Lands Act was the primary instrument through which the Crown alienated public lands. The only lands it did not cover – very limited areas around HBC posts and occupied lands along the Red River as well as the North and South Saskatchewan rivers – formed only a tiny proportion of the Prairie's total land surface. Homesteads, railway lands, lands owed to the HBC, and the small land endowment for schools were all encompassed in a single act and land survey system that covered the whole of the eventual inhabited Prairies.[44]

The Homestead Act of 1862, by contrast, was only one of several US public lands acts, to which it was never reconciled. In the decades after its passage, the US government did not stop selling land; from 1865 to 1875 it sold over 14 million acres.[45] Until 1889, a purchaser could have any amount of land for cash or scrip. After that date, purchases were limited to a maximum of 320 acres. The federal government also gave land grants to states for various purposes, including education and promotion of new railways.

Before the Homestead Act, Americans had long debated how (and whether) those actually intending to settle could get access to public land in ways that would prevent speculators from engrossing the best land available before settlement began. These debates culminated in the 1841 Pre-emption Act, which remained in force until 1891. It allowed a conditional right to occupy up to 160 acres of vacant public lands to develop a farm.[46] The Homestead Act itself provided for "commutation" or purchase of the homestead prior to final entry, which gave the homesteader full ownership of the land.[47]

After the Homestead Act, Congress continued to pass legislation for the disposal of public lands, making no more attempt to reconcile the new legislation with the existing Homestead Act than had been expended reconciling that act with the lands legislation preceding it. The most widely used of the new provisions was the Timber Culture Act (1873), which allowed a person to apply for a free grant of 160 acres on condition of planting trees on a certain proportion of the land within a period of time. For 245,000 original entries, some 37 million acres were conditionally granted. However, only 65,292 entries issued final patents for 9.7 million acres.[48] In practical terms, the Timber Culture Act doubled the initial amount of land a homesteader in a newly opened area could claim, with the act's claim later converted to a purchase by pre-emption.

In 1877 Congress passed the Desert Land Act, which provided that where farmers irrigated part of a 160-acre claim, they could purchase that quarter section for only 25 cents per acre. However, as with the Timber Culture Act, its terms allowed a person first to file an entry on a quarter section to prevent others making a claim and later to convert the claim to a pre-emption purchase.[49] Using both acts, the earlier homesteaders could blanket an area with claims, which could later be purchased or relinquished to latter arrivals for a fee.

Before and after the Homestead Act, Congress passed a great deal of legislation to alienate public lands for a wide variety of purposes: to promote education, to fund internal improvements (roads, canals, railways), to provide reservations for treaty Indians, and to compensate military veterans. Of the total western public lands granted or sold by the United States in the nineteenth century – 1,399,000 acres – homesteaders got only 256 million acres, 18 per cent of the total, by 1930. Between 1860 and 1900, 5,737,000 new farms were established with a total area of 4,514,000 acres.[50] By comparison, up to 1900, only 600,000 homesteads with a total of 80 million acres were patented in this period (1863–1900). Therefore the great majority of the new farms established between the Civil War and the end of the century began with a land purchase. Homesteaders accounted for no more than one in six new farms (possibly as low as one in ten).[51]

It is surprisingly difficult to obtain precise figures on what proportion of new farms on the Canadian Prairies began with (or included) a homestead grant. Table 7.2 shows the numbers of Prairie farms, homestead entries and cancellations from 1891 to 1911. Comparing the census data for new farms in each decade with the total homestead entries and cancellations results in what seems to be an extremely high result.[52]

Table 7.2: Canadian Prairies: farms, homestead entries, cancellations, and proportion of net new farms to homestead entries, 1891–1911.

	New farm occupiers	Total homestead entries	Cancellations	Percentage of entries cancelled	Net new homesteads	New farms as a percentage of new homesteads
1891–1901	29,810	37,286	9,423	25.3	27,863	93.5
1901–1911	148,166	283,943	143,838	50.7	140,105	94.6

Source: M.C. Urquhart and K.A.H. Buckley (eds.), *Historical Statistics of Canada*, 2nd ed., Statistics Canada, Ottawa, 1983, L5-13 to L57-72.

The bias in this data seems to stem, at least in part, from an under-reporting of cancellations. For the "hard" years of 1891–93, there are no data on cancellations. Some sources list different numbers in different places for the same period. For example, the number of "occupiers" is listed as either 29,810 or 23,493 for 1891. There are several problems in how government documents reported data. For example, Saskatchewan and Alberta data are reported combined, not only in the territorial period but also from 1909 to 1912.

As a check on these figures for completed homestead grants, one can compare the total acreage patented with the total acreage patented as homesteads. Doing so shows the changing proportions of public lands patented by Canadian homesteaders to total public lands alienated by the federal government.

How many Canadian Prairie homesteaders patented land as compared to the number of new farmers? The number who proved up can be calculated from the total area patented (that is owned outright) as homestead land divided by the average area of land claimed (usually slightly above or below 160 acres). However, there are a series of difficulties that need to be addressed in using the available data.

The first problem is the time lag. Prairie homesteaders had to be on their land a minimum of three years before claiming a patent. Many had to ask for extensions in time to complete their claim. The number of those who patented shows how many succeeded in getting that far, as compared to just filing for entry, which was the very beginning of the process. In a given period (say a decade) many new farmers would not yet be able to prove up, while others patenting would have begun their farm prior to the decade. When farmers had the option of pre-empting an additional 160 acres, there would be a similar time lag.

Table 7.3: Prairie pre-emption entries and cancellations, 1874–1913.

Year	Entries	Cancellation Notes
1874–1880	6,204	No cancellations given
1881–1890	13,822 (net)	Cancellations shown for only 5 years
1891–1913	2,850	Of pre-1891 entries

Rough estimate of net pre-emption claims: 18,178, which is obviously too high since it exceeds the number of new farmers in 1881–90.

Source: M.C. Urquhart and K.A.H. Buckley (eds.), Historical Statistics of Canada, 2nd ed., Statistics Canada, Ottawa, 1983, L5-13 to L57-72.

The second problem is incomplete data. As previously noted, homestead cancellations were under-reported. Pre-emption cancellations were not recorded at all until 1884, and then fairly regularly from 1886 on. Moreover, there is no separate record of lands patented under pre-emption until 1914.[53] I have therefore assumed that farmers' homestead claims and pre-emption claims are both listed (until 1914) under homestead lands patented. How many homesteaders took pre-emption claims before the option was ended in 1891? The data in Table 7.3 show the Prairie pre-emption entries and cancellations between 1874 and 1913, which allow only rough estimates.

The estimate of 18,178 net pre-emption claims is obviously far too high, since it exceeds the number of new farmers on the Prairies between 1881 and 1890! Nonetheless, if we assume that every homesteader had a pre-emption, then we can estimate that in 1881–90 there were 7,891 homesteaders who patented land. Table 7.4 compares the number of new farms per decade to the number of homesteads patented in that same decade.

The time lag is most striking for 1901–10. It is explained by the late rush in the decade. Alberta had its all-time peak of homestead entries – 17,178 – in 1910. Saskatchewan's entries remained above 20,000 per year from 1909 to 1912. The outbreak of the First World War obviously then slowed the settlement of the Prairies. Consequently the growth of new farms slackened, while those already on the land could complete their homestead entry and file for a patent to give them outright ownership. Thus, although several of these estimates may not be exact, the overall picture is clear: the great majority of Canadian Prairie farms began with a substantial grant of free public lands.

While the influence of the American Homestead Act on the Dominion Lands Act is often remarked on, much less attention has been paid to the

Table 7.4: Prairies: new farms and homestead patents, 1881–1921.

Year	New farms	Homesteads patented
1881–1890	21,161	7,891[1]
1891–1900	23,924	15,041[2]
1901–1910	144,017	13,373
1911–1915	19,360	110,181
1916–1921	37,094	73,799
Totals:	245,566	220,285

Percentage of new farms begun as homesteads: 89.7%

Sources: M.C. Urquhart and K.A.H. Buckley (ed.), Historical Statistics of Canada, 2nd edition, Statistics Canada, Ottawa, 1983, L5-13 to L57-72.

1 For this decade, assuming every homesteader also completed a pre-emption, I used 320 rather than 160 acres. Since everyone did not file for a pre-emption, this is a conservative estimate of the number who "proved up" in this decade. Pre-emption was re-introduced in 1908 with the opening of the Palliser Triangle, but lands patented under these pre-emptions are listed separately.

2 A small, but unknown, number of homesteaders in this decade could have completed a pre-emption claim as well. However, I used 160 acres as the norm, so this estimate would be slightly too high.

influence of Canadian lands policy on American legislation. In the early years of the twentieth century, tens of thousands of Americans began to move north to the Canadian Prairies in search of free or cheap land. The American government responded with a series of attempts to make their own homesteads more attractive, or at least as attractive.[54] The first step came in 1904 when an enterprising Nebraska congressman persuaded Congress to experiment with larger homesteads for the drier western parts of his state. The Kinkaid Act's offer of 640 acres (instead of the usual 160 acres) drew an immediate response of 10,000 new entries. Within a decade, most of the state's remaining public lands had been taken up. In 1908 the Canadian government opened the remaining, driest part of the Prairies for homestead (cancelling ranch leases to do so) and re-introduced the Canadian pre-emption, which amounted to a 320-acre homestead grant. The following year the US Congress replied with the Enlarged Homestead Act, which also granted 320-acre homesteads, initially in nine semi-arid states, later expanded to twelve. However, the American northward exodus continued. In 1912 Congress enacted an amendment to the Homestead Act to shorten the claim period from five years to three, following the lead of the Dominion Lands Act. In the debates around this legislation, congressmen made direct references to the need to match the appeal of Canadian homestead legislation.[55]

The US Homestead Act enabled only a small proportion – perhaps as low as 10 per cent – of new farmers to begin their farm with free

Table 7.5: The Canadian Prairies under the Dominion Lands Act (1872–1930) and the US Public Domain under the Homestead Act (1862–1923).

Allocation of Land	Canada (acres)	Canada (%)	United States (%)
Homesteads[1]	63,005,000	35.2	21.1
Sales[2]	5,624,000	3.1	5.1
Railway grants[3]	31,782,000	17.8	11.3
HBC[4]	7,027,000	3.9	–
Education[5]	9,493,000	5.3	8.2
Indian reserves[6]	3,891,000	2.2	2.5
River lots and Métis scrip	2,605,000	1.5	–
Road allowances	3,734,000	2.1	–
Military bounty[7]	–	–	3.1
Total		71.1%	48.2%

Totals are less than 100% because in neither case is every form of allocation represented (e.g., forest reserves, national parks, etc.)

Sources: Benjamin H. Hibbard, A History of the Public Land Policies, 1924, 570, and Chester Martin, "Dominion Lands" Policy, 228–9.

1 Homesteads including pre-emptions and purchased homesteads.

2 All sales, including those for irrigation and drainage. US sales are after 1862.

3 The CPR still had 563,659 acres unsold in 1930.

4 The HBC had 2.6 million acres unsold by 1930.

5 Education included both school lands and the University of Manitoba. 5.4 million acres of Canadian school lands remained unsold in 1930.

6 Indian Reserves, including what was later surrendered and sold by the federal governments.

7 Military Bounty includes only entries made after 1862.

land paid for by fulfilling the settlement conditions. By contrast, on the Canadian Prairies the great majority of new farms included a homestead grant. Thus, although there has been a great deal of discussion about the western United States as a homestead frontier, in fact Canada provided much greater chances of getting land by homesteading.

Moreover, Canada's different public policies on crown lands produced a strikingly different distribution of those lands compared to the United States. When the total surveyed area of lands fit for cultivation that had been sold or granted in what would become the three Prairie provinces is compared to the extent of lands granted or alienated by the United States after 1862 west of the Mississippi, the differences are striking. Table 7.5 compares the proportions of public lands on the Canadian Prairies and the American West used for various purposes. It shows those proportions (and extent) for public lands to 1928 on the eve of the Canadian federal surrender to the three provinces. It also indicates the proportions of the United States western lands disposed of between 1862 and 1930.

In Canada, 60 per cent more public land went to homesteaders than in the United States. The American federal government sold 60 per cent more public lands than did the Canadian federal government. Canada gave 63.5 per cent more of its Prairie public lands to promote railways than did the United States from its western lands. Both countries gave comparable amounts to support "common schools" (4.9 per cent versus 5.2 per cent). However, in Canada, Prairie public lands supported only the University of Manitoba – the one university on the Prairies in the nineteenth century – while the United States offered support for land grant colleges in all states. The United States had many acts giving out lands for a great variety of public purposes. Above all, the United States continued to sell public lands as a major source of federal revenue. Canadian policy and land grants were highly focused on settlement and railways: homesteads and railways together accounted for the majority of Canadian public lands disposed (53 per cent). In the United States those purposes amounted to less than a third (32.4 per cent).

Canada's Dominion Lands policies on the Prairies largely achieved their intended purposes of financing railway infrastructure and facilitating settlement. The CPR, as by far the largest railway, disposed of its lands efficiently in a way that expedited rapid settlement. That was a striking contrast to the smaller railways, which copied all that was worst in the American practice of railway administration. Modern economic historians consider land grants an inefficient means to finance railways, but have to concede that it was the most politically feasible in that era. While economic costs probably outweighed economic benefits, the social benefit of a national railway more than compensated.

To a surprising degree, the free homestead played a very large part in the start of the great majority of Prairie farms. Private individuals (especially around villages and towns) and land companies (including the Hudson's Bay Company) no doubt got control of land and held it for speculative purposes. But while the most active of these speculators made some financial gains from their activities, across the region as a whole, the farmer – four times out of five – began as homesteader. This is perhaps the greatest contrast with the experience of the American West.

In the course of actual settlement, families from central and eastern Canada found they had to adapt their expectations and practices to the demands of a very different environment. Even with a railway built, could such a short growing season and such a low level of rainfall support commercial agriculture? The family farm in Quebec and Ontario had balanced a subsistence domestic economy of women with production for off-farm sales associated with men. Could that balance and women's roles in the family be sustained where soils were so thin and winters so severe? The Prairies would require more than just new tillage methods and new types of equipment: the farm family itself needed to be reassessed.

Both Canada and the United States acquired their respective western public domains by land surrender treaties signed with the region's native peoples. The Prairies numbered treaties included government promises of assistance for native peoples to take up agriculture on the reserves allocated to them. Consequently these "treaty Indians" would be the first in the region to attempt, on a large scale, the European type of sedentary farming. The problems encountered by reserve agriculture would test not only native adaptability, but also the good faith of Canada's federal government.

Native Farming on the Prairies

Europeans began their approach to the North West with the view that they farmed and that native peoples did not – but should. As early as 1862, in his report on Rupert`s Land, Captain John Palliser had urged that reserves should be set aside at once where Indians could be taught agriculture.[1] While the federal government's treaty commissioners spoke in very general terms about the need for native peoples to take up farming, the texts of the treaties sent out from Ottawa contained no practical assistance to that end. In Alexander Morris's 1880 account of the treaty negotiations and early implementation, natives appear as the passive recipients of the royal bounty. Agriculture is mentioned in Treaty 1 negotiations only as the rationale for the small size of each reserve: 160 acres for each family.[2] Otherwise, farming was seen only as a future option: "where farms shall be required ... should you chose to get your living by tilling."[3] In later correspondence, it is noted in passing by Commissioner W.M. Simpson that "it has been agreed" that natives would get livestock and farming implements, with no indication as to who had initiated that provision.[4] Morris's own comments on treaty implementation certainly would not encourage the idea that natives had shown any initiative. He described them as "tractable, docile, and willing to learn ... Already the prospect of many of the bands turning their attention to raising food from the soil is very hopeful."[5] He felt they only needed farm instructors to enable all bands to be self-supporting.

Half a century later, all such hope was gone. Historian George Stanley concluded that "the Indians were, on the whole, unresponsive to the Government policy."[6] Like Morris, he cited Lieutenant-Governor Archibald at Treaty 1 expressing the Queen's wish that natives "adopt the habits of the whites, to till the land and raise food and store it up against the time of want."[7] But this was only an option: "The Indians, of course, had no desire to settle down."[8] While Ottawa signed treaties through the 1870s with promises of agricultural assistance, it did not readily act on them: "The extermination of the buffalo hastened the adoption of a definite farming policy by the government."[9] But all for naught. "At the outset many, by a display of energy, gave every promise that ere long they might free themselves from dependence upon public assistance ... But the very character of the Indian militated against a rapid advance ... The character moulded by centuries could not be transformed in a few years. Restlessness was inherent in the Indian disposition. His dislike of uncongenial labour was proverbial."[10]

That view became the common coin of non-native discourse. In the 1950s another historian, Grant McEwan, noted Palliser's early recommendation. In his view, Palliser's "faith in the conversion of the savages to agriculturalists has been scarcely justified by the record of the intervening years, although a good deal of progress can be demonstrated."[11] Historian Sarah Carter admitted to being "startled," at the very beginning of her research, when she found that the existing historiography's "standard explanation" – "that Aboriginal people of the Plains never had any inclination to settle down and farm despite concerted government effort and assistance" – was wrong.[12]

In fact, native peoples were the first to introduce agriculture onto the Prairies. Prior to the arrival of Europeans, however, there seem to have been none who based a large part of their livelihood on agriculture, comparable to the Mandan on the Upper Missouri.[13] This early period has been the domain of the anthropologists. What evidence there is of prehistoric native agricultural activity north of the forty-ninth parallel points to limited purposes, tobacco being the most widely grown crop. Its cultivation, at least on a small scale, extended across the region from the Cree to the Blackfoot. Once the fur trade began to supply quantities of better quality, its cultivation seems to have declined.

The Swampy Cree and Saulteaux (or western Ojibwa) made regular harvests of wild rice on a substantial scale. While anthropologists have debated definitions of "agriculture" and "horticulture" relative to native peoples, in this book it is all considered farming.[14] The native custom of throwing some of the harvested rice back as an offering to the divine has been described as "unconscious" planting, leaving the harvesting of wild rice as a gathering activity rather than actual agriculture. However, from about 1800 to 1820 there are reports of the Saulteaux sowing wild rice in the waterways along the Red River and Assiniboine River corridors. Anthropologist Laura Peers noted that the earliest Europeans west of the Great Lakes recognized that agriculture was part of a native multi-source subsistence strategy.[15]

At the beginning of the nineteenth century a new type of agriculture was carried west of the Canadian Shield onto the Prairies. Historical geographers have shown that this was an extension west of an established pattern followed by Algonquian-speaking peoples. But in part it was also adaptation both to climate and of crops. Not only was the traditional maize cultivation carried beyond its prehistoric limit but also the crop mix was broadened by the introduction of potatoes, brought to North America by the Europeans. Native farmers were sufficiently successful that fur traders realized these crops could become items of trade, rather than just native subsistence.

Of the traditional native farming combination of maize, beans, squash, pumpkins, and sunflowers, it was maize that proved the most adaptable on the Prairies. Mandan "flint" maize was short, hardy, and at least partially frost resistant. Fur traders had early traded with the Mandan and endeavoured to grow this corn in trading post gardens. Native farmers on the Canadian Prairies took up a number of root crops from the Europeans, of which turnips and, above all, potatoes were the most widely grown.[16]

The dating of native agriculture's entry onto the Prairies is confined by the limits of history: the survival of written records. At the beginning of our historical horizon is Alexander Henry's 1805 report of an Ottawa band starting to farm at Netley Creek (just below where the Red River enters Lake Winnipeg). He recounts himself as supplying the seed and thereby, perhaps implicitly, the impetus for the growing of maize and potatoes.[17] In fact it is difficult to determine at whose initiative this farming began. Having moved west to follow the fur trade, these Ottawa may not have had any kind of farming in their recent past. But as a people they had been familiar with the use of agriculture as part of a broader subsistence strategy. "It is possible that earlier, unreported efforts at growing crops had been made."[18]

After some years, the Ottawa abandoned the Netley Creek site, partly because of depredations on their gardens, probably also because of the increasing levels of conflict between the HBC and the NWC. It is suggestive to note that they moved from the Red River on one much-used fur trade route, and to Lake of the Woods on another much-used fur trade route. This would suggest that they intended to sell their surplus crops. In this way agriculture was a double addition: it provided a food source and a potential trade resource when fur resources were declining.[19] A degree of market orientation was evident. Immediately after the merger of the two rival companies in 1821, agricultural prices fell. Natives, in the short term, shifted out of agriculture, or at least reduced sales (and, one might infer, reduced production for sale). However, the records of HBC purchases indicate that agriculture seemed to rebound in the later 1820s. The disappearance of the NWC turned out not to be the disappearance of all competition to the HBC. American traders moved west of the Great Lakes seeking to draw furs south.

To fur traders and others, it appeared that the Ottawa had introduced a kind of agriculture to the Red River area, which was taken up by both the Saulteaux and the Cree. Missionaries hoped that the Red River settlers of Lord Selkirk would set an example of farming for natives to follow. The reverse is probably true: "The colonists' crops of wheat and barley failed with predictable regularity due to frost, drought, and grasshoppers, leaving the Europeans largely dependent on the Indians and Métis for food, while the [western] Ojibwa were able to harvest their potato patches and corn fields and maintain a productive fishery during the most difficult years."[20] The repeated failures of the new farmers' crops and the example of the natives' multi-source subsistence strategy may well have led the settlers to strive to balance farming with other occupations, whether as buffalo hunters, contractors or labourers with the HBC.

In the era before Confederation, native farmers adapted to the severities of the Prairie climate much more successfully than did Europeans. The Red River Valley bottomlands were not suited to maize. Fur traders noted that Indians often grew certain crops more successfully than the traders' own gardens adjacent to the fur trade post. This success arose from seeking out what are now recognized as microclimate zones that favoured maize especially. Use of such zones enabled native farmers to extend the crop's range from the parkland into even the forest regions. Such zones had several characteristics. Natives sought out lighter, sandier soils on which maize could mature as much as ten days earlier. These soils were also easier to cultivate with a minimum of tools (hoes rather than plows or harrows). In addition to a particular soil type, native planters also selected locations with great care: southern-facing slopes surrounded by or next to substantial bodies of water. It is striking that a few Selkirk settlers who farmed the natural levees rather than bottomlands also had some success with maize.

Natives farmed on a comparatively small scale for several reasons. The micro-zones they sought to give crops the best chance were not large in extent, and thus sometimes they had several widely dispersed areas under cultivation at the same time. Their tools were limited by their need to be pursuing other food sources. Some natives brought in iron goods to European blacksmiths to be remade into hoes,[21] but investment in heavier equipment would have been uneconomical.

In some native societies there was evidence of a gendered division of labour. Men were often "the hunters," while women were "the gatherers," even when they had planted what was gathered. Among the Saulteaux, Laura Peers noted "there is no evidence to suggest a division of spring activities by sex (men hunting for furs while women, children, and elders made sugar), as would seem to be the case for some earlier groups."[22] However, when it came to short-term resource switching, "women, who did much of the gardening, would have played a crucial role in deciding how to balance these resources each year and how best to compensate for changing weather patterns and water levels."[23] Carter made a different sort of distinction: "In the areas most intensively farmed, men did most of the work, but where agricultural produce was a secondary source of subsistence, women did the most, although the men helped to clear ground and harvest."[24]

In the Confederation era, adaptations of the type of native farming developed in the Red River Valley spread across native communities in the parkland belt. Sometimes this has been seen as no more than extension of the white presence in fur trade posts and mission settlements. Certainly the HBC, to reduce its own expenditures, encouraged not only gardens but even farms at its posts. Fort Carlton's "garden" grew barley, wheat, hops, and potatoes. At the farms for forts Ellice, Pelly, and Qu'Appelle, "Indians were hired to tend the crops, to hay, and to look after the horses and other stock."[25] However the extension west of potato cultivation was not just an extension of the fur trade or missionary work.[26] For over two decades in the Touchwood Hills, the Cree Magpie band, similar to the Mandan, raised maize and potatoes and lived in log houses covered with earth. The Little Bones and Pasquah bands farmed on Leech Lake raising both "gardens" and cattle. In 1861 they bought a plow from the HBC. By 1875, in the midst of the treaty signing process, one band of 36 families had 97 cattle and 57 horses. Sarah Carter suggests that these bands were placing greater reliance on agriculture because the buffalo in their area had already disappeared.[27] Ahtahkakoop's band of Cree, who wintered on the north side of the parkland belt, had begun their shift away from buffalo to potatoes and other garden produce by 1872.[28]

Before Confederation, native farming often succeeded better than white farming around fur trade posts and in the Red River Valley because the natives chose their garden spots specifically for growing, while fur traders tried to raise gardens at sites chosen for trade purposes. Selkirk settlers were often bound to a specific piece of land by the conventions of their society rather than its agricultural potential. Natives also sought to balance one food source with others, rather than relying wholly on farm produce. "Later in the century [western] Ojibwa deliberately planted larger gardens if water levels seemed unfavourable for rice crops in the spring."[29] Moreover, "The gardens provided two partial solutions to the fur and game shortage: they supplemented the diet, thus bolstering game supplies and allowing more time to be spent obtaining furs, and they provided a new product to trade, partial compensation for the decrease in the number and quality of furs."[30] Prior to the treaties and the disappearance of the buffalo from Canada, in some Prairie bands, farming was added to or expanded as an alternate food source to compensate for declines in other areas, not only of buffalo but also other, smaller animals. Given that extent of native farming already present across the Prairies, the treaty commissioners' monolithic view of "the Indian" as someone unfamiliar with farming becomes even more mysterious.

Once a treaty was signed, Ottawa assumed full rights of possession, but was not so anxious to fulfill its treaty obligations. In fact, federal officials took a leisurely attitude toward establishing reserves. Far from insisting that natives take up agriculture, they actually resisted native demands that specific assistance to promote agriculture be included in the treaty agreements.[31]

The first treaty set down some fundamental precedents that weighed heavily on later negotiations. Several chiefs demanded recognition of their sovereign authority, in return for which they were prepared to grant the government corridors through native lands. The federal officials refused to consider any such proposal: the purpose of a treaty was to surrender all sovereignty and all claims to traditional lands. The Cree then countered with a demand for about two-thirds of all Manitoba's lands. Again federal officials insisted that the reserve would be limited to the natives' traditional encampment (in practice, often their wintering place). A crucial development came when a leader of the Pembina band pressed the government agents on the feasibility of a transition to agriculture. Lieutenant-Governor Archibald made a general statement about the need for natives to take up farming, stressing that while the Queen desired this, it was up to the natives to decide when. Henry Prince of the

St Peter's band followed up by asking how natives could support them-selves. Archibald replied, in an apparently offhand way, that the gov-ernment would supply the needed implements, livestock, and seed. In D.J. Hall's view, "This promise by the Governor altered the whole mood of the negotiations ... They now saw an alternative way to secure their future, if the reserves and annuities were not to be increased."[32]

The underlying assumption of officials seems to have been that they had access to all lands and resources not in immediate use, even with-out treaties. Thus, surveyors and roadwork contractors began construc-tion of a road in 1868 from Lake Superior to the Red River without any attempt at consultation with the Saulteaux of the area. The first treaties came in response to native resistance to that trespass. "The Saulteaux of southern Manitoba and the North-West Angle of the Lake of the Woods effectively created the fear of violence against those who might venture into their territory before treaties were negotiated with them."[33] In 1875 workmen on the projected telegraph line from Red River to Fort Edmonton were sent packing by Cree who pointed out that there was yet no treaty in place north of the Saskatchewan River to justify whites cutting trees or putting up telegraph wires.

The same resistance could meet private individuals who behaved in a similar manner. Young John Hines, an Anglican missionary to the Cree north of Fort Carlton, assumed he could choose a site for his mission and begin its construction from local materials before any contact with (much less permission from) the native peoples of the area. He was con-fronted by a group of Cree led by Netmaker who pointed out that they had not asked for a missionary nor given consent to any mission or to the use of either woods or land. An hour's discussion ensued. While Hines rejected demands that he pay either for the trees he cut or a weekly rent on the land, he eventually got consent to reside temporarily.[34]

Succeeding treaties often marginally increased the terms of earlier treaties and sometimes included new provisions, such as a famine clause and the promise of a "medicine chest" on each reserve, which then became general for all treaty Indians. Where the government could avoid such promises, it did. Perhaps due to the absence of many leaders, Treaty 4 did not contain agricultural provisions. Laura Peers suggested that because the Saulteaux had already developed extensive subsistence crops, they "were still economically secure enough to adopt a forceful bargaining strategy for treaty benefits, while the plains-oriented tribes, who faced immediate starvation because of the disappearance of the bison, were forced to comply more readily with the government's terms in order to gain an ally to see them through the immediate crisis."[35] However, at the negotiations for Treaty 6, numerous native leaders attended. Their recent experience with epidemics and the effectiveness of inoculations led to their demand for a "medicine chest" on each reserve.[36] There would be hoes and spades for each family and a plow and harrow for every ten families, as well as livestock, wagons, and carpenter's tools for each band. The fearsome reputation of the Blackfoot Confederacy enabled them to gain even more extensive provisions of land, livestock, and agricultural assistance.[37]

In order to begin farming on reserves, it was necessary to have the land surveyed, natives settled, and sufficient subsistence provided to allow people to focus on clearing, breaking, plowing, and planting. Under Treaty 6, for example, "for the first three years after reserves were surveyed, bands actually cultivating would be granted provisions to the sum of one thousand dollars."[38] However, the commencement of reserve farming across the Prairies did not progress smoothly due to a wide range of factors. Even after signing the first three of the numbered treaties in 1871–73, the federal government was slow to begin surveying. It appeared surprised that natives wanted to begin their transition at once. Selection of reserves did not start until the fall of 1875.

Native peoples in treaty negotiations insisted on provision of assistance to a farming way of life. From many of their leaders came a clear intention (however imperfectly realized in practice) to change their way of life. However, native and white often worked at cross-purposes. Natives often thought in terms of their traditional multi-source approach to subsistence. It was obvious that farming would now play a much larger part, but that did not mean it would necessarily be their exclusive reliance. Whites – such as civil servants and missionaries – often thought and spoke in radically different terms, more akin to religious conversion than cultural adaptation. They urged natives to give up their wandering ways and concentrate wholly on farming. Though very few missionaries and no civil servants knew anything about prairie farming, they all assumed it would provide a more reliable material support than hunting and gathering. That excessively optimistic assumption wrought great havoc in the lives of most Plains Indians confined to the reserve system. Only gradually did the most persistent and aware of the farm instructors and Indian agents come to realize how hazardous an enterprise had been imposed on native peoples.

In the context of the buffalo's disappearance from the Canadian West, the selection of reserves and settling of them became part of a power struggle between the federal government and several native leaders. The government sought to locate native peoples to give them the least power and the government the least expense. For example, it rejected the demands of Piapot, Little Pine, and Big Bear for a large Cree reserve or a tight cluster of reserves around Cypress Hills. As the starvation crisis deepened at the close of the 1870s, both sides tried to gain leverage over the other: the natives by refusing to select or go to reserves (pursued most consistently by Big Bear); the government by withholding food to any but those who obeyed government directions (pursued most vigorously by Indian Commissioner Edgar Dewdney).[39]

Selection of reserve sites was often guided by past experience of wintering – the need for wood (as fuel and construction material), water, fish, and small game for subsistence. Some bands already had wintering grounds to which they returned each year, although some family members – usually those most vulnerable in mobile encampments – inhabited the grounds year-round, cultivating potatoes and fishing through the summer. Native reserve selection sometimes led to conflict within bands. Initially the Saulteaux band, led by a chief known as "The Key" had settled on a reserve on Shoal River, near Swan Lake, well into their traditional parkland winter range. However, a flood in 1880 persuaded the Indian agent that the land could not be cultivated and he directed them to find a new site. While the scouts reported glowingly of a new location on the upper Assiniboine River not far from Fort Pelly, the band split on whether to move. Part of the division may have been caused by a conflict over how decisions should be made: the chief and his supporters seem to have accepted the government's idea of the chief's power, as against more traditional forms of consensus seeking. Only a minority of the band ultimately followed the chief to the new site. The government eventually accepted that the dissident majority would continue on the old reserve as a separate body.[40]

While the multitude of details often differ, the common experience of most natives in their first decade on the reserve was of federal officials who repeatedly failed to deliver promised goods, yet demanded an increasing degree of control over native life. Livestock, equipment, and seed seldom arrived in a timely manner to begin spring activities, harvest time, or even threshing. Part of the reason for this – following from the initial white presumption that the land was theirs – was a common perception by government, and many of the general settler population, that the aid specified in the treaties was not a binding legal obligation, but an act of charity springing from goodwill.

Government officials at all levels sought to read the treaties in the narrowest way. Some bands had expected to start farming immediately, whether or not the government had got around to surveying the reserve's boundaries. However, Indian agents generally refused to deliver any assistance until reserves had been surveyed, the people settled, and farming had begun. Here natives found themselves trapped in the circular logic of the Indian Department: they could not begin farming (on the scale and in the way that the government wanted) until they had oxen, plows, and seed; but over and over, agents refused these until natives had begun farming, somehow, without them. Agents like William Wagner often took up invidious rumours as if they were fact: natives were accused of eating seed grain and draft animals, of selling or neglecting farm equipment issued. By contrast agent Angus MacKay pointed out the consequences of acting on such suspicions: "They could not construct buildings because they had no animals to draw timber and they could not break land until they were supplied with implements and animals. While attempts have been made to do both, little could be accomplished without draft animals."[41]

One consequence of the initial failures of reserve agriculture (and subsequent starvation) was the government's new policy of establishing seventeen "home farms" across the NWT starting in the fall of 1879. What is most striking about their failure to meet the government's overly optimistic expectations is the contrast to the native performance on reserves in the same period as well as later in the decade. "Architects of the program sanguinely hoped that the instructors could, after one year, raise enough grain and root crops to support themselves, their families, and employees. It was hoped that within a short time they could raise a surplus to contribute toward the expense of feeding the Indians."[42] These farms were staffed mainly from Ontario, with families used to agriculture in the European manner. By the time the experiment ended in 1884, not one of these farms had even managed to become self-supporting.

In comparison with the agricultural societies of Upper and Lower Canada and Lord Dalhousie's model farm, the home farms were even greater failures. Dalhousie's farm at least demonstrated that large-scale sheep farming was feasible in Lower Canada, even if it was far beyond the financial resources of all but a few habitants.[43] The agricultural societies promoted diverse new crops and advertised the value of purebred stock whose appeal was severely limited where land was abundant and labour scarce. There were no fences, as cattle were left to forage for themselves in the bush, and consequently no opportunity for controlled breeding.[44]

The home farms could not even meet their minimal goal of becoming self-supporting: the families required government salaries beyond the produce they grew to survive.

The home farm program shared the common assumption behind many government activities, that farming was something that whites knew how to do, but Indians did not. However, even before Confederation, at Red River, it had been clear that the central issue was not farming in its broadest sense, but contrasting ways of farming and contrasting perceptions of the role of farming in providing for the subsistence of a family. In the conflicts of the 1820s and 1830s between a succession of missionaries and the Saulteaux, "it was not simply the growing of crops that the missionaries wished so fervently to teach the Ojibwa. They also wanted the Native people to learn about the growing of European crops (especially wheat), planting in the straight furrows used by European farmers."[45]

Sarah Carter observed that for farming on the Prairies, it might well have been the natives who should have been the teachers: "In many ways their training made them better suited to farming than new arrivals in the West. Although the Plains Indians lacked formal education in agriculture, their highly specialized empirical knowledge of nature approached a science. They were aware of the vegetation in their environment and they knew when and how to harvest it."[46] Examples of that highly specialized knowledge are not hard to find. By careful selection of places with favourable microclimates, the Saulteaux could raise corn 200 miles north of where whites had failed. Contributing to the division in The Key's band was an awareness that the 1880 flooding was an exceptional occurrence, something that the Indian agent who was new to the region could not have known – hence part of the reason for the majority not feeling any need to move.

Through the 1880s, though hampered both by government failure to deliver promised goods and by repeated government interference, a substantial number of native farmers, who were spread through many bands across the Prairies, began to experience their first successes. Carter reminds us, "Through their pioneering efforts to farm west of Manitoba [Red River] on any scale, they were the first to encounter many of the limitations and requirements of prairie farming that were later to baffle and frustrate the homesteaders."[47] Native farmers learned the essential lesson that the short growing season meant time-saving equipment and procedures were all-important. Plowing had to be done in the fall because there was no time in the spring. The wooden plows with iron shares from central Canada might break lighter, sandy soils, but steel plows had to be used to cut prairie sod. Planting had to be done as early as possible, even risking late frosts. Harvest was complicated by the fact that crops matured at the same time that winter hay had to be cut. Consequently, both operations had to be done as quickly as possible – which meant a horse-drawn mower for the hay and a reaper for the grain. The urgency of threshing was the need to utilize the crop, for sale or (more often) for subsistence. Bands repeatedly found themselves with wheat they could not readily eat because there were few gristmills – a problem they shared with whites in the 1870s and 1880s.

In the mid- to late 1880s farming began to flourish on a number of reserves across the Prairies. Under Treaty 2, for example, the Sioux band that settled on the Oak River reserve, who had made little progress in their first decade, made outstanding strides in their second decade. Without the "benefit" of either Indian agent or farm instructor, by 1887 they had 200 acres in wheat – one of the best crop years for the whole of the West. In 1888 they broke another 68 acres and purchased mowers, horse rakes, wagons, and a threshing machine from their off-reserve sales of grain and hay. In 1890 they purchased three binders, six mowers and rakes, and six wagons. In 1891 they bought two new mowers and rakes, five binders, and six plows. By that year, the 42 families had 500 acres in crop and 40 acres in summer fallow.[48] Thus it was not only the Saulteaux and Swampy Cree who succeeded in farming but also the "plains-oriented" natives, who were able to adapt to the new economy. Under Treaty 4, several strong starts were made. By 1884 Pasquah's band had 28 working oxen.[49] It benefited from nearby Fort Qu'Appelle serving as a market. On the Chacachase reserve there was both a large field worked in common and a group of four families who farmed on their own.[50] Perhaps the leading agricultural band under Treaty 6 was Ahtahkakoop's, which sowed 177 acres in the spring of 1884, with 110 acres in wheat.[51]

Just as the treaty concession reflected the reputation of the Blackfoot Confederacy, so too did the implementation of Treaty 7. It had neither a promise of famine relief nor a "medicine chest," but did provide for cattle as well as farm implements.[52] Unlike any other tribes, the Blackfoot continued to receive rations until 1901. Thus agriculture, never a major part of their historic subsistence, did not become an immediate necessity for them. However, many, especially amongst the Piegan, began to grow potatoes, not primarily for subsistence but for sale. In a single year they harvested 50 tons of potatoes as well as smaller crops of turnips and barley.[53] This was commercial farming rather than peasant farming just for subsistence. The sales motive became clear when, consequent to the price falling, they stopped growing potatoes on a large scale. Those who had been able to retain herds of horses in the later 1880s began to expand into cattle.

As native peoples turned to their own resources, they gained the purchasing power to acquire machinery that was really needed to begin agriculture on their reserves. Initially they exploited hay resources, cutting by hand, not only to winter their own livestock but also to sell off the reserve to improve their productive capacity. By 1883 three bands under Treaty 4 had bought horse rakes and mowers to expand their hay production. However, only one reserve had a mechanical reaper in the early 1880s.[54] In August 1884, Treaty 6 chiefs complained they had been given *wild* cattle, not draft or dairy animals. Moreover, "their farmer neighbours had threshing mills, mowers, reapers, and rakes. They believed they were entitled to this sort of machinery and asked that their inferior implements and wild cattle be replaced."[55] While there was some improvement in Indian Department personnel and procedures by the mid-1880s (for example, Indian agents began to realize that seed grain had to be on the reserves to distribute before spring came), those bands that prospered most were those who relied upon their own resources. The Muscowpetung reserve under Treaty 4 sold 200 tons of hay in 1886. With the proceeds, they purchased a mowing machine, a horse rake, seven double wagons, and four double sleighs – all of which would enable them to expand hay production. They also bought reapers and self-binders to ensure their grain crop also came off quickly before frost. In 1888 the File Hills Indian agent pointed out that with 130 acres of wheat the natives would lose their crop without the necessary machinery for an extensive harvest operation. In 1888 the Kahkewistahaw band pooled annuities to make a $55 down payment on a Massey-Harris self-binder. Local merchants extended credit for binder twine as well as the machinery. However, it was not until the late 1880s that agents would approve acquisition of powered threshing machinery. As long as natives had to rely on renting local threshing equipment from outside the reserve, they often got the equipment so late in the year that their sheaves had spoiled and, in the intense cold, those threshing suffered terribly. "Where threshing machines were available, the Indians soon became proficient at operating them, dispelling the concern of some officials that they lacked the ability to operate them properly."[56] In the late 1880s, Indian Department reports praised the purchases of mowers, horse rakes, and threshing machines as evidence that "the Indians were not squandering their earnings."[57]

Livestock holdings also expanded. Once again the government's role in this process was mixed. In 1886 Lawrence Herchmer in the Birtle Indian Agency had begun a program to assist cattle raising on reserves. "A trustworthy individual was loaned a cow and was to raise a heifer, either of which had to be returned to the agent. The animal the Indian kept became his property, although the agent's permission was required to sell or transfer ownership."[58] On a miniature scale, this program reflected the contradictions of much native policy: the idea was to promote an independent spirit (and individualism), yet every sale and purchase was under the agent's control. Moreover, it was the agent who decided who was "trustworthy" enough to benefit, which could only be experienced by native peoples as arbitrary personal favouritism on the agent's part. Carter commented, "The system eroded the practice of holding cattle in common, except perhaps bulls, but it did not give the owners a full degree of ownership."[59] Natives made use of the program, but alongside it also built up herds that were exclusively their own. By 1890, for example, the Ochapowace reserve had 84 "government-controlled" cattle and 28 "private" cattle. Like other prairie farmers of the 1880s, those who persevered through the dismal early 1880s, finally saw better harvests in the latter part of the decade.

Sarah Carter argued persuasively that native agriculture on numerous reserves had succeeded in laying the foundations of a prosperous commercial agriculture by 1890. As the early prairie homesteaders who had endured through hard times – such as W.R. Motherwell of Aberdeen – became well-established grain farmers in the 1890s through use of the evolving dry-land farming techniques and new labour-saving machinery, she believed that native farmers could have had a parallel success in the same decade.

Instead, a new man and a new policy fatally crippled reserve agriculture, leaving natives with little opportunity for an autonomous economic existence. The new man was Hayter Reed, appointed Indian commissioner in 1888 (then department superintendent general in 1893). He had risen rapidly from his first appointment as Battleford Indian agent in 1881. When other agents praised native "energy and curiosity" and attributed early failures "not to the Indians' character and traditions, but to the economic and climatic conditions that made farming a dubious and uncertain undertaking," Reed's reports pursued a different tack.[60] "Reed's explanations for the Indians' limited success at farming were more convenient than those that involved a complex of factors which included climate, geography, oxen, implements, seed, mills, and markets.

They also absolved the government of much responsibility in the matter."[61] The convenience of his explanations undoubtedly had much to do with his rapid rise to favour within the government.

The new policy was to destroy the tribal system (as Reed understood it) by promotion of thoroughgoing assimilation of the so-called advanced Indian and the imposition of an idealized "peasant agriculture" on reserves. Part of the new policy's political appeal was that it promised a substantial reduction of both public expenditure and reserve size (seen as "freeing" land for productive use – by whites). Even before he became Indian commissioner, Reed sought to have natives confined to their reserves, even though there was no legal basis for this and it contradicted treaty provisions that had guaranteed native peoples' access to resources on crown lands.[62] Part of the political pressure on which Reed successfully played were the complaints of some white settlers that native farming had been too successful, in that it threatened to compete with homesteaders in local markets for hay, grain, or lumber.

Reed offered a fairly sophisticated rationale for confining natives to a low level of subsistence. He drew on several prevailing ideas. In the United States, the Dawes Severalty Act had begun a process of dividing reserves into private native holdings, which resulted in these being rapidly sold to non-natives, effectively shrinking reserves dramatically in size. Reed also drew on popular ideas about biological determinism, which underpinned the new "scientific racism" of the late nineteenth century.[63] Reed portrayed natives as an earlier stage of human evolution, who arrogantly thought they could unnaturally begin modern farming without "progressing" through its earlier stages.[64] "Peasants of other countries ... farmed successfully with no better implements than the hoe, rake, cradle, sickle, and flail."[65] By confining each native family to an acre or two, most reserve land could be appropriated for white settlers. Reed prescribed self-reliance for natives, who were to manufacture for themselves all the equipment and tools they needed – or do without. Reed not only wanted all government expenditure on native farming ended but also all private credit, which had been extended to native farmers by white merchants.

Reed's rationale also drew upon a theme of romantic resistance to modern technology. The rural ideal (almost always espoused by urban elites) had the self-reliant yeoman do everything by hand, with little engagement with markets or credit.[66] Reed deplored even the tendency of homesteaders to go heavily into debt to acquire labour-saving machinery to grain farm on a large scale. But he had no power to cripple their livelihood. Treaty Indians were not so fortunate.

From 1889 on, Reed ruthlessly enforced this new policy, firing agents who protested against it. Despite his threats against his own subordinates, more than half a dozen agents protested against at least some aspect of implementing the new policy. Inspector Alex McGibbon pleaded that "it was contrary to common sense to ban universally the use of machinery. Exceptions had to be made and flexibility shown ... The Onion Lake band ... had 500 acres under crop, much of which would be lost if the department insisted it be cut with cradles."[67] Others pointed out that the archaic methods on which Reed insisted could not work on the Prairies: for example, sheaves could not be bound with straw because prairie straw was too short. Reed responded that it was better to lose part of the crop than concede the principle of the new policy. While he made occasional individual concessions and was occasionally overruled by Commissioner Forget, he persisted in enforcing his views. Although natives might continue to use machinery, Reed gradually cut off both their outlet for sales and their access to credit. Carter concluded, "The restrictions had an enormous impact on the agricultural activity of the Indians just when they were beginning to overcome some of the obstacles that had sabotaged their efforts in the past."[68]

Natives protested against the new restrictions vigorously, sending delegations to Ottawa, at times with the support of some local settlers. But Reed had already adopted the department's general view that all who protested were unrepresentative troublemakers. For example, the Oak River Sioux under Treaty 2 had, by 1893, 540 acres under cultivation and 350 head of livestock. They had had neither agent nor farm instructor before 1891. Once appointed, the agent's aim was to end off-reserve sales and any credit to members of the band. He told grain buyers they could only purchase from natives to whom he had given a pass to leave the reserve. Instead of paying native farmers, the proceeds were first to go to pay off implement dealers (who were told to make no further sales to natives), with the balance going to the agent who would pay off any other reserve debts.[69] By 1895 the Indian Agent for the The Key reserve exalted in what he saw as the new policy's success. "All tribal influences have disappeared. It is now every man for himself. Each has his own affairs and if he wants to speak of them he comes to the agent and the matter is settled – no big meetings and waste of time for days."[70] As native farmers' machinery wore out, their markets closed and their credit constricted, as they came under ever more intensive control by government officials, they lost the capacity and sometimes even the will to farm effectively. "In preventing Indians from determining their own course of action and making investments required to mechanize and expand their agricultural operations, the federal government effectively ensured that Indian farmers would be denied entry into the mainstream of the agricultural economy."[71]

When Wilfrid Laurier's Liberals came to power in Ottawa in 1896, they dismissed Reed as Tory appointed. They also slashed all spending on Indian Affairs, cutting personnel and salaries. Formally the ban on machinery was dropped, but not in practice. The Red Pheasant band's request to buy a traction-plowing outfit was rejected in 1902 on the grounds that if it were allowed to make such a purchase, other bands would want to do the same.[72] The new government's main priority in Indian Affairs turned out to be consistent with part of Reed's program: the reduction of reserve size to open more land for whites. At first there was some balancing concern for native welfare as David Laird, one of the department's top civil servants, and Minister of the Interior Clifford Sifton occasionally opposed specific surrenders on the grounds that the Crown as trustee had an obligation to ensure bands retained sufficient resources at least nominally to support themselves. However, Sifton's replacement, Frank Oliver of Edmonton, had no such scruples. His 1906 amendment to the Indian Act provided that 50 per cent (not just 10 per cent) of the surrender purchase price paid for the land could be distributed in cash.[73] That gave individual Indian agents a powerful weapon to persuade bands to agree to land surrenders, trading away their own long-term interests to meet immediate necessities.

This trend culminated during the First World War when a succession of acts allowed federal officials to appropriate reserve lands without the band's consent. The most bizarre of these was the appropriation of native lands for the Soldier Settlement Board – native veterans were not eligible for such lands as returned soldiers. Instead, the government directed that they could be granted a location ticket to exclusive rights over part of the remaining reserve lands (once again, without the band's consent).[74]

A specific example of one such coerced land sale is the 1909 surrender of the The Key reserve. The Crown took 11,500 of its 24,320 acres, for a price fixed at $100 per person on the reserve. With a population of 87, that meant natives had received less than a dollar per acre. None of the land would have sold for less than $3 per acre on the open market. Whether an agent made personal speculative gains or not, native peoples were deprived of their essential land base for a fraction of its true market value. "This surrender appeared to be a defeat for the people in their constant battle against government pressure on their right to the land they had been granted."[75]

In the era after Reed's dismissal, a handful of more entrepreneurial Indian agents sought to create success stories of Indians adapting to agriculture that might advance their individual careers. This was usually done by recruiting a small number of "suitable individuals" (often industrial school graduates) and concentrating the reserve's resources in a white-controlled enterprise. Under Treaty 4 William Morris Graham (File Hills agent since 1897) founded the File Hills Colony in 1901 to be "a showcase of Indian farming." It was manned by graduates of residential and industrial schools, who were kept under rigid discipline (for example, native languages were forbidden). These individuals received four-year loans as well as use of modern farm machinery held in common by the colony (such as two steam-powered threshing outfits). By 1914 the colony had 2,000 acres of wheat and oats. Graham's showpiece earned him promotion, first to inspector, then commissioner for the Prairie provinces.

Under Treaty 7, there was the similar example of W.A. Markle. Appointed Indian agent in 1901, he ended the issue of rations and persuaded the bands to sell substantial amounts of reserve land to raise a fund of capital. The fund was wholly under Markle's control: he decided which individuals would get which land and loans as well as what cattle and heavy machinery would be purchased. "Four paid [white] instructors made all the decisions on planting and harvesting, supervised the operations, and did the bookkeeping. In the fall, the big machines moved through, taking off the crops on all the farmers' plots; the cattle were removed to the hands of a [white] professional stockman."[76] White control was not intended to teach the Blackfoot how to farm efficiently on a large scale (despite the managers being called "instructors"). "It was simply a farm operation, run by white men, which took care of most of the work on individual plots and kept the [native] farmers from learning anything about machinery, costs, profits, productivity."[77] Thirty years later the Blackfoot were still "seeding plots of forty acres, although white farmers in the district needed 640 acres to make money ... Farmers were given the seed grain and paid a wage by the Department to plough and sow."[78] The agent-controlled trust fund was paying out rations (which had been re-introduced for some). It also paid for reserve housing, medical care, and aid to the elderly, which on other Western reserves came out of public funds. As Reed's career had indicated, a successful policy was viewed as one that reduced costs to the federal government.

Beyond these two well-known examples, there were numerous cases of partial applications of these models. Many agents, for example, argued that bands should approve land surrenders to create trust funds, which could finance successful agriculture or more services on the reserve. The integrity of this argument was undermined by the 1906 amendment allowing half the proceeds to be distributed immediately as cash. It was completely overturned in 1915 by a departmental ruling that the cost of farming operations could not be charged to the funds' interest accounts. "This statement must have come as a cruel surprise to Indians in favour of surrender, who had been promised the means to establish themselves in farming. The reasoning of the department was that interest funds were the property of the band as a whole; they could not be used for the advantage of those who farmed because the grain raised was not the property of the whole band."[79] Agents used their control over band assets to favour those who supported government policy, always referred to as the more progressive Indians.

While her research was based largely on the bands under Treaty 2 and Treaty 4, Sarah Carter's conclusion appears to be substantially confirmed by available evidence for bands under other Prairie treaties, such as that of Brian Titley for Treaty 6 and Helen Buckley for Treaty 7.[80] "Indian farmers, who had lost the opportunity to participate in commercial agriculture in the 1890s by not being allowed to raise and dispose of a surplus and invest in higher yielding methods of production, did not regain any ground in the early years of the twentieth century. They fell further behind and became increasingly isolated. They fell behind in technology as well as training."[81]

For much of the Prairies, peasant farming alone could not provide a viable subsistence. The low rainfall and the consequent lack of fertility of much of the soil in the southern short-grass prairie meant that low yields of even root crops would not provide enough to support a family working with only hand tools. Perhaps the ultimate *reductio ad absurdum* was Reed's insistence that natives grind their grain with hand mills. Department officials discovered that such mills were so antiquated that no one any longer produced them.

The native peoples were the first to explore what sort of agriculture could be sustained on the Prairies. The first model included agriculture as part of multi-source subsistence strategy that combined gathering wild rice, planting corn and potatoes in select micro-zones, hunting, and fishing. It ensured the extended family's survival by a balance of sources instead of reliance upon only one.

The second model came with the treaty system, which increasingly restricted movement over time, leading to a sedentary agriculture as the family's predominant food source. Natives were the first, large-scale – if involuntary – group of farmers to test eastern farming methods on the prairie grasslands, as distinct from the river bottoms of the Red and Assiniboine. They followed the mixed farming model of central Canada, raising livestock as well as potatoes, oats, and wheat. Like those from Ontario staffing the home farms, they discovered early on that the wooden plow with an iron share could not cut prairie sod, that the short growing season changed the timing of plowing and seeding, and that harvest had to be done as quickly as possible. Natives had to learn the additional lesson that they must overcome these problems themselves: Ottawa's aid would come too late or not at all. They sought to acquire by their own means the equipment needed to till prairie soils and make the transition to a more commercially oriented farming.

Just when many bands and individual farmers had made the successful adaptations and acquired the necessary machinery, there came the third model. Indian Commissioner Hayter Reed imposed a rigid peasant farming policy that destroyed an autonomous reserve agriculture, ensuring that natives would be dependent on the federal government. A few years later, European settlers with generations of peasant ancestors would choose the parklands for their subsistence potential. They could sustain themselves at least for a period – native peoples had neither their choices nor their cultural resources for any "retreat" into peasant subsistence.

While the Liberals formally rejected that peasant policy after 1896, they continued one of its most invidious aspects: the ongoing reduction of reserve size – to open more land for white settlers. The impoverished state of most reserves after 1920 fed Reed's racial characterization of a primitive people who failed to adapt to agriculture. Next we turn to the federal government's uses of these lands after having extinguished all indigenous land title, at least to its own satisfaction.

9

Prairie Agriculture's Historiographic Debates

Over the past forty years, five interrelated debates have dominated the historiography of Prairie farming. Why did the completion of the CPR in 1885 not bring a rush of settlement into the region? If it was held up by the need to develop new tillage techniques as well as new types of farm machinery, did the cost of that new farm machinery cancel the promise of free homesteads to everyone who wanted to start a farm? Did the extensive scale of farming required by that new machinery push some families onto land where traditional women's roles in eastern Canada as co-producers had to change? Certainly sons' traditional roles had to change when there was no hardwood forest to clear. In the southern Alberta foothills the mild winters held out the promise of ranching on a scale never before seen in Canada. But that ranching frontier fell before the insatiable demand for yet more homestead land. However, that opening of the driest part of the Palliser Triangle showed the limitations of the new tillage techniques and farm implements, since the "dryland disaster" saw most homesteaders leave within two decades of settling. Later decades witnessed an adaptation of both small ranches and mixed farming that could be sustained in that arid region.

Farm families came to the Prairies for land. But the promise of a free homestead could only be kept if, when, and where a series of challenges could be overcome. It could be realized if the family had working capital and a willingness to work, when they arrived early enough to choose their lands, and where they avoided the short-grass prairie. Where the Interior Plains of North America crossed the Alberta Plateau, the farm frontier ran out in the 1920s. That was due not primarily to the lack of land, but ultimately to the rising costs of farm machinery and the instability of farm incomes.

WHY THE DECADE OF DELAY?

What could be commercially produced on the Prairies? As settlers approached the new region with an eye to its agricultural potential, they initially saw it in three zones: the fertile belt, the Palliser Triangle, and the southwestern foothills. In the first and later the second they saw the renewed promise of an old staple – wheat.

Until the 1970s Canadian historians and economic historians broadly agreed on the reasons for the slow pace of Prairie settlement after the completion of the CPR. In the conventional view, it took a conjunction of favourable circumstances in the 1890s to finally bring the rush of settlers at the end of the century, easing the long recession from the 1870s to the late 1890s. A renewal of international trade was reflected in rising wheat prices and a renewal of international migration flows. These factors, combined with a number of technical breakthroughs, led to falling transportation costs (on both railways and the ocean), advancements in milling technology for hard spring wheat, and numerous improvements in wheat production ranging from new, more labour-efficient machinery to earlier-maturing wheat varieties. The specifically North American causes cited for the end of the delay included the increased activity of the federal government in promoting immigration and, above all, the end of the American western frontier.[1] However, few of these explanations have survived critical scrutiny in the last forty years.

Economic historian Kenneth Norrie was the leading figure in overturning the conventional view. His work has been the focus of extended debates amongst both economic historians and historians. Perhaps the dearest cause to the heart of "economic man" has been the market price of wheat, read as a signal to market-oriented farmers that economic opportunity beckoned. However, Norrie pointed out several problems in trying to connect the rate of settlement to the movements of prices. First, if high wheat prices promoted settlement, then the high prices of the mid-1880s should have brought a rush of would-be homesteaders to the Prairies as soon as the CPR was completed. While wheat prices rose in the late 1890s, they were still well below the best prices of the 1880s. Second, the attempts – made several times, by several economic historians including Norrie – to link wheat price *increases* and the increased rate of homestead entries have not been convincing. While rising wheat prices may well have played a role in many families' decisions, no strong statistical relationship has been established between price rises and homestead entries. More broadly, Norrie concluded that labour and capital moved in response to perceptions of future economic opportunities rather than to present conditions.[2]

The various technical breakthroughs also seem out of step with the start of the wheat boom. The most important advance in milling, which greatly increased the demand for hard spring wheat, came around 1880, too long before the boom to be a proximate cause. Railway freight rates and shipping costs fell continuously from the 1870s through the 1890s. That continuous trend means that it does not explain the change: a constant cannot explain a change. The development of an earlier-maturing wheat came in 1909, after the wheat boom was well underway – too late to function as a cause. The succession of improvements in farm implements, especially those relating to planting and harvest, seems much more promising. However, Norrie's own view was that the machinery of greatest importance came after 1900, again too late to explain a change in the mid-1890s.

The influence of the federal government, both in encouraging immigration and in facilitating railway construction has fared somewhat better as an explanation for the boom. Several economic historians have seen some statistical evidence that the increase in government spending after 1896 is positively correlated to the rise in homestead entries. However, they themselves note that not just the amount of money spent but how it was deployed may have been the decisive element (not reducible to quantity of money spent). Land grants and cash subsidies from the federal and Manitoba governments could have helped induce railway companies to build more track, especially the branch lines that often opened more land for settlement than the main lines that crossed long stretches of territory not seen as potential farmland. However, it is extremely difficult to isolate the effect of such subsidies relative to the railway companies' own assessments of the future rate of growth in the farming population.[3]

Norrie brought the greatest clarity to the issue of the American frontier's impact on the timing of settlement in the Canadian Prairies. The announcement by the 1890 director of the US census of the "closing" of the American frontier was long taken as a fact by many Canadian scholars. It seemed logical, then, that once the American frontier had been filled, settlers would begin to stream into the Canadian "last best West." However, a number of historians and economic historians noted that tens of thousands continued to take out homesteads in the United States after 1890. In fact, more land was entered under the American Homestead Act after 1890 than before. Given that large-scale settlement continued and even accelerated in the United States from 1890 to 1914, it was not the "closing" of homestead opportunities there that turned the tide of settlement north.

Yet Norrie pointed out that a certain kind of "frontier" had indeed more or less ended in the United States by 1890. What the westward-moving frontier of settlement reached, and in some places breached, in the late 1880s was the broad transition zone from sub-humid to semi-arid lands that approximately extended from the 100th meridian to the 98th. East of that zone, where rainfall averaged above 20 inches a year, farmers had advanced from the Appalachians to the Mississippi and Missouri rivers using much the same succession of crops, implements, and farming methods. When they tried to move west of that zone into western Kansas, Nebraska, or the Dakota Territory, they could flourish in a series of years with above-average rainfall. But once the inevitable dry cycle came, their crops failed and many lost their homesteads or farms. What had passed in 1890 was the frontier of sub-humid lands. For the frontier to continue its advance, farmers would have to find ways of adapting to a drier, more variable climate.

Norrie concluded that the American frontier continued to advance after 1890 because American farmers developed dry-farming techniques that enabled them to survive the periodic cycles of drought. He argues that the changed nature of the American frontier from sub-humid to semi-arid – not its "closing" – had the effect of increasing the rate of settlement on the Canadian Prairies. As long as there were sub-humid lands open for homestead or sale in the United States, most farmers went there because they could continue the agriculture that they knew. West of the Red River, Canada had little land to offer as sub-humid: try as the expansionists did to create the impression, this was not so. Consequently most *Canadian* farm families who migrated west before 1890 went to the *American* frontier, not the Canadian Prairies. However, after 1890 the Canadian Prairies offered the same semi-arid lands as remained in the United States, and immigrants began to come in increasing numbers, even as larger numbers took up farms on the American semi-arid lands.

For Norrie, then, the keys to explain the timing of settlement on the Canadian Prairies were the end of the American sub-humid frontier and the development of dry-farming techniques to successfully till semi-arid lands on both the Canadian Prairies and the American high plains. Government aid may have fostered this growth rate by its advertising and promotion of railway construction, especially branch lines.

With a few honourable exceptions, most historians and economic historians have believed that those dry-farming techniques developed first on the American western frontier and then spread to western Canada, either by example or in the large wave of American settlers who entered Canada after 1895.[4] However, most of the American adaptations were either irrelevant to the Canadian prairies (e.g., switching from corn and hogs to wheat and cattle) or impractical in the Canadian climate (e.g., winter wheat, sorghum). The essential technique north of the forty-ninth parallel was summer fallow, which was developed and popularized through the network of federal experimental farms, especially by Angus MacKay at the Indian Head Farm. To conserve moisture in the soil, Mackay urged farmers on the short-grass prairie to plant only half of their cultivated land each year. Crops grown on fallowed land not only produced more in good years but also gave some crop even in dry years.

While many Canadian scholars have pointed to the American H.W. Campbell as the leading exponent of summer fallow, in fact he only included it in his "system" in 1902, a decade after MacKay had begun promoting it. Moreover, Campbell dropped it in 1907. However, the extreme claims by Campbell (and others like him) have been fathered onto Mackay. According to David C. Jones, MacKay believed that his technique "virtually guaranteed agricultural production on the arid plains."[5] MacKay's own 1890 report was much more guarded: "The Experimental Farm suffered in company with every other farm in the country ... but dry weather, though reducing the yields, was not so disastrous as to many."[6] In sharp contrast, Campbell declared, "the more arid sections could be made to produce not only two and three times as much fodder and grain as had been heretofore produced in good years, but that good yields could be made certain in dry seasons."[7] The American agricultural historian Mary Hargreaves, noted that only after the First World War did farmers in Montana and western North Dakota begin to summer fallow extensively, following the example of their Canadian neighbours (and even using specific Canadian techniques and equipment).[8] The influence of the extreme dry-farming advocates becomes more critical when we turn to consider the decision to settle the Palliser Triangle.

As MacKay and others were popularizing summer fallow through the mid-1890s, new machinery became available north and south of the border to address another major problem of farmers on the short-grass prairie: low soil fertility in a region with a short growing season. The economic historian Anthony Ward focused his attention on the gradual technological changes that increased labour productivity in grain farming on the Prairies. These changes were gradual in several senses. The inventions took time to become part of the farm practices of working farmers. Invention of the seed drill preceded its commercial production and distribution by several decades. Farmers used a wide range of machinery, which meant that the innovations occurred at different times with different pieces of equipment. Changes in plowing technology and technique could proceed at quite a different pace than harvesting technology and technique, even though the two were sequentially related: you can only harvest where you have plowed. The innovations themselves were usually a succession of gradual changes in a basic machinery type. For example, the self-reaping binder first just dropped cut grain that stookers had to bind with straw before they could form the stook (or stack). Then binders appeared that held the bundles together with wire, only to be replaced by ones that used twine, which was both cheaper and safer for the stookers. At almost every step, however, the common gain of every technical change was a reduction in the amount of labour needed to perform the task.[9]

Ward considered that the short Prairie growing season initially restricted the labour-constrained farmer from cultivating enough land to be profitable. A broad series of technical changes enabled homesteaders to farm much more extensively, generating the greater profits needed to attract settlers to the Prairies. Of the many changes, the key developments came in planting and harvesting, the speed with which each could be done setting the extensive margin of cultivation. Fall plowing served to prepare the soil for as early a spring planting as possible. But the sulky gang plow, with its double shares, introduced in the mid-1890s, enabled the farmer to plow more than twice the acres in a day, halving the time needed for the unavoidable spring plowing. In the early 1890s the Brandon Experimental Farm tested and publicized several types of seed drills, the most effective being the press seed drill. Any effective drill not only put seed into the ground in a more systematic way than broadcasting the seed by hand but also gave it better protection from birds and wind, as well as increased the pace of germination. The common seed drill shortened the period for the grain growing to maturity by 3.8 days; the press seed drill, by 4.8 days. With a short growing season, even such marginal improvements were critical to farm productivity.

Moreover, what was planted had to be harvested promptly. The self-rake reaper of 1880 cut grain quickly but left it to be gathered and bound by hand. Five men could harvest about 10 acres in a day, so it took 0.5 day per acre per man. The twine binder became available in Western Canada from 1884 on. As the machinery was steadily improved (for example, dropping sheaves in groups) and the width of the cut broadened (from 6 to 10 feet), it reduced the labour time of reaping from 0.1 day per acre in 1884 to 0.067 day by 1900 and 0.057 day by 1910. However, the increased amount of grain cut and bound still had to be stooked by hand.

The high moisture content of wheat meant that stooks could only be temporary. The grain had to be threshed before the first hard frost, or wheat especially would lose much of its commercial value. This need was met by a combination of innovations both technological and organizational. Steam-powered threshing machines rapidly replaced horse-powered ones (steam powered 65 per cent of threshing outfits on the Prairies as early as 1899). In the 1880s the output per day of steam threshing outfits was around 600 bushels per day with a crew of fourteen. By 1910 the output had more than doubled to 1,500 bushels per day while the number of men needed to service the machine had declined to five. Moreover, these newer steam threshers were also "traction engines," moving themselves from farm to farm (often creating havoc on rural roads and bridges). Their somewhat problematic mobility led to the organizational innovation of travelling custom thresher outfits.

Threshing crews represented a combination of temporary labour with increasingly efficient technology, from horse to steam to gasoline. Meanwhile, the vital task of stooking remained an almost purely labour matter. The binder might tie the sheaves and even drop them in convenient groups, but there was no mechanical substitute before the end of the First World War for the back-breaking human task of stooking. As the custom threshing crew provided an earlier and more productive threshing of the grain, harvest excursion trains began to bring thousands of men to the Prairies from eastern Canada and eventually even from Britain for the harvest in an attempt to alleviate the most pressing of all the critical labour shortages in western farming.

In assessing the role of harvest labour after 1890, Ward took the numbers reported taking the CPR harvest excursion trains and divided that into the total of all farms in Manitoba and the Territories.[10] While dividing the number of farms by the harvest labour pool may make sense as a model-building statistical procedure, it is unlikely to reflect the actual use of such labour in practice. Ward's averaging method seems to imply that he saw each excursion labourer working on a single farm in a given year rather than on a succession of farms. Certainly it was the interest of the excursionist to do harvest work for as long as he possibly could, since these were generally the highest wages an unskilled worker could get in the course of a year. Some excursionists tried to extend their high-paying stay in the West by moving on to a threshing crew once all the paid harvest labour had been completed.

Ward identifies the self-binding reaper (universally called the "binder") as the great breakthrough in more labour-efficient harvest machinery, enabling the farmer to cut as much as 75 or 80 acres in a day. However, it required three or four stookers to follow it.[11] The statistical procedure that would most closely represent the actual use of harvest labour could not be the arithmetic mean but the mode – just as mode for landholding was 160 acres for each homesteader, not an arithmetic mean of all farmers divided by all occupied land.

Districts without rail service were unlikely to see any harvest excursion labour. John Herd Thompson made this point in noting that the more northerly farms received little excursion labour until the local rail network became denser after the First World War.[12] The CPR excursion trains were not the only way in which harvest labour came into the Prairie West, but they were probably the largest and are certainly the best documented. Those that began in Eastern Canada usually paid less than half the regular fare to the West, which rose over time from $10 in the 1890s to $15 in the 1920s. In the first decade, that fare took the labourer initially to Winnipeg. In 1901 the CPR began "re-ticketing" men further west, as local agents for communities west of Manitoba sought to attract labour to their locale. Until 1912 men could re-ticket to a given cut-off point as far west as Moose Jaw without extra charge. That year the CPR introduced a policy of selling the excursionists a second ticket, at half a cent per mile, to an ultimate destination beyond Winnipeg (as far as Edmonton, Calgary, or Macleod). The extra charge obviously discriminated against places further west. The excursionist of small means had to weigh the extra ticket's cost against the likelihood that wages would be higher at a more westerly destination such as Alberta.[13]

The CPR required the excursionist to have his employers sign his ticket stub to show that he had worked at least 30 days on farms. The reduced return fares were good until 30 November. However, since wages on threshing crews were close to the high level of harvest wages, many men sought to stay on in the West. "Custom threshers with large outfits handled much of the crop in the West, and it was difficult for a harvest excursionist to find a job on a threshing crew. ... Sometimes a transient could catch on, if he had some skill with horses, driving a bundle team loaded with sheaves to the separator or a loaded grain wagon to the farmer's granary or the elevator. Men without experience looked for work as 'field pitchers,' helping drivers fork sheaves from stooks to bundle wagons."[14]

Ernest Ingles noted that the rapid increase in the number of farms on the Prairies in the late 1890s paralleled the expansion in the number of custom thresher outfits. In 1899 there were 402 such outfits on the Prairies, or one for every twenty farms. Within two years the number nearly doubled to 760, but the ratio fell to one for every thirty farms. The need was so great in 1902 that the CPR, partially at the urging of Winnipeg businessmen, offered cheap rates of one cent per mile to threshing outfits (with a limit of six on the crew) to enable them to serve as many farms as possible. By 1908 Saskatchewan had 3,468 outfits (for a ratio to farms of 1:19), Manitoba had 2,287 (for a ratio of 1:20), and Alberta had 890 (for a ratio of 1:34).[15] However, 1908 was a year when the enormous increase in excursionists – from previous highs of around 6,000 to 27,500 – and the very bad publicity they attracted (mobs stealing liquor in towns en route) made it highly unlikely that any significant proportion were taken on as part of threshing crews that fall.[16]

Another important differential in the deployment of harvest excursion labour was the nature of the farms themselves. Those established in the park belt were sometimes largely subsistence oriented for several years. Many newly settled families, especially amongst the Eastern European settlers, farmed for subsistence, growing oats as their grain crop, and relied solely on family labour for harvest.[17] Consequently, these farmers were much less likely to be able to afford harvest labour. Indeed, to meet the unavoidable cash demands that the production of their farms was unable to cover, they were more likely to turn themselves into harvest labour, to make the highest wages offered in a given year. By contrast, the commercially oriented farmers were both more ready to hire extra harvest labour and more likely to be located where such labour would be available, within hauling distance of a railway.

The concentration of available excursion labour on the most commercially oriented of farms would have meant that their harvest operations used the new technology in the most efficient way. Thus the key element of additional labour at harvest would have served to make those commercial farms the most productive in the region. By attracting much of the excursion labour, commercial farmers were not only able to make the most of their labour-efficient machinery but also their successes had a demonstration effect on other farmers, encouraging them to increasingly focus their efforts on becoming commercial grain farmers as well.

As the balance of linkages between the Quebec and Ontario economies shifted, the linkages between the Prairies and central Canada evolved over time. In spite of Mackenzie and Mann's Canadian Northern and several early small banks, the major railways and banks operating in western Canada had their head offices in central Canada. Winnipeg strove to become the West's own metropolis, initially by capturing privileged wholesale freight rates from the CPR. In the Winnipeg Grain Exchange, the city sought a major share in the profits of the region's staple. The Exchange had to fight off challenges from the Grain Growers Grain Company and then the wheat pools. The federal government's entry into the marketing of Canadian wheat in 1930, which led to the creation of the Canadian Wheat Board in 1935, substantially undermined its position.

The need to demonstrate the feasibility of profitable farming caused the decade of delay. The short growing season, thin soil, and low rainfall required both newly adapted farm implements and dry-farm techniques – above all, summer fallow – to conserve moisture. The drill press seeder in the spring and the self-tying binder in the fall enabled the farmer to cultivate extensively enough to overcome the problem of low yields. Assisted by a rising trend in international wheat prices, persevering homesteaders by the 1890s showed that commercial farming on the Prairies could succeed.

DID THE COST OF STARTING A FARM CANCEL THE PROMISE OF A FREE HOMESTEAD?

How much capital did a farmer need to start a homestead? That apparently simple question can be and has been answered in many ways, as much because of the intellectual orientation of the scholars who pose the question as by the time and place to which any given answer pertains. Economic historians, focused on economic man, have been concerned to count all costs (including implicit opportunity costs) to set up a commercial unit of production. Many historians, by contrast, have been concerned primarily with the out-of-pocket costs of establishing a farm that could support the family directly through production of subsistence, indirectly by the production of a cash crop, or by some combination of both on-farm subsistence and off-farm sales or labour. Most of the work on estimating farm-making costs has focused on the capital requirements to establish a commercial farm either immediately or in the near future. However, on the Canadian Prairies, at least in the parkland fertile belt, many families initially arrived seeking land primarily for subsistence. Consequently, a farm family's capital needs varied according to the type of farm they initially intended to establish.

Taking the long view of agriculture in North American history, Wayne Rasmussen argued that there have been two agricultural revolutions. The first was marked by the application of animal power in place of human labour on the farm. Seeding by hand, harvesting by scythe and cradle or sickle, and threshing with flails were replaced by horse-drawn seed drills, reapers then binders, and horse-powered threshing machines. Only the very poorest of the Prairie crofter and peasant settlers had come from farming with hand tools and almost all aspired to move beyond that stage.[18] The capital cost of going from farming with hand tools to farming with horse-drawn machinery was considerable.[19] The grain cradler of the 1850s and 1860s cost about $4–$5, while the self-binding reaper of the 1880s cost around $290.[20] The second revolution replaced horse-power with new power sources, such as steam and then the internal combustion engine. Just as the first revolution made the farm more dependent on external markets to purchase expensive capital items and finance those by regular sale of a substantial cash crop, the second made farms more dependent on external energy sources as wood or coal, diesel or gasoline replaced oats.[21] In the American West relatively few settlers began their farms prior to the first revolution. Canada's broader ethnic mix and the potential of the parklands to be farmed for subsistence made both revolutions relevant for the history of farming on the Prairies.

The fact that few settlers in the American West began their farms prior to the first revolution crippled the American version of the "homestead promise." It was rooted in a particular reading of the frontier thesis, according to which the open western frontier provided an outlet for eastern working-class families. The possibility of this escape from wage labour was supposed to keep wages in the eastern states higher than in Europe and class tensions low, since everyone could see themselves as eventual landowners. As early as 1941, Clarence Danhof questioned this safety valve thesis on empirical grounds: the sums required for farming were beyond the resources of the eastern working class. He found a range of costs for farm-making in the 1850s, from a low of $705 in Minnesota to a range of $850–$2,650 in Iowa, to $2,475 in Michigan, to a range of $2,100–$2,750 in Illinois.[22] In most cases the basic barrier was the price of land. Although public lands were supposed to be

open for auction or pre-emption at $1.25 an acre, these lands were often
not available in any feasible way. Danhof concluded that the total sum
needed ranged from $537 to $2,350. Apart from purchasing the land
(a very significant condition on the eve of the Homestead Act), someone with less than $1,000 might have started a farm on the prairies of
Minnesota or Texas. Danhof conceded that time could substitute for
capital, but he hedged this concession with several significant qualifications. "The farm-maker's wealth could not fall much short of $1,000; to
the degree that it did, the farm-maker was inevitably forced to undertake
farm-making in some round-about fashion, perhaps working part of his
time for wages."[23] While Danhof clearly intended to put the stress on the
greater risks and discomforts of the undercapitalized pioneer, his qualifications indicate an awareness that not everyone proceeded directly to
commercial operation.

Forty years later, Jeremy Atack reviewed the extended debates (including Robert Ankli's work) over farm-making costs and offered his own
empirical evidence from the 1860 census. To a remarkable extent he confirmed Danhof's earlier work. Atack asked "how much capital, on average, a farmer actually had invested in Midwestern farms of specific sizes
in 1859."[24] For 160-acre farms, he found that the aggregate value of all
implements by state ranged from a low of $46 in Minnesota to a high of
$182 in Illinois. However, for the frontier settlements only, he found an
average of $52, with an average livestock value of $303. The latter figure
fell remarkably on the high side within the $156–$508 range of state-
wide averages.[25] Like Danhof, he stressed that these sums meant that
western farms were an unlikely prospect for the eastern working class.
"Even the $1,000 or so necessary for entry-level farming on a 40 acre
plot in the west would place the household in the upper 60 percent of all
households in the wealth distribution and 20 percent of all households
could not even have raised the $400–$500 for a 40 acre farm in Kansas
or Minnesota."[26] Atack's conclusion repeats Danhof's "concession" that
time could substitute for capital.

Like Atack, Lyle Dick, in his estimates of farm-making costs in Saskatchewan for 1882–1914, reviewed the previous literature, especially
the work of Ankli, and then offered his own empirical evidence. However, more than most involved in this discussion, Dick stressed that the
sum required depended on a multiplicity of variables. He pointed to
the settlers' cultural backgrounds, family size, topography, presence of
neighbours, and type of farming practised. He contrasted the experience
of Anglo-Saxon migrants from Ontario who settled around Abernathy,

Saskatchewan, in the 1890s to that of their German counterparts in nearby Neudorf who arrived after 1901. He concluded that the latter started with considerably less capital than the former and often much less than Ankli had assumed necessary. The German settlers gave their housing, in particular, very low values: 46 per cent valued their houses at $100 or less (17 per cent at $50 or less). Dick costed the implements and livestock necessary for a commercial farm: breaking and walking plows, iron harrows, drill seeder, mower, binder, horse rake, sleigh runners; draft horses (where he found Ankli low) or oxen. A team of draft horses would have cost between $150 and $300, versus Ankli's $75 to $100, which reflected the average value of *all* horses rather than *draft* horses. The total for implements also reflected price changes over time, from 1884 to 1914. While some prices rose in that period, others declined significantly: binders from $290 to $150 and mowers from $80 to $52 (*lower* prices for *more* productive machines, it should be noted). Overall, Dick concluded that implement costs probably fell from around $500 in 1884 to $324 by 1915.[27] However, he does not address the replacement of walking plows with the more productive sulky gang plows in the 1890s, or the emergence of steam-powered threshing machines.

Dick offered profiles of three sorts of settlers in terms of their available capital. Those with minimum capital could have begun with between $291 and $562, relying on the cheaper oxen for draft animals and keeping farm implements to an absolute minimum. The average homesteader with capital ranging from $590 to $1,193 would also begin with oxen, but have both mower and rake. The substantial settler would be able to begin commercial production, with capital of between $2,093 and $5,873, which would include not only the full complement of farm machinery but also two teams of horses and six cattle.[28] In contrast to previous writers, Dick believed that there was "a degree of economic democracy" on the Canadian Prairies before the First World War: "A hired man usually earned enough to start farming on free grant land with a year's accumulated wages."[29] However he stressed that it was important to arrive *early* in order to have the chance to get the best land and that the poorest settlers were also the most vulnerable to economic misfortune. The latter stipulation seems somewhat out of place. His examples are of physical barriers (such as an inability to find water or buildings burning down) rather than specifically *economic* misfortune such as a collapse in prices. In fact, the more subsistence-oriented farmer might be less dependent on the market for survival than his commercially oriented counterpart.

Irene Spry's critique of Dick contrasts their respective academic disciplines more than historical reality. She insists on the economic historian's questions about all costs (including opportunity costs) and only the costs of establishing a unit of production, the farm as a business enterprise, not including the family's subsistence. However, she implicitly accepted Dick's contrast of cultural backgrounds. She pointed out that the cost of learning how to farm on the Prairies would have been lower for settlers from the European steppes or the American Great Plains than for those from farms in eastern Canada, to say nothing of urbanites who hoped to become homesteaders. She also embraced the consideration that farmers of minimal capital could gradually work their way up to commercial production over time.[30] Thus there emerges the realization that start-up costs varied greatly depending on what was being started.

Many families came to the Prairies and chose to settle in the parklands because their intention, at least initially, was to build a farm primarily to provide directly for the family's subsistence. At the very beginning, some of the family members commonly worked off the farm to earn subsistence for the others, who remained on the farm building dwellings, breaking land, and putting in crops. The mix of crops and the livestock acquired provided for feeding and clothing the family. In time, cash crops came to supplement off-farm work to provide for the essential cash outlays. Undercapitalized and on the more northerly edge of the arable Prairies, these families may often have chosen oats rather than wheat as their cash crop. Oats matured earlier than wheat, which better protected it from early frosts and also left family members available to earn high harvest wages on commercial wheat farms in their neighbourhood or the region. The exceptionally high wheat yields and prices of 1915–16 may have encouraged such families to switch to wheat once the earlier-maturing Marquis had proven itself. John Herd Thompson's general argument about the war's impact on Prairie farming may have particular salience for the initially undercapitalized, subsistence farmers of the northern parklands.[31]

The acceleration of the second revolution, which was underway by the 1920s, saw tractors and trucks largely replace horses. That meant that power-driven implements replaced the earlier horse-drawn ones. While this machinery greatly increased the scale on which a grain farm could operate, its costs compelled the farm to operate on a much larger scale to pay for it and the fuels needed for tractors and trucks. As the costs and scale of Prairie farming rose after the First World War, so did the barriers to prospective homesteaders.

PRAIRIE FARM FAMILIES: WIVES, DAUGHTERS, AND SONS

In Quebec and Ontario over the generations, farm families had balanced male and female spheres of production. Would it be possible for women to maintain their traditional role of domestic production in the West's harsh environment of short summers, thin soils, and low rainfall? Depending on where on the Prairies a family settled, the farm wife's traditional role within the family could be either sustained or decisively undermined. By way of contrast, the wife's legal standing began with the loss of customary dower rights. Women's groups, mobilized to restore dower, campaigned for other rights as well, but with only limited success.

Moreover, an essential element of the family farm in the East had been to establish a new generation on farms of their own. But when free land could be had by all, would it be necessary to devote family resources to provide for the next generation? The traditional role of sons in increasing the farm's productive capacity changed on Prairie farms. Whether sons could overcome the effects of that loss of role in the farm family depended on when they came of age on the Prairies, since the available homestead land diminished over time.

The writing of women's history has undergone continuous development over the last forty years. The early feminist historians of the 1970s wrote women's history implicitly regarding gender as the primary source of personal identity and the source of social organization. However, by the 1990s, under the pressure of both Marxist and postmodern critics, many of them felt they had to concede both the existence of many possible sources of identity – such as class, race, ethnicity, and language – and a great variety of women's individual experiences. In some cases these points were stressed to disrupt what was seen as a limiting stereotype, as in Sara Brooks Sundberg's attack of the "helpmate" image of pioneer women on homesteads.[32] Sundberg insisted on including in the historical record those women who sought to move West, rather than being taken unwillingly. Some even initiated the move, usually for the perceived benefits for their children. Single women went West with the same spirit of adventure as did young men.

Against that interest in diversity, Kathryn McPherson sought to stress what was common rather than individual in women's experiences. "There is no doubt that luck, personality, and perhaps the serendipity of the documentary record are important elements of explaining women's divergent reactions to agricultural settlement, but recognizing diversity need not preclude analyses of the structures that defined difference."[33]

As well as those structures, Elaine Silverman offered another basis for making valid generalizations about the experiences of women. Silverman pointed out common elements that ran through the diversity of the reflections of some 150 women she had interviewed: "Their stories, as they came together, became not just a random collection of stories, but a collective autobiography."[34] She sought to shape her book as "a collective autobiography about migration and adaptation [in which] ... the voices diverge and recombine to weave subtle patterns."[35] Even in a postmodern world, we can hope to focus on those structures that defined differences for women, as well as the common elements in the life cycles of the women who came to create new homes and families in the West.

As settlement on the Canadian Prairies accelerated at the beginning of the twentieth century, the women who arrived encountered two contrasting images of the farm wife: co-producer and lady of leisured culture. Each was a broad category encompassing variations and each underwent development over time. The farm wife as co-producer was grounded in many generations across Europe when women had worked alongside men in producing from the soil what their families needed to survive. By the eighteenth century in western Europe, complementary roles had emerged for the farmer and his older sons on the one hand, and the farm wife, her daughters, and younger children on the other. The men did the fieldwork and "heavy" work around the farmyard and cared for certain types of livestock such as draft animals. The women and younger children did the work of household maintenance and providing household sustenance (producing and preserving food from the garden, henhouse, orchard, dairy, sheep pen, and pigsty), and, on specific occasions such as planting and harvest, working in the fields. While there was no suggestion of equality between men and women or between their respective roles, each laboured as co-producers to sustain their family.

Transplanted to the Prairies, the co-producer role was read in diverse ways. In the literature of the pioneers and their descendants, the image recurs of the heroic pioneer on the homestead overcoming incredible hardships to provide the essentials for her family. Often the accounts feature women acting beyond the conventional role, extending their co-production into what was regarded as men's sphere.[36] One homesteader's wife, in her husband's absence during the summer to earn wages for the provision of subsistence, hauled the lumber herself (without a draft animal) for miles to build the family a house for the winter rather than spend it in a dugout.[37] The accumulation of such stories has confirmed to some modern observers the view of a number of pioneer women's contemporaries, that the female homesteader was a drudge worn down by a life of unspeakable hardships. Some of that contemporary comment came out of class and ethnic differences – upper-class British travellers remarking on the quaint (or appalling customs) of Scottish crofters or the new "foreign" settlers.[38] However, many of the same remarks were made by Canadian or American commentators on the lives of pioneer homesteaders of their own ethnic background. Yet both images, whether of heroic martyr or drudge, arose from the same role as co-producer on the family farm.

The newer image is often associated with the Victorian era: the middle-class lady of leisure and culture, her contribution to the household a domesticity most frequently associated with flower gardens (in contrast to vegetable gardens, which included an acre of potatoes to hoe, among other things). In Britain this image was associated with the attempt to spread gentility from the landed aristocracy to the rising urban middle class. Its rural counterpart was the advance of the more successful of the yeoman farmers into the ranks of the gentry. Mary Kinnear cites the following rhyme with its telling dates:[39]

1743	Man to the plough,	1843	Man tally ho,
	Girl to the cow,		Miss piano,
	Wife to her yarn,		Lady silk and satin,
	Boy to the barn,		Boy Greek and Latin,
	And the rent will be netted.		And you'll all be gazetted.

Some women's historians have seen the two roles as a sequence, dependent on a farm's growing prosperity: "Formerly, the spinning, weaving, sewing, soap- and candle-making, butchering, and baking by rural women had been essential for the sustenance of their families; their place in the economy was clear. As men turned from agriculture to industry ... some ... became wealthy enough to remove their wives from producing for the domestic family economy. Married to men who could afford wives who did not work for pay or who did not produce household necessities, middle-class women began to lose economic meaning."[40] Some rural women who moved to towns where their husbands took up urban jobs expressed regret at their loss of function even as their access to social amenities had greatly improved.

For those who remained on the farm, the emerging country life movement in the United States at the turn of the century sought to instill a more urban ethos in the rural population as part of its reform of agriculture and to inculcate more domestic values in American farm women by urging them to seek increased investment within their homes. The farm wife was to leave the drudgery of the farmyard to become the angel of domesticity in the house. The achievement of this goal presupposed a successful commercial farm that could not only dispense with her contribution to household subsistence but also provide for the investment of capital in such household improvements as running water, sewage disposal, and electricity to run a myriad of domestic appliances to lighten the load of housework. In the face of a dwindling pool of female rural labour to provide the servants of the Victorian middle-class household, this general trend in public policy – in concert with American advertisers – promoted appliances to greatly diminish the physical work inside the farmhouse. Instead of household help, the thoroughly modern rural housewife would have every modern convenience to take care of the arduous washing of clothes, cleaning of carpets and floors, and preparing of meals.[41]

The American Smith-Lever Act of 1914, as well as providing for county agents to advise farmers on the latest and best in farming methods, offered funds to hire female "home demonstration agents" who would give the farm wife good advice and examples on how to run her household more efficiently. Many farm women sought advice and other resources to expand or improve their production activities, as in the henhouse and dairy, only to learn that this was implicitly the field of men. Quite aside from the cultural conflict latent in young, unmarried university women with cars setting themselves up to offer advice to married farm women with heavy workloads and very little access to any capital, there was a fundamental conflict between the agents' assumption that farm women wanted to retreat from production and those women's determination to improve their families' livelihoods by becoming more efficient producers.

On the Prairies, the provincial universities established "extension divisions" to carry the message of modern housekeeping to women newly arrived on homesteads. "Foreign" women became the special objects of this attention. According to the Anglo-Protestant extension workers, part of the continental immigrants' acculturation to the new society would be learning to cook like Canadians, make clothes like those Canadians wore, and care for their children in an approved Canadian way. Similarly the "home mission" departments of several Protestant churches established schools and medical missions to serve as agents of assimilation in ethnic block settlements.

As part of a general revision of the school curriculum to make it more "practical," each of the Prairie provinces established home economics as a new subject. That few rural schools ever had the resources to offer the subject is of less significance here than the debates that the introduction of the course provoked. As in the United States, many farm women wanted help to expand their home production activities and make them more profitable, yet some educators felt the imperative to promote domesticity rather than domestic production.

What confronted the apostles of domesticity before the First World War was the great diversity of the farm wives' traditional roles, not only encompassing many activities but often carrying them out simultaneously. Women carried the responsibility not only for physical reproduction of the species but also for the reproduction of culture in the rising generation (raising children, sometimes directly providing their schooling) and the physical survival of the home's maintenance and sustenance. This involved cleaning the house (initially coping with earth floors, then wooden, finally linoleum), making and washing clothes, cooking meals, and preserving food. At harvest time and through threshing season, large crews of men – often strangers – had to be fed before the sun rose, during the day in the fields, and after the sun had set when their day's work ended. Reviewing the range of products and activities, it is not surprising to read "the maternal mortality research conducted by the federal government pointed to the collapse of families and of farm operations when the mother died."[42] The loss of the farm wife (through death or prolonged illness) was often the cause of farms failing, because the husband and children could not keep up and co-ordinate all the varied activities on whose results the farm family depended.

Farm women also carried on a wide range of domestic production. The great majority of farms had poultry and dairy cattle. From the henhouse came meat for the table and eggs. With Saskatchewan farms averaging around a hundred poultry, the work of feeding as well as gathering eggs constituted a major commitment of labour. Dairy cattle provided a wide range of products, most of which required some processing activity. Cheese production, at least according to the census, was much less common than cream and butter production, perhaps not surprising given the additional labour required. Most farms had gardens, although the census only imperfectly reflects their contribution; more telling than the values assigned to garden produce were those of the volumes of potatoes produced. About half of all farms kept pigs, often fed with by-products of the dairy and garden. Relatively few farms on the short-grass prairie kept sheep, their maintenance requiring more attention than chickens or pigs. Of those who had sheep, production of wool seems to have been the object in only about half the cases.

Much of this domestic production provided the family's subsistence. In contrast to the United States, Canadian Prairie farms retained a larger portion of subsistence production longer. In 1900 the United States Department of Agriculture estimated that farm families produced about 60 per cent of what they consumed. By 1921 that estimated proportion had fallen to 40 per cent. A 1930 federal study of Prairie farms estimated that farm families produced about 50 per cent of their own needs. As late as 1942 the noted western agricultural journalist Cora Hind held that farm families could supply all of their own necessities,[43] though such broad generalizations overlook important geographic variations within the region.

Some of women's production, however, could be sold, allowing the farm to diversify its earning potential. Given that in Saskatchewan, for example, about one in five farms had no poultry or dairy cattle, there would have been ready local markets for chickens, eggs, and dairy products. The federal government had initiated and subsidized the founding of more than a dozen creameries across the Territories at the turn of the century. After 1905 the new provincial governments continued to promote rural production of dairy products. The "cream cheque" became a small but steady income source for cash-strapped farm families. And while men seldom performed "women's work" in the household, women regularly contributed to field labour. The annual cycle of harvest and threshing drew extra labour from women in feeding substantial numbers of men from outside their own household. Often meals had to be provided in the fields during the day to ensure the most continuous application of labour to tasks that had to be done in a timely way. However, in the early pioneer phase and during recurring periods of economic depression when the farm could not afford to hire, women often did fieldwork themselves. That meant that women had to have the skills of field labour, such as stooking or driving a team of horses, a truck, or a tractor, as well as those of their own sphere.

Where and when on the Prairies a given farm was located had differentiating impacts on what was expected of farm women and what they were able to do. On the short-grass prairie, the rigours of the climate downgraded the domestic economy by severely limiting what could be produced. While the differences were ones of degree, the further south and west – the further into the inner Palliser Triangle – the more extreme the climate became. Long-term low rainfall meant that the soil was lacking in organic matter and greatly increased the effort needed to keep a garden from drying up. The low levels of garden produce, even potatoes, may have contributed to limits on the number of poultry, milk cattle, and pigs able to be kept on farms in southeastern Alberta and southwestern Saskatchewan. The weakness of the domestic economy put much greater demands on the market economy, which may explain why there was sometimes less summer fallow in the driest areas, where one might expect to find the most.

As on the short-grass prairie, so too in the parkland belt a variety of situations could be found. The southern edge of the belt featured localities where the two ecological zones mixed, allowing complementary farming operations to develop. On the northern edge of the park belt, the growing season grew progressively shorter, while rainfall was somewhat more reliable. Thus there was less need for summer fallow but greater need for crops with shorter growing seasons. While many settled there with the aspiration of becoming commercial farmers, others may have had in mind a more balanced farm operation, looking for most of their subsistence needs to be produced by their own hands. Whatever their class or ethnic backgrounds, at least in the early years, the farm wife would most often have been co-producer with her husband and children. But regardless of their goals or intentions, many early settlers, whether Scottish crofters in the 1880s or Ukrainian peasants in the late 1890s, were too poor to begin anything other than under-capitalized, subsistence-oriented farms.

Families from the English middle class found homesteading on the Prairies an extreme shock, no one more so than the wife, as we know from those who recorded their experiences. The enduring English illusion was that the grant of a 160-acre homestead meant an established farm resembling those of England – not a bare stretch of ground without buildings, fences, or cultivated fields.[44] While we have far fewer accounts of the first impressions of Ukrainian peasant families, we know that, in contrast to the English, many marvelled at the extent of their new holdings and soon recreated their familiar domestic architecture in home and barnyard.[45]

Paul Voisey's study of the Vulcan area in southern Alberta reflected the conditions that prevailed in the last phase of settling the southern prairie. The very limited capability of the soils combined with the climate to decisively undermine the female domestic side that had been typical of most farm families across the northern part of North America. The limitations on their productive side encouraged farm women to think of themselves as middle-class ladies of leisure rather than as co-producers. The fact that many had recently arrived from the United States probably also contributed to the influence of the country life movement in southern Alberta. So diminished was the domestic side of farming, that it became feasible to speak of "bachelor homesteaders" not as men briefly single but as men in a permanent condition. Eating the occasional meal in the town café and leaving his dirty clothes at the Chinese laundry, the bachelor farmer could also leave his few working livestock on a neighbour's farm and spend his winters working in BC lumber camps or on railway construction gangs.[46] This was a marked change from the confident nineteenth-century dictum that a farm without a wife could not succeed.

Much more studied has been the campaign for dower right. Originating in the common law tradition as a widow's right to a portion of her deceased husband's estate, in the nineteenth century, dower right came to be part of statute law in both Great Britain and the civil laws of most provinces of Canada. However, in Manitoba during the late 1880s those heavily involved in real estate transactions demanded a much-simplified system of land titles. In the heady days of the Manitoba land boom, the older method of registering land titles seemed cumbersome, slow, and, worst of all, uncertain: "Land speculators were lobbying the government to adopt a new registry system referred to as the Torrens system ... [that] guaranteed uncontested ownership of property upon issue of land titles." In the Red River Valley there were numerous conflicting, often-unresolved issues stemming from "old settlers," Métis, and native land claims: "The new system required the government registry department to settle all claims before issue of title ... A whole series of legislative amendments occurred to clarify and often eliminate claims based upon old laws and agreements."[47] Amongst the claims swept away by the Torrens system was the widow's dower right. This seems to be an instance of a tendency noted by Sandra Rollings-Magnussen: "While it is unlikely that attention was specifically directed at creating legislation to deliberately hitch women to the homestead, the patriarchal nature of society worked hand in hand with this outcome."[48] Along similar lines Jane Ursel observed, "While the general pattern towards extending and protecting married women's property rights was clearly established during the first period [of western settlement], the history of dower in western Canada shows how the power of economic interests determine the parameters within which the transformation of patriarchy occurs."[49]

The Manitoba legislature adopted the Torrens system of land title registration in 1885. The following year, the federal government passed parallel legislation to establish the same system in the NWT. This loss of traditional property rights sparked a forty-year campaign that led some women far beyond reclaiming traditional rights to the espousal of new ones based on the equality of women's labour with men's in creating farms on the Prairies.

Women in the late nineteenth century often viewed dower right much more broadly that either common law or statutory law ever stated. Britain's 1833 law, which applied to Canada, limited dower right to a widow's claim on the estate of her husband if he died without leaving a will (i.e., intestate). The law allowed the husband to dispose of his property as he liked during his lifetime and after his death by drawing up a will. By contrast, at least some Ontario farm wives assumed that they had a legal say in the disposition of the family's principal asset, land. Some refused to consent to the sale of their Ontario farm as a way of objecting to their husbands' desire to go west. However, while the arguments may have been effective within families, they had no standing in law.

Ontario women who moved west assumed they took dower right with them. When they discovered that the law would countenance neither their own broader reading of the common law tradition nor even what the law allowed in Ontario, they began to agitate for the restoration of what they had understood to be their rights. But once women began to ask for the law to change, the actions of organizing and discussing property and female rights caused other issues to emerge. Women began to question collectively, as well as individually, why in the Canadian West they were not able to file for homesteads in their own right, as in the American West. They began to demand that dower right include a say in the disposal of real property while their husbands were still alive. As they made their arguments, women followed two lines of attack, which to some extent mirrored their approaches in the parallel debate over women's suffrage. Based on the traditional concept of dower, they argued that as mothers they needed legal protection for themselves and their families. But this maternalist view ran alongside a much more radical argument that since farm wives contributed jointly to the creation of a family farm from a homestead claim, they were equally entitled to its ownership.

The equal rights argument was pushed furthest in Alberta. In 1910 Emily Murphy enlisted the Alberta Opposition leader R.B. Bennett to introduce a bill to guarantee a wife's interest in her husband's property in his lifetime. Premier A.L. Sifton responded with a Married Women's Relief Act that was much less sweeping: a widow could go to court if the will left her with less than if the husband had died without a will.[50] Across the three Prairie provinces, the legislative and legal campaigns proved long and arduous. In Saskatchewan a Farmers Anti-Dower Law Association directly opposed the campaign of the women's organizations.[51] Although by 1920 all three provinces had responded to the demands of a variety of women's groups, it took longer for the courts to accept the new definitions of women's rights.

The tensions between the two economies of the family farm – women's domestic economy oriented to subsistence and men's cash crop economy oriented to the market – became visible in several ways in relation to women's ownership of property, above all, land. There is some evidence that certain married women attempted to use their newly acquired right to protect the assets of their domestic economy from the risks run by their husbands' engagement in the market economy. Several Manitoba legal cases turned on the wife claiming ownership of certain family assets that creditors could not seize for the payment of their husbands' debts (in one case money borrowed to purchase farm machinery). It is unclear if this was a jointly pursued strategy between husbands and wives or whether these wives were independently trying to protect the home place from the risks undertaken by their husbands in pursuit of cash crops.

In January 1917 the United Farm Women of Alberta (UFWA) passed a dower law resolution. In May of the same year, the Alberta Liberal government passed a Dower Act. It provided that the wife's historic claim was preserved in the form of her guaranteed use of the family homestead after her husband's death. However, rural women widened the debate, arguing that farm wives should have an equal share in family property. Despite the strong role played by the UFWA in the election of 1921, the new United Farmers of Alberta government did not pass new legislation. Women continued to press for action through the 1920s, but by 1926 a legislative committee that included Irene Parlby, Nellie McClung, Emily Murphy, and Henrietta Edwards sadly concluded that there would not be an extension of equal rights: "Notwithstanding the pioneering partnership, public opinion was against [the adoption of community of property]."[52]

Margaret McCallum considers that the maternalist argument undermined that of equal rights. "Supporters of a dower law were not contesting the predominant role which custom and law gave to men in conducting the business and financial affairs of the family ... They were asking merely that the law set some limits on the absolute power of a man to dispose of his property, in recognition of the rights of his wife and children."[53] While this maternalist legal goal would have put further limits on the hitherto unfettered discretion of husbands and fathers, it also showed how narrowly the law, as an expression of social norms, saw the roles of women.

The perceived shortage of land for homestead in the years leading up to 1914 had an impact on gender relations. When every hired hand had the opportunity to begin his own homestead, the social distance between the hand and the farmer family narrowed to the point that marriage to the farmer's daughter was unexceptionable. However, as the opportunity for land closed off, the social distance not only greatly increased, it also came to be enforced by resort to law. Even when daughters wanted to marry, their fathers sued for seduction and abduction to prevent either having a member of the family marry down the social scale or giving a share of land to an unwanted son-in-law.[54]

Sons who grew up on Prairie farms did not have the traditional forest-clearing roles of eastern Canada and thus had less claim to the traditional family support. Clearing hardwood forest was the work of a lifetime. The sons' years of labour in that task earned them a reasonable expectation of support in establishing farms of their own – even though such expectations could not always be met. Sod busting – even clearing aspen groves and underbrush in the parklands – could be accomplished in months (at most a few years). With the spread of power machinery on the prairies, that time could be reduced to a matter of days. The family's sons continued to contribute to the farm's successful operation, but did not build up the productive capacity in a substantial enough way as to create a major family obligation to them.

If the obligation seemed less, the necessity also seemed less. When free homesteads were available to everyone, the farmer's son could file his entry just like anyone else. The family would provide start-up working capital such as livestock, implements, and even some labour to put up the first buildings. However, as land on the treeless Prairie grew scarce, sons' options became more restricted. Cohesive ethnic groups that had arrived early, such as the Mennonites (whose solidarity was at first powerfully reinforced by a communal religious ethos) and the Canadiens of Montcalm, were able to transplant two or three generations of sons.[55] But even these were ultimately stopped by what was seen as the shortage of land.

As families moved to the Canadian Prairies, the traditional roles within them sometimes had to adjust, as did their implements and tillage practices, in order to cope with a different environment. Some wives and all sons found their traditional roles undermined, compelling them to adjust to different expectations. Whether the farm wife could maintain her traditional role as co-producer or took on a new role as lady of the house, she eventually regained and to some extent improved her legal standing, although it never reached that of equality except at the ballot box. Without hardwood forest to clear, sons found their traditional contribution to building up the farm's long-run productive capacity gone, and with it much of their claim on the family's resources to begin farms of their own. As long as they could homestead, this need not have been a major problem. But when it seemed that land for homesteads had become scarce, sons could be at a significant disadvantage. That same fear of scarcity meant daughters could find their marriage choices constricted by the social standing of the successful family farm and their fathers' determination to enforce the borders of that standing.

CATTLE AND OTHER LIVESTOCK

Over the years, cattle raising on the Prairies has given rise to three successive schools of thought. The first saw livestock in general and cattle in particular playing a key role on the advancing edge of settlement. The second stressed the distinctively Canadian rather than American patterns in large-scale livestock raising, breeding, and marketing, while the third school reasserted American connections to qualify that picture of an Anglo-British elite controlling the Prairie cattle industry. The three schools emerged sequentially as explanations of cattle raising on the Prairies, but rather than being rivals, each explains specific places and phases of the industry.

In the first view, which arose in the 1920s and 1930s, raising cattle and other livestock was a phase in the advancing settlement frontier across the Prairies, inevitably replaced by an exclusive focus on farming crops.[56] The pioneers used livestock as a means of converting their field crops into cash in the absence of any ready transportation facilities, since grain-fed livestock could be walked to market.

While railways were sometimes built ahead of settlement, it was also often the case that local settlement went ahead of planned branch lines. When the inevitable delays occurred, settlers intent on commercial farming had to find ways to market their produce at a considerable distance from the nearest railhead. During the "Manitoba Boom" of 1879–82, hundreds of settlers took up homesteads across the southwestern corner of the province beyond the Mennonite Western Reserve. Most of this settlement was spurred by the strong conviction that branch lines were about to be constructed that would offer direct market access to the grain crops confidently expected in a few years' time. However, when boom turned to bust, new farms were left without the transportation on which they were premised.

Farmers' first object had to be the family's subsistence, as they could not expect to buy provisions on a regular basis or easily market the anticipated grain crop. While there were a very substantial number of homestead cancellations, and doubtless some outright abandonments, for those who remained and struggled on, the market access problem had to be overcome one way or another. In addition, the new homesteaders encountered another problem: early frosts, hail, and other natural disasters limited their production of top-quality grain. The solution to both problems was the turn to livestock, mainly cattle but also in some cases pigs. A frost-damaged crop that would have been unsaleable, even if there had been an adjacent railway, could be fed to animals, which could then be walked to market. This solution's outcome was far from optimal: travel over prairie trails (even apart from the hazards of the journey posed by gopher holes and fording creeks) entailed weight loss in animals.[57] Yet for a commercially oriented farm, this practice provided a stop-gap until the railhead appeared and until farmers found the crops that could best survive in the short, sometimes unpredictable growing season. By the 1890s two branch lines had extended into that corner of Manitoba, giving farmers direct market access. Then, at the very least, they had the alternative of taking a grain crop directly to market or disposing of livestock in a more economical way.

A potential bounty of being one of the earliest settlers in a district lay in the often-abundant grass on nearby unclaimed crown (or HBC or railway) lands. The homesteader on the frontier of settlement could graze his livestock, especially cattle, horses, and even sheep, on the free grass until the district was sufficiently settled for the need to pay for grazing permits to such lands.[58] White Cap's band of Sioux settled south of the future Saskatoon, raising cattle that grazed on the grasslands around their reserve. But this became increasingly difficult once new settlers had homesteaded on the prairie surrounding the reserve.[59] A.S. Morton told his students about horse ranches that used the unclaimed brushland on the opposite side of the South Saskatchewan as free pasture into the early twentieth century. As late as 1919, James M. Minifie's father grazed twenty head of cattle over the summer on the open range south of his homestead and pre-emption near Vanguard, Saskatchewan.[60]

The second school of thought around the livestock industry on the Prairies arose in response to a popular perception of southern Alberta as a mere northern extension of the American cattle industry of the Great Plains. Establishing the existence of a distinctively Canadian ranching frontier in the Alberta foothills was a major historiographic achievement. In a series of scholarly articles and books, Lewis G. Thomas, Sheilagh Jameson, and David Breen emphasized the importance of the federal government; its creations, the North West Mounted Police (NWMP) and the CPR; and above all, the central role played by eastern Canadian and British investors in creating a thriving cattle industry in southern Alberta. The result was a conservative "cattle compact" quite different from the American Wild West.[61]

While some American whisky smugglers reinvented themselves as cattle ranchers after the arrival of the NWMP (in part to supply their former presumed opponents), within five years a predominantly Anglo-Canadian ranching community had proved the feasibility of open-range ranching in the southern Alberta foothills. Even though I.G. Baker of Fort Benton retained the major contract for supplying beef to both the NWMP and Indian Affairs until 1884, the cattle increasingly came from the Canadian-owned herds. By 1880 there were around 6,000 head of cattle on about two hundred ranches in the foothills.[62]

The closure of the British market to the entry of live cattle from the United States in 1879 and the prospect of the CPR connecting Calgary to Winnipeg sparked the Canadian beef bonanza of the early 1880s. Senator Matthew Cochrane prodded the federal government into offering highly favourable leases (though not as favourable as he had been led to expect) by the end of 1881. Within three years the federal government had issued 47 leases covering 1,785,690 acres. By 1888, 111 leaseholders held a peak of 3,252,378 acres.[63] By 1890, they reported 91,822 cattle and 11,471 horses on their properties, while non-leaseholders reported 17,476 cattle and 3,001 horses.[64] Of the ten largest companies, British investors owned four, Canadians five, while Americans controlled only one. While the cowboys and cattle initially came from the United States, the capital and the control remained in the hands of a distinctively Anglo-Canadian elite.

Purchased in Montana, many of these cattle had come from eastern Oregon and Washington. Canadian buyers preferred these "westerns," which came from a Durham-Shorthorn cross, to the stereotypic "Texas Longhorn" driven north up the Great Plains. Not content with purchasing grade cattle, the leading Alberta ranch owners imported pedigree bulls to improve the quality of their herds. Cochrane shipped 125 Hereford bulls to his extensive ranch, while Fred Stimson bought 21 Polled Angus for the North-West Cattle Company of which he was manager and part-owner.[65] These efforts did not always succeed. In 1886 a substantial portion of purebred stock sickened and died on their trip from Britain to Canada. Once on the range, the purebred bulls could not always compete successfully with the "scrub bulls" born on the range. Open-range ranching that gathered the cattle only twice a year gave ranchers little opportunity to control breeding. However, their orientation to the British market and their determined attempts to promote the quality of Alberta beef distinguished Alberta ranchers from their American counterparts who valued quantity over quality and focused primarily on their domestic market.

The Alberta cattle industry depended much more, and more directly, on the federal government than did its American counterpart. The cattlemen relied on government to give them some security over their open-range grazing, first through long, "closed" leases (i.e., "closed" to homestead entry) and then through a system of stock-watering reserves. The government allowed leaseholders to import cattle from the United States duty free in the early 1880s. When those leaseholders became worried about possible American competition crowding "their" open range in the mid-1880s and asked the government to end free entry, the government obliged.[66] Most contentiously, the government upheld the closed nature of leases by supporting the NWMP eviction of squatters who tried to claim homesteads within leased areas. When this tension eventually grew too costly in political terms, the government created stock-watering reserves, which achieved the same goal for ranchers without the territorial disputes that arose from closed leases. A limited degree of violence marked the Canadian ranching frontier: some cowboys pulled down settlers' homes and fences, while some frustrated evicted settlers may have set fire to the prairie grass essential to grazing (and perhaps even some haystacks). But there was nothing comparable to the deadly range wars of the American Great Plains.[67]

Breen sees the Alberta cattle industry in terms of the metropolitan staples model. Not only were the ranch owners (and some of the managers) British and Anglo-Canadians from eastern Canada, but their enterprise was tied to the CPR and a British export market. The demands of that market led to the ranchers' concern for a quality product. Breen suggests that the success of their staple – the one dynamic element in Canada's foreign trade in the late 1880s and early 1890s – reinforced the federal government's disposition to favour ranchers in considering the increased demands from settlers.[68] The negative side of that export orientation was that Alberta ranchers saw the local domestic market in the West as a place to send cattle of inferior quality.[69] When foreign markets closed or became more costly, the Alberta cattle industry had to turn to a domestic market too long scorned to respond readily by purchasing local beef.

The analysis of the southern Alberta foothills cattle industry has shown the distinctively Canadian character and British orientation of the major investors and owners.[70] However, some conflict remains over the relative weight to be apportioned to an American social ambience and an Anglo-Canadian one on the cattle frontier. Warren Lopfson has stressed the continuing American presence amongst ranch managers as well as cowboys.[71] Simon Evans has shown that the later phase of open-range grazing had a much larger and more direct American presence as the geographic scope of the southwestern Prairie livestock industry expanded beyond the southern end of the District of Alberta to include the western end of the District of Assiniboia.[72]

The distinctive contribution of the third school of Prairie livestock historiography has been to look at the whole of the Prairie livestock industry's history; once the scope of inquiry is expanded beyond the foothills, it becomes clear that there was an element of truth in the older view of the Canadian cattle industry as an extension of the American.[73] As well as the minor American presence in the foothills, for a brief period there was a much larger American incursion into the grasslands of western Assiniboia. As pressure on the American open range increased at the end of the nineteenth century, both from overstocking (partially checked by the deadly winter of 1886–87) and from settlers' encroachments, large- and small-scale American ranchers began to move their operations into the short-grass prairie between Cypress Hills and the Missouri Coteau, up to and even beyond the South Saskatchewan River. After limited entry in the mid-1880s, several large outfits began in earnest to move north of the forty-ninth parallel at the end of the century. Some of this movement bordered on the illegal: cattle "drifted" north of the line on the unfenced open range from ranches just south of the boundary. In 1899, American Turkey Track and T-Bar Down ranch hands rounded up some 12,000 head south of the Cypress Hills. As large-scale leases again became available after 1900, a few large American outfits moved into

Canada in a major way. In 1903, 30,000 cattle and some 4,000 horses were shipped into the Sounding Lake area north of the South Saskatchewan River. The Turkey Track and T-Bar Down brought in 20,000 and 10,000 head respectively. The enormous Matador Ranch took 150,000 head across Saskatchewan Landing. Some of this stock came from as far away as the Dakotas, Texas, and even Mexico. By the end of 1903, twenty-two American leaseholders held a total of 60,000 acres, or 30 per cent of the lands leased for grazing by the federal government.[74] There were also a multitude of medium- and smaller-scale ranchers, forming a short-distance migration out of an increasingly crowded open range in Montana. Such movements showed again the great mobility of the open-range cattle industry whose capital was almost entirely confined to the cattle themselves.

After the deadly winter of 1906–07, in the "carrion spring" of 1907, the newly arrived herds of the American cattlemen bore the heaviest losses. Above Saskatchewan Landing, over half of all the livestock died. The ecological catastrophe largely ended the open-range phase of Canadian ranching. Those who survived had in part done so because they had already begun the transition toward much smaller-scale stock farming. The foothills also provided more shelter than the open grasslands. But cattlemen who had smaller herds, some winter forage, and even fences had been able to prevent the drifting and starvation that decimated the very large herds on the open range.

Between 1890 and 1914 live cattle grew to become one of Canada's principal staples, accounting for 20 per cent by value of exports to the United Kingdom in 1906.[75] Over half of these cattle came from the Prairies, channelled through Winnipeg by a combination of Patrick Burns of Calgary and Gordon, Ironside and Fares of Winnipeg. Burns did the buying in southern Alberta, took the rough cattle for his own business of supplying railway construction crews and lumber camps and sent the best on to Winnipeg for shipment across the Atlantic.[76] By owning their own ranches and feedlots in both Alberta and Manitoba; feeding their own cattle; operating their own slaughterhouses in Alberta, Saskatchewan, and Manitoba – as well as shipping cattle overseas – the two firms between them had completely integrated operations with forward and backward linkages. They were able to make profits at every turn of the market. For example, when there was a glut of cattle offered in the fall, they bought cheap (keeping their own cattle off the market); when cattle were in short supply, they used their own cattle to keep input costs down. However, as the expanding settlement cut into ranch land

and the First World War closed some export markets, Gordon, Ironside and Fares lost their control to a Toronto-based company that eventually took over their Winnipeg plant. Burns on the other hand continued to supply local markets across western Canada.

With the 1908 Homestead Act, the federal government turned away from its historic role of protecting ranchers and set the scene for what some describe as another ecological catastrophe by opening the heart of the Palliser Triangle to homesteaders. However, on the southern-most limit of the Canadian grasslands, smaller-scale ranchers persisted even as the last of the large outfits closed down. Around the Cypress Hills and across Pilot Butte to Wood Mountain they continued ranching by raising more forage crops and providing fences and shelter for their livestock. As the homestead "experiment" failed, ranchers sought to expand again to the northern slope of the continental divide, reclaiming the marginal lands farmers had abandoned. Eventually, under the Prairie Farm and Rehabilitation Act (PFRA) of 1935, the ranchers would again get tangible assistance from the federal government. This time it took the form of creating community pastures out of desiccated farms, stock-watering dams, and limited irrigation projects to promote the growth of forage crops within the region. These measures provided some security against the climatic extremes of the southern-most grasslands.[77]

While the post-war drought and that of the 1930s drove out many of the homesteaders whom the government had encouraged to enter the dry belt, some remained. Repeated crop failures taught them that wheat could not be relied upon. Gradually the survivors turned toward a mixed farming with a growing livestock side that could benefit from the PFRA's land-reclamation and water-control projects. The once highly divergent homestead and ranch enterprises slowly and unevenly began to converge on a mixed farm/stock farm middle ground that sought to cope with the region's extreme climate changes by diversified risk taking.

While historians have sometimes thought of the ranching frontier as "passing," that stage was not the end of livestock production on the Prairies. In both the foothills of southern Alberta and part of the grasslands of western Assiniboia (which became, with provincial status, partly southwestern Saskatchewan and partly southeastern Alberta), medium-scale ranches evolved into stock farms. These farms continued to focus on livestock production supplementing forage crops with grazing on lands that were sub-marginal for farming. A similar development appeared on the eastern edge of the Canadian Shield, where failed mixed farms of the Interlake region became dairy farms, supplying milk to the West's metropolis, Winnipeg.

What had definitely passed was open-range ranching, especially on the large scale pioneered by Senator Cochrane and his generation. A.B. McCullough has estimated that the ten largest ranches represented an investment of about $2.5 million in 1891.[78] In their best years they had paid out dividends of 20 per cent and better. Large ranches with well-connected owners could secure the leases that gave some security to grazing on crown lands at a penny an acre a year. As well as cheap grass, these ranches benefited from low labour costs. While there were one or two men for every 100 to 300 cattle on smaller ranches, the ratio could be as high as 1,000 cattle per man on large ones.[79] However, the medium-scale rancher was not without advantages, especially evident in hard times. With between 1,000 and 2,000 head ranged over 5 to 15 sections of grazing land, this rancher had much more control over breeding than the large outfits, and over the long term he could prevent the degeneration of his herd. Another potential advantage of smaller scale arose from being able to raise more horses proportionately than the big outfits. Horse breeding required more specialized care (which the more labour-intensive small ranch could provide) while yielding from two to five times the return per animal over cattle.[80] In 1890 in the southwestern corner of the Territories, horses made up 14.6 per cent of the livestock held by non-leaseholders but only 11.1 per cent amongst the leaseholders.[81] Hard times led smaller-scale ranchers to increase their holdings of horses. For example, after suffering heavy losses with dairy cattle, Pascal Bonneau Sr of Willow Bunch re-established his herd with 400 cattle and 400 horses.[82]

Although almost all the literature on livestock production focuses on cattle, with minor asides on horses, other types of livestock were being raised in large numbers on the Canadian Prairies. Sheep provoked the most controversy, since ranchers viewed them as destroyers of the open range. The different cropping practice of sheep meant that they put much more pressure on grassland vegetation. Early on, Senator Cochrane, who pioneered large cattle operations in southern Alberta, reflected the cattleman's distaste for sheep ranching. In 1882 he was among those who welcomed the ban on sheep grazing on crown lands. However, when cattle did not thrive as expected on his lease west of Calgary, Cochrane changed his mind.[83] In 1884 he had 5,000 sheep brought in on foot from Montana and Wyoming. The following year his company shipped out 70,000 pounds of wool.

Table 9.1: Prairie sheep holdings, selected years.

	Number of sheep
1881	6,419
1891	100,758
1901	95,512
1911	265,000
1921	1,277,000
1924	435,078 (post–First World War low)
1931	1,346,700
1947	1,080,000 (post–Second World War decline began)

Source: Census of Canada, 1880–81, vol. 3, 130–2; 1890-91, vol. 4, 118, 220.
Canada Year Book, 1913, 160; 1922–23, 262; 1933, 245; 1943–44, 225; 1948–49, 225.

Alarmed cattlemen demanded that sheep be confined to the northern range of grazing marked by Sheep Creek, 30 miles south of Calgary. In 1884 the federal government prohibited sheep south of the Bow and Highwood rivers. While sheep numbers declined to 1890, in that year sheep men began to enter western Assiniboia as well as the area around Cardston. In 1893 the federal government revised its prohibitions on sheep grazing. They were now only to be allowed east of St Mary's River and south of the South Saskatchewan. The late 1890s saw increased demand for mutton in southern BC mines, which led not only to expansion of flocks – numbered at 230,000 in 1900 – but also import of some 70,000 sheep in 1901 alone. That expansion led to increased conflict over who could graze where. Then heavy sheep losses in the spring of 1903 led some sheep men to switch over to cattle. While there had also been cattle losses that spring, they represented less capital investment and labour input: "The sheep industry was very labour intensive, needing a shepherd at all times with the flock; it was expensive, too, for the sheep required lambing sheds and buildings for refuge against severe winters."[84] The carrion spring of 1907 would show that cattle, too, required more capital investment to survive climatic extremes. Table 9.1 shows Prairie sheep holdings for selected years.

The growth in the total numbers of sheep on the Prairies after 1903 likely represents the impact of European immigrants, especially Scandinavians and Ukrainians, for whom a small herd of sheep provided the family with both meat and wool. For the first time, sheep began to appear in numbers north of the Red Deer River in the newly settled areas. In Saskatchewan, sheep in small numbers were common in the parklands, but farms on the short-grass prairie typically had either no

Table 9.2: Prairie hogs holdings, selected years.

	Number of hogs
1881	20,133
1891	70,460
1901	200,375
1911	285,120
1921	1,231,798
1924	2,249,367
1931	2,380,988 (inter-war peak)
1940	1,941,000
1941	2,705,200
1943	4,969,000 (wartime peak)

Source: Census of Canada, 1880–81, vol. 3, 130–2; 1890–91, vol. 4, 118, 220.
Canada Year Book, 1913, 160; 1922–23, 262; 1933, 245; 1943–44, 225; 1948–49, 225.

sheep or hundreds rather than thousands. Most prairie rural municipalities had none. Yet the Maple Creek census district in 1916 had one-third of all sheep in the province, with average holdings over 300; Moose Jaw came second with an average over 140. On the prairie, sheep were not part of a family's subsistence but the principal product of a few large-scale operators.[85] Throughout the 1930s, the total number of sheep on the Prairies never went below 1 million, but immediately after the war, sheep holdings began a long decline. Their numbers clearly indicate that they formed a substantial part of the Prairie livestock industry. However, sheep have yet to find a historian of their own.

The other major livestock animal on the Prairies was the humble pig. The Red River settlement from its earliest days had counted both sheep and pigs amongst its livestock holdings. The growth of hog production over the period of Prairie settlement bears more resemblance to general population growth than does that of sheep. Table 9.2 indicates the number of hogs on the Prairies for selected years.

The number of hogs, like sheep, expanded with the very rapid rise in Prairie population between 1901 and 1906. From then until 1913, there was a steady increase in hogs, and production stayed above 1 million throughout the First World War. After a sudden fall in 1920, there was steady expansion to the peak of 1924. However, hog production never went below 1.5 million during the later 1920s and the 1930s (after the brief peak in 1931 and 1932). After a wartime peak in 1943, hog production fell steadily until 1952, when it again went over 2 million. Like sheep, hogs have no historian who has sought to relate their numbers to either their function in the farm economy (for family subsistence or market) or their role in the region's total livestock production.

An overview of all livestock holdings should alert us to another problem with the phrase "ranching frontier." Problematic as the oft-repeated, oft-abused phrase "mixed farming" may be, farmers on parkland and prairie (to differing degrees) resorted to a variety of animals for a variety of purposes, not all captured in the model of commercial farming. Some raised substantial numbers of cattle, horses, or sheep as their principal production, or at least as a major cash source. Reasons for this orientation ranged from a phase of necessity for would-be commercial grain farmers temporarily without the immediate railway access to markets, to farmers (and sometimes ranchers) adapting their product mix to local soils or climate, to exploitation of open grazing in a favourable climate that made winter shelter or forage seem unnecessary. But many more farmers raised a wider variety of animals – including pigs, poultry, and dairy cattle – as part of their farm's domestic economy for family subsistence. The adaptability of such mixed farming, almost always urged by the best-qualified agricultural scientists, lay, first, in allowing farm families to subsist through periods of adverse markets or climate cycles and, second, in allowing commercially oriented farm enterprises to cope with the unforeseen – whether it be failure of expected transportation facilities to materialize or damage, such as rust or early frost, to cash crops (making such crops saleable, even if at reduced returns, as livestock feed). The mixed farming model may not have been cost-efficient in terms of maximizing a farm's cash income, but it could often serve as an insurance against the complete loss of an unmarketable cash crop.

On the margins of agricultural settlement, cattle played several different roles that are less easily captured if the term "ranching frontier" is limited to cattle ranching in southern Alberta and western Assiniboia. Human settlement spread across the Prairies from east to west in a kind of ecological succession of pioneer adaptations. As the first scholarly analysis of cattle and other livestock established, settlers, especially homesteaders, often took up lands well in advance of any transportation link to the larger world and its markets, and so depended on livestock until field crops became a dependable source of income. Many areas across the Prairies had such a transitional "ranching" phase, and the phenomenon itself is perhaps more deserving of the name "ranch frontier" than southern Alberta and western Assiniboia, where the particular geographic resources in the long term encouraged a permanent livestock industry to develop and flourish.

The contribution of the second historiographic school to analyze cattle was to overturn the popular perception of southern Alberta's cattle industry as nothing more than an extension into Canada of the American "Wild West" frontier. By establishing who initiated and carried forward the establishment of the large ranches, Jameson and Breen demonstrated the Anglo-Canadian dominance of the cattle compact. The third school added nuance to that picture by highlighting the American presence amongst the staff and management of those Canadian- or British-owned companies as well as the much greater and more direct involvement of American ranchers in the last phase of the open-range frontier in western Assiniboia. Together the three schools give us a detailed and well-documented understanding of the Prairie cattle industry. Beyond that, to complete our understanding of livestock of all varieties on the Prairies, needs to be added the roles other livestock and other enterprises besides ranches played.

HOMESTEADING THE PALLISER: A PREDICTABLE DISASTER

In the decade between 1897 and 1907, tens of thousands of new settlers took up parkland and prairie, just as the National Policy had long promised. New machinery and farming techniques held out the promise of prosperous farming even on the drier prairie that lay south of the parkland fertile belt. Sulky gang plows, drill press seeders, and binders made it possible in a short growing season to plant and harvest on such a large scale that even low-yield soils could be profitable. Summer fallow every other year in the more arid areas appeared to conserve enough moisture to make a reasonable return even in dry years. Years of success both fed and combined with a rising demand for more land open for homesteading, not only from a mounting wave of immigrants but also from many eastern Canadians. In 1908, on the eve of a federal election, the Laurier government gave way to these demands. It cancelled the remaining grazing leases, thus opening up the driest parts – the heart – of the Palliser Triangle.[86] The government attempted to exercise some caution by amending the Dominion Lands Act to reinstate the pre-emption provision that had been dropped. Thus the pioneer heading to the driest portion of the Canadian prairie was enabled (even implicitly advised) to operate a 320-acre farm.

Another factor in the decision to open more of the short-grass prairie to homestead might be called the issue of degree. When successful grain farms were in operation on the mixed-grass prairie, it did not seem any great change to argue for the development of similar farms a few dozen miles further south, on the short-grass prairie. There were no sharp natural boundaries to the Palliser Triangle, as shown by the great variety of even current attempts to map it.[87] In 1908, during a wet cycle on the Prairies, the ranchers' argument that the Triangle was only fit for grazing carried less weight than it does in retrospect. Laurier's government can be criticized for not giving enough weight to the knowledge then available that wet and dry cycles alternated. Homesteaders could not count on an unending wet cycle to sustain their farms in the long run. Of course, if Voisey is right that many of the late-arriving settlers, like those of Vulcan, themselves intended only a short-run speculation, this criticism would carry less weight.

In contrast to governments, railways were much more cautious about the region's prospects. There was no local repeat of lines built ahead of settlement. Branch lines only began to be built after the region had suffered its first severe climate test at the end of the First World War, and then tended to run only along the edge of the short-grass prairie, not into its driest areas. Consequently, another burden for the marginal farms of the region was the long distance to any railhead, and the resulting higher costs in time and money for transportation.

Those entering this last grassland frontier had the strongest motives to seek out and believe the most extreme promoters of dry-land farming who had promised (like the prophet Isaiah of old) that "the desert shall rejoice and blossom as the rose."[88] In order to seize their opportunity to "cash in" (as Voisey would have it) or succeed in establishing their farm, families like that of writer Wallace Stegner had to believe the odds were low enough to make their gamble worthwhile.[89] However, several other factors combined to make their gamble far more of a long shot than most could have realized.

The almost universal desire of these last pioneers on the short-grass prairie was to establish a successful grain farm. Few, if any, attempted small-scale peasant farming for family subsistence. Low-yield soils, scanty rain, and lack of any wood resources made any such attempt obviously impracticable by 1908. In the long run it would be the stock farm that had the best chance of success in this region, but that entailed even higher capital costs and a much wider skill set than the "straight grain" farm. Even the latter's capital costs had become much more substantial as the advance of agricultural technology combined with the onset of inflation at the start of the new century (after nearly half a century of deflation) to raise the capital costs of a new grain farm considerably. The result was a much greater financial burden on the increasingly marginal farm, which had less prospect of sustaining itself in the long run.

An important second factor that undercut the new farm's viability was the region's severe limits on the domestic side of the farm's economy, which had underwritten the farm family's survival in Quebec and Ontario, as distinct from the farm enterprise's commercial viability. The soil's poverty, the extreme climate, and persistent desiccating winds meant that families could not rely on their own gardens, poultry, dairy, or pigs to feed them. Census data show that farms at the heart of the Triangle seldom had the full range of domestic production, often lacking any pigs or cattle. John Hubbard, Saskatchewan's foremost promoter of beekeeping in this period, had to admit that "bees would be a failure on the open prairie, where there is no shelter-belt of trees and no bee-pasturage."[90] Not even the lowly potato, which often provided not merely a major part of the family's subsistence but also by-products for domestic animals such as pigs, could be grown in sufficient quantity in dry years. Thus the family's subsistence, almost as much as its commercial success, rested on its field crop.[91] This may partially explain why the driest parts of the prairies had relatively the least land in summer fallow: everything depended on the field crop's success.

In less than a decade, over 130,000 people had established 30,000 new farms and put 4 million acres into crop. However, when drought set in after 1917, many (like the Stegners) left as quickly as they had come. The most dramatic evidence was the large-scale abandonment of farms in southeastern Alberta; southwestern Saskatchewan saw both a smaller number and a smaller proportion of homesteads abandoned. The return of rain and the rise in grain prices through the 1920s brought stability to both parts of the region and a measure of recovery. But then the much longer and more severe drought of the 1930s (the decade of depressed wheat prices, and the near strangulation of international trade) left the region physically devastated, its human and animal populations depleted.

Several historians have condemned the Laurier government's 1908 decision to open the Palliser Triangle to homesteaders. David C. Jones refers to it as the "Prairie Dryland Disaster" and entitled his book on the subject *The Empire of Dust*.[92] Both Jones and Paul Voisey blame "the experts" for promoting exaggerated notions of what dry farming could accomplish.[93] Barry Potyondi points to the same "culprits" as do Jones and Voisey: "Many believed the oft-repeated federal government argument that 'proven' dryland farming techniques could make their dry homesteads produce bountiful crops."[94] That critique needs to be

examined from several perspectives. What was the actual advice given
by the best-qualified Canadian agricultural scientists employed by Canadian governments? To what extent was that advice heeded? In the long
term, was the cultivation of the Palliser Triangle justifiable in terms of its
role in Canada and the larger world community?

The critics of cultivation have attributed the decisions of governments
and individuals to the mistaken advice of agricultural experts. It is necessary, however, to look closely both at the specific advice and the particular experts who gave it. Jones claimed that Angus MacKay of the Indian
Head Experimental Farm believed summer fallow "virtually guaranteed agricultural production on the arid plains."[95] But MacKay, in fact,
made no such assertion.[96] Rather, he maintained that it could provide
some crop in a dry year, though not necessarily enough to offset the lost
production of the fallow year.[97] In sharp contrast, the American H.W.
Campbell declared that by his "system," "the more arid sections could be
made to produce not only two and three times as much fodder and grain
as had been heretofore produced in good years, but that good yields
could be made certain in dry seasons."[98] While it seems highly probable
that at least some of the last homesteaders on the prairie did listen to the
more extreme dry-farm exponents, their choice cannot be used to fault
the more carefully weighed advice given by the best qualified of the Canadian agricultural scientists.

To what extent was *all* of the best advice followed? Perhaps the
most continuous element in the advice that intending farmers received
was the call for mixed farming. Some experts might concede that a
"straight grain" operation, with its lower start-up capital costs, might
be necessary to begin with, but virtually all urged as rapid a transition
as possible to more balanced farm production. There was undoubtedly confusion over the mixed farming advice offered. Some of the
advice was about a farm enterprise producing both grain and livestock
for sale. But there were two other roles that animals could play that
would enhance the farm's adaptability. Some advice was clearly about
the value of animals and their by-products as essential to the farm's
domestic side, for family subsistence (not necessarily sales). Another
important theme was the value of animals in offering the potential
to shift away from exclusive reliance on growing top-quality grain
toward producing some income from a field crop that was damaged or
harvested in a year of extremely low grain prices by feeding it to the
livestock on hand. Local studies such as Voisey's and available census
statistics both suggest that most of the pioneers entering the heart of

the Palliser Triangle in the first decade disregarded that advice in whole or in part; most farms lacked the "full complement" of animals necessary for the farm family's subsistence.

The severe production and marketing crises at the end of the First World War created a second opportunity for agricultural scientists to persuade farmers to adopt a more complex strategy to cope with the region's lack of resources and the vagaries of its climate. In Alberta, large-scale farm abandonment in the area most seriously affected meant that most of the provincial government's efforts became focused on the collapse of whole communities and a social infrastructure that was often less than a decade old.[99] However, in Saskatchewan there was a greater concerted effort to change farm practices to stabilize and sustain agriculture in the region. In July 1920 the Saskatchewan government held a "Better Farming" Conference at Swift Current to promote necessary adaptations to the dry cycle. Some of these were well-worn repetitions, such as the need to pursue mixed farming rather than wheat monoculture. The Agriculture Department's annual report for 1920 noted that "in numerous cases their cattle and hogs carried them over and supplied them with the necessities of life which they could not have secured for any system of grain farming during the last three years."[100]

However, the conference and the royal commission that paralleled it did address several problems pointed up urgently in recent experience. To counter the effects of soil drifting on summer fallow, agricultural scientists recommended practices such as ridging the soil at right angles to the prevailing wind's direction and keeping a cloddy surface to avoid breaking up finely textured soils that contained little organic matter. To correct the latter condition, they advised farmers to plant hay crops or to plow under green crops as "green manure." They also promoted growing protective crops such as sweet clover and winter rye, as well as leaving stubble over the winter to catch the snow. Closely spaced windbreaks of trees or hedges were also recommended. The dense inrush of homesteaders meant that farmers who survived the drought and had livestock could find little grazing in the summer. To remedy this as well as to reclaim abandoned farmlands, the province organized community pastures open to all. These were managed by grouping cattle by type and moving them from one area to another to prevent over-grazing.[101] The province also took steps to improve livestock marketing by enabling groups of farmers to ship their cattle together. Both the conference and commission attracted much local attention in 1920–21, which seemed to be followed by shifts in farming practice.

The most immediate effect was the expansion in winter rye, increasing from 46,909 acres to 773,499 acres. The provincial government facilitated this by distributing free seed after the poor crops of 1921. Grazing co-ops got government leases to operate community pastures on both abandoned farmlands and former ranch leases. Farmers increased their holdings of dairy cattle and showed great interest in dairy meetings organized by local agricultural representatives. In 1925 three new privately owned dairies were established in the region. However, the shift in farming practice did not last.

The return of high wheat prices, beginning in 1924, and the promise of the wheat pool movement to sustain high prices and ease cash flow led many farmers to return to a near-exclusive reliance on wheat. Crop districts 3 and 4 and the corresponding census districts showed livestock holdings declining from 1926 to 1931. A 1930 provincial royal commission reported that "few engaged in mixed farming beyond their immediate needs."[102] It is important to avoid confusion here over mixed farming: the commission was conceding that at least some farmers held at least some livestock for their family's subsistence, but beyond that, "they simply did not subscribe to the view, expressed by many government officials, that to engage in mixed farming was to hedge their bets in a tenuous business venture that combines environmental unpredictability with economic uncertainty."[103] In the second chance of 1920–22, then, agricultural scientists were clearly not at fault. Their recommendations for long-term farm management were tried and rejected in favour of short-term market opportunities.

Several critics of the 1908 decision to open the Palliser Triangle have stated (or implied) that it was an unjustifiable mistake because the region should only ever have been used for grazing. Most historians agree with the verdict of the front page series run by the *Winnipeg Free Press* in September 1919: the Triangle should never have been opened for settlement. The modern concern for respecting the integrity of ecosystems has added weight to that view. However, there are counter-arguments. James H. Gray opened his *Men against the Desert* declaring that "Canada could not have existed without the settling and farming of the Palliser Triangle."[104] While he later qualifies this somewhat, he holds that settlement was essential to hold onto all of the land north of the forty-ninth parallel: without settlement, American ranchers could have taken the Palliser Triangle into the United States, Oregon-style.

Moreover, Gray pointed to the 50,000 people who stayed as playing a key role in reclaiming a vast stretch of agricultural land from being "a weed-covered wasteland and short-grass cattle range."[105] The over-coming of the effects of the 1930s ecological disaster made Canada a world leader in agricultural science. He asked how, in a world of rapidly rising populations needing to be fed, the abandonment of such a large wheat-growing area could be justified. To confine the region perma-nently to grazing would mean a lower production of calories per acre compared to grain farming. As Gray stressed, in its years of bumper crops the short-grass prairie produced yields of 30–40 bushels per acre, against the Prairie average in such years of 26 bushels per acre.[106]

Since the Second World War the region has largely maintained a sort of ecological equilibrium with much land in community pastures, as well as in stock farming and some grain farming. With much of abandoned homestead land now in the public domain, it is available not only for grazing, but also for periodic farming. In wet cycles, when world wheat prices are high, it can still make economic sense for a grain farmer to lease some of that crown land for a couple of years in the hopes of taking off several good harvests before either the wet cycle or the high prices fade. In eastern Colorado, where a similar pattern has developed, Americans speak of "suitcase farming":[107] it allows a grain farmer to substantially increase his sown acreage with no long-term costs to the farm enterprise, providing a much greater scale of operation over which to spread his machinery costs (which have continued to mount past his ancestors' imagining). This long-term pattern of land use allows the short-grass prairie to maximize its grain production when it is possible and most profitable to do so, while allowing its grazing potential to be sustained through the years when grain growing would require more than the soil can sustain.

INTERCONNECTIONS OF THE FIVE HISTORIOGRAPHIC DEBATES

The above five debates over Prairie agricultural settlement are inter-related in complex ways. Put in simplest terms, the delay in settlement after railways opened up the area was caused in part by the need to develop specialized machinery, whose costs raised the question of whether that expense had become a substantial barrier to starting a homestead before the First World War. The machinery made possible farming on a much more extensive scale, which drew more and more families onto the mixed grass and short-grass prairie, where the farm wife's traditional role came into question. The Prairies offered opportunities as well as challenges: southern Alberta's foothills promise of mild winters created Canada's largest ranches. However, the drive for more farms compelled the cancellation of the remaining ranch leases, when the heart of Palliser Triangle opened for homestead in 1908. The "dryland disaster" eventually resulted in a convergence of small-scale stock farms and mixed farming that has proved sustainable in the long run.

Beyond those simple connections, there are several other more complex factors for consideration. The primary reasons for the delay in the settlement of the Prairie West after the completion of the CPR were the need for tillage practices to conserve moisture and for specialized machinery to make extensive cultivation of thin soils with low productivity commercially feasible. The federal experimental farms, especially Indian Head under the direction of Angus MacKay, developed and promoted summer fallow in alternate years as the essential practice, especially on the dry prairie. The plow with the chilled steel blade could open the prairie sod where eastern wood and iron plows could not. The press seed drill could bury the seed deep enough to avoid the depredations of birds and other predators, to draw more moisture, and to germinate more rapidly. The binder could cut and bind the grain in sheaves, ready for the last labour-intensive task of stooking. Steam-powered threshing outfits could convert stooks into ready cash before the snow came. In time, steam-powered tractors could even break the virgin sod at previously unheard of rates. But this latter innovation came after the others had come into general use in the mid-1890s, making commercial farming on an extensive scale efficient enough to promise success.

However, the new machinery made farming much more costly than the eastern type with horses or oxen pulling wooden plows with iron shares, broadcasting seed by hand, harvesting with sickle or even scythe, and threshing by hand through the winter. However, just as new types of machinery made commercial farming potentially profitable, the long-term trend of falling wheat prices that had characterized the second half of the nineteenth century reversed into a long-term rise in the general price level. Prices for the new machinery rose as well. Where Lyle Dick saw machinery costs *falling* from 1884 to 1914, he also noted that there were different levels at which a homesteader could begin. From a minimum of $291 to $562 for an under-capitalized grain farm, costs could rise to $2,093–$5,873 to immediately begin a commercial grain farm.[108] Irene Spry insisted on including opportunity costs (beloved of economists) and discounted costs of the subsistence side of the operation, but she agreed with Dick's comments about start-up costs varying by ethnic and social-class expectations.[109] Scottish crofter and Ukrainian peasant families whose immediate goal was subsistence often began with far less capital in hand that even Dick's lowest estimates.

In time, some of those who began seeking subsistence by settling in the parkland were drawn into more commercially oriented agriculture. Initially many worked away from their homesteads to earn money for needs their farms could not yet provide. By growing oats to adapt to the shorter growing season of the parkland, they could take off their own crops, and then work as harvest labour on the later-maturing wheat crops of commercial farmers. The peak prices of a year like 1915 may well have encouraged those whose farms had been largely subsistence-oriented to enter more fully into the commercial wheat economy.

Even commercial farms needed a complementary domestic economy to provide initially for their families and then potentially for off-farm sale to augment the main cash crop. Traditionally, the farm wife's role was to direct the labour of her children and any hired girls the family could afford. In good years, the garden, sheepfold, pigsty, chicken coop, and dairy reduced demands on the farm's cash income. In bad years, they could ensure the family's survival. Paul Voisey questions this, but one of his own sources said, "those cattle and chickens were all that kept us afloat in hard times."[110] Voisey takes "afloat" to mean cash income, whereas the reference may well have been to the family's physical survival.

Given the thinness of prairie soils and the usual low yield per acre, Prairie farming had to operate on an extensive scale to be profitable. Consequently, the size of farms continually expanded as new implements made this possible and their cost made it necessary. The drive for more land came not only from newcomers to the region but also from those already in the region seeking to expand their scale of operations. As this pressure pushed more and more families onto the treeless prairie, farm wives found it more and more difficult to sustain domestic production. The soil was too thin, the rain too scanty, the desiccating winds too incessant to raise enough to feed a family, with no hope of clothing it from resources on the farm. The situation was structurally conducive for an exchange of the co-producer role for that of lady of the house.

The farm family's sons had no such alternate role. Most grew up, like generations before them, with the expectation of becoming farmers themselves. If homestead land was running out, so had their chance of "land that I can own."[111] That scarcity could also narrow daughters' marriage prospects where their fathers put the family's social standing above the call of true love.

Most writing about livestock on the Prairies has focused on those operations in which cattle or horses were the principal, or even the only, concern. Yet the pure ranch too quickly discovered that it also needed a subsistence side. Warren Lopfson pointed to the irresistible drift toward variations on stock farming, growing crops for human as well as animal consumption. Much less attention has been devoted to the other roles that livestock played in Prairie agriculture. Most farms kept a diverse range of animals primarily for their own subsistence needs: cattle (including dairy), sheep, pigs, chickens (and other kinds of fowl), as well as goats (which did not catch the census-takers' notice but appear in early photos of pioneer farms). The fact that holdings varied from farm to farm (with some having no chickens and others no pigs, for example), strongly suggests that there were local markets at least for exchange if not for sale. As the transportation network improved, meat, wool, and dairy products could find wider markets.

On the outer edge of homestead settlement, the practice of small-scale open grazing on local unoccupied lands was common. That initial low-cost animal feed encouraged larger herds. Where the farm was distant from any railhead, such animals could provide a means to take a crop to that distant market. Even after settlement grew more dense, livestock offered an alternative way to make at least some cash from a damaged cash crop. Cattle fattened on wheat hit by an early frost could be sold when there was no market for that wheat, even as feed grain.

The federal government's decision to open the heart of the Palliser Triangle to homestead entailed a series of risks that were neglected or minimized at the time. In an arid climate with thin soils, the family farm could not depend on its domestic economy to provide insurance against market and weather fluctuations. Consequently, the greater knowable risk (of recurring drought) became multiplied: the cash crop had to not only pay as a commercial operation but also provide much of the family's subsistence. Moreover, in the more arid climate, farmers needed even greater investment in livestock (as well as fences and buildings) in order to move toward the stock farm that proved to be the type of operation that could survive in this region in the long term (with ample grazing available beyond the farm itself). The straight grain farm had the least capital costs but also the least chance of being viable. Thus, in the Palliser Triangle, the risks to the under-capitalized homesteader multiplied beyond any reasonable hope of long-term success. As Voisey observed, the farmers who benefited most were those who "sold up" as soon as they could.[112] Aside from

Table 9.3: Estimates of gross agricultural wealth in the Prairie provinces, 1929.

| | Gross wealth ($000s) | | | | |
	Land	Buildings	Machinery	Livestock	Poultry
Manitoba	315,245	115,005	67,472	66,472	5,358
Saskatchewan	877,042	216,398	178,676	134,950	7,240
Alberta	523,221	121,765	98,812	123,133	6,785

Source: Canada Year Book, 1931, 217.

Table 9.4: Area and value of field crops in the Prairie provinces, 1925.

| | Field crops | |
	Area (in acres)	Value
Manitoba	5,941,066	$93,191,235
Saskatchewan	18,758,471	$368,274,521
Alberta	8,516,917	$157,227,282

Source: Canada Year Book, 1931, 217.

that sort of speculative gain, there was little prospect of success from an under-capitalized investment.

The heart of the Palliser Triangle witnessed the ultimate *reducto ad absurdum* of Prairie settlement. The very machinery and tillage techniques that had overcome the difficulties of farming prairie sod constituted a capital cost that overstretched or exhausted many homesteaders' financial resources. Often heavily in debt, they found their under-capitalized straight grain farms lacked both the necessary subsistence provided elsewhere by the domestic economy and the balance that larger livestock holdings might have provided. The adaptations that had worked well in the parkland and mixed-grass prairie were less possible and their absence posed much greater risks in the region's driest zone.

While the Dominion Lands Act's implicit pledge of a free homestead was (at least initially) ridden into the ground in the Palliser Triangle, that should not obscure that the promise proved true for the tens of thousands of families who settled elsewhere. Even after the onset of the Great Depression beginning in 1929, the 1931 census showed 54,199 farms in Manitoba, 97,408 in Alberta, and 136,497 in Saskatchewan.[113] Table 9.3 shows the gross agricultural wealth of those farms in 1929. Just before the Depression their gross agricultural wealth was estimated in the hundreds of millions, land being worth more than all the other assets combined.

Table 9.4 indicates the area and value of field crops in 1925. In the mid-1920s, between the post-war depression and the later Roaring Twenties, each of the three provinces had a broad developed land base yielding substantial revenue in field crops.

A great many pioneers found the homestead promise true. Their families built farms that endured through two wars and two depressions. In doing so, they created not only family farms but also the rural society of the Prairies.

The Prairies had its own frontier. Unlike Quebec and Ontario, the feasible limit of cultivation was not defined primarily by geography but by economics. The Great Plains extend north of Edmonton as the parklands reach up in the direction of the Peace River watershed. The twentieth century began with public controversy over whether commercial agriculture in the Peace River country was possible due to cold weather.[114] However, just as farming had to adapt to (relative) dry (and found a benefit – less rain to wash nutrients out of the soil), so it could adapt to (relative) cold (and find a benefit – more hours per day of sunshine). After the harsh experiences of the short-grass prairie following the First World War, people increasingly looked north for new opportunities. "In 1928, 4,400 new homesteads were filed in Peace River's and Grand Prairie's Dominion land offices, comprising 34% of all western Canada's homesteads filed that year."[115] The critical factor in the expansion of the open-land frontier on the Prairies turned out to be not the availability of free land for homesteads, but the availability of credit to farm on a commercial scale.[116]

What Historiographic Debates Can Tell Us

Most historians today live in cities. That simple fact has a strong tendency to shape what they assume – even unconsciously – to be "normal" or most important. A history of cities in British North America in the nineteenth century, for example, would focus on only a small part of the region's population. Ideas about dominant urban elites building the country or the importance of working-class revolutionary potential, while apparently far apart ideologically, in fact share a common misperception about the importance of urban populations at the time.

Nationalism may be articulated by elites, but it is fuelled by much broader social and economic needs or desires. The farm family's need for land on which to plant the rising generation was just such a desire. A little-noticed but substantial part of the ongoing conflicts between what would become Quebec and Ontario arose from the different stages of their agrarian economies by the mid-1800s. Canadian history has been shaped by agriculture, and to grasp the form of that shaping, we need to take into consideration the changing dynamics of the family farm.

Agriculture was a family business; for many it was a way of life. Much of the mystery, not to say controversy, over the wheat staple and around commercial farming is resolved by understanding the family farm. Whether the farm was pioneer, peasant, or (in almost all cases, to some degree) commercial, it contained two complementary economies. The balance between those two greatly depended on the type of farm and sometimes on the region. The male economy produced the much-studied wheat staple. That economy was primarily oriented to producing grain for the family or off-farm sale or to creating capacity for such production. But often conditions – weather, prices, tariff policies – meant that revenue from the sale of grain could not be the sole support for a farm. What enabled commercial farms as well as pioneer and peasant farms to

survive was the female economy of domestic production. As well as raising the next generation, the farm wife directed the labour of daughters
and younger males to produce food and clothing. On pioneer and especially on peasant farms, the domestic economy loomed larger than the
goal of increasing future productive capacity or potential off-farm sales.

A further dimension to the farm family's life projected into the future:
the hope of providing land to reward the children (usually only the sons)
for their years of unpaid labour on their parents' farm. While most families aspired to this, it was not a universal practice since many families
lacked the means. Depending on the extent of the parents' land base, the
type of farming, and the number of surviving sons, sometimes the goal
could feasibly be achieved for at least one generation through division
of the parental lands. But more commonly, well-established farmers
looked to purchase, lease, secure a grant on, or at least rent land – usually uncleared – on which their sons could begin farms of their own. In
addition to land, sons could hope for additional gifts of food and at least
loans of working livestock and implements to get their clearing underway. Obviously the more distant the move, the less likely was that sort
of start-up support.

Finding land for each new generation to begin farms of their own
was a running pulse through the process of agricultural settlement on
Canada's open land frontiers. Where forest prevailed, it became the first
physical barrier to farm families. Where immigration was slow, as in
New France (which became Quebec in 1763), the rate of expansion was
largely influenced by the rate of population growth, which set the rate of
forest clearing. Britain's strong demand for wheat after 1770 encouraged
a faster rate of forest clearing to expand output for exports, although
after the turn of the century that pace of rising exports slackened.

A second physical barrier emerged in the geographical limits of the St
Lawrence Valley. The decades after 1800 saw continuous forest clearing,
but it was increasingly on less-fertile soils. Once the best lands of the
Quebec District had been occupied, many young, single people or young
families went west to the best lands on the Montreal plain. As those were
taken up, people moved onto more marginal lands in the Montreal District. When even those were gone, there was a substantial rural population shift back to the Quebec District to take up its marginal lands,
despite the shorter growing season.

The third barrier to finding farms for sons was not a physical one.
Culture in its many facets formed a permeable barrier that severely limited agrarian migration onto better lands, although it did not stop it. For

Canadiens, the seigneurial system provided a social framework in which they conducted their economic as well as their social lives. As an occupier rather than owner, who faced a substantial tax if he tried to sell that "occupation right," the habitant had little scope for moving his accumulated wealth out of a seigneury or out of agriculture. This substantial economic barrier was compounded by the obvious social barriers of leaving friends, kinship networks, and religious community. The habitant who sought to move onto new land would have depended heavily on those friends and kin to make even a meagre beginning as a pioneer possible. The more distant he was from them, the harder the task.

Moreover, the clerical nationalism that dominated Quebec's intellectual life from the 1840s on preached an agrarian mission for Canadiens. To abandon the soil was the first step toward abandoning one's faith. Farming became more than just a way of life: it was a religious duty. Some energetic clergy took the lead in promoting colonization as new areas opened to create farms for young families. However, while Canadiens began to move beyond the limits of the seigneurial system to new lands, their moves were usually short-distance ones, onto lands as marginal as those they had left in the last settled parts of the seigneuries.

Pioneers in what became Ontario faced the forest barrier and eventually the geographic barrier as well. A high level of immigration, which sometimes came in rapid spurts, pushed the settlement frontier much more rapidly than in Quebec. As in Quebec, farm families sought to establish their children (again, mostly their sons) on farms of their own. As in late eighteenth-century Quebec, mid-century Ontario saw wheat emerge as the major agricultural export. The international collapse of wheat prices in 1857 brought a corresponding collapse in Ontario land prices. While many farm families found short-term responses, among the long-term ones was a demand for the annexation of Rupert's Land to create a new open land frontier.

The diversity of peoples settling in Ontario meant that cultural factors there were much more diverse and played much less of a role than in Quebec. Experienced pioneers such as the late Loyalists judged the quality of the soil by its tree cover: no trees meant the land was not worth having. Thus they were slow to take up land in the oak plains west of Hamilton, preferring to chop down trees rather than plow up grass meadows. Irish settlers, Protestant and Catholic, followed patterns of chain migration that led them to cluster together in certain areas. Until 1826, settlers could get a location ticket, a conditional right to occupy and clear a specific lot of 100 acres. If they fulfilled the conditions, they could apply for a patent and gain outright ownership. Newcomers from Britain who received their location ticket went to their lot and began clearing. Only if they found a squatter on the lot were they likely to return the ticket and ask for another. Those born in British North America or the United States tended to take their ticket and go to look over the lot. If it was not to their liking, they returned the ticket and asked for another.

By the middle of the nineteenth century, the agricultures of Quebec and Ontario, while each was diverse, had some striking parallels. A substantial minority amongst Quebec's farmers had begun a transition to more intensive tillage oriented to livestock and dairy. In the area around Montreal, this type of farmer predominated. But at the other end of the spectrum were a great many subsistence-oriented farms that struggled even to provide for their families. Increasingly, one or two members had to work for wages off the farm to earn the balance of the family's subsistence needs. The transition out of farming (at first into forestry) had already begun. Nationalist elites and the clergy preached *la patrie* to a decreasingly receptive audience.

Ontario too had a large minority of commercial farmers, many of whom began to shift into livestock after the rude shock of collapsing wheat prices in 1857. In the Ottawa Valley, Irish and British farmers sold their lands and moved elsewhere as the forest industry moved to the Upper Ottawa and the type of agriculture they sought did not seem to flourish. Canadiens bought some of their land, and prospered by pursuing a different type of agriculture. Farms began to come into operation further north beyond the geographic limits of commercial farming. The owners of these marginal operations pursued farming as a way of life, for the status of being farmers and landowners rather than for any idea that they would ever be successful commercial farmers. By contrast, in southern Ontario the sons of prosperous farmers expected one day to have prosperous farms of their own. The question at mid-century was: where?

The contrasting land-hungry nationalisms of Quebec and Ontario profoundly shaped the settlement of Rupert's Land. Quebec's clerical nationalist elite, well represented at Ottawa, sought to reserve a place in the new region for emigrant Canadiens, especially those already in the United States. In Ontario there had been an expansionist movement for over a decade demanding annexation to open a new agrarian frontier. The first conflict between the two opposing interests arose over the terms of entry and the first institutions provided for the new region. The Manitoba envisioned by George-Étienne Cartier was a bilingual, bicultural province, with two equal school systems – Catholic and Protestant – in which 1.4 million acres would be set aside for the Métis, and in which (shortly) there would be extensive blocks of land reserved for the settlement of Canadiens.[1] As Parliament passed the Manitoba Act, the federal government sent a military expedition with a British commanding officer and British troops, but including Ontario militia, to hunt down the local government with which it had just finished negotiating.

The second conflict involved the settlement of Manitoba. At the behest of the leading Quebec politicians in Ottawa, at one time the immigration department's six full-time agents were all in New England trying to persuade Canadien factory hands to take up the federal government's offer to homestead on the Prairies. Despite two decades of work, as well as direct appeals in Quebec by Manitoba's Bishop of St Boniface, only a few thousand came – not enough to hold the reserved lands, which all reverted to the general pool of lands available for homestead. By contrast, the 1881 census for Manitoba's population showed that 19,125 had been born in Ontario; by 1891 it was 46,620. The much greater pent-up demand in Ontario for land and the relative prosperity of many Ontario farms meant that it was that province, not Quebec, that would provide the great majority of Canadian-born settlers to Manitoba between 1871 and 1891.

The third conflict was the triumph of local initiative over federally imposed cultural institutions. Along the way, in the Laurier-Sifton Agreement of 1897, the door had been accidentally left ajar for the use of languages other than English for instruction. It was not the relatively stable number of French-speaking Roman Catholics or the small number of German-speaking Mennonites, but the completely unexpected influx of Ukrainians who tested the strength of Manitoba's accidental tolerance by establishing 114 Ukrainian school boards by 1914. The majority's answer, in 1916, was the suppression of all languages other than English for instruction in schools, to which attendance was made compulsory.

While local initiatives made short work of Ottawa's attempt at imposing cultural institutions on the Prairies, the federal government's control over the allocation of land gave it the decisive role in the region's economic development. The fact that the Dominion Lands Act (1872) resembled the American Homestead Act (1862) and that Canadian land grants to railways after 1878 resembled American railway grant policy before 1870 has misled most historians and economic historians into thinking that the land grant policies and outcomes of the two countries were quite similar. This was not the case for either farms or railways. What almost all previous scholars have missed is the legal contexts in which Canadian and American homestead and railway policies operated.

When the United States Congress passed the Homestead Act in 1862, it simply added it as one of the many ways in which federal land could be obtained. Congress continued to add further legislation creating routes to land ownership in all or parts of the area covered by the Homestead Act with no attempt to reconcile all these various pieces of legislation. It was a major task for the would-be farmer to locate which public lands were open for entry.

The Dominion Lands Act provided a single unified system of land granting – a context that delivered outcomes far closer to the American ideals of land for homesteaders and railway land grants to speed settlement. Nearly 90 per cent of Prairie farmers began with a free homestead grant, compared to only about one in six in the American West. The CPR held 80 per cent of all railway lands, which were sold to farmers early and on easy terms. In contrast to its supposed American model, the Dominion Lands Act concentrated most public lands on homesteads and railways – 53 per cent versus 32 per cent in the American West.

The federal government's imposition of the numbered treaties in the 1870s cut short First Nations' own early adaptations to agriculture. Treaty Indians found themselves forced into the first large-scale attempt at European sedentary farming on the prairies. Just as they began successful adjustment, a peasant farming model came into force that destroyed their efforts, leaving them wholly dependent on the federal government.

The harsher Prairie climate – more severe winters and hotter, drier summers – compelled newcomers to adapt. That slowed the anticipated flood of settlement for a decade after completion of the CPR had provided direct rail access coast to coast. New techniques had to be found and demonstrated – above all summer fallow – to conserve enough moisture to give a reasonable expectation of a fair crop. New and improved implements – steel plows, press seed drills, self-tying binders – enabled a farmer to cultivate on a large enough scale in the short growing season to make low-yield soils a paying proposition. Did those equipment costs put prairie farming out of the homesteader's reach? That depended to some extent on individual backgrounds and expectations; the lower the expectations, the more feasible the ambition. But the later a homesteader arrived after 1900, the more difficult it became to get land on the tree-less Prairie.

While men worried about summer fallow and seed drills, women had to struggle with growing the family's food on thin soils with low rainfall. In the parkland, women could maintain their traditional range of domestic animals and extensive gardens, but on the short-grass prairie it was extremely difficult. As land for homesteads on the southern prairie became more scarce, daughters and sons sometimes found their life prospects more limited, in different ways. The promise of mild winters in the foothills of southern Alberta and the prospect of virtually free grass drew large-scale ranchers to that short-grass prairie. Despite periodic winter catastrophes, ranching endured until it fell before the desperate scramble for more lands to homestead. In 1908, the federal government cancelled ranch leases and opened the heart of the Palliser Triangle to homesteading, while re-introducing pre-emptions, which gave the implicit advice to the prospective homesteader that put half his land in summer fallow. It would not be enough. Within a decade, tens of thousands of families had left the dryland disaster. Settlers had overcome many challenges of the prairie climate and adapted to others, but some challenges were simply too great for most. Thousands of farm families abandoned at the end of the First World War what they had only begun after 1908. There were others who hung on, even in the Palliser, by virtue of mixed farming, coming to resemble their one-time political enemies – those ranchers who also had endured by raising forage crops and keeping close watch on smaller herds. Both types benefited from the conversion of abandoned homesteads into community pastures.

But what of the Prairies' own frontier? The northward expansion of the Prairie frontier in the 1920s was stopped by the escalating cost of farm machinery as the second revolution in agriculture accelerated and by the banks' growing reluctance to supply credit to pioneer farmers. A further problem lay in the lack of opportunity for paid off-farm labour in the isolated areas where homesteads were available. One contemporary noted, "More and more it is becoming necessary for the settlers to depend on their small initial capital to carry them through the first few years of lean living."[2] The running pulse of the open land frontier failed, and could not be revived by either the Soldier Settlement Board after the First World War or the Veterans Land Act after the Second World War.[3] Even in the 1950s, agriculture in the Peace River developed very slowly.

What do we learn from these major debates about Canadian agriculture from late eighteenth-century Quebec to the early twentieth-century

Prairies? I believe there are at least three overall themes to be drawn from a close review of these debates: links between regions, policy in relation to application, and how we can best learn our past.

I have argued that several major debates in agricultural history can be linked together to reveal important connections between the histories of three Canadian regions. One of this book's central contentions has been that differences in the relative pace of agricultural change between Quebec and Ontario decisively shaped both public policy toward culture (as in schools) and economic development (in land granting) on the Prairies. Thus, this is a work of synthesis that seeks to draw together – in a non-oppressive way – threads derived from social history (not limited to agricultural history). My hope is to create a coherent larger narrative of Canada's rural past. I would have preferred to write a synthesis that was national in scope but that was not where the evidence led me.

A second theme deals with policy and its application. The central issues in agrarian societies are: Who controls the land? Who makes the rules by which the land is distributed? Apart from any controversy, Fernand Ouellet had an undeniable point to make: eventually, demographic growth would exceed the fixed limits of the seigneuries. Where English land tenure prevailed, the issues were land speculation, land sales, and free grants. The free grants (up to 1826 in Upper Canada) came with fees that grew to equal the price of some lands in the western states. It is unclear whether speculators (public ones like the Crown and Clergy Reserves, private ones like the Canada Company, or private individuals) made substantial profits in the long run. Certainly the unoccupied blocks of land dispersed settlement and hindered rural development. On the Prairies, the Dominion Lands Act did a far more effective job of providing free land to homesteaders. Land sales by the CPR were early, cheap, and not a barrier to development. But at the other end of the scale was the Canadian Northern Railway, which took a long time in choosing its land, tying up reserved blocks, and then held out for the highest prices.

However, in addition to the top-down questions, we need to ask the bottom-up question: to what extent were the rules of land acquisition obeyed? Whether they were habitants squatting on the edges of the Eastern Townships; Canadians born in Upper Canada squatting on to Canada Company land; or Ukrainian newcomers moving into Manitoba's Riding Mountain Timber Reserve, insisting on being near their countrymen on the only vacant land available, squatters collectively bent the law by clearing land and farming.[4] A new appreciation of the squatters' roles demonstrates the virtues of open academic debate. The contemporary nineteenth-century polemic about land speculation had entered academic discourse largely unexamined, providing underlying assumptions and even setting parameters for research.[5] However, on closer examination, the large-scale speculators in some cases were revealed not as all-powerful but as trying to persuade squatters to accept leases in a last hope of getting something rather than nothing.

A third theme involves how we learn about our past. The ongoing reassessment of public policy in terms of its application (as just outlined with land and squatters) is one instance of that method of learning. Another example is the examination of how the successive married women's property acts actually changed the patterns of women holding real property in their own names.[6] The federal government's policy of developing a self-sufficient reserve agriculture proved, in application, completely self-defeating. To return to the example of the major historiographic controversy with which this book began, the acrimonious tone of the debate over whether, or when, Quebec had an agricultural crisis has been oft lamented. But the real damage appears in the Quebec-France colloquia, where most Quebec contributors avoided so much as mentioning Ouellet's name even while addressing the issues that he had raised. The result was often shadowboxing; Ouellet's theses were reduced to caricatures, and his supporting arguments have been ignored. However, some contributors have acknowledged at least part of Ouellet's case, allowing them to directly address his arguments whether or not they agreed with them.[7] It is best to directly address the arguments you oppose than simply to ignore them.

Throughout the nineteenth century, agriculture was the common employment of most Canadians. No surprise then that the contrasting paces of change in the rural societies of the St Lawrence strongly influenced the emerging rural society on the Prairies. But public policy (whether set in Quebec City or Ottawa) did not always determine actual practice (whether in the seigneuries or on the Prairies). The debates themselves have an importance beyond their subject matter. The quality of academic exchange has much to do not only with how we learn but also how well we learn. The future of Canadian agricultural history needs continuing open debate that at its best can draw in new sources of evidence, new methods, and new scholars.

Notes

1 The "open land frontier" advanced at the speed with which Crown land was appropriated by farmers, as distinct from the rate at which forest was cleared or prairie sod opened.

2 Jean Hamelin and Fernand Ouellet, "Crise agricole dans le Bas-Canada (1802–1837)," *Etudes rurales*, 1962, 36–57.

3 This appears in its most striking form in the nine volumes of the Quebec-France colloquia held over the last thirty years. While the issues Ouellet raised are discussed in more than seventy papers, Ouellet is seldom mentioned and his arguments rarely addressed directly. The fullest exposition of an Ouellet thesis and an unusual case of direct citation by a *French* graduate student appear in the first volume. Dominique Joulia, "Pratiques successorales en milieu rural, 1795–1870: étude comparative de cas France de l'Ouest-Québec," in Joseph Goy and J. Wallot (eds.), *Société rurale dans la France de l'Ouest et du Québec (XVIIe-XXe siécles)*, Université de Montréal/École des Hautes Etudes en Sciences Sociales, Montréal, 1981, 93–139. No *Quebec* contributor ever gave as much space or so direct a reference to Ouellet. Most commonly, Ouellet is referred to obliquely as "the traditional historiography": J.-P. Wallot and Gilles Paquet, "Les Habitants de Montréal et de Québec," F. Lebrun and N. Séguin (eds.), *Sociétés villageoises et rapports villes-campagnes*, Presses Universitaires de Rennes, Rennes, 1985, n101, and their "Crédit et Endettement," G. Bouchard and J. Goy (eds.), *Famille, économie et société rurale en contexte d'urbanisation (17e–20e siècles)*, Centre interuniversitaire SOREP École des hautes études en sciences socials, Chicoutimi, 1990, 251.

4 Béatrice Craig made the point that you cannot always deduce *mentalities* from conduct: "Pour une approche comparative de l'étude des societies rurales nord-américaines," *Histoire sociale/Social History*, vol. 23, no. 46, November 1990, 266.

5 J.M.S. Careless, "George Brown and the Mother of Confederation," *Canadian Historical Association Annual Report*, 1960, 71.

CHAPTER ONE

1 I have developed this argument at length for the settlement process after 1815 in my *"Here We Are Laird Ourselves": Attitudes to Social Structure and Social Mobility in Upper Canada, 1815–1840*, Edwin Mellen Press, Queenston, 1990. David Vickers, "Competency and Competition: Economic Culture in Early America," *William and Mary Quarterly*, vol. 47, no. 1, 1990, 3–29, uses the term "competency" as another contemporary term for what I found described as "independence."

2 Russell, 13–26, and Vickers, 10, on the equation of wage labour and "dependency."

3 The rather large literature on the transplantation of peasant cultures or "the household mode of production" has been reviewed by several scholars: on the European origins, T. Shanin, *Defining Peasants: Essays Concerning Rural Societies*, Blackwell, Oxford, 1990; on the American debates, Allan Kulikoff, "The Transition to Capitalism in Rural America," *William and Mary Quarterly*, vol. 46, January 1989, 120–44. Allan Kulikoff, *From British Peasants to Colonial American Farmers*, University of North Carolina, Chapel Hill, 2000. There have been several Canadian reviews of this literature: Beatrice Craig, "Pour une approche comparative de l'étude des societies rurales nord-americanes," *Histoire sociale/ Social History*, vol. 23, November 1990, 249–70; Catherine Desbarats, "Agriculture within the seigneurial regime of the 18th century: Some thoughts on the recent literature," *Canadian Historical Review*, vol. 73, no. 1, March 1992, 1–29; and Ruth Sandwell, "Rural Reconstruction: Towards a new synthesis in Canadian History," *Histoire sociale/Social History*, vol. 27, May 1994, 1–32.

4 Amongst those who see the farmer as entrepreneur have been James Lemon, *The Best Poor Man's Country*, Johns Hopkins University Press, Baltimore, 1972; Edwin Perkins, *The Economy of Colonial America*, 2nd edition, Columbia University Press, New York, 1988; and Winnifred Rothenberg, *From Market Place to Market Economy*, University of Chicago Press, Chicago, 1992, and "Early Stages of Economic Development:

Massachusetts, 1642–1770," in Clara Eugenia Nunez (ed.), *Land, Labor, and Tenure: Institutional Arrangements*, Fundacion Fomento De La Historia Economica, Madrid, 1998, 41–51. For two different perspectives, see Gilles Paquet, "Économie et Histoire: Les liaisons dangereuses d'Hermes et de Clio," and Ruth Dupre, "Cliometrie, Économies et Histoire: Un ménage à trois," *Revue d'histoire de l'Amérique Français*, vol. 46, no. 4, Spring 1993, 629–43 and 645–60.

5 There is an older "social history" that dwelt much on "the pioneer," such as Robert L. Jones, *History of Agriculture in Ontario*, University of Toronto Press, Toronto, 1946, and G. deT. Glazebrook, *Life in Ontario, A Social History*, University of Toronto Press, Toronto, 1968 (especially 17–42). This needs to be set alongside newer work such as Roland Berthoff, "Peasants and Artisans, Puritans and Republicans: Personal Liberty and Communal Equality in American History," *Journal of American History*, vol. 69, no. 3, December 1982, 579–98; K. Conzen, "Peasant Pioneers: Generational Succession among German Farmers in Frontier Minnesota," in S. Hahn and J. Prude (eds.), *The Countryside in the Age of Capitalist Transformation*, University of North Carolina Press, Chapel Hill, 1985, and "German-Catholic Communalism and the American Civil War," in Elizabeth Glaser-Smith and Herman Wellenreuther (eds.), *Bridging the Atlantic: Europe and the United States in Modern Times*, Cambridge University Press, Cambridge, 2002, 119–44; and D.H. Akenson, *The Irish in Ontario – A Study in Rural History*, McGill-Queen's University Press, Montreal, 1984.

6 See, for example, Employment and Immigration's *National Occupational Classification*, 1992, entry 8251 for "Farmers and Farm Managers." On our problems in reading nineteenth-century occupational labels, see Gérard Bouchard, "Les categories socio-professionnelles: une nouveau grille de classment," *Labour/Le Travail*, vol. 15, 1985, 145–63.

7 Russell, *"Here We Are Laird Ourselves,"* 19–26.

8 Farm households did not necessarily specialize in farming: Béatrice Craig, Judith Rygiel, and Elizabeth Turcotte, "Survival or Adaptation? Domestic Rural Textile Production in Eastern Canada in the Later 19th century," *Agricultural History*, vol. 49, no. 2, 2001, 147–50; Jacques Mathieu, "Les relations ville-campagne: Québec et sa region au XVIIIe siècle," in Joseph Goy and J. Wallot (eds.), *Société rurale dans la France de l'Ouest et du Québec (XVII–XX siècles)*, Actes des colloques de 1979 et 1980, University of Montreal, Ecole des Hautes Etudes en Sciences Sociales, 1981, 197, found that not only were 25 per cent of Quebec's apprentice shoemakers from rural areas, but 58 per cent of those returned to the countryside,

36 per cent of them to their parish of origin. John Howison, *Sketches of Upper Canada*, George B. Whittaker, Edinburgh, 1825, 253, noted that "Mechanics cannot fail to do well in Upper Canada; for, when not engaged in clearing lands, they will find it easy to gain a little money by working at their professions." On the theoretical debates over "protoindustrialization" see: Hans Medick, "The Proto-Industrial Family Economy: The Structural Function of Household and Family during the Transition from Peasant Society to Industrial Capitalism," *Social History*, vol. 3, 1976, 291–315; Sonya O. Rose, "Proto-Industry, Women's Work and the Household Economy in the Transition to Industrial Capitalism," *Journal of Family History*, vol. 13, no. 2, 1988, 181–93; Stanley L. Engerman, "Expanding Protoindustrialization," *Journal of Family History*, vol. 17, no. 2, 1992, 241–51, and Ulrich Pfister, "The Protoindustrial Household Economy: Toward a Formal Analysis," in the same issue of the same journal, 201–32. David Levine, *Family Formation in an Age of Nascent Capitalism*, Academic Press, New York, 1977.

9 See Normand Séguin, "Paysans et monde forestier: nouvelles reflexions sur le monde rurale québécois au xixe siècle," *Cahiers des annals de Normandie*, vol. 24, 1992, 177–87, and his *Conquête du sol au 19e siècle*, Boreal Express, Sillery, 1977. See also John Willis, "Urbanization, Colonization and Underdevelopment in the Bas-Saint-Laurent : Fraserville and the Témiscouata in the Late Nineteenth Century," *Cahiers de Géographie du Québec*, 28, 73–4, April–September 1984, 125–61.

10 Rusty Bitterman, Graeme Wynn, and Robert McKinnon, "Of Inequality and Interdependence in the Nova Scotia Countryside, 1850–1870," CHR, vol. 74, no. 1, March 1993, 1–43, and Ruth W. Sandwell, "Peasants on the Coast? A Problematique of Rural British Columbia," paper presented to the BC Studies Conference 1994.

11 The last of the three labels, it must be confessed, was chosen more for alliteration than for its reflection of current usage amongst scholars. In the historical literature, it has been most common to refer to these farmers as either "capitalist farmers" or "commercial farmers" (including variants such as "commercially oriented farmers"). The term "profit maximize" describes only one of several possible goals that neo-classical microeconomists prescribe for an economic unit. Economists recognize that firms can choose to maximize other things besides profits (whether short term or long term), such as sales. In addition, some economists have put forward a variety of non-maximizing theories to explain the behaviour of firms in the market place. There have been extensive debates over commercial farming and agrarian capitalism, some focused in particular

journals such as the *Journal of Economic History* – multiple exchanges between Winifred B. Rothenberg, "The Market and Massachusetts Farmers, 1750–1855," *Journal of Economic History*, vol. 41, no. 2, June 1981, 283–314, and Rona S. Weiss, "The Market and Massachusetts Farmers: Comment," *Journal of Economic History*, vol. 43, no. 2, June 1983, 475–78, drawing in comment – Michael A. Bernstein and Sean Wilentz, "Marketing, Commerce and Capitalism in Rural Massachusetts," *Journal of Economic History*, vol. 44, no. 1, March 1984, 170–8; Andrew H. Baker and Holly V. Izard, "New England Farmers and the Marketplace, 1780–1865," *AH*, vol. 65, no. 3, Summer 1991, 29–52; the *Journal of Peasant Studies* for more than a decade starting with Robert Albritton, "Did Agrarian Capitalism Exist?," *Journal of Peasant Studies*, vol. 20, no. 3, April 1993, 419–41, drawing multiple replies from Mike Zmolek, "The Case for Agrarian Capitalism: A Response to Albritton," *Journal of Peasant Studies*, vol. 27, no. 4, July 2000, 138–59, which continued down to 2004. See also J. Cooper, "In Search of Agrarian Capitalism," *Past and Present*, vol. 80, August 1978, 20–65; Joyce Appleby, "Commercial Farming and the 'Agrarian Myth' in the Early Republic," *Journal of American History*, vol. 68, no. 4, March 1982, 833–49; Susan Archer Mann and James M. Dickinson, "One Furrow Forward, Two Furrows Back: A Marx-Weber Synthesis for Rural Sociology?," *Rural Sociology*, vol. 52, no. 2, 1987, 264–85; Patrick M. Mooney, "Desperately Seeking: One-Dimensional Mann and Dickinson," *Rural Sociology*, vol. 52, no. 2, 1987, 286–95; Susan Archer Mann and James M. Dickinson, "Collectivizing Our Thoughts: A Reply to Patrick Mooney," *Rural Sociology*, vol. 52, no. 2, 1987, 296–303; Susan Archer Mann, *Agrarian Capitalism in Theory and Practice*, University of North Carolina Press, Chapel Hill, 1990; Sue Headlee, *The Political Economy of the Family Farm: The Agrarian Roots of American Capitalism*, Praeger, New York, 1991; John Rule, "The Agrarian Path to Capitalism?," *Journal of Peasant Studies*, vol. 16, no. 3, April 1989, 443–9; Charles Post, "The Agrarian Origins of US Capitalism: The Transformation of the Northern Countryside Before the Civil War," *Journal of Peasant Studies*, vol. 22, no. 3, April 1995, 389–445.

12 S.M. Miller (ed.), *Max Weber*, T.Y. Crowell, New York, 1963, 27–31.

13 James Henrietta, "Families and Farms: *Mentalité* in Pre-Industrial America," *William and Mary Quarterly*, vol. 35, January 1978, 3–32; Robert E. Mutch, "Yeoman and Merchant in Pre-Industrial America," *Societas*, vol. 7, Autumn 1977, 279–307; and Michael Merrill, "Cash is Good to Eat: Self-sufficiency and Exchange in the Rural Economy of the United States," *Radical History Review*, vol. 3, Winter 1977, 42–72.

14 William Thomas Wien, "Peasant Accumulation in a Context of Colonization – Riviére-du-Sud, Canada, 1720–1775," doctoral dissertation,
McGill University, Montreal, chapter 5.

15 Béatrice Craig pointed out that farmers could also use the market for
family purposes: "Pour une approche comparative de l'étude des sociétés
rurales nord-américaines," *Hs/SH*, vol. 23, no. 46, November 1990, 266.

16 See, for an example, "Reminiscences of Mrs. White," *Ontario Historical
Society Proceedings and Records*, vol. 7, 1906, 154–5.

17 Mrs. Agnes Turnbull to Mrs. W. W. Baldwin, 12 February 1838, W.W.
Baldwin Papers, Toronto Public Library, Toronto.

18 Marjorie Griffin Cohen, *Women's Work, Markets, and Economic
Development in 19th Century Ontario*, University of Toronto Press,
Toronto, 1988, 76–7.

19 Russell, *Here We Are Laird Ourselves*, 88–97. Barbara C. Murison, "The
Search for the 'Best Poor Man's Country': Shifting Emigration Patterns
from Scotland in 1830s and 1840s," paper presented to the Canadian
Historical Association, 1991.

20 There is a large literature on the problems of commercial farmers in the
twentieth century trying to achieve both high and stable cash incomes.
A brief introduction from an economist's perspective is R.L. Heilbroner,
The Economic Problem, 4th ed., Prentice-Hall, Englewood Cliffs, 1975,
121–33.

21 On the complex problems of farm accounting, see Clarence Danhof, "The
Farm Enterprise: The Northern United States, 1820–1860s," *Research in
Economic History*, vol. 4, 1979, 134–9.

22 Certainly in Upper Canada, the pioneer life was seen as beyond the capacity of a single man. At least some Americans shared that view. See the
Christian Guardian article reprinted from the upstate New York *Genesse
Farmer*, on the necessity of a wife and the need for husbands to attend to
their side of the gender-defined work boundary, 7 December 1836.

23 Paul Voisey, *Vulcan – The Making of a Prairie Community*, University of
Toronto Press, Toronto, 1988, 18–21, 93–4.

24 Ibid., 37–41.

25 V.C. Fowke, "The Myth of the Self-Sufficient Canadian Pioneer," Transactions of the Royal Society of Canada, 3rd series, vol. 56, June 1962,
23–37. For New England, see Bettye Hobbs Pruitt, "Self-Sufficiency and
the Agricultural Economy of 18th Century Massachusetts," *William and
Mary Quarterly*, vol. 41, no. 3, July 1984, 334–64.

26 W.L. Mackenzie attacked farm debt as undermining the farmer's
independence: *Colonial Advocate*, 27 May 1824; 8 August 1827;

Correspondent and Advocate, 16 July 1835. For a more positive, modern view of the value of credit to farmers, see Douglas McCalla, *Planting the Province: The Economic History of Upper Canada, 1784–1870*, University of Toronto Press, Toronto, 145–51.

27 K.M. Stampp, *The Peculiar Institution*, A.A. Knopf, New York, 1969, 282–9. J.W. Blassingame, *The Slave Community*, Oxford University Press, New York, 1979, 251, 254. Allan Kulikoff, "The Beginnings of the Afro-American Family in Maryland," in K.K. Sklar (ed.), *Women and Power in American History*, Prentice-Hall, Englewood Cliffs, 1991, 72–89.

28 Donald H. Akenson, *The Irish in Ontario: A Study in Rural History*, McGill-Queen's University Press, Montreal, 1999, 202–3.

29 M.L. Magill, "William Allan: A Pioneer Business Executive," in F.H. Armstrong (ed.), *Aspects of Nineteenth-Century Ontario*, University of Western Ontario Press, London, 1974, 102. See also T.W. Acheson, "The Nature and Structure of York Commerce in the 1820s," CHR, vol. 50, no. 4, December 1969, 409–10, and McCalla, *Planting*, 146–7.

30 See, for examples, Craig, 33–45, and Desrosiers, 151–6.

31 Examples are Douglas Dowd, *U.S. Capitalist Development since 1776*, M.E. Sharpe, Armonk, 1993; Rona Weiss, "Primitive Accumulation in the U.S.: The Interaction between Capitalist and Non-Capitalist Class Relations in 17th Century Massachusetts," *Journal of Economic History*, vol. 42, March 1982, 77–82; and her illuminating response to W. Rothenberg, "The Market and Massachusetts Farmers, 1750–1850," *Journal of Economic History*, vol. 41, June 1981, 283–314, which appeared in the same issue, 475–8. On the teleological aspect, see Colin A.M. Duncan, "Agriculture and the Industrial Teleology of Modern English History," *Canadian Papers in Rural History*, vol. 7, 1990, 335–62.

32 See, for examples, Olive Dickason, *Canada's First Nations*, McClelland and Stewart, Toronto, 1992, 36–43, and Bruce Trigger, *The Huron: Farmers of the North*, Harcourt, Brace, Jovanovich, Fort Worth, 1990, as well as his *The Children of the Astaentsic: A History of the Huron People to 1600*, McGill-Queen's University Press, Montreal, 1987. For the development of Native agriculture in the Prairie region see D. Wayne Moodie and Barry Kaye, "The Northern Limit of Indian Agriculture in North America," *Geographic Review*, vol. 59, 1969, 513–29, and their "Indian Agriculture in the Fur Trade Northwest," *Prairie Forum*, vol. 11, no. 2, Fall 1986, 171–84.

33 The traditional/modern dichotomy in other social sciences can be seen in any number of introductions to sociology – H.C. Bredemeir and R.M. Stephenson, *The Analysis of Social Systems*, Holt, Rinehart, Winston,

New York, 1962, 22–4, 142; R S. Denisoff and Ralph Wahrman, *An Introduction to Sociology*, Macmillan, New York, 1983, 559–62; or W. Feigelman (ed.), *Sociology Full Circle*, Holt, Rinehart, Winston, New York, 1980; Daniel Lerner, "Modernization – The Grocer and the Chief," 465–83 – and critically reviewed in anthropology, as in Richard R. Wink, *Household Ecology, Economic Change, and Domestic Life among the Kekchi Maya in Belize*, University of Arizona Press, Tucson, 1991, especially xv–xx.

34 This assumption is so profound, it shapes the very vocabulary we use: the economy of the nineteenth century (indeed of *any* previous century) is commonly described at "pre-industrial." As we experience significant change within our own era, we struggle with neologisms such as "post-industrial" or "post-modern." Always "industrial" and "modern" are the norms against which everything is implicitly measured. Anyone who described modern industrial Canada as "post-agricultural" would be thought either perverse or eccentric.

35 This aphorism is cited in many places, but Roger Wines (ed.), *Leopold von Ranke – The Secret of World History*, Fordham University Press, New York, 1981, n30, gives the original citation.

36 B.H. Slicher van Bath, "Agriculture in the Vital Revolution," in E.E. Rich and C.H. Wilson (eds.), *Cambridge Economic History of Europe*, vol. 5, Cambridge University Press, Cambridge, 1977, 57–103.

37 Danhof, 127–91, especially 129, 130–1. Béatrice Craig traced the common North American pattern of the pioneers who begin with little labour and a lot of land evolving, as land became scare, to market integration or forced migration: "Pour une approche comparative de l'étude des societies rurales nord-américaines," *HS/SH*, vol. 23, no. 46, November 1990, 254.

38 Ibid.

39 Ibid., 134–5. See also Voisey, *Vulcan*, 85–6.

40 This is a domestic example of what economists call gains from trade, which flow from specialization and the division of labour. See Craig, Rygiel, Turcotte, 147–50.

41 Cohen, *Women's Work*, 34–91. See also Allan Greer, *Peasant, Lord, and Merchant: Rural Society in Three Quebec Parishes, 1740–1840*, University of Toronto Press, Toronto, 1985, 28–34, 52–6.

42 See J. Wallot and Giles Paquet, "Stratégie foncière de l'habitant: Québec (1790–1835)," *Revue historique d'Amérique Français*, vol. 39, no. 4, Spring 1986, 555, on "bounded rationality." On the nature of peasants and their adaptations to North America see Teodor Shanin, *The*

Awkward Class, Political Sociology of Peasantry in a Developing Society: Russia, 1910-1925, Clarendon Press, Oxford, 1972, and *Defining Peasants - Essays concerning Rural Societies, Exploratory Economies, and Learning from Them in the Contemporary World,* Basil Blackwell, Oxford, 1990; V. Chayanov, *The Theory of Peasant Economy,* edited by Daniel Thorner, Basil Kerblay, and R.E.F. Smith, Richard D. Irwin Publishers, Homewood, 1966; Jon Gjerde, *From Peasants to Farmers: The Migration from Bolestrand, Norway to the Upper Middle West,* Cambridge University Press, Cambridge, 1985; David Peal, "Purposeful Peasants? A Review Essay," *Peasant Studies,* vol. 14, no. 1, Fall 1986, 39-53.

43 Adam Smith, *The Wealth of Nations,* Edwin Cannan (ed.), Methuen, London, 1961, vol. 2, 179.

44 Harold Innis, "Conclusion" from his *Fur Trade in Canada,* reprinted in Gordon Laxer (ed.), *Perspectives on Canadian Economic Development,* Oxford University Press, Toronto, 1991, 50-1.

45 McCalla, *Planting,* 46-66, 72-82.

46 Rothenberg, "Markets and Massachusetts Farmers," 300-5.

47 Vickers, 3-29.

48 Fernand Ouellet, *Economic and Social History of Quebec, 1760-1850,* Gage Publishing, Toronto, 1980, documented the strong habitant response to market signals from the 1770s to the 1790s (83-9, 113-18, 157-163), as well as the growing crisis after the turn of the century (186, 256-72).

49 Wallot and Paquet conceded that there was an habitant ethos according to which farm families adapted to change, but they wanted to deny that it was what determined the habitants' actions, "Strategie fonciére," 551-81, n555.

50 Fernand Ouellet, "Le mythe de l'Habitant sensible au marché," *Recherches sociographiques,* vol. 17, 1976, 115-32 – the article's title alone was a gift to his enemies.

51 Fernand Ouellet, "La sauvegarde des patrimoines dans le District de Québec," RHAF, vol. 26, no. 3, December 1972, 319-74.

52 Greer, 202-9.

53 Christian Dessureault, "Les Fondements de la Hierarchie Sociale au sein de la Paysannerie: Le cas de Saint-Hyacinthe, 1760-1815," doctoral dissertation, University of Montreal, 1985; his "L'Egalitarisme paysan dans l'ancienne société rurale de la vallée Saint-Laurent: element pour une ré-interpretation," RHAF, vol. 40, no. 3, Winter 1987, 373-407; and his "Crise ou Modernisation? La société rurale maskoutaine Durant le premiere tiers du xixe siècle," RHAF, vol. 42, no. 3, Winter 1989, 359-87. See

also T. Wien, "Visites paroissiales et production agricole au Canada vers la fin du XVIIIe siècle," F. Lebrun and N. Séguin, *Sociétés villageoises et rapports villes-campagnes au Québec et dans la France de l'Ouest, XVII–XXe siècles* (Actes du colloque de Québec, 1985), Trois-Rivières: Centre de recherché en etudes québécoises, UQTR, 1987, 183–93.

54 Normand Séguin, *La Conquête du sol au 19e siècle*, Boreal Express, Montreal, 56–63.

55 Guy Boisclair's review essay of J.I. Little's *Nationalism, Capitalism and Colonization*, in the *Journal of Eastern Township Studies*, no. 3, Fall 1993, 71–85. See also Little's reply, *Journal of Eastern Township Studies*, no. 4, Spring 1994, 74–86.

56 Gérard Bouchard, "Co-intégration et reproduction de la société rurale. Pour un modèle saguenayen de la marginalité," *Recherches socio-graphiques*, vol. 29, no. 2–3, 1988, 283–310.

57 John McCallum, *Unequal Beginnings: Agriculture and Economic Development in Quebec and Ontario until 1870*, University of Toronto Press, Toronto, 1980, 24.

58 Marvin McInnis, "Marketable Surpluses in Ontario Farming, 1860," *Social Science History*, vol. 8, no. 4, Autumn 1984, 395–424.

59 Frank Lewis and Marvin McInnis, "Agricultural Output and Efficiency in Lower Canada, 1851," *Research in Economic History*, vol. 9, 1984, 45–87. However, one should note the critique of Robert Armstrong, "The Efficiency of Quebec Farmers in 1851," *HS/SH*, vol. 17, no. 33, May 1981, 149–63.

60 Douglas McCalla, "The Wheat Staple and Upper Canadian Development," paper presented to the Canadian Historical Association, 1978, 34–45.

61 McCalla, *Planting*, 82, 87–8.

62 Marjorie Griffin Cohen, *Women's Work, Markets and Economic Development in 19th century Ontario*, University of Toronto Press, Toronto, 34–5.

63 G.F. Stanley, *The Birth of Western Canada*, University of Toronto Press, Toronto, 1961, 6–8.

64 Dennis Sprague, *Canada and the Métis*, Wilfrid Laurier University Press, Waterloo, 1988, and his "The Manitoba Land Question, 1870–1882," in R.D. Francis and H. Palmer (eds.), *The Prairie West – Historical Readings*, Pica Pica Press, Edmonton, 1992, 118–35.

65 Frederick John Shore, "The Canadians and the Métis: The Re-Creation of Manitoba, 1858–1872," doctoral dissertation, University of Manitoba, Winnipeg, 1991.

66 John Friesen, "Expansion of Settlement in Manitoba," in D. Swainson (ed.), *Historical Essays on the Prairie Provinces*, McClelland and Stewart, Toronto, 1970, 120.

67 Gerhard Ens, "Dispossession or Adaptation? Migration and Persistence of the Red River Métis," in Francis and Palmer, *Prairie West*, 136–61. See also Thomas Flanagan and Gerhard Ens, "Métis Land Grants in Manitoba: A Statistical Study," *HS/SH*, vol. 27, no. 53, May 1994, 65–87, and Thomas Flanagan, *Métis Lands in Manitoba*, University of Calgary Press, Calgary, 1991.

68 Peter A. Russell, "The Far-From-Dry Debates: Dry Farming on the Canadian Prairies and the American Great Plains," *AH*, vol. 81, no. 4, Fall 2007, 493–521. See also Friesen, "Expansion," 124–6.

69 Paul Voisey, *Vulcan – The Making of a Prairie Community*, University of Toronto Press, Toronto, 1988, 98–127; Cecilia Danysk, *Hired Hands*, McClelland and Stewart, Toronto, 1995, 26–58; and Tony Ward, "The Origins of the Canadian Wheat Boom, 1880–1910," *Canadian Journal of Economics*, vol. 27, no. 4, November 1994, 865–83.

70 Cash crop need not always mean wheat monoculture: grain and livestock raising were often combined.

71 Voisey, 77–97, and John Herd Thompson, *The Harvests of War: The Prairie West, 1914–1918*, Oxford University Press, Toronto, 1998, 66–8.

72 For examples, see B.G. Smillie (ed.), *Visions of the New Jerusalem – Religious Settlement on the Prairies*, NeWest Press, Edmonton, 1983, 109–53, and M. Lupul (ed.), *A Heritage in Transition: Essays in the History of Ukrainians in Canada*, McClelland and Stewart, Toronto, 1982, 32–48.

73 Sarah Carter, "'Two acres and a Cow': 'Peasant' Farming for the Indians of the Northwest, 1889–1897," in J.R. Miller (ed.), *Sweet Promises, A Reader on Indian-White Relations in Canada*, University of Toronto Press, Toronto, 1991, 353–77, and her "Agriculture and Agitation on the Oak River Dakota Reserve, 1875–1895," *Manitoba History*, vol. 6, 1983, 2–9.

74 On the limits and opportunities for subsistence, see Peter A. Russell, "Subsistence, Diversification and Staple Orientations on Saskatchewan Farms: Parkland vs. Prairie, 1911–1926," *Saskatchewan History*, vol. 57, no. 2, Fall 2005, 15–28.

75 John Weaver, *The Great Land Rush and the Making of the Modern World, 1650–1900*, McGill-Queen's University Press, Montreal, 2003, 44–5, 207–8, 251–2.

76 Although, as William Lyon Mackenzie said, "the price of free land is the fees."

77 After 1826 some free grants continued to be made in Upper Canada. Some privileged speculators received large grants in the Eastern Townships.

78 Most Prairie lands for sale were offered through the railways and the Hudson's Bay Company. Chester Martin, *Dominion Lands' Policy*, Macmillan, Toronto, 1938.

79 Ibid., 207–8.

80 Ibid.

CHAPTER TWO

1 Jean Hamelin and Fernand Ouellet, "Crise agricole dans le Bas-Canada (1802–1837)," *Études rurales*, 1962, 36–57.

2 Fernand Ouellet, *Economic and Social History of Quebec, 1760–1850: Structures and Conjonctures*, Gage Publishing, Toronto, 1980, 84–5. See also Jacques Mathieu, "Les relations ville-campagne: Québec et sa région au xviiie siècle," in Joseph Goy and J.-P. Wallot (ed.), *Société rurale dans la France de l'Ouest et au Québec (xvii–xxe siècles)*, University of Montreal Ecole des Hautes Etudes en Sciences Sociales, Montreal, 1981, 198–9.

3 The "minot de Paris" was a unit of volume, equal to 34.277 litres. The arpent as a measure of area was equal to 3,400 square metres or 0.84 acres.

4 Ouellet, *Economic and Social History*, 84–5.

5 Ibid., 90–3, 118–20, 164–8, 195–203, 310–13. See also Mario Lalancette, "Description et analyse du rapport pêche/seigneuriale canadienne á l'Ile-aux-Coudes au xviiie siècle," 203–16 and Aliette Geistdoerfer, "S'approprier la mer aux Iles de la Madeleine (Québec) et á Saint-Pierre-et-Miquelon," in Joseph Goy and J.-P. Wallot (ed.), *Évolution et éclatement du monde rural: structures, fonctionnement evolution des societies françaises et québécoises, xviie–xxe siècles*, University of Montreal Press, Montreal, 1986, 499–505.

6 See Louise Duchêne, *Habitants and Merchants in Seventeenth Century Montreal*, McGill-Queen's University Press, Montreal, 1992, 117–22, and Allan Greer, *Peasant, Lord, and Merchant: Rural Society in Three Quebec Parishes, 1740–1840*, University of Toronto Press, Toronto, 1985, 177–93.

7 G. Ramsay Cook, "La Survivance French-Canadian Style," *The Maple Leaf Forever*, Macmillan, Toronto, 1971, 129–40.

8 Ouellet, *Economic and Social History*, 668.

9 Ibid., 160, 194, 258, 344. See also *Lower Canada*, 350, which shows the
   decline in per capita output for the best years from 1774 to 1831.
10 Fernand Ouellet, "L'Agriculture bas-canadienne vue á travers la dîme
   et la rente en nature," *Histoire sociale/Social History*, 1971, 5–44, and
   Lower Canada, 1791–1840: Social Change and Nationalism, McClelland
   and Stewart, Toronto, 1980, 406. For his critics' case, see J.-P. Wallot and
   Gilles Paquet, "Rentes foncières, dîmes et revenues paysans: Le cas canadien," in Joseph Goy and Emmanuel Le Roy Ladurie (ed.), *Prestations
   Paysans, Dîmes, Rente Foncière et Mouvement de la Production Agricole
   á l'Epoque Preindustrielle*, Editions de l'Ecole Des Hautes Etudes en Sciences Sociales, Paris, 1982, 749–61.
11 These are largely taken at face value in R.L. Jones, "French-Canadian
   Agriculture in the St Lawrence Valley, 1815–1850" and "The Agricultural
   Development of Lower Canada, 1850–1867," in *Agricultural History*,
   vol. 16, 1942, 137–48, and vol. 19, 1945, 212–24, respectively.
12 Ouellet, *Economic and Social History*, 228, from three francophone wit-
   nesses and one anglophone witness.
13 Thomas Wien, "'Les Travaux Pressants,' Calendrier Agricole, Assolement
   et Productivité au Canada au XVIIIe siècle," *Revue d'histoire de Amérique
   Français*, vol. 43, no. 4, Spring 1990, 538.
14 Christian, "L'Égalitarism paysan dans l'ancienne société rurale de la
   Vallée du Saint-Laurent: Éléments pour une ré-interprétation," *Revue
   Historique d'Amérique Français*, vol. 40, no. 3, Winter 1987, 395 – no
   species of animal was found on all farms, not even the largest, implying a
   local trade in animal products. However, see Corinne Beutler, "Le role du
   blé à Montréal sous le régime seigneurial," *RHAF*, vol. 36, no. 2, September 1982, 241–62.
15 Greer, 177–93.
16 Ouellet, *Lower Canada*, 122. In his 1976 book, Ouellet put more explicit
   emphasis on intensive cropping as a cause of declining wheat yields.
17 Ibid., 282.
18 Fernand Ouellet, *Economy, Class, and Nation in Quebec: Interpretive
   Essays*, Copp Clark Pitman, Toronto, 1991, 126. On marginal lands in
   the Montreal District being taken up, see Réal Bélanger, *Social and Economic History of St-Lin, 1805–1883 and the Importance of the Laurier
   Family*, National Historic Parks and Sites Branch, Environment Canada,
   Ottawa, 1980; and on the turn to the marginal lands of the Trois-Rivieres
   District, see Colin M. Coates, *Metamorphoses of Landscape and Community in Early Quebec*, McGill-Queen's University Press, Montreal,
   2000; and the return to the Quebec District's marginal lands, see Lynda

Villeneuve, "La Socio-économie de Charlevoix au debut des Annes
1830," master's thesis, University of Laval, Quebec, 1992, and her *Paysage, mythe et territorialité: Charlevoix au xixe siècle: pour une nouvelle approche du paysage*, Laval University Press, Quebec, 1999.

19 Ouellet, *Economic and Social History*, 361. See also his *Lower Canada*, 57.

20 Ibid., 228.

21 Ibid., see for example 267.

22 Ibid., 160, 226, 260–3, 344, and 464.

23 Ouellet, *Lower Canada*, 278, 331.

24 Ibid., 354.

25 Ouellet was more explicit in 1976, *Lower Canada*, 122, 143.

26 Fernand Ouellet, "La sauvegarde des patrimoines dans le District de Québec Durant la premier moitié du xixe siècle," RHAF, vol. 26, no. 3, December 1972, 319–74.

27 Christian Dessureault on St Hyacinthe's marginal lands: "Les Fondements de la Hierarche Sociale au sein de la Paysannerie: Le cas de Saint-Hyacinthe, 1760–1815," unpublished doctoral dissertation, University of Montreal, 1985, and Jean Lafleur, Gilles Paquet, J.-P. Wallot, "Préliminaires á une étude de la géographie des prix du sol. La région de l'Assomption, 1792–1835," in Gérard Béaur, Christian Dessureault, and Joseph Goy (ed.), *Familles, Terre, Marchés Logiques économiques et stratégies dans les milieu ruraux (XVIIe–XXe siècles)*, Presses Universitaires de Rennes, Rennes, 2004, 222–4.

28 Ouellet, *Economic and Social History*, 342, against W.H. Parker, "A Revolution in the Agricultural Geography of Lower Canada, 1833–1838," *Revue de géographie de Montréal*, vol. 11, December 1957, 189–94, and his "A New Look at Unrest in Lower Canada in the 1830s," *Canadian Historical Review*, vol. 40, 1959, 209–17.

29 Ouellet, *Economic and Social History*, 349–53.

30 Homespun was not always for domestic use: some very poor families produced it to supplement their farm's meager income. Béatrice Craig, Judith Rygiel, Elizabeth Turcotte, "Survival or Adaptation? Domestic Rural Textile Production in Eastern Canada in the Later 19th Century," AH, vol. 49, no. 2, 2001, 140–71, especially 159.

31 Ibid., 355.

32 Ibid., 199–200. Author's translation.

33 Ibid., 186–8. See also R. Cole Harris and John Warkentin, *Canada before Confederation: A Study in Historical Geography*, Carleton University Press, Ottawa, 81–2, on the accelerated clearing of the eighteenth century,

and their view that "wheat exports reached their peak in 1802–1803 and declined rapidly thereafter," 83.

34 Ibid., 187.

35 Ibid., 204–15.

36 Ibid., 316–31.

37 Michel Brunet, "Trois Dominantes de la Pensée canadienne-française" in his *La Prèsence Anglaise et les Canadians*, Beauchemin, Montreal, 1964, 126.

38 Abbé Groulx, "The French Canadian Family" in Susan Mann Trofimenkoff, *Abbé Groulx – Variations on a Nationalist Theme*, Copp Clark, Toronto, 1972, 116.

39 Brunet, 124.

40 J.-P. Wallot and Gilles Paquet, "Aperçu sur le commerce international et les prix domestiques dans le Bas-Canada (1793–1812)," *RHAF*, vol. 21, 1967–68, 447–73; "Canada, 1760–1850: Anamorphoses et prospective," in *Economie québécoise*, R. Comeau (ed.), University of Quebec Press, Sillery, 1969, 278–80; "Le Bas-Canada au début du XIXe siècle: une hypothèse," *RHAF*, vol. 25, June 1971, 39–61; "Crise Agricole et tensions socio-ethniques dans le Bas-Canada, 1802–1812: éléments pour une ré-interprétation," *RHAF*, vol. 26, September 1972, 185–236; "International Circumstances of Lower Canada, 1786–1810: Prolegomenon," *CHR*, vol. 52, December 1972, 371–401. See also J.-P. Wallot, *Un Québec Qui Bourgeait*, Boreal Express, Montreal, 1972, especially 36–7, n44.

41 J. Wallot and Giles Paquet, "Crise agricole et tensions socio-ethniques dans le Bas-Canada, 1802–1812: éléments pour une reinterpretation," *RHAF*, vol. 26, no. 2, September 1972, 196–222.

42 Ibid., 234–5.

43 Ibid., 198–200.

44 Ibid., 199, 200.

45 Ibid., 217. For a map of the seigneurial zone see Serge Courville, *Quebec : A Historical Geography*, UBC Press, Vancouver, 2005, 139, 142; or R. Cole Harris, *Two Societies – Life in Mid-Nineteenth Century Quebec*, McClelland and Stewart, Toronto, 1976, 10.

46 Corinne Beutler, "La Modernisation de l'equipement agricole dans la région de Montréal: Recherches sur l'origine des nouveaux modeles de charrue d'aprés des inventaires après deces, 1792–1835," in Gérard Bouchard and Joseph Goy (ed.), *Famille, Economie et Société Rurale en context d'urbanisation (17e–20e siècle)*, Centre interuniversitaire SOREP, Chicoutimi, 1990, 273–92. Robert-Lionel Séguin, "L'équipement aratoire

prémachineiste aux xviie, xviiie, et xixe siècles," Claude Galarneau and Elzéar Lavoie (ed.), *France et Canada Français du xvie au xxe siècles*, University of Laval Press, Quebec, 1963, 121–38.

47 Wallot and Paquet, "Crise Agricole," 217.

48 Greer, 212–15.

49 Wallot and Paquet, "Crise Agricole," 221. Except for the last eight words, this could be a rough summary of an important part of Ouellet's thesis. Is the dispute, then, essentially one about timing?

50 Wallot and Paquet, "International Circumstances," 384–7.

51 J. Wallot and Giles Paquet, "Le Bas-Canada au début du xixe siècle: une hypothèse," *RHAF*, vol. 25, no. 1, June 1971, 54–8.

52 T.J.A. Le Goff, "The Agricultural Crisis in Lower Canada, 1802–1812: Review of a Controversy," *CHR*, vol. 55, March 1974, 6.

53 Ibid., 8.

54 Ibid.

55 Ibid., 29.

56 Ibid., 14.

57 Ibid., 13.

58 Ibid., 16.

59 Ibid., 22.

60 Ibid., 29.

61 Ibid., 30.

62 J. Wallot and Gilles Paquet, "The Agricultural Crisis in Lower Canada, 1802–1812: *mise au point*. A Response to T.J.A. Le Goff," *CHR*, vol. 56, no. 2, June 1975, 133–61; italics added.

63 Ibid., 137.

64 Ibid., 138.

65 Ibid., 144.

66 T.J.A. Le Goff, "A Reply," *CHR*, vol. 56, June 1975, 167.

67 Fernand Ouellet, "Le Mythe de 'L'Habitant Sensible au Marché,'" *Recherches sociographiques*, vol. 17, no. 1, 1976, 115. Wallot and Paquet, in 1986, would qualify their own perspective to allow for an ethos amongst peasant farmers who made choices within a "bounded rationality" rather than irrationally: "Stratégie Foncière de l'Habitant," *RHAF*, vol. 39, no. 4, spring 1986, n555.

68 Ouellet, "Mythe," 127–8.

69 The 20.9 per cent figure comes from using Innis's data: H.A. Innis and A.R.M. Lower (ed.), *Selected Documents in Canadian Economic History, 1783–1885*, University of Toronto Press, Toronto, 1933, 265–6. Wallot and Paquet calculated 10 per cent: "Crise Agricole," 192. Ouellet in

Lower Canada, 349, offered five- and ten-year moving averages (1793–1842) to show the trend of decline more clearly.

70 The graph also shows the rising peaks and valleys in exports until after the turn of the century and then the falling peaks and valleys, leading up to the end of wheat exports in the 1830s. Wallot and Paquet want to reserve the word "crisis" for the final collapse of wheat exports, as against the "crisis in the sense of Ouellet," which marks the beginnings of the downward trend. Ouellet, *Economic and Social History*, 668, gives a graph for wheat and flour production that was actually the export figures.

71 J.-P. Wallot and Gilles Paquet, "Strategie foncière de l'Habitant: Québec (1790–1835)," RHAF, vol. 39, no. 4, Spring 1986, n559.

72 J.-P. Wallot and Gilles Paquet, "Les Inventaires après décès á Montreal au Tournant du XIXe siècle: Préliminaires á une analyse," RHAF, vol. 30, no. 2, September 1976, 163–224. Christian Dessureault, "L'inventaire après désès et l'agriculture bas-canadienne," *Material History Bulletin/Bulletin d'histoire de la culture matérielle*, no. 17, National Museums of Canada, Ottawa, 1983, 127–38, and Lorraine Gadoury, "Les stocks des habitants dans les inventaires après décès," 139–47 in the same issue.

73 By the late 1970s Europeans had begun to apply quantitative techniques in the use the post-mortem inventories and to reflect on that source's difficulties, a debate in which Wallot and Paquet took part. See Ad van der Woude and Anton Schuurman (ed.), *Probate Inventories – A New Source for the Historical Study of Wealth, Material History, and Agricultural Development*, HES Publishers, Utrecht, 1980; M. Baulant (ed.), *Inventaires Aprés-Décès et Ventes de Meubles – Apports á une histoire de la vie économique et quotidienne, XIVe – XXe siècle*, Academia, Louvain-la-Neuve, 1988; and J.-P. Wallot and Gilles Paquet, "Une Spectrographie des Genre de Vie dans la société rurale Bas-Canadienne (1792–1835)," 243–56.

74 Yves Morin, "La répresentativité de l'inventaire après décès – l'étude d'un cas: Québec au debut du XIXe siècle," RHAF, vol. 34, 1981, 515–33.

75 Wallot and Paquet, "Les Inventaires après Décès," 173–83, and their "Strategie fonciere," 564–5.

76 For examples, see J. Wallot and Giles Paquet, "Structures socials et niveau de richesse dans les campagnes du Québec, 1792–1812," *Material History Bulletin/Bulletin d'histoire de la culture matérielle*, no. 17, National Museums of Canada, Ottawa, 1983, 249, as well as Wallot and Paquet, "Strategie fonciére," n564.

77 Morin, 515.

78 Dessureault, "Fondements," 206.

79 Christian Dessureault, "Crise ou modernization? La société rurale maskoutaine Durant le premier tiers du XIXe siècle," *RHAF*, vol. 42, no. 3,
winter 1989, 373–4.

80 Wallot and Paquet, "Strategie fonciére," 570.

81 J. Wallot and Gilles Paquet, "Les habitants de Montréal et de Québec
(1790–1835): contexts geo-économiques differents, meme strategie fonciére," *RHAF*, vol. 39, no. 4, spring 1986, 105.

82 Louis Michel, "Endetement et société rurale dans la region de Montréal
au dix-huitième siècle. Premières approches et éléments de réflexion,"
in François Lebrun and Normand Séguin (ed.), *Sociétés Villageoise et
Rapports Villes-Compagnes au Québec et dans la France de l'Ouest,
XVIIe–XXe siècles*, Actes du Colleque Franco-Québecois, 1985, University
of Quebec at Trois-Riviéres, Trois-Riviéres, 1987, 171–80.

83 J. Wallot and Giles Paquet, "Crédit et endettement en milieu rural bas-
canadien," *Famille, Économie et Société Rurale en Context d'Urbanisation (17e–20e siècle)*, Centre interuniversitaire SOREP, Chicoutimi,
1990, 251–70.

84 J. Wallot and Giles Paquet, "Reproduction sociale et crédit en milieu
rural: une approche socio-économique au cas du Québec, 1790–1835,"
*Transmettre, Hériter, Succéder – Le Reproduction Familliale en mileux
Rural France-Québec, XVIIIe–XXe siècles*, University of Lyons Press, Lyon,
1992, 175–88.

85 Jean Lefleur, Gilles Paquet, and J. Wallot, "Le coût du sol dans la région
de l'Assomption, 1792–1825: enrichissement, enchérissement et liens au
marché," *Famille et Marché, XVIe–XXe siècles*, Septentrion, Quebec, 2003,
95–114.

86 Jean Lefleur, Gilles Paquet, and J. Wallot, "Preliminaires a une étude de
la géographie des prix du sol. La région de l'Assomption, 1792–1835,"
*Familles, Terre, Marchés Logiques économiques et stratégies dans les
milieu ruraux XVIIe–XXe siècles*, University Press of Rennes, Rennes,
2004, 211–25.

87 Paquet and Wallot, "Rentes fonciéres," 753 point to increases from 10
to 15 livres in 1808–1810 for new concessions to 20 to 24 livres around
1820. See also Ouellet, *Economic and Social History*, 286–7, and Christian Dessureault, "Fondements," 99.

88 Claude Pronovost notes that merchants seldom saw actual currency or
coin: "Marchands et crédit marchand au debut du XIXe siècle,"
G. Bouchard and J. Goy (eds.), *Famille, économie et société rurale en
contexte d'urbanisation (17e–20e siècles)*, Centre interuniversitaire

SOREP École des hautes études en sciences socials, Chicoutimi, 1990, 245.

89 Jean Lefleur, "Le marché de la terre dans la région de Montréal, Saint-Sulpice, 1792–1835," *Familles, Terres*, 199–209.

90 An exception was Pierre Guy.Joanette Ginette, "Pierre Guy, marchant-negociant de Montréal: Les multiples activities d'un bourgeoise canadien-français dans la second moitie du XVIIIe siècle," master's thesis, University of Montreal, Montreal, 1985. The larger the merchant's scale of operations the more likely he was to speculate in "wild" lands, the less likely to deal in cleared land: Gérald Bernier and Daniel Salée, "Appropriation Foncière et Bourgeoisie Marchande: éléments pour une analyse de l'économie marchande du Bas-Canada avant 1846," *RHAF*, vol. 36, no. 2, September 1982, 163–94. George Bervin, "Les marchands-négociants et la diversité de leurs activités économiques à Québec entre 1800 et 1825," doctoral dissertation, University of Montreal, Montreal, 1989, and his *Québec au XIXe siècle: L'activité économique des grands marchands*, Septentrion, Quebec, 1991. Martine Cardin, "Jean Leroux dit Provençal, marchand à Sorel au XVIIIe siècle," master's thesis, University of Montreal, Montreal, 1987. Jean Lafleur, "Capital marchand et transition vers le capitalism: étude sur les marchands montréalais au cours du premier tiers du XIXe siècle," master's thesis, University of Montreal, Montreal, 1989. Claire Lapointe, "Les marchands ruraux anglophones de la région de Montréal entre 1765 et 1840: niveau de vie et activités commerciales," master's thesis, University of Montreal, Montreal, 1991. Claude Pronovost, *La bourgeoisie marchande en milieu rural (1720–1840)*, University of Laval Press, Quebec, 1998. Katy Tari, "Les marchands ruraux de la Paroisse Saint-Joseph de Chambly (1796–1850): etude socio-économique," master's thesis, University of Montreal, Montreal, 1989.

91 Lise Saint-Georges, "Transactions foncières dans la paroisse de Pointe-aux-Trembles sur l'île de Montréal, entre 1821 et 1861," *Transmettre, Hériter, Succéder*, 91–100.

92 Several other articles on land markets in the same volume do not bear on conditions in the seigneurial zone: Marc Saint-Hilare, "Marché foncier et transmission familiale dans un terrior neuf: Saint-Fulgence," 101–14, covered a later period in a colonization parish outside the seigneurial zone. Similarly, "Essai de synthèse," 115–20, which he co-authored with Saint-Georges and Gérard Béaur, tried to draw patterns from three areas too different to be comparable. Jacques Mathieu, Alain Laberge, Lina Gouger, and Geneviève Postolec's study of the first half of the eighteenth century focused on initial settlement and whether pioneers attempted a "land

monopoly," i.e., disproportionate landholding: "L'accaparement foncier et la reproduction sociale dans la vallée du Saint-Laurent au xvIIIe siècle," 121–34.

93   Lefleur, Paquet, Wallot, "Le coût du sol," 109.

94   Ibid., 101. Compare to Sylvie Depatie, "La transmission du patrimoine au Canada (xvII–xvIIIe siecles): qui sont les defavorises?," *RHAF*, vol. 54, no. 4, Spring 2001, 557–70.

95   Fernand Ouellet, "Les classes dominantes au Québec, 1760–1840. Bilan historiographique," *RHAF*, vol. 38, no. 2, Autumn 1984, n233. And again in his *Economy, Class, and Nation*, n158. In an oblique reference, apparently directed at Christian Dessureault, who used all post-mortem inventories not a sample, Ouellet commented: "Even if a lot of caution is necessary in using probate records the fact is that all of this confirms my conclusions of 25 years ago derived from other sources," *Economy, Class, and Nation*, 137.

96   J. Wallot and Gilles Paquet, "Stratégie foncière de l'habitant: Québec (1790–1835)," *RHAF*, vol. 39, no. 4, Spring 1986, n564.

97   Ibid., n565.

98   Fernand Ouellet, *L'Ontario Français dans le Canada français avant 1911*, Prise de parole, Sudbury, 2005, 366–7.

99   Serge Gagnon, *Quebec and Its Historians: The 20th Century*, Harvest House, Montreal, 1985, 103. Earlier in his career, Gagnon had espoused a relativist "sociology of knowledge" akin to postmodernism: Serge Gagnon, "La nature et le role de l'historiographie: postulats pour une sociologie de la connaissance historique," *RHAF*, vol. 26, no. 4, March 1973, 479–531; which drew a strong response – Hubert Watelet, "Connaissance et Sociologie de la Connaissance chez les Historiens," *RHAF*, vol. 27, no. 4, March 1974, 571–8. Although Gagnon renounced that approach (*Le passé composé: De Ouellet à Rudin*, vLB éditeur, Montreal, 1999), something very like it would be taken up twenty years later by Ronald Rudin, "La quête d'une societé normale: critique de la réinterprétation de l'histoire du Québec," *Bulletin d'histoire politique*, vol. 3, no. 2, 1995, 9–42, and his *Making History in 20th Century Quebec*, University of Toronto Press, Toronto, 1997; which drew considerably more reaction – John A. Dickinson, "Commentaires sur la critique de Ronald Rudin," *Bulletin d'histoire politique*, vol. 4, no. 2, 1995, 21–4; Jean-Paul Bernard, "Histoire Nouvelle et Révisionnisme," 53–5; Gilles Bourque, "Du révisionnisme en histoire du Québec," 45–51; and Brian Young, "Y a-t-il une nouvelle histoire du Québec?," 7–11 in the same issue; Fernand Harvey and Paul-André Linteau, "Les étranges lunettes de Ronald

Rudin," *RHAF*, vol. 51, no. 3, Winter 1998, 419–29; and Michel Sarra-Bournet, "Pour une histoire postrévisionniste," *Bulletin d'histoire politique*, vol. 4, no. 2, 1995, 25–9.

100 Ibid., 130, emphasis added.

101 Ibid., 139, emphasis added.

102 Ibid., 146.

103 Ibid., 120.

104 Ibid., 123.

105 Ibid.

106 Ibid., 126.

107 Ibid., 132.

108 Ibid., 149.

109 Ibid., 160.

110 Ibid.

111 The tithe is widely used to estimate trends in crop yields in France, despite suffering from a host of problems not found in Lower Canada, such as whether it was collected by the priest or his delegated agent (who kept part of what was paid as a fee), whether it was paid in kind or in cash, and what local variations were in the rate. Much is made of the claim that in France the tithe was collected in the field, but this was often not the case in Lower Canada. Emmanuel LeRoy Ladurie and Joseph Goy, *Tithe and Agrarian History from the 14th to the 19th Centuries*, Cambridge University Press, Cambridge, 1982, 15–31. See also M.T. Lorcin, "La fraude des décimables: movement court ou movement long?," in Joseph Goy and Emmanuel LeRoy Ladurie (ed.), *Prestations Paysans, Dîmes, Rent Foncière et Mouvement de la Production Agricole à l'Epagnes Preindustrielle*, vol. 2, Editions de l'École des Hautes Études en Sciences socials, Paris, 1982, 599–606.

112 Ibid., 160–1; emphasis added.

113 Ibid., 127.

114 Ouellet, *Lower Canada*, 349, 350.

115 Serge Courville, "Croissance Villageoise et industries rurales dans les seigneuries du Québec (1815–1835)," *Sociétés Villageoise*, 210–16; "La crise agricole du Bas-Canada: éléments d'une réflexion géographique," *Cahiers de géographie du Québec*, vol. 24, 1980, 193–224; "Villages and Agriculture in the Seigneuries of Lower Canada: Conditions of a Comprehensive Study of Rural Quebec in the First Half of the Nineteenth Century," *Canadian Papers in Rural History*, vol. 5, 1986, 121–49; and *Entre Ville et Campagne – L'essor du village dans les seigneuries du Bas-Canada*, University of Laval Press, Quebec, 1990. See also Rene Hardy, Pierre

Lanthier, and Normand Séguin, "Les industries rurales et l'extension du reseau villageois dans le Mauricie pre-industrielle: l'example du comte de Champlain Durant la seconde moitie du xixe siècle," *Sociétés Villageoisies*, 239–53, who argue for larger village populations by increasing the number of farmers counted as living in villages; Paul Labonne, "Structuration de l'espace et économie villageoise: Deux études de cas: Saint-Martin de l'Ilse Jesus et l'Abord-à-Plouffe," master's thesis, University of Montreal, Montreal, 1994; and Jocelyn Morneau, *Petits pays et grands ensembles: les articulations au monde rurale au xixe siècle: l'example du lac Saint-Pierre*, University of Laval Press, Quebec, 1999, 30–40. When the census shows an unwelcome decline in the number of blacksmiths, it is dismissed as an error of under-reporting, 82.

116 Against the proto-industrialization thesis, see Jean-Pierre Kesteman, "Une bourgeoisie et son espace: industrialization et développement du capitalism dans le district de Saint-Francis, Québec, 1823–1879," doctoral dissertation, University of Quebec at Montreal, Montreal, 1985, and Christian Dessureault, "Industrie and société rurale: Le cas de la seigneurie de Saint-Hyacinthe," *HS/SH*, vol. 25 (no. 55), May 1995, 100–1, and Michel Boisvert, "Les parameters socioculturels de l'industrie textile au Bas-Canada au xixe siècle," in Serge Courville and Normand Séguin (ed.), *Espace et culture/Space and Culture*, University of Laval Press, Quebec, 1994, 305–18.

117 Ouellet, *Economy, Class, and Nation*, 138.

118 Serge Courville, Jean-Claude Robert, and Normand Séguin, "The Spread of Rural Industry in Lower Canada, 1831–1851," *Journal of the Canadian Historical Association*, 1991, 57.

119 Louise Duchêne, "Observations sur l'agriculture du Bas-Canada au début du xixe siècle," *Evolution et eclatement*, 198. As to which fly, see Art Borkent, "A review of the wheat blossom midge, *Sitodiplosis mosellana* (Géhin) (Diptera: Cecidomyiidae) in Canada," Agriculture Canada, Research Branch, Technical Bulletin 1989-5E, Ottawa, 1989.

120 John D. Post, *The Last Great Subsistence Crisis in the Western World*, Johns Hopkins University Press, Baltimore, 1977, 55, 61, 127, 167, 192.

121 Allan Greer, like Louise Duchêne, was a graduate student of Fernand Ouellet.

122 Dessureault, "Fondements," 257.

123 Greer, 249.

124 J.S. Piché, "La modernization de l'agriculture dans la région de Soulanges de la fin de xviiie siècle au milieu du xixe siècle," University of Montreal, master's thesis, Montreal, 1992, 18–19.

125 Greer first notes wheat production had fallen, as Ouellet inferred from export and tithe records. However, he argued this could not be read as a fall in agricultural productivity. After all, habitants had devoted their land to other crops. He then offers a "diachronic comparison" of the years 1764 and 1831 as "a more straightforward way of gauging changes in agricultural productivity." For Sorel and St Denis, this method shows only a slight decline in the wheat grown per farm for the first seigneury, and a substantial increase for the second. However, Greer seems not to want the reader to take these figures at face value. Instead he turns his attention to the most precise measurement of agricultural productivity.

126 Greer, 213.

127 Ouellet, *Economy, Class, and Nation*, 135. His immediate reference was to the work of Lorraine Gaboury on post-mortem inventories in the District of Montreal.

128 Dessureault, "Fondements," 318, 333.

129 A homespun mix of linen and wool could be bartered or even sold locally. Béatrice Craig, Judith Rygiel, and Elizabeth Turcotte, "The Homespun Paradox: Market-Oriented Production of Cloth in Eastern Canada in the 19th Century," *AH*, vol. 76, no. 1, Winter 2002, 28–57.

130 Greer, 228.

131 Ibid., 225.

132 For a map of the Eastern Townships, see J.I. Little, *Nationalism, Capitalism and Colonization*, McGill-Queen's University Press, Montreal, 1989, 2; Margaret Bennett, *Oatmeal and the Catechism – Scottish Gaelic Settlers in Quebec*, McGill-Queen's University Press, Montreal, 1998; or R. Cole Harris, *Two Societies – Life in Mid-Nineteenth Century Quebec*, McClelland and Stewart, Toronto, 1976, 10.

133 Sylvie Dépatie, Mario Lalanchette, and Christian Dessureault, *Contributions à l'étude du régime Seigneurial Canadien*, Hurtubise HMH, Montreal, 1987, 201.

134 Christian Dessureault, "L'évolution de la productivité agricole dans la plaine de Montréal, 1852–1871 – Grandes and petites exploitations dans un système familial d'agriculture," *HS/SH*, vol. 38 (no. 76), November 2005, 235–65.

135 Piché, 18.

136 Ibid., 19.

137 Greer, 38.

138 From the second half of the eighteenth century to the 1830s, depending on location, the proportion of the plowless varied from 20 per cent to 40 per cent. Beutler, "Modernisation," 273–92. Séguin, "L'équipement,"

121–38. See also Christian Dessureault with John A. Dickinson, "Farm Implements and Husbandry in Colonial Quebec, 1740–1840," in Peter Bones (ed.), *New England/New France, 1600–1850*, Boston University, Boston, 1992, 100–21.

139 Wien, *Peasant Accumulation*, 237–8.

140 This certainly fits the data of both Thomas Wien, "Peasant Accumulation in a Context of Colonization – Riviére-du-Sud, Canada, 1720–1775," doctoral dissertation, McGill University, Montreal, 1988, and Sylvie Depatie, "La transmission du patrimoine au Canada (xviie–xviiie siècle): qui sont les défavorisés?," *RHAF*, vol. 54, no. 4, Spring 2001, 557–70. However, as Depatie noted, the existing inequalities were aggravated and increased as the impact of the market became greater.

141 Greer, 228.

142 Ouellet, *Economy, Class, and Nation*, 135.

143 Christian Dessureault, "L'égalitarisme paysan dans l'ancienne société rurale de la Vallée-Saint-Laurent: éléments pour une ré-interpretation," *RHAF*, vol. 40, no. 40, Winter 1987, 518.

144 Piché, 131.

145 Ibid., 120.

146 Wien points out that the effective limit on the area of actual cultivation was the growing season, "Travaux Pressants," 537–8.

147 Ibid., 120.

148 Greer, 230.

149 Wien, 227.

150 Dessureault, "Fondements," 386–7. See also his "Fortune paysanne et cycle de vie. Le cas de la seigneurie de Saint-Hyacinthe (1795–1844)," *Histoire et Sociétés Rurales*, no. 7, 1997, 73–96.

151 Christian Dessureault, "Parenté et stratification sociale dans une paroisse rurale de la vallée de Saint-Laurent au milieu du xixe siècle," *RHAF*, vol. 54, no. 3, Winter 2001, 411–47, and "Mobilité sociale et généalogie: la descendance de Joseph Plamondon et de Marguerite Marest, de 1741 à 1876," *Mémoires de la société généalogique canadienne-français*, no. 1, cahier 231, Spring 2002, 55–70.

CHAPTER THREE

1 Paul Phillips, "Land Tenure and Economic Development: A Comparison of Upper and Lower Canada," *Journal of Canadian Studies*, vol. 9, no. 2, 1974, 36.

2 Ibid., 44.

3 Phillips, 42. Against this view see J.I. Little, "Ethnicity, Family Structure, and Seasonal Labour Strategies on Quebec's Appalachian Frontier," *Journal of Family History*, vol. 17, no. 3, 1992, 289–302.

4 Ibid.

5 Ibid., 39.

6 John Isbister, "Agriculture, Balanced Growth, and Social Change in Central Canada since 1850: An Interpretation," in Douglas McCalla (ed.), *Perspectives on Canadian Economic History*, Copp Clark Pitman, Toronto, 1987, 64.

7 Ibid., 67.

8 Ibid.

9 John McCallum, *Unequal Beginnings: Agriculture and Economic Development in Quebec and Ontario until 1870*, University of Toronto Press, Toronto, 1980, 44. Béatrice Craig's comparison of North American societies missed that point about culture and mobility: "Pour une approche comparative de l'étude des sociétés rurales nord-américaines," *Histoire sociale/Social History*, vol. 23, no. 46, November 1990, 252.

10 Ibid., 38–9, 113–14.

11 Ibid., 4.

12 Ibid., 20.

13 Ibid., 116.

14 Marvin McInnis and Frank Lewis, "The Efficiency of the French-Canadian Farmer in the 19th Century," *Journal of Economic History*, vol. 40, no. 3, September 1980, 514.

15 R.M. McInnis, "Perspectives on Ontario Agriculture, 1815–1930," *Canadian Papers in Rural History*, vol. 8, 1992, 79–80.

16 Ibid., 81.

17 Ibid., 79.

18 J. David Wood, *Making Ontario: Agricultural Colonization and Landscape Re-Creation before the Railway*, McGill-Queen's University Press, Montreal & Kingston, 2000, 160.

19 Robert Armstrong strongly disputes McInnis's use of econometrics: "The Efficiency of Quebec Farmers in 1851," *Histoire sociale/Social History*, 1984, vol. 17, no. 33, 149–63. See also his *Structure and Change: An Economic History of Quebec*, Gage, Toronto, 1984, but also José E. Igartua, "Le Québec de Pangloss: Structure and Change: An Economic History of Quebec," *Revue d'histoire de l'Amérique Français*, vol. 39, no. 2, Autumn 1985, 253–61.

20 Donald Kerr and William J. Smyth, "Agriculture, Balanced Growth, and Social Change in Central Canada since 1850: Some Comments toward

a More Complete Explanation," *Economic Development and Cultural Change*, vol. 28, no. 3, April 1980, 617.

21 Ibid.

22 Ibid., 619. Examples of unreported animals in the nineteenth century census are poultry and goats.

23 Ibid., 620.

24 J.I. Little, "Agricultural Progress in Canada East/Quebec: Problems in Measuring Relative Productivity during the Grain-Dairy Transition Period," *HS/SH*, vol. 18, no. 36, November 1985, 427. There have been attempts in Europe to apply the calorie approach in more sophisticated ways: B.J. van Bavel and E. Thoen (eds.), *Land Productivity and Agro-Systems in the North Sea area, Middle Ages – 20th Century, Elements for Comparison*, Brepolis, Turnhaut, 1999, and B.M.S. Campbell and M. Overton (eds.), *Land, Labour, and Livestock*, Manchester University Press, Manchester, 1991, especially 10–32.

25 Little, "Agricultural Progress," 425.

26 Ibid., 428.

27 Ibid., 426.

28 Robert Armstrong, "The Efficiency of Quebec Farmers in 1851," *HS/SH*, vol. 17, no. 33, May 1984, 163.

29 Morris Altman, "Land Tenure, Ethnicity, and the Condition of Agricultural Income and Productivity in Mid-Nineteenth Century Quebec," *Agricultural History*, vol. 72, no. 4, Autumn 1998, 738.

30 See Fernand Ouellet, *L'Ontario français dans le Canada français avant 1911*, Prise de parole, Sudbury, 2005, 158–9 and 27–9. Gordon Darroch and Lee Soltow, *Property and Inequality in Victorian Ontario: Structural Patterns and Cultural Communities in the 1871 Census*, University of Toronto Press, Toronto, 1994.

31 See Ibid., 145, and more generally, 141–6.

32 Ibid., 151.

33 Ibid., 154.

34 Ibid., 158.

35 Ibid., 160–9. See also McInnis, "Perspectives," 78–81.

36 Ibid., 179.

37 Ouellet agrees with Akenson's "reasonable" view on this point, against Darroch's claim that there was little support for whether late entry into a land market held one back: Ibid., 323.

38 Ibid., 407.

39 Ibid., 408.

40 Ibid., 307.

41 Ibid., 355.

42 Ibid., 173.

43 Ibid., 174–5.

44 Ibid., 180.

45 In particular, he quotes McInnis for suggesting an immediate move from wheat to cattle. Ibid., 158–9.

46 Heather Menzies, "Technology in the Craft of Ontario Cheesemaking: Women in Oxford County *circa* 1860," *Ontario History*, vol. 87, no. 3, September 1995, 295.

CHAPTER FOUR

1 Harry Johnson, "Canadian Contributions to the Discipline of Economics Since 1945," in Garden F. Boreham (ed.), *Contemporary Economic Thinking*, Holt, Rinehart and Winston of Canada, Toronto, 1971, 77, and Robin Neill, "Rationality and the Informational Environment: A Reassessment of the Work of Harold Adams Innis," *Journal of Canadian Studies*, vol. 22, no. 4, winter 1987–88, 80–1. But see also William Christian (ed.), *The Ideal File of Harold Adams Innis*, University of Toronto Press, Toronto, 1980, viii.

2 H.A. Innis, "An Introduction to the Economic History of Ontario from Outpost to Empire," in Mary Q. Innis (ed.), *Essays in Canadian Economic History*, University of Toronto Press, Toronto, 1956, 108–22.

3 Louise Duchêne's findings for Montreal and its rural surroundings in the seventeenth century call this into question: Duchene, *Habitants et marchands de Montreal au XVIIe siècle – essai*, Boreal, Montreal & Kingston, 1988, 338–47, 484–8.

4 H.A. Innis, "Unused Capacity as a Factor in Canadian Economic History," in Mary Q. Innis, 146, 153. McCalla questions this in *Planting the Province: The Economic History of Upper Canada, 1784–1870*, University of Toronto Press, Toronto, 1993, 62.

5 Innis, "Introduction," 116.

6 F.W. Burton, "Staple Production and Canada's External Relations," in H.A. Innis (ed.), *Essays in Political Economy*, University of Toronto Press, Toronto, 1938, 48.

7 H.A. Innis (ed.), *The Dairy Industry in Canada*, Ryerson Press, Toronto, 1937, ix.

8 M.Q. Innis (ed.), *Essays*, 67. See also, Innis, *Dairy Industry*, vi, as well as Innis, "Economic History of Ontario," 113.

9 Innis, *Dairy Industry*, xv.

10 H.A. Innis and A.R.M. Lower (eds.), *Select Documents in Canadian Economic History, 1783–1885*, University of Toronto Press, Toronto, 1933, 23.

11 Large-scale cheese production on family farms had begun before American factory technology came to Ontario: Innis overestimated the need for that technology. See Heather Menzies, "Technology in the Craft of Ontario Cheesemaking: Women in Oxford County circa 1860," *Ontario History*, vol. 87, no. 3, September 1995, 293–304.

12 Innis, *Dairy Industry*, xxii, 7, 10.

13 Ibid., viii–ix.

14 Vernon Fowke, *Canadian Agricultural Policy*, University of Toronto Press, Toronto, 1946, 79–80; emphasis added. Paul Phillips, "The Hinterland Perspective: The Political Economy of Vernon C. Fowke," *Canadian Journal of Political and Social Theory*, vol. 2, no. 2, Spring-Summer 1978, 73–95.

15 Ibid.

16 Ibid., 105; see also 110.

17 Vernon Fowke, *The National Policy and the Wheat Economy*, University of Toronto Press, Toronto, 1957, 13.

18 Ibid., 17.

19 Fowke, *Agricultural Policy*, 107. See also Phillips, "Hinterland Perspective," 73–96, especially 77–8.

20 Ibid., 128. In comparison with Norman Séguin's *agro-forestier* thesis, Fowke blamed the government as well as the lumber companies. Normand Séguin, *La Conquête du sol au 19e siècle*, Boreal Express, Sillery, 1977; *Agriculture et colonization au Québec*, Boréal Express, Montreal, 1980. "L'agriculture de la Mauricie et du Québec, 1850–1950." *Revue d'histoire de l'Amérique Français*, vol. 35, no. 4, March 1982, 537–62; "Paysans et monde forestier: nouvelles reflexions sur le monde rurale québécois au xixe siècle," *Cahiers des annals de Normandie*, vol. 24, 1992, 177–87.

21 William L. Marr and Donald Paterson, *Canada: An Economic History*, University of Toronto Press, Toronto, 1980: Most diagrams appear designed to show that historical data can be analyzed using neo-classical economics, rather than showing how we could better understand the data itself. If none of the diagrams (or related discussion) appeared, the text would not be diminished as a history of the Canadian economy. Richard Pomfret, *The Economic Development of Canada*, Methuen, Toronto, 1981, has graphs and equations, as well as maps. In Kenneth Norrie and Douglas Owram, *A History of the Canadian Economy*, Harcourt Brace

Jovanovich Canada, Toronto, 1991, the economic analysis is presented in an introduction, leaving the reader largely to relate it to the history.

22 Marr and Paterson, 87.

23 Ibid.

24 Ibid.. 88.

25 Ibid., 90.

26 Ibid., 92.

27 Ibid., 92, 94.

28 Ibid., 88.

29 Ibid., 95–6.

30 Pomfret, *Economic Development*, 30. He presents staples as one of several competing theories of economic development, 42–8 (more space than he dedicated to agriculture in Ontario or Quebec).

31 Norrie and Owram, 110. They note the rise of local crops such as tobacco in Essex and Kent in the early 1820s when wheat seemed unable to breach the British market.

32 Douglas McCalla, "The Ontario Economy in the Long Run," *Ontario History*, vol. 90, no. 2, Autumn 1998, n112. K.J. Rea, *A Guide to Canadian Economic History*, Canadian Scholars' Press, Toronto, 1991, 13–42, is another introductory survey from a staples perspective, although the bibliography includes a citation for one of R.M. McInnis's attacks on the staples thesis.

33 Vernon Fowke, "The Myth of the Self-Sufficient Canadian Pioneer," *Transactions of the Royal Society of Canada*, vol. 56, June 1962, 72.

34 Ibid., 24–5.

35 Ibid., 26.

36 Ibid., 34.

37 Ibid., 27.

38 Ibid., 36.

39 Ibid., 37.

40 The Rowell-Sirois Report (1940) recommended changes to the balance of federal and provincial powers in the Canadian constitution.

41 Leo Johnson, "New Thoughts on an Old Problem: 'Self-Sufficient Agriculture in Upper Canada," paper given at the Canadian Historical Association, Guelph, 1984, 21. See also Leo A. Johnson, "Independent Commodity Production: Mode of Production or Capitalist Class Formation?," *Studies in Political Economy*, no. 6, Autumn 1981, 93–112; Harriet Friedmann, "Simple Commodity Production and Wage Labour in the American Plains," *Journal of Peasant Studies*, vol. 6, 1978, 71–100; and Jacques M. Chevalier, "There is Nothing Simple about Simple

Commodity Production," *Journal of Peasant Studies*, vol. 10, no. 4, 1983, 153–86.

42   Mel Watkins, "A Staple Theory of Economic Growth," *Canadian Journal of Economics and Political Science*, vol. 29, May 1963, 141–58. See also Gilles Paquet, "Some Views of the Pattern of Canadian Economic Development," in T.N. Brewis (ed.), *Growth and the Canadian Economy*, McClelland and Stewart, Toronto, 1968, 34–64.

43   Ibid., 83.

44   C.B. Macpherson, reviewing *The Canadian State: Political Economy and Political Power*, in *Canadian Journal of Political and Social Theory*, vol. 3, Summer 1979, 134–8.

45   David McNally, "Technological Determinism and Canadian Political Economy: Further Contributions to a Debate," *Studies in Political Economy*, no. 20, Summer 1986, 162.

46   On the methods war see Erick Grimmer-Solem, *The Rise of Historical Economics and Social Reform in Germany*, Clarendon Press, Oxford, 2003, 246–84; Geoffrey M. Hodgson, *How Economics Forgot History – The Problem of Historical Specificity in Social Science*, Routledge, London, 2001, 79–134; Kiichiro Yagi, "Carl Menger and the Historicism in Economics," and D. E. Moggridge, "Method and Marshall," both in Peter Koslowski (ed.), *Methodology of the Social Sciences, Ethics and the Economics of the Newer Historical School*, Springer, Berlin, 1999, 231–58, 342–70.

47   As will be apparent, I think that Neill is mistaken in his quarrel with "theory." Indeed, he himself did not sustain this stance. Twelve years later he even suggested that it was possible to derive testable hypotheses from Innis, particularly from his later work on communications and the informational environment (Neill, "Rationality," 85–9). What is at issue is the degree of *generality* that is being claimed: a *universal* claim as compared to a pattern that helps us to better understand a particular country or other historically rooted entity. Innis developed his staple thesis to explain the economic history of Canada. Subsequently, others have sought to increase its generality, not just to other European settlement colonies, but to explain Third World, ex-colonial economies in general. Still others have sought to fit his historically rooted thesis into larger theoretical schemas that claim to be universal – whether neo-classical partial equilibrium theory or some version of Marxism. R.E. Caves, for example, sought to show Innis's staple thesis as only a particular instance of a more general economic model, the "unlimited-supply-of-labour" model from the "vent-for-surplus" model of trade and growth.

One might expect conflicts to arise when such models with their universal claims attempt to incorporate a model not intended to make universal claims (Caves, "Vent for Surplus Models of Trade and Growth," in *Trade, Growth and the Balance of Payments,* in R.E. Baldwin (ed.), Rand McNally, Chicago, 1965, 95–115, especially 97–104.

48 Hugh G.J. Aitken, "Myth and Measurement: The Innis Tradition in Economic History," *JCS,* vol. 12, no. 5, Winter 1977, 98.

49 Edward Vickery, "Exports and North American Economic Growth: 'Structuralist' and 'Staple' Models in Historical Perspective," *Canadian Journal of Economics,* vol. 7, no. 1, February 1974, 32–58. Aitken does not touch the question raised by Thomas Kuhn's use of "paradigm" in his *Scientific Revolutions,* as to how one gets from one paradigm to another: Are they "rationally commensurate"? How does one know, at least, that a predominant myth or paradigm is on its way out (if not what will replace it)? Karl Popper has offered the test of "falsification" to replace the positivist "verification." If successive and diverse hypotheses derived from a paradigm fail, people will tend to lose faith in that paradigm, an opening for the formulation of a new paradigm or myth.

50 McCalla, "The Wheat Staple and Upper Canadian Development," *Canadian Historical Association Papers,* 1978, 33–4.

51 Ibid.

52 McCalla, *Planting,* 62, 64.

53 Innis, "Introduction," 116.

54 McCalla, *Planting,* 124.

55 Ibid., 126.

56 Ibid., 180.

57 Ibid., 181.

58 McCalla, "Wheat Staple," 35.

59 McCalla, *Planting,* 81.

60 Ibid., 49.

61 Ibid., 52.

62 Ibid., 60.

63 Ibid., 61.

64 Ibid., 51.

65 Ibid., 65.

66 Ibid.

67 Ibid., 23, 25.

68 Ibid., 75.

69 Ibid., 89.

70 Ibid., 131–2.

71   Ibid., 113.

72   Ibid., 93, 274–5.

73   Ibid., 113.

74   Douglas McCalla, "The Economic History of Nineteenth-Century Ontario: Approaches, Reflections, and an Agenda for Research," in David and Rosemary Gagan (eds.), *New Directions for the Study of Ontario's Past*, McMaster University, 1988, Papers of the Bicentennial Conference on the History of Ontario, 40.

75   McCalla, *Planting*, 411, 413.

76   Ibid., 415.

77   Ibid., 10.

78   Ibid., 22.

79   Ibid., 186.

80   Ibid., 181.

81   Ibid., 191.

82   Ibid., 91.

83   R.M. McInnis, "Perspectives on Ontario Agriculture, 1815–1930," *Canadian Papers in Rural History*, vol. 8, 1992, 67.

84   On the absence of winter wheat in the Quebec District and its limited role in the Montreal District, see Thomas Wien, "'Les Travaux Pressants,' Calendrier Agrocole, Assolement et Productivité au Canada au XVIIIe sièle," *Revue historique d'Amérique Français*, vol. 43, no. 4, Spring 1990, 554–8.

85   Donald Akenson's work on the "infilling" of even the unpromising lands of Leeds and Lansdowne township indicates that this may not be entirely sound.

86   Ibid., 54.

87   R.M. McInnis, "A Reconsideration of the Role of Wheat in Early Ontario Agriculture," 13th Conference on Quantitative Methods in Canadian Economic History, Waterloo, March 1984, 13.

88   Ibid.

89   Ibid., 14.

90   Ibid.

91   McInnis, "Perspectives," 67.

92   Ibid., 56.

93   Ibid., 62. Not knowing what the omitted components are undermines one's confidence in the figures, as does the thought that they might be as much as one-third in error. It seems implicit from his presentation, that one farm product that was omitted from his calculations was the increased value from land clearing.

94 Ibid., 74. If the missing components are actually unmeasurable, how could anyone know whether they were more or less?

95 By the end of the century, the Ontario norm would be around 75 per cent of land cleared.

96 Ibid., 65.

97 Ibid., 69.

98 Ibid.

99 McCalla, *Planting*, 221.

100 William Marr, "The Allocation of Land to Agricultural Uses in Canada West, 1851: A View from the Individual Farm," *Canadian Papers in Rural History*, vol. 10, 1996, 193.

101 Ibid.

102 Ibid., 197.

103 R.M. McInnis, "The Size Structure of Farming, Canada West, 1861," *Research in Economic History*, Supplement, vol. 5, 1989, 323.

104 R.M. McInnis, "Marketable Surpluses in Ontario Farming, 1860," *Social Science History*, vol. 8, no. 4, Fall 1984, 413.

105 Ibid., 415.

106 Ibid., 422.

107 William L. Marr, "Tenant vs. Owner Occupied Farms in York County, Ontario, 1871," *CPRH*, vol. 4, 1984, 68–9.

108 William L. Marr, "The Distribution of Tenant Agriculture: Ontario, Canada, 1871," *Social Science History*, vol. 11, no. 2, Summer 1987, 175.

109 For example, if the owner and tenant shared the crop equally, they had an equal share in the risk of crop failure.

110 Ibid., 762.

111 Catherine Anne Wilson, *Tenants in Time – Family Strategies, Land, and Liberalism in Upper Canada, 1799–1871*, McGill-Queen's University Press, Montreal & Kingston, 2009, 54.

112 Ibid., 162.

113 J. David Wood, *Making Ontario: Agricultural Colonization and Land-scape Re-creation before the Railway*, McGill-Queen's University Press, Montreal & Kingston, 2000, 56.

114 Kenneth Kelly, "The Impact of Nineteenth-Century Agricultural Settlement on the Land," in J. David Wood (ed.), *Perspectives on Landscape and Settlement in Nineteenth-Century Ontario*, Carleton Library Series, Ottawa, 1975, 68, 80.

115 Wood, *Making*, 87, 91.

116 Ibid., 102.

117 John Clarke, *Land, Power, and Economics on the Frontier of Upper Canada*, McGill-Queen's University Press, Montreal & Kingston, 2001, xxxiii. In fact he declares that he had to avoid consideration of settlement "if only to gain perspective or remain sane." However, together with H.W. Taylor and W.R. Wightman, he offered a comparison of land acquisition with actual development of farms in "Contrasting Land Development Rates in Southern Ontario to 1891," CPRH, vol. 5, 1986, 50–72.

118 Ibid., 159–61.

119 Ibid., 160. See also J.I. Little, "Contested Land: Squatters and Agents in the Eastern Townships of Lower Canada," CHR, vol. 80, no. 3, September 1999, 381–412.

120 Clarke, 374–5.

121 Ibid., 239.

122 Ibid., 259.

123 Richard Pomfret, "The Mechanization of Reaping in Nineteenth-Century Ontario: A Case Study of the Pace and Causes of the Diffusion of Embodied Technical Change," in Douglas McCalla (ed.), *Perspectives on Canadian Economic History*, Copp Clark, Toronto, 1987, 86.

124 William L. Marr, "Did Farm Size Matter? An 1871 Case Study," CPRH, vol. 6, 1988, 283.

125 D.A. Lawr, "The Development of Ontario Farming, 1870–1914: Patterns of Growth and Change," *Ontario History*, vol. 64, no. 4, December 1972, 239–51.

126 William L. Marr, "The Wheat Economy in Reverse: Ontario's Wheat Production, 1887–1917," *Canadian Journal of Economics*, vol. 14, no. 1, February 1981, 136–45.

127 Robert E. Ankli and Wendy Millar, "Ontario Agriculture in Transition: The Switch from Wheat to Cheese," *Journal of Economic History*, vol. 42, no. 1, March 1982, 207–15.

128 R.M. McInnis, "The Changing Structure of Canadian Agriculture, 1867–1897," *Journal of Economic History*, vol. 42, no. 1, March 1982, 191–8.

129 McCalla, *Planting*, 74.

130 Ibid., 224.

131 Frank D. Lewis and M.C. Urquhart, "Growth and the Standard of Living in a Pioneer Economy: Upper Canada, 1826 to 1851," *William and Mary Quarterly*, 3rd series, vol. 56, no. 1, January 1999, 152.

132 Ibid., 159.

133 Ibid., 160.

134 Ibid., 172.

135 Ibid., 165.

136 John McCallum, *Unequal Beginnings*, University of Toronto Press, Toronto, 1980, 4.

137 Ibid., 13–14.

138 Ibid., n14.

139 Ibid., 11.

140 Ibid., 12.

141 Ibid., 13.

142 Ibid., 15.

143 Ibid., 15–16. .

144 Ibid., 22.

145 Ibid., 21.

146 Ibid.

147 Ibid., 7.

148 Ibid., 116.

149 Ibid.

150 Ibid., 4.

151 Marjorie Griffin Cohen, *Women's Work, Markets, and Economic Development in Nineteenth-Century Ontario*, University of Toronto Press, Toronto, 1988, 24. See also Lee A. Craig, *To Sow One Acre More: Childbearing and Farm Productivity in the Antebellum North*, Johns Hopkins University Press, Baltimore, 1993.

152 Ibid., 68. See also Gérard Bouchard, "Family reproduction in new rural areas: Outline of a North American Model," CHR, vol. 75, no. 4, December 1994, 475–510.

153 Ibid., 8.

154 Ibid., 59.

155 Ibid., 36. See also Greer, *Peasant, Lord, and Merchant*, 203–9.

156 Ibid., 36.

157 Ibid., 40. For more recent debate see Leslie Page Moch et. al., "Family Strategy: A Dialogue," *Historical Methods*, vol. 20, no. 1, Summer 1987, 113–25. Theo Engelen, "Labour Strategies of Families: A Critical Assessment of an Appealing Concept," *International Review of Social History*, vol. 47, no. 3, December 2002, 453–64. Jan Kok, "The Challenge of Strategy: A Comment," *International Review of Social History*, vol. 47, no. 3, December 2002, 465–85.

158 Ibid., 69. See also Darrett B. Rutman, "Assessing the Little Communities of Early America," *William and Mary Quarterly*, 3rd series, vol. 43, no. 2, April 1986, 163–78, and Richard L. Rudolph, "The European Peasant Family and Economy: Central Themes and Issues," *Journal of Family History*, vol. 17, no. 2, 1992, 119–38.

159 Ibid., 74.

160 Ibid., 70.

161 Ibid.

162 Ibid., 77.

163 Ibid., 82. McCalla, *Planting*, 100, showed that as late as 1861, two-thirds of all small farmers and three-quarters of all large farmers kept sheep. David Gagan would identify here an indication of the 1857 agricultural crisis, as farm families sought greater self-sufficiency to off set "hard times" – sometime in the 1850s; at least the later 1850s – that suddenly moved farm households backwards, toward greater self-sufficiency.

164 Ibid., 85.

165 Cohen, 82.

166 Ibid., 89.

167 Ibid., 91.

168 Cynthia Wallace-Casey, "'Providential Openings': The Women Weavers of Nineteenth-Century Queens Country New Brunswick," *Material History Review*, vol. 49, Fall 1997, 29–44.

169 Béatrice Craig, Judith Rygiel, and Elizabeth Turcotte, "'The Homespun Paradox': Market-Oriented Production of Cloth in Eastern Canada in the Nineteenth Century," *Agricultural History*, vol. 76, no. 1, Winter 2002, 42.

170 Wallace-Casey, "'Providential Openings,'" 31–9.

171 Béatrice Craig, et. al., 44.

172 Women's role in dairying and its decline can be seen in many countries: Joanna Bourke, "Dairywomen and Affectionate Wives: Women in the Irish Dairy Industry, 1890–1914," *Agricultural History Review*, vol. 38, 1990, 149–64; Bodil K. Hansen, "Rural Women in Late Nineteenth-Century Denmark," *Journal of Peasant Studies*, vol. 9, 1982, 225–40; Joan Jensen, "Butter Making and Economic Development in Mid-Atlantic America from 1750–1850," *Signs*, vol. 13, Summer 1988, 813–29; Jennie Kitteringham, "Country Work Girls in Nineteenth-Century England," in Raphael Samuel (ed.), *Village Life and Labour*, Routledge and Kegan Paul, London, 1975, 73–138; Sally McMurry, "Women's Work in Agriculture: Divergent Trends in England and America, 1800–1930," *Comparative Studies in Society and History*, vol. 34, April 1992, 248–70; and Deborah Valenze, "The Art of Women and the Business of Men: Women's Work and the Dairy Industry c. 1740–1840," *Past and Present*, no. 130, February 1991, 142–69.

173 Ibid., 106.

174 Ibid., 108.

175 Ibid., 113. See also Bernadine Dodge, "'Let the Record Show': Women
and the Law in the United Counties of Durham and Northumberland,
1845–95," *Ontario History*, 92, autumn 2000, 127.

176 Cohen argued that historians need to examine the power relations within
the family unit. Courts consistently upheld the view that "the labour of a
single woman provided on the property of a male relative generally was
understood to have been freely provided and did not provide the woman
with either a claim on the property or a claim to a wage." This feminist analysis of power can be contrasted to the Marxist reading of power
in labour market relations: "In this respect the issue of ownership of
property in the family economy is considerably more all-encompassing
than the power over labour exercised by capitalist ownership." Wives
and daughters of farmers, to whom the law granted no claim on family
assets while the male head of household lived, could not have expected
much compensation once he was dead. The long-term impacts of married women's property acts and inheritance patterns, down to the First
World War, reveal a much different pattern from Cohen's suggestive
sample from the pre-Confederation period. Kris Inwood and associates
found both an increased number of women owning property in their own
names and a pattern of inheritance that gave more to widows and more
equal treatment to daughters. Kris Inwood and Sara Van Sligtenhorst,
"The Social Consequence of Legal Reform: Women and Property in a
Canadian Community," *Continuity and Change*, vol. 19 no. 1, 2004,
and Susan Ingham and Kris Inwood, "Property Ownership by Married
Women in Victorian Ontario," *Dalhousie Law Journal*, 2000, 429.

177 Lena Sommestad, in "Gendering Work, Interpreting Gender: the Mas-
culinization of Dairy Work in Sweden, 1850–1950," *History Workshop
Journal*, issue 37, 1994, 57–75, shows that the comparatively slow retreat
of women from dairying in Sweden meant that it was women who
became the "industrial dairymaids" who graduated from government-run
vocational schools equipped to manage and run the power machinery
of highly modernized butter and cheese factories after the First World
War.

178 Cohen, 108.

179 Ibid., 107.

180 Ibid., 114. The same cultural association between women and milk as
part of nature, in a much stronger form, existed in Sweden: see Sommestad, 59–62.

181 Ibid., 116.

182 Heather Menzies, "Technology in the Craft of Ontario Cheesemaking: Women in Oxford County circa 1860," *Ontario History*, vol. 87, no. 3, September 1995, 293–304.

183 Margaret Derry, "Gender Conflicts in Dairying: Ontario's Butter Industry, 1880–1920," *Ontario History*, vol. 90, no. 1, Spring 1998, 31–47. See also McInnis, "Changing Structures," 196.

184 Ibid.

185 The proportion of the simplest dairy product of all – fluid milk – exceeded that of the much-touted cheese until 1899–1902. R.M. McInnis, "The Changing Structure of Canadian Agriculture, 1867–1897," *Journal of Economic History*, vol. 42, no. 1, March 1982, 193.

186 McCalla, *Planting* 243.

187 McInnis, "Perspectives," 81.

188 Ibid., 82.

189 Ibid.

190 Ibid., 83.

CHAPTER FIVE

1 Compare George Emery and José Igartua, "'David Gagan's 'The 'Critical Years' in Rural Canada West': A Critique of the Methodology and Model," *Canadian Historical Review*, vol. 62, no. 2, 1981, 189, to both J. Wallot and Gilles Paquet, "Crise agricole et tensions socio-ethniques dans le Bas-Canada, 1802–1812: éléments pour une réinterprétation," *Revue d'histoire de l'Amérique Français*, vol. 26, no. 2, September 1972, 218, and Serge Courville, *Quebec: A Historical Geography*, UBC Press, Vancouver, 2008, n123 and 124.

2 Peter Russell, *Attitudes to Social Structure and Mobility in Upper Canada, 1815–1840*, Edwin Mellen, Lewiston, 1990, 88–97. John Clarke, *The Ordinary People of Essex – Environment, Culture, and Economy on the Frontier of Upper Canada*, McGill-Queen's University Press, Montreal & Kingston, 2010, 44, suggests land concentrations held by speculators "cast doubt on the prevailing image [of a poor man's country]," but then (49) concludes, "This was the country's gift to the poor – that, within a very short time span, a labourer might expect to become a freeholder."

3 Robert E. Ankli and Ken J. Duncan, "Farm Making Costs in Early Ontario," *Canadian Papers in Rural* History, vol. 4, 1984, 37–9; H. Pearson Gundy, "The Family Compact at Work: The Second Heir and Devisee Commission of Upper Canada, 1805–1814," *Ontario History*,

vol. 66, 1974, 140; and Barbara C. Murison, "The Search for the 'Best Poor Man's Country': Shifting Emigration Patterns from Scotland in 1830s and 1840s," paper presented to the Canadian Historical Association, 1991. Clarke, *Ordinary People*, 366–9, 370–2. However the sympathy for squatters was not universal: James Harvey to W.W. Baldwin, 2 March 1837, W.W. Baldwin Papers, Toronto Metropolitan Library, Toronto, and Susanna Moodie, *Roughing It in the Bush*, Carleton University Press, Ottawa, 1988, 67.

4 George Forbes to John Forbes, 20 April 1850, Forbes Papers, Scottish Public Record Office, Edinburgh.

5 David Gagan and Herbert Mays, "Historical Demography and Canadian Social History: Families and Land in Peel County, Ontario," CHR, vol. 54, no. 1, March 1973, 27–47.

6 Ibid., 27.

7 Ibid.

8 Ibid.

9 Ibid., 28.

10 Ibid., 29.

11 David Gagan, *Hopeful Travellers*, University of Toronto Press, Toronto, 1981, 24. However in Chinguacousy Township in 1842, the assessment roll showed that non-residents still held 22 per cent of all lands.

12 Michael Katz, *The People of Hamilton*, Harvard University Press, Cambridge, 1975. See also Gordon Darroch, "Migrants in the Nineteenth Century: Fugitives or Families in Motion?," *Journal of Family History*, vol. 6, no. 3, 1981, 257–77; "Class in Nineteenth-Century, Central Ontario: A Reassessment of the Crisis and Demise of Small Producers during Early Industrialization, 1861–1871," *Canadian Journal of Sociology*, vol. 13, nos. 1 and 2, Winter-Spring 1988, 49–71; and with Lee Soltow, "Inequality in Landed Wealth in Nineteenth-Century Ontario: Structure and Access," *Canadian Review of Sociology and Anthropology*, vol. 29, no. 2, 1992, 167–90.

13 David Gagan, "Geographical and Social Mobility in Nineteenth-Century Ontario: A Microstudy," *Canadian Review of Sociology and Anthropology*, vol. 13, no. 2, 1976, 153.

14 Ibid., 155.

15 Ibid., 160.

16 Ibid.

17 Ibid., 161.

18 Ibid., 162. See also David Gagan, "'The Prose of Life': Literary Reflections of the Family, Individual Experience and Social Structure in

Nineteenth-Century Ontario," *Journal of Social History*, vol. 9, no. 3, Spring 1976, 367–81; "The Indivisibility of Land: A Microanalysis of the System of Inheritance in Nineteenth-Century Ontario," *Journal of Economic History*, vol. 36, no. 1, 1976, 126–48, and R.M. McInnis, "Comment on Paper by Gagan," *Journal of Economic History*, vol. 36, no. 1, 1976, 142–6.

19 Ibid., 295.

20 Ibid., 297. By contrast Toronto Gore Township had an average of three children per family. Compare to C. Alexander Ross, "Delaying the Fertility Decline: German Women in Saginaw County, Michigan," *Journal of Family History*, vol. 14, no. 2, 1989, 157–70, and Maris A. Vinovskis, "Socioeconomic Determinants of Interstate Fertility Differentials in the United States in 1850 and 1860," *Journal of Interdisciplinary History*, vol. 6, no. 3, Winter 1976, 375–96.

21 A.R.M. Lower, *Canadians in the Making*, Longmans Canada, Toronto, 1958, 336–7.

22 David Gagan, "Land, Population and Social Change: The 'Critical Years' in Rural Canada West," CHR, vol. 59, no. 3, 1978, 305.

23 Ibid., 307. See also David Gagan, "The Indivisibility of Land: A Microanalysis of the System of Inheritance in Nineteenth-Century Ontario," *Journal of Economic History*, vol. 36, no. 1, 1976, 126–48. See also Sonya Salamon and F.V. Carroll, "Share and Share Alike – Inheritance Patterns in Two Illinois Farm Communities," *Journal of Family History*, vol. 13, no. 2, 1988, 219–32.

24 Majorie Griffin Cohn, *Women's Work, Markets, and Economic Development*, University of Toronto Press, Toronto, 1988, 49–58, 159–62.

25 Gagan, *Hopeful Travellers*, 55.

26 Ibid., 90.

27 Ibid.

28 Gagan, "Land, Population and Social Change," 307.

29 Gagan had not been aware of that fact in 1980: Gagan, *Hopeful Travellers*, 73.

30 Gagan, "Land, Population and Social Change," 308. On the role of women in Upper Canada more generally, see Katherine M.J. McKenna, "The Role of Women in the Establishment of Social Class in Early Upper Canada," *Ontario History*, vol. 83, no. 3, September 1990, 179–205, and Russell, 51–61.

31 Gagan, "Land, Population and Social Change," 311.

32 Ibid., 313.

33 Herbert J. Mays, "Families and Land in Toronto Gore Township, Peel County, Ontario, 1820–1890," unpublished doctoral dissertation, McMaster University, Hamilton, 1979, 5. This township took its name from its highly unusual shape: a triangle. For the layout of the standard township, see G.M. Craig, *Upper Canada: The Formative Years, 1784–1841*, McClelland and Stewart, Toronto, 1963, 27.

34 Ibid., 106–8.

35 Peter Russell, "Emily Township: Pioneer Persistence to Equality?," *Histoire sociale/Social History*, vol. 22, November 1989, 317–31.

36 Ibid., 111.

37 Catherine A. Wilson, *Tenants in Time – Family Strategies, Land, and Liberalism in Upper Canada, 1799–1871*, McGill-Queen's University Press, Montreal & Kingston, 2009, 173–89. See also William L. Marr, "Tenant vs. Owner Occupied Farms in York County, Ontario, 1871," *Canadian Papers in Rural History*, vol. 4, 1984, 50–71; "The Distribution of Tenant Agriculture: Ontario, Canada, 1871," *Social Science History*, vol. 11, no. 2, Summer 1987, 169–86; and "Nineteenth-Century Tenancy Rates in Ontario's Counties, 1881 and 1891," *Journal of Social History*, vol. 21, no. 4, Summer 1988, 753–64.

38 Herbert J. Mays, "Families, Land, and Permanence in Toronto Gore Township," *Canadian Historical Association Papers*, 1980, 198.

39 Ibid193.

40 Ibid., 208.

41 Ibid., 203. See also Donald R. Leet, "Human Fertility and Agricultural Opportunities in Ohio Counties: From Frontier to Maturity, 1810–1860," in D.C. Klingman and R.K. Vedder (eds.), *Essays in Nineteenth-Century Economic History – The Old Northwest*, Ohio University Press, Athens, 1975, 138–58, and "The Determinants of the Fertility Transition in Antebellum Ohio," *Journal of Economic History*, vol. 36, no. 2, June 1976, 359–78.

42 Ibid.

43 Ibid.

44 Ibid., 204–5. Compare to Stephen John Gross, "Handing Down the Farm: Values, Strategies, and Outcomes in Inheritance Practices among Rural German Americans," *Journal of Family History*, vol. 21, no. 2, April 1996, 192–217.

45 Wilson, 147, 152.

46 McCalla, *Planting*, 69.

47 Ibid.

48 George Emery and José Igartua, "David Gagan's 'The "Critical Years" in Rural Canada West': A Critique of the Methodology and the Model," *CHR*, vol. 62, no. 2, 1981, 189.

49 Ibid., 191.

50 This point was also later made by McCalla, see *Planting*, 144.

51 Emery and Igartua, 192.

52 Ibid., n194. If Gagan treated each category of a nominal variable (e.g., type of will) as a separate dichotomous variable, he had not said so. But, in a footnote, they observe that if he did, it would explain why in some cases he appeared to get "over" 100 per cent.

53 Ibid., 195.

54 Ibid.

55 Ibid., 196.

56 Ibid.

57 David Gagan, "Under the Lamp Post: A Reply to Emery and Igartua," *CHR*, vol. 62, no. 2, 1981, 197.

58 For example Gagan cited the work of Richard Easterlin, "Does Human Fertility Adjust to the Environment?," *American Economic Review*, vol. 61, no. 2, May 1971, 399–407, and "Farm Production and Income in Old and New Areas at Mid-Century," in David C. Klingman and Richard K. Vedder (eds.), *Essays in Nineteenth-Century Economic History – The Old Northwest*, Ohio University Press, Athens, 1975, 77–117; "Population Change and Farm Settlement in the Northern United States," *Journal of Economic History*, vol. 36, no. 1, March 1976, 45–75; "Factors in the Decline of Farm Family Fertility in the United States: Some Preliminary Results," *Journal of American History*, vol. 63, no. 3, December 1976, 600–14; and with Glen H. Elder Jr., "Family History and the Life Course," *Journal of Family History*, vol. 2, no. 4, Winter 1977, 279–304. See also Donald R. Leet, "Human Fertility and Agricultural Opportunities in Ohio Counties: From Frontier to Maturity, 1810–1860," in Klingman and Vedder, 138–58, and "The Determinants of the Fertility Transition in Antebellum Ohio," *Journal of Economic History*, vol. 36, no. 2, June 1976, 359–78.

59 Gagan, "Lamp Post," 198. For an example of the "metropolitan" approach see T.W. Acheson, "The Nature and Structure of York Commerce in the 1820s," *CHR*, vol. 50, no. 4, December 1969, 406–28.

60 Darrell A. Norris, "Migration, Pioneer Settlement, and the Life Course: The First Families of an Ontario Township," *CPRH*, vol. 4, 1984, 130–51.

61 Gagan, "Lamp Post," 201. John W. Bennett, "Adaptive Strategy and Processes in the Canadian Prairies," in Richard Allen (ed.), *A Region of the*

Mind, Canadian Plains Studies, no. 1, Canadian Plains Research Center, University of Regina, Regina, 1973, 181–99, as well as John W. Bennett and Seena B. Kohle, *Settling the Canadian-American West, 1890–1915 – Pioneer Adaptation and Community Building – An Anthropological History*, University of Nebraska Press, Lincoln, 1994.

62 David Levine, *Reproducing Families: The Political Economy of English Population History*, Cambridge University Press, Cambridge, 1987, 25, on peasant land hunger in England.

63 One possible solution to that problem could be to cross-reference the deeds with land tax assessment rolls, which show how much land was cleared.

64 Ibid., 206.

65 Emery and Igartua argued that in whatever way the male population was counted, it should be compared to a more specific measure of land in agricultural use: the number of improved, or cropped, acres or the number of acres in wheat. Unless he found a better measure than occupied acres, they argued, one could read his results as being merely a drive to increase the proportion of occupied acres *cropped* (i.e., an alternative hypothesis could explain his data). Gagan took note of the latter part of their argument.

66 Gagan, *Hopeful Travellers*, 45, table 9.

67 Ibid., 205, compare to Gagan, "Land, Population and Social Change," 305, table v.

68 Ibid., 53.

69 Raymond Roy, Christian Pouyez, and François Martin, "Le jumelage des données nominatives dans les recensements: problèms et méthods," *HS/SH*, vol. 13, no. 25, May 1980, 173–93, especially 186–9. In the same issue, Ian Winchester offered a more general comment on both: "Review of Peel County History Project and the Saguenay Project," 195–205, mainly to chide Gagan for turning away from statistical argument to the use of more traditional sources in describing his findings.

70 McInnis, "Perspectives," 69.

71 Ibid., 74.

72 McCalla, *Planting*, 6.

73 Ibid., 215.

74 Ibid., 218.

75 Ibid., 219 This would be an instance of not taking into account the critique of Roy, Pouyez, and Martin.

76 See for examples, Donald H. Akenson, *The Irish in Ontario: A Study in Rural History*, McGill-Queen's University Press, Montreal & Kingston, 1999, n335, and Ian Winchester, "Review," 197, 199.

77　Gordon Darroch and Lee Soltow, *Property and Inequality in Victorian Ontario: Structural Patterns and Cultural Communities in the 1871 Census*, University of Toronto Press, Toronto, 1994, 20.

78　Ibid., 35, emphasis added.

79　Ibid., 40.

80　Ibid., 63.

81　Glenn Lockwood, "Irish Immigration and the 'Critical Years' in Eastern Ontario: The Case of Montague Township, 1821–1881," *CPRH*, vol. 4, 1984, 171.

82　Ibid., 174.

83　Ibid., n335.

84　Ibid.

85　Akenson, *Irish in Ontario*, 260.

86　Bruce Elliot, *Irish Migrants in the Canadas*, 2nd ed., McGill-Queen's University Press, Montreal & Kingston, 2004, 256.

87　Gordon Darroch, "Class in Nineteenth-Century, Central Ontario: A Reassessment of the Crisis and Demise of Small Producers during Early Industrialization, 1861–1871," *Canadian Journal of Sociology*, vol. 13, issue 1–2, Winter/Spring 1988, 49–72.

88　On the Irish and their settlement patterns, see Alan G. Brunger, "Geographical Propinquity among Pre-Famine Catholic Irish Settlers in Upper Canada," *Journal of Historical Geography*, vol. 8, no. 3, 1982, 265–82, and Edward J. Hedican, "Irish Farming Households in Eastern Canada: Domestic Production and Family Size," *Ethnology*, vol. 42, no. 1, Winter 2003, 15–37.

89　Gagan, "Land, Population and Social Change," 313. See also David Gagan, "The Relevance of 'Canada First,'" *Journal of Canadian Studies*, vol. 5, no. 4, November 1970, 36–44.

90　The concentration then continued further west and south of Lake Michigan into Wisconsin and Illinois. There was another cluster on the upper Mississippi spanning Wisconsin and Minnesota. From 1850 to 1860 the number of Canadians in these five states rose 39.6 per cent. In the next decade it rose 53.6 per cent and the rate continued to accelerate, to reach 80.5 per cent by 1890. The census of that year gave the occupations of Canadian emigrants in the United States, showing farmers and farm labourers making up almost one-quarter of all Canadians living in the United States (compared to lumbermen at 3 per cent).

91　*Abstract of the Tenth Census: 1880*, Government Printing Office, Washington, 1884, vol. 1, 492.

92 *Statistical View of the United States ... Being a Compendium of the Seventh Census*, J.D.B. DeBow, Government Printing Office, Washington, 1854, (1990 reprint, Norman Ross Publishing, New York) vol. 1, xxxvi (the first to note foreign place of birth); *Population of the United States in 1860; Compiled from the Original Returns of the Eighth Census*, Joseph C.G. Kennedy, Government Printing Office, Washington, 1864, (1990 reprint, Norman Ross Publishing, New York) 620; *Abstract of the Ninth Census: 1870*, Government Printing Office, Washington, 1874, vol. 1, 397; *Abstract of the Tenth Census: 1880*, Government Printing Office, Washington, 1884, vol. 1, 492; *Abstract of Eleventh Census: 1890*, part II, Government Printing Office, Washington, 1894, cxlvi, 36.

93 McCalla, *Planting*, 231.

94 Donald H. Akenson, *Irish in Ontario*, 283–331.

95 Ian Drummond, *Progress without Planning: The Economic History of Ontario from Confederation to the Second World War*, University of Toronto Press, Toronto, 1987, 28, 442.

96 Ibid., 30: Ontario's farms increased from 172,258 in 1871 to 216,191 in 1891, while the area cultivated rose from 6.5 million acres in 1871 to 10.4 million in 1926.

97 David Gagan, "Class and Society in Victorian English Canada," *British Journal of Canadian Studies*, vol. 4, no. 1, 1989, 76–7.

98 Drummond, 30.

99 R. Douglas Francis, "'Rural Ontario West': Ontarians in Alberta," in H. Palmer and T. Palmer (eds.), *The Peoples of Alberta: Portraits of Cultural Diversity*, Western Producer Prairie Books, Saskatoon, 1985, 123–42.

CHAPTER SIX

1 A.I. Silver, "Some Quebec Attitudes in an Age of Imperialism and Ideological Conflict," *Canadian Historical Review*, vol. 57, no. 4, 1976, 440–60. Silver's Quebec imperialism is more limited than what I call "Quebec nationalism." His idea is confined to the defence of language and religion in Prairie schools. While he notes the often self-defeating efforts of western clergy to encourage settlement, he is primarily concerned to point up the paradox of Quebec leaders opposed to settlement yet trying to defend rights that only substantial settlement could have sustained.

2 Alastair Sweeny, *George-Etienne Cartier*, McClelland and Stewart, Toronto, 1976, 201–10. Donald Creighton, *John A. Macdonald – The Old Chieftain*, Macmillan, Toronto, 1955, 65–8. Maurice Prud'homme,

"The Life and Times of Archbishop Taché," *Historical and Scientific Society of Manitoba Papers*, 3r series, no. 11, 1956, 7–14. Lionel Dorge, "Bishop Taché and the Confederation of Manitoba," *Historical and Scientific Society of Manitoba Papers*, 3r series, no. 26, 1969–70, 93–109.

3 David Levine, *Reproducing Families: The Political Economy of English Population History*, Cambridge University Press, Cambridge, 1987, 25, on peasant land hunger in England, 25.

4 John Weaver, *The Great Land Rush and the Making of the Modern World, 1650–1900*, McGill-Queen's University Press, Montreal & Kingston, 2003, 251. Of course this does not rule out violence altogether: see the careers of the Cree Almighty Voice and the Blackfoot known as "Charcoal," as well as systemic racism in the legal system, as in Lesley Erickson, *Westward Bound: Sex, Violence, the Law and the Making of Settler Society*, UBC Press, Vancouver, 2011, 44–77. But Beth La Dow, *The Medicine Line, Life and Death on a North American Borderland*, Routledge, New York, 2001, to minimize Canadian-American differences, stretches her evidence too far, 80–4.

5 A.S. Morton, *History of Prairie Settlement*, Macmillan, Toronto, 1938, 42.

6 George F. Stanley, *The Birth of Western Canada*, Longmans Green, London, 1936, 8.

7 Marcel Giraud, *The Métis in the Canadian West*, George Woodcock (trans.), University of Alberta Press, Edmonton, 1986, vol. 2, 163, 165. On the actual problems of farming at Red River, see Barry Kaye, "'The Settlers' Grand Difficulty': Haying in the Economy of the Red River Settlement," *Prairie Forum*, vol. 9, no. 1, Spring 1984, 1–12.

8 W.L. Morton, "Introduction," *Alexander Begg's Red River Journal*, The Champlain Society, Toronto, 1956, 2.

9 Donald Creighton laid out his views most sharply in "John A. Macdonald, Confederation, and the Canadian West," in Craig Brown (ed.), *Minorities, Schools, and Politics*, University of Toronto Press, Toronto, 1969, 1–9.

10 Ralph Heintzman, "The Spirit of Confederation: Professor Creighton, Biculturalism, and the Use of History," CHR, vol. 52, no. 3, September 1971, 245–75. Heintzman's was not the first response to Creighton's attack on biculturalism: see Cornelius Janen, "Creighton, Confederation and Conspiracy," *Canadian Dimension*, vol. 4, no. 4, May-June 1967, 22–5. D.J. Hall came to Creighton's defence in "'The Spirit of Confederation,' Ralph Heintzman, Professor Creighton, and the Bicultural Compact Theory," *Journal of Canadian Studies*, vol. 9, no. 4, November 1974, 24–43.

11 Stanley, 194–206.

12 W.L. Morton, *Manitoba: A History*, University of Toronto, Toronto, 1957, 66–8. W.L. Morton, (ed.), "Introduction," *Alexander Begg's Red River Journal*, The Champlain Society, Toronto, 1956, 16.

13 Douglas N. Sprague and R. Mailot, "Persistent Settlers: The Dispersal and Resettlement of the Red River Métis, 1870–1885," *Canadian Ethnic Studies*, vol. 17, no. 2, 1985, 1–30. See also W. Leland Clark, "The Place of the Métis within the Agricultural Economy of the Red River during the 1840s and the 1850s," *Canadian Journal of Native Studies*, vol. 3, no. 1, 1983, 69–84; Arthur J. Ray, "Reflections on Fur Trade Social History and Métis History in Canada," *American Indian Culture and Research Journal*, vol. 6, no. 2, 1982, 91–107; Olive Patricia Dickason, "From 'One Nation' in the Northeast to 'New Nation' in the Northwest: A Look as the Emergence of the Métis," *American Indian Culture and Research Journal*, vol. 6, no. 2, 1982, 1–21; Carol M. Judd, "Mixed Bloods of Moose Factory, 1730–1981: A Socio-Economic Study," *American Indian Culture and Research Journal*, vol. 6, no. 2, 1982, 65–88, and "Moose Factory Was Not Red River: A Comparison of Mixed-Blood Experiences," in Duncan Cameron (ed.), *Explorations in Canadian Economic History, Essays in Honour of Irene M. Spry*, University of Ottawa Press, Ottawa, 1985, 251–68.

14 Gerhard Ens, *Homeland to Hinterland: The Changing Worlds of the Red River Métis in the Nineteenth Century*, University of Toronto Press, Toronto, 1996, and "Métis Agriculture in Red River during the Transition Period from Peasant Society to Industrial Capitalism: The Example of St. Francis Xavier, 1835–1870," in R.C. Macleod (ed.), *Swords and Ploughshares – War and Agriculture in Western Canada*, University of Alberta Press, Edmonton, 1993, 239–62. See also his "Kinship, Ethnicity, Class, and the Red River Métis: The Parishes of St Francis Xavier and St Andrews," University of Alberta, unpublished doctoral dissertation, 1989, as well as his "Dispossession or Adaptation? Migration and Persistence of the Red River Métis, 1835–1890," *Canadian Historical Association Historical Papers*, 1988, 120–44. Thomas Flanagan, *Métis Lands in Manitoba*, University of Calgary Press, Calgary, 1991; "The Case Against Métis Aboriginal Rights," *Canadian Public Policy*, vol. 9, no. 3, September 1983, 314–25; and with Gerhard Ens, "Métis Land Grants in Manitoba: A Statistical Study," *Histoire sociale/Social History*, vol. 27, no. 53, May 1994, 65–87; Nicole J.M. St-Onge, *Saint-Laurent, Manitoba: Evolving Métis Identities, 1850–1914*, Canadian Plains Research Center, University of Regina, 2004, and "Race, Class, and Marginality – A Métis

Settlement in the Manitoba Interlake, 1850–1914," University of Manitoba, unpublished doctoral dissertation, 1990. See also, "The Dissolution of a Métis Community: Pointe à Grouette," *Studies in Political Economy*, no. 18, Autumn 1984, 149–72. See also H.S. Sprenger, "The Métis
Nation: Buffalo Hunting vs. Agriculture at the Red River Settlement," in
A.S. Lussier and B.B. Sealey (eds.), *The Other Natives: The/Les Métis*,
Manitoba Métis Federation Press, Winnipeg, 1978, 158–78.

15 The question of separate schools had indeed been discussed in the federal
house, from problems arising in New Brunswick where Catholics found
that the guarantees of section 93 of the BNA Act had not proven effective
in protecting their Catholic separate schools, which had existed by custom rather than by law at the time of Confederation. P.B. Waite, *Canada,
1874–1896: Arduous Destiny*, Oxford University Press, Toronto, 1996,
40–2. See also Peter M. Toner, "The New Brunswick Separate Schools
Issue, 1864–1876," University of New Brunswick master's thesis,
1967.

16 A Conservative senator would later allege that there had been a "Grit
conspiracy" to introduce the amendment into the House to please the
Catholics, only to have it quietly defeated in the Senate. If there had been
such a "conspiracy," it failed, in large part because of the Conservatives'
dominance held over from Macdonald's time.

17 See for examples, A.H. deTremaudan, *Hold High Your Heads (History
of the Métis Nation in Western Canada)*, translated by Elizabeth Maguet,
Pemmican Publications, Winnipeg, 1982 (originally published in 1936),
and Donatien Frémont, *Les Français dans L'Ouest Canadien*, Les Editions de la Liberté, Winnipeg, 1959.

18 In a story replete with ironies, Jules-Paul Tardivel had been born and
raised in a Protestant community in the United States. DCB, vol. 13,
1009–12. In the 1870s he wrote for *Le Courier de Sainte-Hyacinthe* and
La Minerve. In 1883 he established his own ultra-Catholic paper, *La
Verite*.

19 Of greatest scandal in the West was his eventual espousal of French-
Canadian settlement in eastern and northern Ontario in preference to
Manitoba. Mathieu Girard, "La Pensée Politique de Jules-Paul Tardivel,"
Revue d'histoire de l'Amérique Français, vol. 21, 1967, 397–428.

20 A.I. Silver, "French Canada and the Prairie Frontier, 187–1890," CHR, vol.
50, no. 1, March 1969, 11–36.

21 Andre Lalonde, "The French Canadians of the West: Hope, Tragedy,
Uncertainty," in D.R. Lauder and Eric Waddell (eds.), *French America*,
Louisiana State University Press, Baton Rouge, 1991, 102.

22 Kenneth M. Sylvester, *Limits of Rural Capitalism: Family, Culture, and Markets in Montcalm, Manitoba, 1870–1940*, University of Toronto Press, Toronto, 2001, 12–31.

23 Robert Painchaud, *Un rêve français dans le peuplement de la Prairie*, Éditions des Plaines, Saint-Boniface, 1987.

24 Carl Dawson, *Group Settlement: Ethnic Communities in Western Canada*, Macmillan of Canada, Toronto, 1936, 344. His study was based on St Albert, Alberta, and Ste Rose, Manitoba, where the 1921 census recorded 3,745 and 1,749 "French and Belgians" respectively.

25 Nicole J.M. St-Onge, "Race, Class and Marginality: A Métis Settlement in the Manitoba Interlake, 1850–1914," doctoral dissertation, University of Manitoba, Winnipeg, 1990.

26 The province of Quebec itself had launched a small and largely ineffectual colonization program designed to draw French Canadians back from the United States to their homeland and traditional vocation. J.I. Little, "La Patrie: The Repatriation Colony, 1875–1880," in his *Nationalism, Capitalism, and Colonization in Nineteenth-Century Quebec, The Upper St Francis District*, McGill-Queen's University Press, Montreal & Kingston, 1989, 158–73. On their target population, see George F. Theriault, "The Franco-Americans of New England," in Mason Wade (ed.), *Canadian Dualism – Studies in French-English Relations*, University of Toronto Press, Toronto, 1960. On the longer-term quest, see Gabriel Dussault, *Le Curé Labelle: Messianisme, utopia et colonization au Québec, 1850–1900*, Hurtubise, Montreal, 1983.

27 Ibid., 103.

28 See, for example, Robert Painchaud, "French-Canadian Historiography and Franco-Catholic Settlement in Western Canada, 1870–1915," *CHR*, vol. 59, no. 4, December 1974, 447–66. Albert Faucher, "L'Émigration des canadiens français au XIXe siècle: position du problem et perspectives," *Recherches sociographiques*, vol. 5, no. 3, September-December 1964, 27–317, and his *Québec en Amérique au XIXe siècle*, Fides, Montreal, 1972. Gilles Paquet and Wayne R. Smith, "L'Émigration des canadiens français vers les États-Unis, 1790–1940: problématique et coups de sonde," *L'Actualité économique*, vol. 59, no. 3, September 1983, 423–53. Gilles Paquet, "L'Émigration des canadiens français vers la Nouvelle-Angleterre, 1870–1910: Prises du vue quantitative," *Recherches sociographiques*, vol. 5, no. 3, September-December 1964, 319–70. Yves Roby, "Quebec in the United States: A Historiographical Survey," *Maine Historical Society Quarterly*, vol. 26, no. 3, Winter 1987, 126–59.

29 Allen Green, Mary MacKinnon, and Chris Minns, "Conspicuous by their Absence: French Canadians and the Settlement of the Canadian West," *Journal of Economic History*, 2005, vol. 65, no. 3, 822–49.

30 See Leon E. Truesdell, *The Canadian Born in the United States*, Yale University Press, New Haven, 78–9 for French Canadians in 1890 working in Michigan, Wisconsin, and Minnesota. Painchaud, 453, had raised the question tangentially as an unexplored hypothesis: "French Canadians had neither the money nor the inclination to pursue agriculture occupations in the late nineteenth century."

31 Several rural counties had populations of over 1,000 francophones as late as 1930. See Ibid., 54, 206, for Michigan, Wisconsin, and Minnesota.

32 Bruno Ramirez, *On the Move, French-Canadian and Italian Migrants in the North Atlantic Economy, 1860–1914*, McClelland and Steward, Toronto, 1991, 26–7. See also Faucher, "L'émigration des canadiens français," and Paquet, "L'émigration des canadiens français" ; James Allen, "Migration Fields of French Canadian Immigrants to Southern Maine," *Geographic Review*, vol. 62, no. 3, July 1972, 366–83; Frances H. Early, "The Rise and Fall of Felix Albert: Some Reflections on the Aspirations of Habitant Immigrants to Lowell, Massachusetts in the late nineteenth century," in Raymond Breton and Pierre Savard (eds.), *Quebec and Acadian Diaspora in North America*, Multicultural History Society of Ontario, Toronto, 1982, 25–38; Paquet and Smith, "L'émigration des canadiens français," 423–53; and Roby, "Les canadiens français," *Revue historique d'Amérique Français*, vol. 41, no. 1, Summer 1971, 3–22.

33 Douglas Owram, *The Promise of Eden: The Canadian Expansionist Movement and the Idea of the West, 1856–1900*, University of Toronto Press, Toronto, 1980, 62–74.

34 Ibid., 60.

35 In just over a year during the peak of the pre-war land rush (1909–1910) at Saskatchewan's main point of rail entry from the United States, 5.6 per cent were returning Canadians. Just over half were from North Dakota. Less than 10 per cent had been living in Minnesota, and an even smaller proportion had travelled through the United States from Ontario. Randy Widdis, "American Resident Migration to Western Canada at the Turn of the 20th Century," in Gregory P. Marchildon (ed.), *Immigration and Settlement, 1870–1939*, Canadian Plains Research Centre, Regina, 2009, 347–51.

36 This discussion is largely focused on Rupert's Land and not the whole of the Canadian West. The substantial French Catholic Métis population and the near absence of any previous form of government created a

seeming political vacuum, not thought to exist in British Columbia. It was a British colony with representative (if not yet in possession of "responsible") government, a settled European population almost wholly English and Protestant. It was admitted to Confederation not only without any requirement of biculturalism of any kind but also with even its crown lands vested in the provincial government (while the Prairie provinces had to wait until 1930 to receive theirs). The extension of biculturalism to Rupert's Land was, in part, recognition of an existing French Catholic population and, in part, an open question as to future cultural orientation where there was as yet no substantial settled European population.

37 W.L. Morton, 196–7. Gerald Friesen, "Homeland to Hinterland: Political Transition in Manitoba, 1870–1879," *Canadian Historical Association Historical Papers*, 1979, 33–47. For the earlier debates, see Robert Fletcher, "The Language Problem in Manitoba Schools," *Manitoba Historical and Scientific Society Transactions*, no. 6, 1951, 52–6, and Anthony Herriot, "School Inspectors in the Early Days in Manitoba," *Manitoba Historical and Scientific Society Transactions*, no. 4, 1947–48, 26–36. See also Ron G. Bourgeault, "The Indian, the Métis and the Fur Trade: Class, Sexism and Racism in the Transition from Communism to Capitalism," *Studies in Political Economy*, no. 12, Fall 1983, 45–80, and David Boisvert and Keith Turnbull, "Who are the Métis?," *Studies in Political Economy*, no. 18, Autumn 1985, 107–47.

38 W.L. Morton, "Manitoba Schools and Canadian Nationality, 1890–1923," in Craig Brown (ed.), *Minorities, Schools, and Politics*, University of Toronto Press, Toronto, 1969, 10–18.

39 Lovell Clark (ed.), *Manitoba School Question: Majority Rule or Minority Rights?*, Copp Clark, Toronto, 1968, and Paul E. Crunican, *Priests and Politicians: Manitoba Schools and the Election of 1896*, University of Toronto Press, Toronto, 1974, 8.

40 J.R. Miller, "D'Alton McCarthy, Equal Rights, and the Origins of the Manitoba School Question," CHR, vol. 54, no. 4, December 1973, 369–92, and his *Equal Rights – The Jesuit Estates Act Controversy*, McGill-Queen's University Press, Montreal & Kingston, 1979, 118–19. T.S. Mitchell, "Forging a New Protestant Ontario on the Agricultural Frontier: Public Schools in Brandon and the Origins of the Manitoba Schools Question, 1881–1890," *Prairie Forum*, vol. 11, no. 1, Spring 1986, 33–50.

41 It may be that the Greenway government sought a powerful issue to rebuild its popularity after a scandal over railways. J.A. Jackson, "Railways and the Manitoba School Question," *Manitoba Historical Society Transactions*, no. 30, 1973–74, 81–8.

42 D.J. Hall, *Clifford Sifton, The Young Napoleon*, vol. 1, UBC Press, Vancouver, 1981, 117.

43 Sifton had not heretofore displayed any partiality to either Mennonites or any other linguistic minority in Manitoba.

44 S.W. Horrall, "Sir John A. Macdonald and the Mounted Police for the North-West Territories," CHR, vol. 53, no. 2, 1972, 179–200. When recruiting Métis seemed impractical, Macdonald turned to Canadiens to have a francophone presence in the new police force.

45 "Richard Hardistry," in J.M. Bumsted, *Dictionary of Manitoba Biography*, University of Manitoba Press, Winnipeg, 1999. B.A. Stacey, "D.W. Davis, Whiskey Trader to Politician," *Alberta History*, 38, no. 3, Summer 1990, 1–11.

46 Mackay lost by 44 votes. He was eventually elected in 1911. John Hawkes, *The Story of Saskatchewan and Its People*, vol. 2, Clark, Chicago, 1924, 1179–81.

47 However, a thorough legislative review in the 1960s by the Bilingualism and Biculturalism Commission discovered that the assembly ordinance had never actually been proclaimed by the lieutenant-governor. Consequently, while the assembly's action determined subsequent practice of monolingual documents, that action was never given force of law. It has been argued that the Autonomy Bills of 1905, in carrying forward whatever had been in the 1875 NWT Act which had not been explicitly amended or revoked by either the federal or territorial legislatures, entrenched the legal right to the use of French in both provinces. See also Kenneth Munro, "Official Bilingualism in Alberta," *Prairie Forum*, vol. 12, no. 1, Spring 1987, 37–47. For the use of French in schools, see Keith Alwyn McLeod, "A History of the Status of the French Language in the Schools of the NWT, 1870–1905 and in Saskatchewan, 1905–1934," master's thesis, University of Saskatchewan, Saskatoon, 1966.

48 Grant MacEwan, *Frederick Haultain, Frontier Statesman of the Canadian Northwest*, Western Producer Prairie Books, Saskatoon, 1985, 122–32, 144–6, 155–7.

49 On the problems of French-language instruction in Saskatchewan, see Ray Huel, "The French Canadians and the Language Question, 1918," *Saskatchewan History*, vol. 23, no. 1, Winter 1970, 1–15; "The Teaching of French in Saskatchewan Public Schools, A Curious Infraction of the Provisions of the School Act in Ethier S.D. No. 1834, 1921–1923," *Saskatchewan History*, vol. 24, no. 1, Winter 1971, 13–24; and "The Dilemmas of French Language Education in Saskatchewan: L'Association Interprovincial and the Recruitment of Bilingual Teachers, 1917–1925,"

Canadian Ethnic Studies, vol. 20, no. 2, 1988, 20–35; for a leading opponent, see the work of Gordon Barnhart, "The Prairie Pastor: E.O. Oliver," *Saskatchewan History*, vol. 37, no. 3, Autumn 1984, 81–94, and Michael Owen, "'Building the Kingdom of God on the Prairies': E.H. Oliver and Saskatchewan Education, 1913–1930," *Saskatchewan History*, vol. 40, no. 1, Winter 1987, 22–34.

50 As examples, the checkerboard pattern of homesteading meant the few Arab settlers were scattered, but even the numerous Swedes and Norwegians who settled together seldom showed a resistance to assimilation: Mildred A. Duncanson, "Uncle Sam Jamha," *Alberta History*, vol. 28, no. 3, Summer 1980, 7–17; Gilbert Johnson, "The Syrians of Western Canada," *Saskatchewan History*, vol. 12, no. 1, Winter 1959, 31–2; and Habeeb Salloum, "The Urbanization of an Arab Homesteading Family," *Saskatchewan History*, vol. 42, no. 2, Spring 1989, 79–83. Katharine Farnham, "The Westlings: Swedish Pioneers," *Alberta History*, vol. 46, no. 1, Winter 1998, 10–14. Kenneth O. Bjork, "Scandinavian Migration to the Canadian Prairie Provinces, 1893–1914," *Norwegian-American Studies*, vol. 26, 1974, 3–30; and Daisy Lucas, "A Pioneer Norwegian Family," *Alberta History*, vol. 41, no. 4, Autumn 1993, 16–19. This can be compared to a view of the American experience: Jon Gjerde, *The Minds of the West, Ethnocultural Evolution in the Rural Middle West, 1830–1917*, University of North Carolina Press, Chapel Hill, 1997.

51 See Roberto Perin, "Clio as an Ethnic," in Carl Berger (ed.), *Contemporary Approaches to Canadian History*, Copp Clark, Toronto, 1987, 201–21; Martin L. Kovacs, "Ethnic Canadians: Synoptic Comments," in Martin L. Kovacs (ed.), *Ethnic Canadians: Culture and Education*, University of Regina Canadian Plains Studies Center, Regina, 1978, 473–95; G. Carter Bentley, "Ethnicity and Practice," *Comparative Studies in Society and History*, vol. 29, no. 1, 1987, 24–55; S. S. Halli et al. (ed.), *Ethnic Demography, Canadian Immigrant, Racial and Cultural Variations*, Carleton University Press, Ottawa, 1990; Edward N. Herberg, *Ethnic Groups in Canada: Adaptations and Transitions*, Nelson, Toronto, 1989; Dirk Hoerder, "Ethnic Studies in Canada from the 1880s to 1962: A Historiographic Perspective and Critique," *Canadian Ethnic Studies*, vol. 26, no. 1, 1994, 1–18; and Frederick Luebke (ed.), *Ethnicity on the Great Plains*, University of Nebraska Press, Lincoln, 1980.

52 Anthony Becker, "The Germans from Russia in Saskatchewan and Alberta," *German-Canadian Yearbook*, vol. 3, 1976, 106–19; Kurt Tischler, "The Efforts of the Germans in Saskatchewan to Retain their Language before 1914," *German-Canadian Yearbook*, vol. 6, 1981; and

Gerhard Bossler, "Problems and Perspectives in German-Canadian Historiography," in K.R. Gurttler (ed.), *Annals 5 Problem, Project, Perspective Symposium 1985*, Colloques DEAM, Montreal, 1986, 1–19.

53 Heinz Lehmann, *The German Canadians, 1750–1937: Immigration,
Settlement and Culture*, Jesperson Press, St John's, 1986, 194–247.
Arthur Grenke, "Settlement Patterns of German-Speaking Immigrants on
the Canadian Prairies, 1817–1914," *German-Canadian Yearbook*, vol.
14, 1995, 1–16.

54 The Prairie standard township provided alternate sections for homesteads, with railway, school, and Hudson Bay lands. See John A. Archer,
Saskatchewan: A History, Western Producer Books, Saskatoon, 1980, 57;
D.G.G. Kerr, *A Historical Atlas of Canada*, Thomas Nelson, Don Mills,
1966, 62; Martin, 18.

55 George Woodcock and Ivan Avakumovic, *The Doukhobors*, Oxford University Press, Toronto, 1968. John W. Friesen and Michael M. Verigin,
Community Doukhobors: A People in Transition, Borealis Press, Ottawa,
1989. Koozma J. Tarasoff, *Plakun Trava, The Doukhobors*, Mir Publication Society, Grand Forks, 1982. Sam George Stopnikoff, *Historical
Saga of the Doukhobor Faith, 1750s–1990s*, Apex Graphics, Saskatoon,
1992. Victor O. Buyniak, "Documents in Western History, Doukhobor
Immigration: The Potato Dilemma," *Saskatchewan History*, vol. 37, no.
2, 1985, 72–8. Andrew Donskov et al., *The Doukhobor Centenary in
Canada*, Slavic Research Group, University of Ottawa Press, Ottawa,
2000. Ashleigh Androsoff, "A Larger Frame: 'Redressing' the Image of
Doukhobor-Canadian Women in the 20th century," *Journal of the Canadian Historical Association*, vol. 18, no. 1, 2007, 81–105. S.J. Sommer-
ville, "Early Icelandic Settlement in Canada," *Manitoba Historical Soci-
ety Transactions*, no. 1, 1944–1945, 25–35. A group of Jewish colonists
attained substantially the same concessions on a much smaller scale at
Narcisse/Bender, Manitoba in 1903. Yossi Katz and John C. Lehr (eds.),
The Last Best West, Magnes Press, Jerusalem, 1999, chapter 2, "Jewish
Pioneer Agricultural Settlements," 48–57. Max Rubin, "Alberta's Jews:
The Long Journey," in Howard and Tamara Palmer (eds.), *Peoples of
Alberta: Portraits of Cultural Diversity*, Western Producer Prairie Books,
Saskatoon, 1985, 328–47.

56 Donald E. Willmott, "Ethnic Solidarity in the Esterhazy Area, 1882–
1940," in Kovacs, *Ethnic Canadians*, 167–76. N.F. Dreisziger (ed.), *Struggle and Hope: The Hungarian-Canadian Experience*, McClelland and
Stewart, Toronto, 1982, 61–78.

57 Palmer and Palmer, 4–5.

58 Ibid., Robert Macdonald, "The Hutterites in Alberta," 348–64. John W. Friesen, "Pacifism and Anastasia's Doukhobor Village," *Alberta History*, vol. 41, no. 1, Winter, 1993, 14–19.

59 Dreisziger, 68, 78.

60 Arnold Dashefsky, "Theoretical Frameworks in the Study of Ethnic Identity" and John W. Berry, "Finding Identity: Separation, Integration, Assimilation, or Marginality?," both in Leo Driedger (ed.), *Ethnic Canada: Identities and Inequalities*, Copp Clark, Toronto, 1987, 172–80, 223–39.

61 One well-documented example, from an urban setting, was Slovak immigrants who sought to avoid assimilation by English-language schools, just as they had kept their children from German-language schools imposed in Slovakia. See Peter D. Chimbos, "A Comparison of the Social Adaptation of Dutch, Greek and Slovak Immigrants in a Canadian Community," *International Migration Review*, vol. 6, no. 3, Autumn 1972, 230–44; Joseph J. Barton, *Peasants and Strangers: Italians, Rumanians and Slovaks*, Harvard University Press, Cambridge, 1975; M. Mark Stolarik, "Immigration, Education, and the Social Mobility of Slovaks, 1870–1930," in Randall M. Miller and Thomas D. Marzik (eds.), *Immigrants and Religion in Urban America*, Temple University Press, Philadelphia, 1977, 103–16; and John Bodnar, "Schooling and the Slavic-American Family, 1900–1940," in Bernard J. Weiss (ed.), *American Education and the European Immigrant: 1840–1940*, University of Illinois Press, Urbana,1982, 78–96.

62 M.R. Lupul, *The Roman Catholic Church and the North-West School Question*, McClelland and Stewart, Toronto, 1974; J. Skwarok, *The Ukrainian Settlers in Canada and Their Schools*, Basilian Press, Edmonton, 1958; and Dreisziger, 78–81.

63 William Kostash and Fred Hannochko, "Education and Teachers," in Nicholas Holubitsky et al., *Ukrainians in Alberta*, Ukrainian News Publishers, Edmonton, 1975, 190–5, on the "Ukrainian Schools Crisis" of 1912–13.

64 John C. Lehr, "The Rural Settlement Behaviour of Ukrainian Pioneers in Western Canada, 1891–1914," in Brenton M. Barr (ed.), *Western Canada Research in Geography*, Tantalus Research, Vancouver, 1975, 52.

65 Michael Ewanchuk, *Spruce, Swamp, and Stone – A History of the Pioneer Ukrainian Settlements in the Gimil Area*, Derksen Printers, Steinbeck, 1977.

66 John C. Lehr, "The Landscape of Ukrainian Settlement in the Canadian West," *Great Plains Quarterly*, vol. 2, no. 2, Spring 1982, 94–105.

Francis Swyripa, *Wedded to the Cause: Ukrainian-Canadian Women and Ethnic Identity, 1891–1991*, University of Toronto Press, Toronto, 1993.

67 John C. Lehr, "Governmental Coercion in the Settlement of Ukrainian Immigrants in Western Canada," *Prairie Forum*, vol. 8, no. 2, Fall 1993, 179–94.

68 Radomir Borislow Bilash, "The Colonial Development of East Central Alberta and its Effect on Ukrainian Immigrant Settlement to 1930," University of Manitoba, master's thesis, 1983.

69 "Ruthenian" and "Galician" were terms used for Ukrainians before the First World War. Conflicts with the Catholic archbishop, which interacted with denominational conflicts within the Ukrainian community, and the domestic needs of a cabinet minister led to the school being moved to Brandon. A separate school for training Polish teachers took its place in Winnipeg, under the archbishop's watchful eye.

70 Skwarok, 87–94.

71 W.L. Morton, "Manitoba Schools and Canadian Nationality, 1890–1923," in Brown, Minorities, 14–18. Sybil Shock, "The Immigrant Child in the Manitoba Schools," *Manitoba Historical Society Transactions*, no. 30, 1973–74, 17–32. The same pattern followed in provinces further west: Manfred Prokop, "Canadianization of Immigrant Children: The Role of the Rural Elementary School in Alberta, 1900–1930," *Alberta History*, vol. 37, no. 2, Spring 1989, 1–10. R. Bruce Shepard, "The Little 'White' Schoolhouse: Racism in a Saskatchewan Rural School," *Saskatchewan History*, vol. 39, no. 3, Autumn 1986, 81–93. Bill Maciejko, "Ukrainians and Prairie School Reform, 1896–1921: Ethnic and Domestic Ideologies in Modern State Formation," *Canadian Ethnic Studies*, vol. 22, no. 2, 1990, 19–40. Marilyn J. Barber, "Canadianization through the Schools of the Prairie Provinces before World War One: The Attitudes and Aims of the English-Speaking Majority," 281–94, and Raymond Huel, "The Public School as Guardian of Anglo-Saxon Traditions: The Saskatchewan Experience, 1913–1918," 295–303, both in Martin L. Kovacs (ed.), *Ethnic Canadians: Culture and Education*, Canadian Plains Studies, Regina, 1978.

72 While Poles benefited from the special teacher training school, a 1914 survey of Manitoba's bilingual schools showed only two in which the second language was Polish and five in which both Ukrainian and Polish were used (compared to 87 that used only Ukrainian). Henry Radecki, *A Member of a Distinguished Family: The Polish Group in Canada*, McClelland & Stewart, Toronto, 1976, 87.

73 On the other side, it has been suggested that the Hungarians were "put
    up" to attack the archbishop by elements in the Liberal Party that wanted
    to weaken the intransigent ultramontane archbishop whose refusal to
    accept Laurier's compromises on Manitoba schools had been an on-going
    sore point for the government. Martin L. Kovas, "The Hungarian School
    Question" in Kovacs, 176, 333–58.

74 René Rottiers, "Mgr. Gaire: missionnaise-colonisator des prairies," in
    Pierre-Yves Mocquais et al., *La langue, la culture et la société des franco-
    phones de l'Ouest*, Institute de recherche du Centre D'Études Bilingues,
    Regina, 1984, 37–57, where the priest recruited from Alsace saw himself
    as founding French Catholic settlement and settlements, and so came into
    conflict with Bishop Lègal who demanded that he learn English.

75 The new Irish bishops got rid of their French clergy within a few years.
    Not all of them went quietly: Henry L. Wostenberg, "Exiled but Not
    Silent: The Factum Letter of Father Henri Voisin," *Alberta History*, 58,
    no. 2, Spring 2010, 17–25.

76 Clinton O. White, "Education among German Catholic Settlers in Sas-
    katchewan, 1903–1918: A Reinterpretation," *Canadian Ethnic Studies*,
    vol. 16, no. 1, 1984, 78–95; "Pre-War Elementary Education Develop-
    ments among Saskatchewan's German Catholics: A Revisionist View,"
    Prairie Forum, vol. 18, no. 2, Fall 1993, 171–96; "Pre-World War I Sas-
    katchewan German Catholic Thought Concerning the Perpetuation of
    their Language and Religion," *Canadian Ethnic Studies*, vol. 26, no. 2,
    1994, 15–45; "Maintaining Anglo-Celtic Cultural Hegemony in Sas-
    katchewan: Rev. E.H. Oliver, Provincial Education Policy and the Ger-
    man Catholics," *Historical Studies in Education*, vol. 6, no. 2, Fall 1994,
    253–80; "German Catholic Parochial Schools in St Peter's Colony: Their
    Buildings, Equipment and Finances," *Saskatchewan History*, vol. 48, no.
    2, Fall 1996, 26–47.

77 Gloria Romaniuk, "The Legacy of Monsignor Philip Ruh (1883–1962):
    Rich Beyond Measure," *Western Oblate Studies*, vol. 15, 1999, 175–94.

78 In the great struggles between the Roman Catholic and Greek Ortho-
    dox faiths in the sixteenth century, Ukraine marked the frontier zone.
    Each faith was backed at one time or another by major powers: Cath-
    olic Poland and Catholic Austria on one side, Orthodox Russia on the
    other. In 1596, reflecting the ascendancy of the Catholic powers, under
    the Union of Brest-Litovsk, a substantial portion of the Ukrainian Ortho-
    dox accepted papal authority, which in turn recognized their "East-
    ern rite" liturgy as well as married priests. In 1686, reflecting the rising
    power of Orthodox Russia, the remainder of the Ukrainian Orthodox

Church accepted the primacy of the Moscow patriarch, which secured their Orthodox liturgy at the cost of Moscow appointing Ukrainian bishops. These high-level politics had their practical impacts on the tens of thousands of Ukrainian peasants from Galicia and Bukovina who arrived in Canada before the First World War. Most Ukrainians from Galicia adhered to the Ukrainian Greek Catholic (or Uniate) Church, viewing the Roman Catholic Church as the ally of the Polish (and latterly Austrian) nobility who oppressed them economically and socially. Ukrainians of Bukovina were divided between Greek Catholic and Russian Orthodox. Compounding these complexities was a ruling from the pope in 1895 that married Greek Catholic clergy would not be allowed to minister in North America. Since about 95 per cent of the Galician Ukrainian Greek Catholic clergy were married, it meant that the Ukrainian Catholics almost always arrived without any clergy to accompany them.

79 Andrii Krawchuk, "Between a Rock and a Hard Place: Francophone Missionaries among Ukrainian Catholics" and Mark G. McGowan, "'A Portion for the Vanquished': Roman Catholics and the Ukrainian Catholic Church," both in L. Luciuk and S. Hryniuk (eds.), *Canada's Ukrainians, Negotiating an Identity*, University of Toronto Press, Toronto, 1991, 206–17, 218–37.

80 John W. Friesen, "School and the Doukhobor Experience," in Tarasoff and Klymasz, 137–46.

81 William Janzen, *Limits of Liberty: The Experience of Mennonite, Hutterite, and Doukhobor Communities in Canada*, University of Toronto Press, Toronto, 1990, 36–59.

82 M.R. Lupul (ed.), *Heritage in Transition*, McClelland and Stewart, Toronto, 1982, 275. Radecki, 95.

83 Luciuk and Hryniuk, 262, for a study of greater Toronto.

84 For a contrasting view – that minimizes the cultural impact of English-language dominance – see David Smith, "Instilling British Values in the Prairie Provinces," Marchildon, 441–56.

CHAPTER SEVEN

1 The brief steamboat era (1878–85) on the North and South Saskatchewan amply demonstrated that both were too shallow to function as transportation routes in spite of their apparent natural link to Winnipeg.

2 J. Murray Beck (ed.), *Joseph Howe: Voice of Nova Scotia*, McClelland and Stewart, Toronto, 1964, 124, 130.

3 However, J.M. Beck, *Joseph Howe*, vol. 2, *The Briton Becomes 1848–1873*, McGill-Queen's University Press, Montreal & Kingston, 1983, 125–6, 143–4, wanted to make an exception for his hero. P.B. Waite, *Canada, 1874–1896: Arduous Destiny*, McClelland and Stewart, Toronto, 1971, 219–21; Dale C. Thomson, *Alexander Mackenzie: Clear Grit*, Macmillan, Toronto, 1960, 218–20; and Brian Young, *Georges-Etienne Cartier, Montreal Bourgeois*, McGill-Queen's University Press, Montreal & Kingston, 1981, 64–5. Ken Cruikshank, "Working for the People's Railway: The Intercolonial Railway in the Maritime Economy," paper read at the Canadian Historical Association, 1992.

4 Robert S. Henry, "The Railroad Land Grant Legend in American History Texts," 121–44; Charles S. Morgan, "Problems in the Appraisal of the Railroad Land Grants," 163–73, and Paul W. Gates, "The Railroad Land-Grant Legend," 175–9, all in V. Carstensen (ed.), *The Public Lands: Studies in the History of the Public Domain*, University of Wisconsin Press, Madison, 1963.

5 Chester Martin, *"Dominion Lands" Policy*, Lewis H. Thomas (ed.), Carleton Library Series, McClelland & Stewart, Toronto, 1973 (1938), 38.

6 Lloyd J. Mercer, *Railroads and Land Policy – A Study in Government Intervention*, Academic Press, New York, 1982, 60–7.

7 Martin, 74–97.

8 Martin, 47.

9 Martin, 55–8, and Donald C. Petker, "The Irrigation Frontier in Southern Alberta, 1885–1915: Expectation, Adaptation, and Diversification," master's thesis, University of Calgary, Calgary, 1996.

10 Martin, 47.

11 Ibid., 69.

12 Mercer, 29.

13 Robert W. Fogel, *The Union Pacific Railroad: A Case in Premature Enterprise*, Johns Hopkins Press, Baltimore, 1960, 91–110.

14 Ibid.

15 Albert Fishlow, *American Railroads and the Transformation of the Ante-Bellum Economy*, Harvard University Press, Cambridge, 1965, 163–204.

16 Mercer, 138.

17 Ibid., 147. See also Fogel, 91–110.

18 Martin, 140.

19 Ibid., 152.

20 Ibid., 82, 92.

21 Ibid., 153.

22 Ibid., 155. If land companies can only sell in a boom, they could do no more than an individual in a depressed market. Their technique lay wholly in good timing.

23 Only for a brief period could Canadians enter for a second homestead in the nineteenth century (1883–86). Pre-emptions could be had only at the very beginning and the very end of Prairie settlement.

24 William J. Stewart, "Speculation and Nebraska's Public Domain, 1863–1872," *Nebraska History*, vol. 45, no. 3, 1964, 265–71; Allan Bogue and Margaret Beattie Bogue, "'Profits' and the Frontier Land Speculator," *Journal of Economic History*, vol. 17, no. 1, 1957, 8–24; and Robert Swierenga, "Land Speculation and Its Impact on American Economic Growth and Welfare: A Historiographic Review," *Western Historical Quarterly*, vol. 8, no. 3, July 1977, 283–302.

25 That "Liberal Organ" was the *Manitoba Free Press*, 3 March 1906.

26 "Fake Homesteading," UBC Special Collections Pamphlet, n.p., n.d. [1908].

27 Ibid., 174, 169, 172.

28 Paul Voisey, *Vulcan, The Making of a Prairie Community*, University of Toronto Press, Toronto, 1988, 38.

29 Ibid., 39.

30 Ibid., 41. Land values did not return to pre-1920 values until after 1945.

31 Ibid., 44.

32 Ibid., 44–5.

33 Peter B. Waite (ed.), *The Confederation Debates in the Province of Canada, 1865*, McClelland & Stewart, Toronto, 1963, 56.

34 House of Commons, Debates, 1869, 484.

35 House of Commons Debates, 1878, 209.

36 See, for examples, Martin, 17, 116–19, 142–5; R.C. Brown, "For the Purposes of the Dominion: Background Paper on the History of Federal Lands Policy to 1930," in J.G. Nelson et al. (ed.), *Canadian Public Land Use in Perspective*, Proceedings of a Symposium Sponsored by the Social Science Research Council of Canada, Ottawa, 1973, 9. Comparisons have not be limited to those between Canada and the USA: Paul F. Sharp, "Three Frontiers: Some Comparative Studies of Canadian, American, and Australian Settlement," *Pacific Historical Review*, vol. 24, no. 4, November 1955, 369–77; Carl Solberg, *The Prairies and the Pampas, Agrarian Policy in Canada and Argentina, 1880–1930*, Stanford University Press, Stanford, 1987; as well as Jeremy Adelman, "The Social Bases of Technical Change: Mechanization of the Wheatlands of Argentina and

Canada, 1890 to 1914," *Comparative Study of Society and History*, vol. 34, no. 2, April 1992, 271–300, and his *Frontier Development – Land, Labour, and Capital in the Wheatlands of Argentina and Canada, 1890–1914*, Clarendon Press, Oxford, 1994.

37 See, for examples, Sheryll Patterson-Black, "Women Homesteaders on the Great Plains Frontier," *Frontiers: A Journal of Women's Studies*, vol. 1, no. 2, Spring 1976, 68; Kathryn Llewellyn Harris, "Women and Families in Northwestern Colorado Homesteads, 1873–1920," doctoral dissertation, University of Colorado, 1983; H. Elaine Lindgren, "Ethnic Women Homesteading on the Plains of North Dakota," *Great Plains Quarterly*, vol. 9, Summer 1989, 157–73; and Paula Bauman, "Single Women Homesteaders in Wyoming, 1880–1930," *Annals of Wyoming*, vol. 58, Spring 1986, 39–53. But see also, Sherry L. Smith, "Single Women Homesteaders: The Perplexing Case of Elinore Pruitt Stewart," in Sandra K. Schackel (ed.), *Western Women's Lives, Continuity and Change in the 20th Century*, University of New Mexico Press, Albuquerque, 2003, 161–82.

38 Shelia McManus, *The Line which Separates*, University of Nebraska Press, Lincoln, 2005, 40.

39 Sandra Rollings-Magnusson, "Spinsters Need Not Apply: Six Single Women Who Attempted to Homestead in Saskatchewan Between 1872 and 1914," *Prairie Forum*, 34, no. 2, Fall 2009, 357–80.

40 Rod Bantjes, *Improved Earth – Prairie Space as Modern Artefact, 1869–1944*, University of Toronto Press, Toronto, 2005, 118.

41 John Warkentin (ed.), *The Western Interior of Canada*, McClelland and Stewart, Toronto, 1964, 201; see also 216, 221; and compare Hind to Palliser (178) and Hector (167, 171) – who stressed the clay soil rather than rainfall.

42 Ibid., 223.

43 They did not mention the Canadian Shield as a barrier comparable to that presumed desert.

44 The plan of Prairie township is available in several places: John Archer, *Saskatchewan: A History*, Western Producer Books, Saskatoon, 1980, 57; D.G.G. Kerr, *Historical Atlas of Canada*, Thomas Nelson, Don Mills, 1975, 62; and Martin, 18.

45 Benjamin H. Hibbard, *A History of the Public Land Policies*, Macmillan, New York, 1924, 113.

46 Ibid., 3, 136–8.

47 Roy M. Robbins, *Our Landed Heritage, The Public Domain, 1776–1936*, University of Nebraska Press, Lincoln, 1962, 236–55.

48 Paul W. Gates, *History of Public Land Law Development*, Zenger Publishing, Washington (DC), 1968, 402–21.

49 Robbins, 236–51. Paul W. Gates, *History of Public Land Law Development*, Zenger Publishing, Washington, 1968, 401–15. Fred A. Shannon, *The Farmer's Last Frontier Agriculture, 1860–1897*, Holt, Rinehart and Winston, New York, 1945, 57–60.

50 Shannon, 51. Zachariah L. Boughn, "The Free Land Myth in the Disposal of the Public Domain in South Cedar County, Nebraska," *Nebraska History*, vol. 58, no. 3, 1977, 359–69. Lawrence B. Lee, "The Homestead Act: Vision and Reality," *Utah Historical Quarterly*, vol. 30, no. 1, 1962, 215–34.

51 These global statistics are borne out in studies at the local level. Yosuo Okada found that in Gage County, Nebraska, homesteaders received about 15.4 per cent of the available public lands, while education scrip took up 40 per cent. Railway land grants were often highly uneven in their distribution. Some states – South Dakota and Oklahoma – had no railway lands at all. In Gage County they accounted for only 4.7 per cent of public lands alienated. Homesteaders in the county did substantially better at "proving up" their entries than the national average, 60 per cent compared to 41 per cent. About 10 per cent "commutated" (i.e., purchased their homestead at the government price of $1.25 per acre), which was very close to the national average. However, Okada found that 54 of the 82 cancellations (40 per cent) were "relinquishments," where the homesteader was allowed to give up one homestead entry and preserve his right to begin another. Since the homesteader could often claim compensation for improvements from whoever took over his 160 acres, this became a means of selling the right to occupy as well. Okada Yasuo, *Public Lands and Pioneer Farms, Gage County, Nebraska, 1850–1900*, Keio Economy Society, Tokyo, 1971.

52 Martin, 157–72, 178–81, 227–32.

53 I have not included the minor categories such as purchased homesteads and soldiers' grants in the totals given.

54 K.D. Bicha, "The Plains Farmer and the Prairie Province Frontier, 1897–1914," *Journal of Economic History*, vol. 25, June 1965, 263–70. Sandford F. Borins, "Western Canadian Homesteading in Time and Space," *Canadian Journal of Economics*, vol. 15, no. 1, 1982, 18–27. Michael B. Percy and Tamara Woroby, "American Homesteaders and the Canadian Prairies, 1899 and 1909," *Explorations in Economic History*, vol. 24, 1987, 77–100.

55 Hibbard, 395ff. Gates, 507. Martin, 157–8. Robbins, 343.

CHAPTER EIGHT

1 Irene Spry (ed.), *The Papers of the Palliser Expedition, 1857–1860*, Champlain Society, Toronto, 1968, 33, 77, 517.

2 Alexander Morris, *The Treaties of Canada with the Indians of Manitoba and the North-West Territories including the Negotiations*, Belfords, Clarke & Company, Toronto, 1880, 29.

3 Ibid.

4 Ibid., 40.

5 Ibid., 288–9. His first example was St Peter's Parish in the Red River Valley, the Ottawa/Saulteaux settlement on Netley Creek where farming had gone on and off since 1805.

6 George F. Stanley, *The Birth of Western Canada*, University of Toronto Press, Toronto, 1960 (1936), 209.

7 Ibid.

8 Ibid., 218. See Liz Bryan, *The Buffalo People, Prehistoric Archaeology on the Canadian Plains*, University of Alberta Press, Edmonton, 1991. Michael Stephen Kennedy (ed.), *The Assiniboines*, University of Oklahoma Press, Norman, 1961. D'Arcy Jenish, *Indian Fall, The Last Great Days of the Plains Cree and the Blackfoot Confederacy*, Viking, Toronto, 1999.

9 Ibid., 237.

10 Ibid., 238–9.

11 Grant MacEwan, *Between the Red and the Rockies*, University of Toronto Press, Toronto, 1952, 38.

12 Sarah Carter, "'We Must Farm to Enable Us to Live': The Plains Cree and Agriculture to 1900," in R. Bruce Morrison and C. Roderick Wilson (eds.), *Native Peoples: The Canadian Experience*, 3rd ed., Oxford University Press, Don Mills, 2004, 320–1. I, too, was "startled" in the early 1970s when Noel Dyck tried to explain to me that the federal government caused the failure of reserve farming: "Administration of Indian Aid in the North-West Territories, 1878–1886," unpublished master's thesis, University of Saskatchewan, Saskatoon, 1970, and "An Opportunity Lost: The Initiative of the Reserve Agricultural Programme in the Prairie West," in F.L. Barron and J.B. Waldram (eds.), *1885 and After: Native Society in Transition*, Canadian Plains Research Centre, Regina, 1986, 121–38.

13 W. Raymond Wood and Lee Irwin, "Mandan," *Handbook of North American Indians*, William C. Sturtevant (general editor), vol. 13, part 1 or 2, Raymond J. DeMallie (vol. editor), Smithsonian Institution, Washington, 2001, 349–64.

14 Mary J. Adair, "Plains Plants" and C. Margaret Scarry and R.A. Yarnell, "Domestication of Plants in the East," both in D.H. Ubelaker (ed.), *Environment, Origins, and Population*, vol. 3, W.C. Sturtevant (general editor), *Handbook of North American Indians*, Smithsonian Institution, Washington (DC), 2006, 365–74, 428–38, and E.S. Roger, "Southeastern Ojibwa," in Bruce G. Trigger (ed.), *Northeast*, vol. 15, W.C. Sturtevant (general editor), *Handbook of North American Indians*, Smithsonian Institution, Washington (DC), 1978, 760–71. Thomas R. Wessel, "Agriculture, Indians, and American History," *Agricultural History*, vol. 50, 1976, 9.

15 Laura Peers, *The Ojibwa of Western Canada, 1780–1870*, University of Manitoba Press, Winnipeg, 1994, 70–1. See also Olive Patricia Dickason, *Canada's First Nations*, Oxford University Press, Don Mills, 2002, and James A. Clifton (ed.), *Being and Becoming Indian: Biographical Studies of North American Frontiers*, Dorsey Press, Chicago, 1989.

16 D. Wayne Moodie and Barry Kaye, "Indian Agriculture in the Fur Trade Northwest," *Prairie Forum*, vol. 11, no. 2, Fall 1986, 171–2.

17 D.W. Moodie and Barry Kaye, "The Northern Limit of Indian Agriculture in North America," *The Geographical Review*, vol. 59, 1969, 516–17.

18 Peers, 70.

19 Ibid., 81–2. Harold Hickerson, "Fur Trade Colonialism and the North American Indians," *Journal of Ethnic Studies*, vol. 1, no. 2, 1973, 15–44.

20 Ibid., 133.

21 Moodie and Kaye, 1969, 517.

22 Peers, 80.

23 Ibid., 70.

24 Sarah Carter, *Lost Harvests*, University of Manitoba Press, Winnipeg, 1989, 37.

25 Ibid., 41.

26 This is asserted by Moodie and Kaye, 1986, 181. See D.W. Moodie, "Agriculture and the Fur Trade," in C.M. Judd and A.J. Ray (eds.), *Old Trails and New Directions*, University of Toronto Press, Toronto, 1980, 272–90. See also Thomas C. Buckley (ed.), *Rendezvous, Selected Papers of the Fourth North American Fur Trade Conference, 1981*, North American Fur Trade Conference, St Paul, 1984.

27 Carter, *Lost*, 42–4.

28 Deanna Christensen, *Ahtahkakoop, The Epic Account of a Plains Cree Head Chief, His People, and their Struggle for Survival, 1816–1896*, Aktahkakoop Publishing, Shell Lake, 2000, 153.

29 Peers, 70.

30 Ibid., 72.

31 D.J. Hall, "'A Serene Atmosphere'? Treaty 1 Revisited," *Journal of Native Studies*, vol. 4, no. 2, 1984, 326. See also Jean Friesen, "Magnificent Gifts: The Treaties of Canada with the Indians of the Northwest, 1869–1876," *Transactions of the Royal Society of Canada*, fifth series, vol. 1, 1986, 41–51, and John Leonard Taylor, "Canada's North-West Indian Policy in the 1870s: Traditional Premises and Necessary Innovations," in J.R. Miller (ed.), *Sweet Promises, A Reader on Indian-White Relations in Canada*, University of Toronto Press, Toronto, 1991, 207–11. Douglas N. Sprague, *Canada's Treaties with Aboriginal People*, University of Manitoba Faculty of Law, Winnipeg, 1991.

32 Hall, "Serene Atmosphere," 326. Hall notes that in the Treaty 1 negotiations the federal representatives had not yet learned to speak with one voice, with Commissioner W.M. Simpson trying to interrupt Archibald's responses when he feared them too generous or unguarded. In future, it would be the native leaders who would be divided.

33 Carter, *Lost*, 54.

34 Christensen, 166. For an insight into the missionaries' approach to native peoples, see Sarah Carter, "The Missionaries' Indian: Publications of John McDougall, John Mclean, and Egerton Ryerson Young," *Prairie Forum*, vol. 9, no. 1, 1984, 27–44. Of course not all white incursions were peaceful: P. Goldring, "The Cypress Hills Massacre: A Century's Retrospect," *Saskatchewan History*, vol. 26, no. 3, Autumn 1973, 81–102.

35 Peers, 196.

36 Rebecca Brain, "Invisible Demons: The Impact of the 1870–1871 Small Pox Epidemic on the Plains Cree," paper read at the Canadian Historical Association, 2005.

37 Walter Hildebrandt, Dorothy First Rider, Sarah Carter, and Treaty 7 Elders and Tribal Council, *The True Spirit and Original Intent of Treaty 7*, McGill-Queen's University Press, Montreal, 1996, 235–6.

38 Carter, *Lost*, 57.

39 John L. Tobias, "Canada's Subjugation of the Plains Cree, 1879–1885," in Miller, 212–27. Hugh A. Dempsey, *Big Bear, The End of Freedom*, University of Nebraska Press, Lincoln, 1984.

40 Harry Miller, *These Too Were Pioneers: The Story of the Key Indian Reserve 65, and the Centennial of the Church (1884–1984)*, Seniors Consultant Service, Melville, 1984, 17–22.

41 Carter, *Lost*, 65.

42 Ibid., 83.

43 *DCB*, vol. 7, 725.

44 Robert L. Jones, *History of Agriculture in Ontario*, University of Toronto Press, Toronto, 1946, 157–74.

45 Peers, 134.

46 Carter, *Lost*, 44.

47 Ibid., 94.

48 Sarah Carter, "Agriculture and Agitation on the Oak River Dakota Reserve, 1875–1895," *Manitoba History*, vol. 6, 1983, 4. See also James H. Howard, *The Canadian Sioux*, University of Nebraska Press, Lincoln, 1984, 67–8, 181–5.

49 Carter, *Lost*, 112.

50 Ibid., 114.

51 Christensen, 465.

52 Hildebrandt, 706.

53 Hugh Dempsey, *Crowfoot, Chief of the Blackfoot*, Hurtig, Edmonton, 1972, 146.

54 Carter, *Lost*, 97–9.

55 Ibid., 118.

56 Ibid., 165.

57 Ibid., p.148.

58 Ibid.

59 Ibid., 169.

60 Ibid., 101.

61 Ibid., 102. For a somewhat different perspective on Reed, see Friesen, 44.

62 Ibid., 150–6.

63 For scientific racism, see Kenan Malik, *The Meaning of Race*, New York University Press, New York, 1996, 89–91, 106–23. Robert Miles, *Racism*, Routledge, London, 1989, 30–40. Pierre L. Van Den Berghe, "Ethnicity and the Sociobiology Debate," in John Rex and David Mason (eds.), *Theories of Race and Ethnic Relations*, Cambridge University Press, Cambridge, 1988, 246–63.

64 Carter, *Lost*, 213.

65 Ibid., 109–10.

66 On the peasant farming ideal and the Romantic resistance to modernity, see Fiona MacCarthy, *William Morris, A Life for Our Time*, Faber and Faber, London, 1994, 154–6, 266–8 on medievalism and 603–4 on the influence of Morris in the United States. G.K. Chesterton, *On Lying in Bed and Other Essays*, Bayeux Arts, Calgary, 2000, 344–88; *What's Wrong with the World*, Sherwood Sugden and Company, Peru (Illinois), 1994, 19–36; and *William Cobbett*, Hodder and Stoughton, London,

1925. Ian Dyck, *William Cobbett and Rural Popular Culture*, Cambridge University Press, New York, 1992.

67 Carter, *Lost*, 220.

68 Ibid., 158.

69 Ibid., 224.

70 Miller, *These Too Were Pioneers*, 32.

71 Dyck, 71–2.

72 Carter, *Lost*, 243.

73 Ibid., 245.

74 Ibid., 250–2.

75 Miller, *These Too Were Pioneers*, 38–9. On the longer-term impact, see Noel Dyck, *What Is the Indian "Problem?" Tutelage and Resistance in Canadian Indian Administration*, Institute of Economic and Social Research, St John's, 1991.

76 Helen Buckley, *From Wooden Ploughs to Welfare – Why Indian Policy Failed in the Prairie Provinces*, McGill-Queen's University Press, Montreal, Montreal, 1992, 64.

77 Ibid.

78 Ibid., 65.

79 Ibid., 254.

80 Brian Titley, "Transition to Settlement: The Peace Hills Indian Agency, 1884–1890," *Canadian Papers in Rural History*, vol. 8, 1992, 175–94, and Buckley, especially 61–6.

81 Carter, *Lost*, 54–5.

CHAPTER NINE

1 William Marr and M. Percy, "The Government and the Rate of Prairie Settlement," *Canadian Journal of Economics*, vol. 11, November 1978, 757–67; Frank D. Lewis, "Farm Settlement on the Canadian Prairies, 1898–1911," *Journal of Economic History*, vol. 41, no. 3, September 1981, 517–35; Pierre Berton, *The Promised Land, Settling the West, 1896–1914*, McClelland & Stewart, Toronto, 1984; J. Arthur Lower, *Western Canada – An Outline History*, Douglas and McIntyre, Vancouver, 1983.

2 Kenneth Norrie, "Cultivation Techniques as a Response to Risk in Early Canadian Prairie Agriculture," *Explorations in Economic History*, vol. 17, 1980, 386–99. See also his earlier "The Rate of Settlement of the Canadian Prairies, 1870–1911," *Journal of Economic History*, vol. 25, June 1975, 410–27; "Dry Farming and the Economics of Risk Bearing: The Canadian Prairies, 1870–1911," *Agricultural History*, vol. 31, 1977,

134–48; and "The National Policy and the Rate of Prairie Settlement: A Review," *Journal of Canadian Studies*, vol. 14, 1979, 63–76. Recall that Douglas McCalla, *Planting the Province: The Economic History of Upper Canada, 1784–1870*, University of Toronto Press, Toronto, 1993, made the same point for Upper Canada.

3   Jack C. Stabler, "Factors Affecting the Development of a New Region: The Canadian Great Plains, 1870–1897," *Annals of Regional Science*, vol. 7, June 1973, 82; Charles M. Studness, "Economic Opportunity and the Westward Migration of Canadians during the Late 19th Century," *Canadian Journal of Political Science and Economics*, vol. 30, November 1964, 570–84; and Penelope Hartland, "Factors in the Economic Growth of Canada," *Journal of Economic History*, vol. 15, no. 1, 1955, 21.

4   The exceptions are Ernest B. Ingles, "Some Aspects of Dry-Land Agriculture in the Canadian Prairies to 1925," master's thesis, University of Calgary, 1973, and David D. Harvey, *Americans in Canada: Migration and Settlement since 1840*, Edwin Mellon Press, Lewiston, 1991.

5   David C. Jones, "The Canadian Prairie Dryland Disaster and the Reshaping of 'Expert' Farm Wisdom," *Journal of Rural Studies*, vol. 1, no. 2, 1985, 136.

6   Angus MacKay, "Report of A. MacKay, Superintendent, Experimental Farm for the North-West Territories," Canadian House of Commons, *Sessional Papers*, 1890, no. 6c, 126, 133.

7   H.W. Campbell, *Campbell's 1907 Soil Culture Manual*, Campbell Soil Culture Company, Lincoln, 1907, 75. He had earlier condemned summer fallow in 1895: "Many tons more moisture can be retained in the subsoil by thorough cultivation of a growing crop than by summer fallowing." See also Mary Hargreaves, *Dry Farming in the Northern Great Plains, 1900–1925*, Harvard University Press, Cambridge, 1957, 87.

8   Leslie Hewes, "The Great Plains One Hundred Years after Major J.W. Powell," in.Brian W. Blouet and Merlin P. Lawson (eds.), *Images of the Plains*, University of Nebraska Press, Lincoln, 1975, 203–14; Mary Hargreaves, *Dry Farming in the Northern Great Plains: Years of Readjustment, 1920–1990*, University of Kansas Press, Lawrence, 1990, 48.

9   Anthony Ward, "The Origins of the Canadian Wheat Boom, 1880–1910," *Canadian Journal of Economics*, November 1994, 865–83.

10   Anthony Ward, "Extensive Development of the Canadian Prairies: A Micro Analysis of the Influence of Technical Change," doctoral dissertation, University of British Columbia, 127–8.

11   Ceclia Danysk, *Hired Hands, Land and the Development of Prairie Agriculture, 1880–1930*, : McClelland & Stewart, Toronto, 1995, 29.

12 John Herd Thompson, "Bringing in the Sheaves: The Harvest Excursionists, 1890–1929," *Canadian Historical Review*, vol. 59, no. 4, 1978, 467–89. See also the older literature, especially Edmund W. Bradwin, *The Bunkhouse Man, A Study of Work and Pay in the Camps of Canada*, University of Toronto Press, Toronto, 1972.

13 Thompson, "Bringing in the Sheaves," 478.

14 Ibid., 479.

15 Ernest Ingles, "The Custom Threshermen of Western Canada, 1890–1925," in David C. Jones and Ian MacPherson (eds.), *Building beyond the Homestead: Rural History on the Prairies*, University of Calgary Press, Calgary, 1985, 137.

16 W.J.C. Cherwinski, "The Incredible Harvest Excursion of 1908," *Labour/ Le Travailler*, vol. 5, Spring 1980, 60. See also his "In Search of Jake Trumper: The Farm Hand and the Prairie Farm Family," in Jones and MacPherson, *Building beyond the Homestead*, 111–33.

17 Cherwinski, "Incredible Harvest," 77.

18 Fred Stambrook and Stella Hryniuk point out that not *all* peasants had been without agricultural equipment in their homelands nor did all arrive penniless: "Who Were They Really? Reflections on East European Immigrants to Manitoba Before 1914," in Gregory P. Marchildon (ed.), *Immigration and Settlement, 1870–1939*, Canadian Plains Research Center, Regina, 2009, 462–4. Wayne Norton, *Help Us to a Better Land, Crofter Colonies in the Prairie West*, Canadian Plains Research Center, Regina, 1994.

19 Wayne Rasmussen, "The Impact of Technological Change on American Agriculture, 1862–1962," *Journal of Economic History* vol. 22, 1962, 578–83.

20 Jeremy Atack, "Farm and Farm-Making Costs Revisited," *AH*, vol. 56, no. 4, October 1982, 673; Lyle Dick, *Farmers "Making Good" – The Development of Abernethy District, Saskatchewan, 1880–1920*, University of Calgary Press, Calgary, 2008, and his "Estimates of Farm Making Costs in Saskatchewan, 1882–1914," *Prairie Forum*, vol. 6, no. 2, Fall 1981, 193.

21 R. Bruce Shephard, "Tractors and Combines in the Second Stage of Agricultural Mechanizations on the Canadian Plains," *Prairie Forum*, vol. 11, 1986, 253–71, and with T.D. Isern, "Adoption of the Combine on the Canadian Plains," *American Review of Canadian Studies* vol. 16, 1986, 455–64.

22 Clarence Danhof, "Farm-Making Costs and the 'Safety Valve': 1850–1860," *Journal of Political Economy*, vol. 49, 1941, 327.

23 Ibid., 354–5.

24 Atack, "Farm and Farm-Making Costs Revisited," 664; Robert Ankli, "Farm-Making Costs in the 1850s," *AH*, vol. 48, January 1974, 51–70; Robert Ankli and Robert Litt, "The Growth of Prairie Agriculture: Economic Considerations," *Canadian Papers in Rural History*, vol. 1, 1978, 35–64; and Judith L.V. Klein, "Farm-Marking Costs in the 1850s: A Comment," *AH*, vol. 48, January 1974, 71–4. See also Alan L. Olmstead, "The Mechanization of Reaping and Mowing in American Agriculture, 1833–1870," *Journal of Economic History*, vol. 35, no. 2, June 1975, 327–52; Gould P. Colmon, "Innovation and Diffusion in Agriculture," *AH*, vol. 42, no. 3, July 1968, 173–88; Alan G. Bogue, "Pioneer Farmers and Innovation," *Iowa Journal of History*, vol. 56, January 1958, 1–36; and Irwin Feller, "Inventive Activity in Agriculture, 1837–1890," *Journal of Economic History*, vol. 22, 1962, 560–77.

25 Atack, "Farm and Farm-Making Costs Revisited," 671.

26 Ibid., 676.

27 Dick, "Estimates of Farm Making Costs," 192.

28 Ibid., 197.

29 Ibid., 198.

30 Irene Spry, "The Cost of Making a Farm on the Prairies," *Prairie Forum*, vol. 7, no. 1, Spring 1982, 95–9; Lyle Dick, "A Reply to Professor Spry's Critique 'The Cost of Making a Farm on the Prairies,'" *Prairie Forum*, vol. 7, no. 1, Spring 1982, 101–2. A.J. Cotton was a farmer who took an alternate route of renting land and had great success; see Wendy Owen, "The Cost of Farm-Making in Early Manitoba: The Strategy of Almon James Cotton as a Case Study," *Manitoba History*, vol. 18, September 1989, 4–11.

31 John Herd Thompson, *The Harvests of War: The Prairie West, 1914–1918*, McClelland & Stewart, Toronto, 1978, 85–6.

32 Sara Brooks Sundberg, "Farm Women on the Canadian Prairie Frontier: The Helpmate Image," in Carol Fairbanks and Sara Brooks Sundberg (eds.), *Farm Women on the Prairie Frontier: A Sourcebook for Canada and the United States*, Scarecrow Press, Metuchen, 1983, 71–90. See also Sundberg's "A Female Frontier: Manitoba Farm Women in 1922," *Prairie Forum*, vol. 16, Fall 1991, 185–204.

33 Kathryn McPherson, "Was the 'Frontier' Good for Women? Historical Approaches to Women and Agricultural Settlement in the Prairie West, 1870–1925," *Atlantis*, vol. 25, no. 1, Fall/Winter 2000, 79.

34 Elaine Silverman, *The Last Best West – Women on the Alberta Frontier, 1880–1930*, 2nd ed., Fifth House, Calgary, 1998, 4.

35 Ibid., 6.

36 Aileen C. Moffatt, "Great Women, Separate Spheres, and Diversity: Comments on Saskatchewan Women's Historiography," in David De Brou and Aileen Moffatt (eds.), *"Other" Voices: Historical Essays on Saskatchewan Women*, Canadian Plains Research Centre, Regina, 1995, 10–26.

37 Anne Woywitha, "The Homesteader's Woman," *Alberta History*, vol. 24, no. 2, Spring 1976, 20–4.

38 Wayne Norton notes that some crofters settled near Saltcoats began with less than £50: *Help Us To A Better Land: Crofter Colonies in the Prairie West*, Canadian Plains Research Centre, Regina, 1994, 29. Majorie Harper, "Enigmas in Hebridean Emigration: Crofter Colonists in Western Canada," in Phillip Buckner and R.D. Francis (eds.), *Canada and the British World*, UBC Press, Vancouver, 2006, 198–214. Michael Ewanchuk noted five parties of Ukrainians in 1897–98 that came with $25 to $60 per person: *Spruce, Swamp, and Stone: A History of the Pioneer Ukrainian Settlements in the Gimli Area*, Derksen Printers, Steinbeck, 1977, 24.

39 Mary Kinnear, *Daughters of Time*, University of Michigan Press, Ann Arbor, 1982, 114.

40 Silverman, *The Last Best West*, 8.

41 A further development of the Victorian lady came in the rise of numerous women's organizations to promote missionary work and social reform. From the Lady Bountiful image sprang dozens of women's organizations not only to provide a wide range of services for the poor but also to lobby governments for action on an even wider range of issues. The most famous of these issues have been prohibition and women's suffrage. But women's missionary societies also began to stipulate that the missionaries they supported be women. The Canadian National Council of Women played a major role in launching the Victorian Order of Nurses (expanding opportunities for women in a newly established profession) as well as successfully pressing the federal government to introduce prison matrons for the oversight of women in federal prisons. This maternal feminism had its limits and blind spots, often arising from its origin in a narrowing view, particularly of what rural women could do on their farms.

42 Nanci Langford, "Childbirth on the Canadian Prairies, 1880–1930," in Catherine A. Cavanaugh and Randi R. Warne (eds.), *Telling Tales – Essays in Western Women's History*, UBC Press, Vancouver, 2000, 168. This needs to be weighed against Paul Voisey's evidence for bachelor farmers in the last phase of settlement in southern Alberta before the First World War, *Vulcan – The Making of a Prairie Community*, University of Toronto Press, Toronto, 1988, 93–4.

43 Mary Kinnear, *A Female Economy: Women's Work in a Prairie Province, 1870–1970*, McGill-Queen's University Press, Montreal & Kingston, 1998, 90.

44 See, for an example, Marjorie W. Campbell, *The Silent Song of Mary Eleanor: A Daughter's Tribute to a Reluctant Pioneer*, Western Producer Books, Saskatoon, 1983, 22–3.

45 John C. Lehr, "The Landscape of Ukrainian Settlement in the Canadian West," *Great Plains Quarterly*, vol. 2, 1982, 97–101, and his "Ukrainian Houses in Alberta," *Alberta History* 21, no. 4, Autumn 1973, 9–15. See also Radomir B. Bilash, "The Colonial Development of East Central Alberta and Its effect on Ukrainian Settlement to 1930," University of Manitoba master's thesis, 1983, 103.

46 Voisey, *Vulcan*, 93–4; compare to Kinnear, *Female Economy*, 88, on the higher rate of failure amongst bachelor homesteaders and Peter A. Russell, *Here We Are Laird Ourselves: Attitudes to Social Mobility in Upper Canada, 1815–1840*, Edwin Mellon Press, Lewiston, 1986, 105, on earlier expectations that a bachelor could not succeed in making a farm out of "the bush" on his own.

47 Jane Ursel, *Private Lives, Public Policy – 100 Years of State Intervention in the Family*, Women's Press, Toronto, 1992, 102.

48 Sandra Rollings-Magnussen, "Hidden Homesteaders: Women, the State and Patriarchy in the Saskatchewan Wheat Economy, 1870–1930," *Prairie Forum*, vol. 24, no. 2, Fall 1999, 113.

49 Ursel, *Private Lives*, 103–4.

50 Cavanaugh, *Telling Tales*, 210.

51 Ibid., 211.

52 Catherine Cavanaugh, "The Limitations of the Pioneering Partnership: The Alberta Campaign for Homestead Dower, 1909–1925," *CHR*, vol. 74, no. 2, June 1993, 224.

53 Margaret McCallum, "Prairie Women and the Struggle for a Dower Law, 1905–1920," *Prairie Forum*, vol. 18, no. 1, Spring 1983, 31.

54 Lesley Erickson, *Westward Bound: Sex, Violence, the Law, and the Making of a Settler Society*, UBC Press, Vancouver, 2011, 127–37.

55 Royden Loewen, *Family, Church, and Market: A Mennonite Community in the Old World and the New, 1850–1930*, University of Illinois Press, Urbana, 1993, and Kenneth Sylvester, *Limits of Rural Capitalism: Family, Culture, and Markets in Montcalm, Manitoba, 1870–1940*, University of Toronto Press, Toronto, 2001.

56 R.W. Murchie and H.C. Grant, *Unused Lands of Manitoba*, Manitoba Department of Agriculture and Immigration, Winnipeg, 1926, 14–15, 38,

123, 126, 153. James B. Hedges, *Building the Canadian West*, Macmillan Company, New York, 1939, 295. C.M. MacInnes, *In the Shadow of the Rockies*, Rivingtons, London, 1930, 259–61. A.S. Morton, *History of Prairie Settlement*, Macmillan Company of Canada, Toronto, 1938, 113–14.

57 Donald M. Loveridge, "'The Garden of Manitoba': The Settlement and Agricultural Development of the Rock Lake District and the Municipality of Louise, 1878–1902," University of Toronto doctoral dissertation, 1978, 567–9.

58 Wilfrid Eggleston tells of the "lucky" homesteader who grazed his livestock on Hudson Bay land for the thirteen years he was on his farm since the Company never sold it: "The Old Homestead: Romance and Reality" in Howard Palmer (ed.), *The Settlement of the West*, University of Calgary Press, Calgary, 1977, 124–5.

59 Peter Douglas Elias, *The Dakota of the Canadian Northwest: Lessons for Survival*, University of Manitoba Press, Winnipeg, 1988, 167–9.

60 James M. Minifie, *Homesteader – A Prairie Boyhood Recalled*, Macmillan of Canada, Toronto, 1972, 205–6.

61 Lewis G. Thomas, "The Ranching Tradition and the Life of the Ranchers," University of Alberta master's thesis, 1935, and Patrick A. Dunae (ed.), *Ranchers' Legacy: Alberta Essays by Lewis G. Thomas*, University of Alberta Press, Edmonton, 1986. Sheilagh S. Jameson, "The Ranching Industry of Western Canada: Its Initial Epoch, 1873–1910," *Prairie Forum*, vol. 11, no. 2, Fall 1986, 229–42. David H. Breen, *The Canadian Prairie West and the Ranching Frontier, 1874–1924*, University of Toronto Press, Toronto, 1983.

62 Breen, *Canadian Prairie West*, 11.

63 Ibid., 77.

64 Ibid., 63, 65.

65 Simon Evans, "Stocking the Canadian Range," *Alberta History*, vol. 26, no. 3, Summer 1978, 4.

66 Breen, *Canadian Prairie West*, 55.

67 Ibid., 43–54. Gloria J. Toole, "Rich Man, Poor Man: Competition for Access to Land in Southwestern Alberta, 1875–1907," *Alberta History*, vol. 56, no. 4, Fall 2008, 2–7.

68 Ibid., 66–9.

69 Max Foran, "Mixed Blessings: The Second 'Golden Age' of the Alberta Cattle Industry, 1914–1920," *Alberta History*, vol. 46, no. 3, Summer 1995, 17–18, and "Hands and Fists across the Border: Canadian and American Cattlemen in the Twentieth Century," *Alberta History*, vol. 56, no. 2, Spring 2008, 2–8.

70 This continues to be a point of dispute, at least over matters of degree in both the labour force and "social ambiance." See, for examples, W.M. Lopfson, "The Myth of Ranching in Southern Alberta," Canadian Historical Association Annual Meeting, 1995, and his "Adapting to the Frontier Environment: The Ranching Industry in Western Canada, 1881–1914," *CPRH*, vol. 8, 1992, 307–27, as well as Simon Evans et al. (eds.), *Cowboys, Ranchers and the Cattle Business – Cross-Border Perspectives on Ranching History*, University of Calgary Press, Calgary, 2000.

71 Warren M. Lopfson, *Cowboys, Gentlemen and Cattle Thieves: Ranching on the Western Frontier*, McGill-Queen's University Press, Montreal & Kingston, 2000, and *Frontier Cattle Ranching in the Land and Times of Charlie Russell*, McGill-Queen's University Press, Montreal & Kingston, 2004.

72 Simon Evans, "Stocking," 1–8; "American Cattlemen on the Canadian Range, 1874–1914," *Prairie Forum*, vol. 4, no. 1, Spring 1979, 121–36; "The End of the Open Range Era in Western Canada," *Prairie Forum*, vol. 8, no. 1, Spring 1983, 71–88; and "The Origin of Ranching in Western Canada – American Diffusion or Victorian Transplant?," in L.A. Rosenwall and S.M. Evans, *Essays on the Historical Geography of the Canadian West*, University of Calgary Press, Calgary, 1987, 70–94. This is not to suggest that Evans has neglected the "British presence" as he devoted a book to the late Prince of Wales: *Prince Charming Goes West – The Story of the E.P. Ranch*, University of Calgary Press, Calgary, 1993.

73 Lopfson insists the American presence was in some ways greater than Jameson or Breen allow. See his "The Myth of Ranching." Simon Evans has argued a similar point, drawing on 1891 and 1901 census data in his "Observations on the Labour Force of the Canadian Ranching Frontier during its Golden Age, 1882–1901," *Great Plains Quarterly*, vol. 15, no. 1, Winter 1995, 3–18.

74 Evans, "American Cattlemen," 131. See also Henry C. Klassen, "The Conrads in the Alberta Cattle Business, 1875–1911," *AH*, vol. 64, no. 3, 1990, 31–59.

75 A.B. McCullough, "The Winnipeg Ranchers: Gordon, Ironside and Fares," *Manitoba History*, issue 41, Spring/Summer 2001, 18–26.

76 Warren Lopfson, "Other People's Money: Patrick Burns and the Beef Plutocracy, 1890–1914," *Prairie Forum*, vol. 32, no. 2, Fall 2007, 235–50.

77 D.M. Loveridge and Barry Potyandi, *From Wood Mountain to the White Mud: A Historical Survey of the Grasslands National Park Area*, National Historic Parks and Sites Branch, History and Archaeology #67, Parks

Canada, Ottawa, 1983, 148, 180–1. See also C.M. Williams, "Always the Bridesmaid: The Development of the Saskatchewan Beef Production System," *Saskatchewan History*, vol. 42, no. 3, Autumn 1989, 106–18.

78 A.B. McCullough, "Eastern Capital, Government Purchases, and the Development of Canadian Ranching," *Prairie Forum*, vol. 22, no. 2, Fall 1997, 215.

79 Breen, *Canadian Prairie West*, 163.

80 Ibid., 131.

81 Ibid., 62–5.

82 Loveridge and Potyondi, *Wood Mountain to the White Mud*, 129.

83 Breen, *Canadian Prairie West*, 41–2.

84 Peter Hawks, "Sheep and Sheep Men in Alberta," *Alberta History*, vol. 36, no. 2, Spring 1988, 22.

85 Peter A. Russell, "Subsistence, Diversification, and Staple Orientations on Saskatchewan Farms: Parklands vs. Prairie, 1911–1926," *Saskatchewan History*, vol. 57, no. 2, Fall 2005, 22.

86 "Heart" is one of several terms used for the short-grass prairie – "dry belt," "inner," "core" are also used. See Gregory P. Marchildon, Jeremy Pittman, and David J. Sauchyn, "The Dry Belt and Changing Aridity in the Palliser Triangle, 1895–2000," *Prairie Forum*, vol. 34, no. 1, Spring 2009, 31–44.

87 Marchildon, Pittman, and Sauchyn, "Dry Belt," 32–40, show how aridity changed over the longer term on the Prairies, changing the size and shape of the dry belt. *Encyclopedia of Saskatchewan*, Canadian Plains Research Center, Regina, 2005, 678, gives three different outlines for Palliser's Triangle. See also R.L. Gentilcore (ed.), *Historical Atlas of Canada*, vol. 2, University of Toronto Press, Toronto, 1993, Plate 3, and D.G.G. Kerr, *Historical Atlas of Canada*, 3rd ed., Thomas Nelson, Don Mills, 1975, 41.

88 Isaiah 35:1, King James Version.

89 Wallace Stegner, *Wolf Willow, A History, A Story, and A Memory of the Last Plains Frontier*, Viking Press, New York, 1955, 254–9.

90 John Hubbard, "Possibilities of Beekeeping in Saskatchewan," Saskatchewan Department of Agriculture, Regina, 1922, 2. His own farm was near Grenfell in the Qu'Appelle River Valley.

91 Clinton N. Westman, "Homesteading in Northern Alberta During the Great Depression: A Life History Approach," *Prairie Forum*, vol. 32, 1, Spring 2007, 178–81, contrasted the abundance of subsistence in the Peace River country compared to the short-grass prairie in the 1930s.

92 David C. Jones, *Empire of Dust: Settling and Abandoning the Prairie Dry Belt*, University of Alberta Press, Edmonton, 1987. See also his *"We'll all*

be buried down here": The Prairie Dryland Disaster, 1917–1926, Alberta Records Publication Board, Historical Society of Alberta, Calgary, 1986.

93 Voisey, *Vulcan*, 99.

94 Barry Potyondi, *In Palliser's Triangle, Living in the Grasslands, 1850–1980*, Purich Publishing, Saskatoon, 1995, 84.

95 David C. Jones, "Canadian Prairie Dryland Disaster," 136.

96 MacKay, *1890*, 133.

97 Angus MacKay, "Report of the Superintendent of the Indian Head Experimental Farm," Canadian House of Commons, *Sessional Papers*, 1896, no. 6, 369; *Sessional Papers*, 1897, no. 6, 976; *Sessional Papers*, 1908, 37. Voisey, *Vulcan*, 104–5, cites very late direct connections between Campbell and Saskatchewan's Minister of Agriculture W.R. Motherwell during the First World War and the Alberta Department of Agriculture in 1919.

98 Campbell, *Soil Culture*, 75.

99 Gregory P. Marchildon, "Institutional Adaptation to Drought and the Special Areas of Alberta, 1909–1939," *Prairie Forum*, vol. 32, no. 2, Fall 2007, 258–9. It was part of the government's program to assist farm families to leave the area, although loans were provided to larger farms that seemed more viable (while for others, reductions and write-offs of land mortgages were arranged)..

100 Saskatchewan Department of Agriculture Annual Report – 1920, as cited in Barry Potyondi, *In Palliser's Triangle*, 99.

101 Carl Anderson, "'Dominion Lands' Policy, Drought and Saskatchewan's 'Better Farming' Commission, 1920," *Saskatchewan History*, vol. 61, no. 1, Spring 2009, 4–21.

102 Saskatchewan Royal Commission on Immigration and Settlement – 1930, as cited in Potyondi, *In Palliser's Triangle*, 111.

103 Ibid.

104 James H. Gray, *Men against the Desert*, Western Producer, Saskatoon, 1978, i.

105 Ibid., vii.

106 Ibid., 12.

107 Leslie Hewes, *The Suitcase Farming Frontier, A Study in the Historical Geography of the Central Great Plains*, University of Nebraska Press, Lincoln, 1973.

108 Dick, *Farmers*, 93.

109 Spry, "Cost," 95–9.

110 Voisey, *Vulcan*, 91.

111 From the title of an English immigrant's daughter's family memoire, Edna Tyson Parson, *Land I Can Own*, Westboro Printers, Ottawa, 1981.

112 Voisey, *Vulcan*, 38.

113 *Canada Year Book*, 1934, 299.

114 W.A. Waiser, "A Bear Garden: James Melville Macoun and the 1904 Peace River Controversy," CHR, vol. 67, no. 1, 1986, 42–61.

115 Westman, "Homesteading," 171.

116 Not all frontiers can be forced: the attempt to extend ranching further north, whether based on buffalo or muskoxen, failed. John Sandlos, *Hunters at the Margin: Native People and Wildlife Conservation in the Northwest Territories*, UBC Press, Vancouver, 2007.

CONCLUSION

1 Robert Painchaud, "French-Canadian Historiography and Franco-Catholic Settlement in Western Canada, 1870–1915," *Canadian Historical Review*, vol. 59, no. 4, December 1978, 450. This was true at least in the 1870s.

2 C.A. Dawson assisted by R.W. Murchie, *Settlement of the Peace River Country: A Study of a Pioneer Area*, Macmillan, Toronto, 1934, 111. See also Clinton N. Westman, "Homesteading in Northern Alberta during the Great Depression: A Life History Approach," *Prairie Forum*, vol. 32, no. 1, Spring 2007, 167–90.

3 On the Soldier Settlement Board, see Desmond Morton and Glenn Wright, *Winning the Second Battle: Canadian Veterans and the Return to Civil Life*, University of Toronto Press, Toronto, 1987, 146–51. The Board had facilitated land acquisition for 25,433 veterans by 1921, but only 5,662 settled on a 320-acre free grant, assisted by an average loan of $4,035. The remoteness and forest cover of the Peace River country and Saskatchewan's Porcupine Forest Reserve discouraged prospective settlers. In the case of the latter, those conditions defeated 40 per cent of those who tried to settle. See Herbert R. Harris, *Porcupine Soldier Settlement and Adjacent Areas*, Shand Agricultural Society, Porcupine Plain, 1967. Peter Neary and J.L. Granatstein (eds.), *The Veterans Charter and Post-World War II Canada*, McGill-Queen's University Press, Montreal & Kingston, 1998, 66, 74–5. The Veterans Land Act put 50,000 returned soldiers on the land with loans of $6,000, and as well, provided training (even for troops who had yet to leave Europe) for those who wanted to begin farming. It had greater success than the agricultural settlement provided by the United States: Suzanne Mettler, *Soldiers to Citizens: The G.I. Bill and the Making of the Greatest Generation*, Oxford University Press, New York, 2005. Even the offer of 360 acres on a ten-year lease with a cash advance for equipment could not attract more than a few

hundred veterans to the Peace River area in the years after the war. See Donald G. Wetherell and Irene R.A. Kmet, *Alberta's North, A History, 1890–1950*, University of Alberta Press, Edmonton, 2000, 250–2.

4 J.I. Little, "Contested Land: Squatters and Agents in the Eastern Townships of Lower Canada," CHR, vol. 83, no. 3, September 1999, 397, 406–9; John Clarke, *The Ordinary People of Essex – Environment, Culture and Economy on the Frontier of Upper Canada*, McGill-Queen's University Press, Montreal & Kingston, 2010, 369, 372. Peter A. Russell, *"Here We Are Laird Ourselves": Attitudes to Social Structure and Social Mobility in Upper Canada, 1815–1840*, Edwin Mellen, Lewiston, 1990, 20; John L. Tyman, *By Section, Township and Range: Studies in Prairie Settlement*, Assiniboine Historical Society, Brandon, 1972, 79–82.

5 W.A. Langton (ed.), *Early Days in Upper Canada: Letters of John Langton*, Macmillan Company of Canada, Toronto, 1926, 52–4 – John Langton's confidence that land speculation was risk free was reprinted in both P.B. Waite (ed.), *Canadian Historical Document Series*, vol. 2, *Preconfederation*, Prentice-Hall of Canada, Scarborough, 1965, 100–1, and V.R. Robeson (ed.), *Upper Canada in the 1830s*, Ontario Institute for Studies in Education, Curriculum Series 22, Toronto, 1977, 25–6. See also John Clarke, "The Role of Political Position and Family and Economic Linkage in Land Speculation in the Western District of Upper Canada, 1788–1815," *Canadian Geographer*, vol. 19, no. 1, 1975, 18–34.

6 Kris Inwood and associates found both an increased number of women owning property in their own names and a pattern of inheritance that gave more to widows and more equal treatment to daughters. Kris Inwood and Sara Van Sligtenhorst, "The Social Consequence of Legal Reform: Women and Property in a Canadian Community," *Continuity and Change*, vol. 19, no. 1, 2004, and Susan Ingham and Kris Inwood, "Property Ownership by Married Women in Victorian Ontario," *Dalhousie Law Journal*, 2000.

7 As examples: Thomas Wien, "Visites paroissiales et production agricole au Canada vers la fin du XVIIIe siècle," 183; Christian Dessureault, "La propriété rurale et la paysannerie dans la plaine maskoutaine, 1795–1814," 39; and Mario Lalancette, "Essai sur la Répartition de la propriété foncière a la Malbaie au pays de Charlevoix," 75, all in F. Lebrun and N. Séquin (eds.), *Sociétés villageoises et rapports villes-campagnes*, Presses Universitaires de Rennes, Rennes, 1985, citing Ouellet's 1972 article against the common belief in inevitable fragmentation of land holdings.

Other Sources Used

QUEBEC

Bédard, Éric. "Genèse des nations et cultures du *Nouveau Monde*: le *magnum opus* de l'historiographie moderniste." *Bulletin d'histoire politique* 9, no. 2 (2001): 160–74.

Bouchard, Gérard. "Les categories socio-professionelles: une nouveau grille de classment." *Labour/Le Travail* 15 (1985): 145–63.

– "L'histoire sociale au Québec. Réflexion sur quelques paradoxes." *Revue historique d'Amérique Français* 51, no. 2 (summer 1997): 243–69.

– *Genèse des Nations et Cultures du Nouveau Monde*, Montreal: Boreal Express, 2001.

– with Alain Roy. *La culture québécoise est-elle en crise?* Montreal: Boreal Express, 2007.

– with Bernard Andrés (ed.). *Mythes et Sociétés des Amériques*. Montreal: Quebec Amérique, 2007.

Breton, Raymond and Pierre Savard (eds.). *Quebec and the Acadian Diaspora in North America*, Toronto: Multicultural History Society of Ontario, 1982.

Chodos, Robert and Eric Hamovitch. *Quebec and the American Dream.* Toronto: Between the Lines, 1991.

Courville, Serge. "La crise agricole du Bas-Canada: éléments d'une réflexion géographique." *Cahiers de géographie du Québec* 24 (1980): 193–224.

– "Villages and Agriculture in the Seigneuries of Lower Canada; Conditions of a Comprehensive Study of Rural Quebec in the First Half of the Nineteenth Century." *Canadian Papers in Rural History* 5 (1986): 121–49.

– "A Mari Usque Ad Mare – La Grande Saga Canadienne." *RHAF* 42, no. 3 (winter 1989): 429–39.

– *Entre Ville et Campagne – L'essor du village dans les seigneuries du Bas-Canada.* Quebec: University of Laval Press, 1990.

– *Immigration, Colonisation et Propaganda – Du rêve américain au rêve colonial.* Quebec: Editions Multi Mondes, 2002.
– *Quebec: A Historical Geography.* Vancouver: UBC Press, 2008.
– with Jean-Claude Robert, and Normand Séguin. "Population et espace rural au Bas-Canada: L'exemple de l'axe laurentien dans la première moitié du XIXe siècle." *RHAF* 44, no. 2 (autumn 1990): 243–62.
– with Normand Séguin. *Rural Life in Nineteenth-Century Quebec,* Canadian Historical Association Historical Booklet, no. 47, Ottawa, 1989.
– with Norman Séguin (eds.). *Espace et Culture/Space and Culture.* Sainte-Foi: University of Laval Press, 1995.
Craig, Béatrice. "Pour une approche comparative de l'étude des sociétés rurales nord-américains." *Histoire sociale/Social History* 23 (November 1990): 249–70.
– "Débat: à propos de deux manuels récents d'histoire du Canada." *RHAF* 51, no. 4 (spring 1998): 549–77.
Dechêne, Louise. "Coup d'oeil sur l'historiographie de la Nouvelle-France." *Études canadiennes/Canadian Studies* 3 (1977): 45–58.
– "La transmission du patrimoine dans les terroirs en expansion: un exemple canadien au XVIIIe siècle." *RHAF* 44, no. 2 (autumn 1990): 171–98.
– (ed.), *Vingt ans après Habitants et marchands. Lectures de l'histoire des XVIIe et XVIIIe siècles canadiens.* McGill-Queen's University Press, Montreal & Kingston, 1998.
Depatie, Sylvie. "La transmission du patrimoine au Canada (xvii-xviiie siècle): qui sont les défavorisés?" *RHAF* 54, no. 4 (spring 2001): 557–70.
Desbarats, Catherine. "Agriculture within the Seigneurial Regime of the 18th century: Some thoughts on the recent literature." *Canadian Historical Review* 73, no. 1 (March 1992): 1–29.
Dessureault, Christian, with Thomas Wien and Gérard Bouchard. "Débat à propos de Quelques arpents d'Amérique de Gérard Bouchard." *RHAF* 50, no. 3 (winter 1997): 401–35.
Dever, Alan R. "Economic Development and the Lower Canadian Assembly, 1828–1840." Master's thesis, University of McGill, Montreal, 1976.
Dickinson, John A. with Christian Dessureault and Thomas Wien. "Living Standards of Norman and Canadian Peasants, 1690–1835." In A. Schuurman and L.S. Walsh (eds.), *Material Culture: Consumption, Lifestyle, Standard of Living (16th–19th centuries).* Milan: Università Bocconi, 1994, 95–114.
Dubuc, Alfred. "L'influence de l'école des Annales au Québec." *RHAF* 33, no. 3 (1979): 357–86.

Dumont, Fernand (ed.). *La société Québécoise après 30 ans de changements.* Quebec: Institut Québécois de recherché sur la culture, 1990.

Hardy, Jean-Pierre, Gilles Paquet, David-Thiery Ruddel, and J.-P. Wallot. "Culture matérielle et société au Québec, 1792–1835." *Material History Bulletin/ Bulletin d'histoire de la culture matérielle,* no. 17, National Museums of Canada, Ottawa, (1983): 25–44.

Hill, Robert Andrew. "Robert Sellar and the *Huntingdon Gleaner*: The Conscience of Rural Protestant Quebec, 1863–1919." Doctoral dissertation, University of McGill, Montreal, 1970.

Kerr, Linda. "Quebec: The Making of an Imperial Mercantile Community, 1760–1768." Doctoral dissertation, University of Alberta, Edmonton, 1992.

Kesteman, J.R., Peter Southam, and Diane Saint-Pierre. *Histoire des Cantons de l'Est,* Institut québécois de recherché sur la culture, Quebec: University of Laval Press, 1998.

Landry, Yves et al. (eds.). *Les chemins de la migration en Beligique et au Québec, XVII-XX siècles,* Louvain-la-Neuve: Editions Académia, 1995.

LaRose, André. "Seigneurie de Beauharnois, 1729–1867." Doctoral dissertation, University of Ottawa, Ottawa, 1987.

Lauder, Dean R. and Eric Waddell (eds.). *French America, Mobility, Identity and Minority Experience across the Continent.* Baton Rouge: LSU Press, 1993.

Lavallée, Louis. *La Prairie en Nouvelle-France, 1647–1760.* Montreal & Kingston: McGill-Queen's University Press: 1992.

Linteau, Paul-André. "De l'équilibre et de la nuance dans l'interprétation de l'histoire du Québec." *Bulletin d'histoire politique* 4, no. 2 (1995): 13–19.

Little, J.I. "The Social and Economic Development of Settlers in two Quebec Townships, 1851–1870." *CPRH* 1 (1978): 89–113.

– "Colonization and Municipal Reform in Canada East." *HS/HS* 14, no. 27 (May 1981): 93–121.

– "Agricultural Progress in Canada East/Quebec: Problems in Measuring Relative Productivity during the Grain-Dairy Transition Period." *HS/SH* 18, no. 36 (November 1985): 425–31.

– Nationalism, Capitalism, and Colonization in 19th Century Quebec: The Upper St Francis District, Montreal & Kingston: McGill-Queen's University Press, 1989.

– "Ethnicity, Family Structure, and Seasonal Labour Strategies on Quebec's Appalachian Frontier." *Journal of Family History* 17, no. 3 (1992): 289–302.

– "Response to Guy Boisclair's Review of *Nationalism, Capitalism and Colonization*." *Journal of Eastern Township Studies,* no. 4 (spring 1994): 75–86.

- "Contested Land: Squatters and Agents in the Eastern Townships of Lower Canada." CHR 80, no. 3 (September 1999): 381–412.
- "'In the desert places of the wilderness': The Frontier Thesis and the Anglican Church in the Eastern Townships, 1799–1841." HS/SH 36, no. 71 (May 2003): 31–54.

Migner, Robert. "Á propos de la crise agricole dans le Bas-Canada." RHAF 27, no. 1 (June 1973): 79–83.

Miquelon, Dale (ed.). *The Debate on the Bourgeoisie and Social Change in French Canada, 1700–1850*. Toronto: Copp Clark, 1977.

Morisset, Michel. *L'Agriculture Familiale au Québec*. Paris: Editions L'Harmatten, 1987.

Noël, Francoise. "Seigneurial Survey and Land Granting Policies." CPRH 5 (1986): 150–80.
- *The Christie Seigneuries: Estate Management and Settlement in the Upper Richelieu Valley, 1760–1854*. Montreal & Kingston: McGill-Queen's University Press, 1992.

Ouellet, Fernand. "La mentalité et l'outillage économique de l'habitant canadien (1760) – Á propos d'un document sur l'encan." *Bulletin des recherché historiques* 62 (1956): 131–9.
- *Élément d'histoire sociale du Bas-Canada*. Montreal: Cahiers du Québec, Hurtubise HMH, 1972.
- "La sauvegarde des patrimoines dans le District de Québec Durant la premier moitié du XIXe siècle." RHAF 26, no. 3 (December 1972): 319–74.
- "Le mythe de l'Habitant sensible au marché." *Recherches sociographiques* 17 (1976): 115–32.
- *Lower Canada, 1791–1840: Social Change and Nationalism*. Toronto: McClelland and Stewart, 1980.
- *Economic and Social History of Quebec, 1760–1850*. Toronto: Gage Publishing, 1980.
- "D.G. Creighton et les Racines de la Nation." *Canadian Forum* (September 1980): 11–12.
- "Les prix agricoles dans les villes et les campagnes du Québec d'avant 1850: aperçus quantatifs." HS/SH 14 (May 1982): 83–127.
- "Économie colonial et économie international: le commerce de la vallée du Saint-Laurent avec l'Espagne, le Portugal, et leurs possessions atlantique (1760–1850)." *Transactions of the Royal Society of Canada* 22 (1984): 167–204.
- "Les classes dominantes au Québec, 1760–1840: Bilan historiographique." RHAF 38, no. 2 (autumn 1984): 223–43.

- "La modernization de l'historiographie et l'émergence de l'histoire sociale." *Recherches sociographiques* 26, nos. 1–2 (1985): 11–83.
- *The Socialization of Quebec Historiography Since 1960.* Toronto: Robarts Centre for Canadian Studies, 1988.
- *Economy, Class, and Nation in Quebec: Interpretive Essays.* Toronto: Copp Clark Pitman, 1991.
- "Review Essay: Language, Schooling, and Cultural Conflict." *Ontario History*, vol. 82, no. 1, March 1989, 59–68.
- *L'Ontario français dans le Canada français avant 1911.* Sudbury: Prise de Parole, 2005.
- with Jean Hamelin, "La crise agricole dans le Bas-Canada, 1802–1837." *Rapport annuel de la Société Historique du Canada* (1962): 17–33.
- with Jean Hamelin, "La crise agricole dans le Bas-Canada, 1802–1837." *Études rurales*, no.7 (October-December 1962): 36–57.
- with Jean Hamelin, "Le mouvement des prix agricoles dans la province de Québec, 1760–1851." In Claude Galarneau and Elzéar Lavoie (eds.), *France et Canada Français du XVI au XXe siècles.* Quebec: Laval University Press, 1963, 35–48.
Paquet, Gilles. "L'Émigration des canadiens français vers la Nouvelle-Angleterre, 1870–1910: Prises du vue quantitative." *Recherches sociographiques* 5, no. 3 (September-December 1964): 319–70.
- "Some Views on the Pattern of Canadian Economic Development." In T.N. Brewis (ed.), *Growth and the Canadian Economy.* Toronto: McClelland and Stewart, 1968, 34–64.
- "Économie et Histoire: Les liaisons dangereuses d'Hermes et de Clio." RHAF 46, no. 4 (spring 1993): 629–43.
- with Wayne R. Smith. "L'Émigration des canadiens français vers les États-Unis, 1790–1940: Problématique et coups de sonde." *L'Actualité économique* 59, no. 3 (September 1983): 423–53.
- with J. P. Wallot. "Le Bas-Canada au début du XIXe siècle: une hypothèse." RHAF, 25, no. 1 (June 1971): 30–61.
- "Crise agricole et tensions socio-ethniques dans le Bas-Canada, 1802–1812: éléments pour une réinterpretation." RHAF 26, no. 2 (September 1972): 185–237.
- "Une critique en porte-à-faux." RHAF 27, no. 1 (June 1973): 84–6.
- "Groupes sociaux et pouvoir: le cas canadien au tournant du XIXe siècle." RHAF 27, no. 4 (March 1974): 509–64.
- "Pour une méso-histoire du XIXe siècle canadien." RHAF 33, no. 3 (December 1979): 387–425.

- "Sur quelques discontinuities dans l'expérience socio-économique du Québec: une hypothèse." *RHAF* 35, no. 4 (March 1982): 483–521.
- "Le système financier bas-canadien au tournant du xixe siècle." *L'Actualité économique* 59, no. 3 (September 1983): 456–513.
- "Nouvelle-France/Quebec/Canada: A World of Limited Identities." In N. Canny and A. Padgen (eds.), *Colonial Identity in the Atlantic World.* Princeton: Princeton University Press, 1987, 95–114.
- *Lower Canada at the Turn of the Nineteenth Century: Restructuring and Modernization.* Canadian Historical Association Booklet no. 45, Ottawa, 1988.

Christian, Raymond Roy and Gérard Bouchard. "La mobilité géographique en milieu rural: le Saguenay, 1852–1861." *HS/SH* 14, no. 27 (May 1981): 123–50.

Roy, Louis and Michel Verdon. "East-Farnham's Agriculture in 1871: Ethnicity, Circumstances, and Economic Rationale in Quebec's Eastern Townships." *CHR* 84, no. 3 (September 2002): 374–95.

St-Georges, Lise. "Le village de l'Assomption, 1748–1791." Master's thesis, University of Quebec at Montreal, Montreal, 1984.

- "Commerce, crédit et transactions foncières: practiques de la communauté marchand du bourg de l'Assomption, 1748–1791." *RHAF* 39, no. 3 (winter 1986): 323–43.

Séguin, Maurice. "La Conquête et la vie économique des Canadiens." In Robert Comeau (ed.), *Les Cahiers de l'université du Québec.* Sillery: University of Laval Press, 1969, 345–61.

Séguin, Normand (ed.). *La Conquête du sol au 19e siècle.* Sillery: Boreal Express, 1977.

- *Agriculture et colonization au Québec.* Montreal: Boréal Express, 1980.
- "L'agriculture de la Mauricie et du Québec, 1850–1950." *RHAF* 35, no. 4 (March 1982): 537–62.
- "Paysans et monde forestier: nouvelles reflexions sur le monde rurale québécois au xixe siècle." *Cahiers des annals de Normandie* 24 (1992): 177–87.

Silver, Arthur I. "French Canada and the Prairie Frontier, 1870–1890." *CHR* 50, no. 1 (March 1969), 11–36.

- "Some Quebec Attitudes in an Age of Imperialism and Ideological Conflict." *CHR* 57, no. 4 (December 1976), 440–60.
- *The French-Canadian Idea of Confederation, 1864–1900.* Toronto: University of Toronto Press, 1982.

Tousignant, Pierre. "Le Bas-Canada: Une étape importante dans l'oeuvre de Fernard Ouellet." *RHAF* 34, no. 3 (December 1980): 415–31.

Wade, Mason (ed.). *Canadian Dualism, Studies in French-English Relations.* Toronto: University of Toronto Press, 1960.

Wallot, Jean-Pierre. *Un Québec qui Bougeait*, Montreal: Boreal Express, 1972.

– "Le Bas-Canada: Une histoire mouvante – Du conservatism atavique à rationalité limitée." *Cheminements Conferences*, Centre de recherche en civilization canadienne-française, CIEQ, University of Ottawa, 2000, 5–18.

– et al. (eds.). *Constructions Identitaires et Practiques socials*. Ottawa: University of Ottawa Press, 2002.

Wien, William Thomas. "Peasant Accumulation in a Context of Colonization – Riviére-du-Sud, Canada, 1720–1775." Doctoral dissertation, McGill University, Montreal, 1988.

– "'Les travaux pressants': Calendrier agricole et régime d'assolement au Canada au XVIIIe siècle." *RHAF* 43, no. 4 (1990): 535–58.

Willis, John. "Urbanization, Colonization and Underdevelopment in the Bas-Saint-Laurent: Fraserville and the Témiscouata in the late nineteenth century." *Cahiers de Géographie du Québec* 28, nos. 73–74 (April-September 1984): 125–61.

– "On and Off the Island of Montreal, 1815–1867: The Transport Background of Town-Country Relations in the *plat pays* of Montreal." In Serge Courville and Normand Séguin (eds.), *Espace et culture/Space and Culture*. Quebec: University of Laval Press, 1994, 343–54.

Young, Kathryn A. *Kin, Commerce, Community: Merchants in the Port of Quebec, 1717–1745*. New York: Peter Lang, 1995.

ONTARIO

Baskerville, Peter A. *Ontario: Image, Identity, Power*. Toronto: Oxford University Press, 2002.

– "Chattel Mortgages and Community in Perth County, Ontario." *CHR* 87, no. 4 (December 2006): 583–619.

Cameron, Wendy, Sheila Haines, and Mary McDougall Maude (eds.). *English Immigrant Voices – Labourers' Letters from Upper Canada in 1830s*. Montreal & Kingston: McGill-Queen's University Press, 2000.

Darroch, Gordon. "Scanty Fortunes and Rural Middle-Class Formation in 19th century Rural Ontario." *CHR* 79, no. 4 (December 1998): 621–59.

Dewar Boyce, Betsy. *The Rebels of Hastings*. Toronto: University of Toronto Press, 1992.

Di Matteo, Livio and George, Peter. "Canadian Wealth Inequality in the Late Nineteenth Century: A Study of Wentworth County, Ontario, 1872–1902." *CHR* 73 (1992): 453–83.

Gaffield, Chad. *Language, Schooling, and Cultural Conflict – The Origins of the French-Language Controversy in Ontario.* Montreal & Kingston: McGill-Queen's University Press, 1987.

– "Children, Schooling, and Family Reproduction in Nineteenth-Century Ontario." CHR 72, no. 2 (1991): 157–91.

Gee, Ellen M. Thomas. "Marriage in 19th Century Canada." *Canadian Review of Sociology and Anthropology* 19, no. 3 (1982): 311–25.

Glazebrook, G.P. deT. *Life in Ontario, A Social History.* Toronto: University of Toronto Press, 1968.

Hall, Roger et al., (eds.) *Patterns of the Past, Interpreting Ontario's History.* Toronto: Dundurn Press, 1988.

Hall, Roger. "The Impact of the Canada Company upon Upper Canada, 1826–1843: The Circumstances of the Commission of Inquiry of 1840." Paper presented to the Canadian Historical Association, 1975.

Innis, Harold A. *The Fur Trade in Canada: An Introduction to Canadian Economic History.* New Haven: Yale University Press, 1930.

– *Problems of Staple Production in Canada.* Toronto: Ryerson Press, 1933.

– (ed.). *The Dairy Industry in Canada.* Toronto: Ryerson Press, 1937.

– (ed.). *Labour in Canadian-American Relations.* Toronto: Ryerson Press, 1937.

– with A.F.W. Plumptre (eds.). *The Canadian Economy and Its Problems.* Toronto: Canadian Institute of International Affairs, 1934.

– (ed.). *Essays in Canadian Economic History.* Toronto: University of Toronto Press, 1956.

Innis, Mary Q. *An Economic History of Canada.* Toronto: Ryerson Press, 1935.

Kelly, Kenneth. "The Transfer of British Ideas on Agriculture to Nineteenth-Century Ontario." In Brian S. Osborne (ed.), *The Settlement of Canada: Origins and Transfer.* Kingston: Queen's University Press, 1976, 70–91.

Langman, R.C. *Patterns of Settlement in Southern Ontario.* Toronto: McClelland and Stewart, 1971.

McCalla, Douglas and Peter George. "Measurement, Myth, and Reality: Reflections on the Economic History of Nineteenth-Century Ontario," *Journal of Canadian Studies* 21, no. 3 (1986): 71–86.

McDonald, Terry. "'Come to Canada While You Have a Chance': A Cautionary Tale of English Emigrant Letters in Upper Canada." *Ontario History* 91, no. 2 (autumn 1999): 111–30.

McInnis, Marvin. "Comment on Paper by Gagan." *Journal of Economic History* 36, no. 1 (1976): 142–6.

– "Childbearing and Land Availability: Some Evidence from Individual Household Data." In R.D. Lee et al. (eds.), *Population Patterns in the Past.* New York: Academic Press, 1977, 201–27.

- "Some Pitfalls in the 1851–1852 Census of Agriculture of Lower Canada." *HS/SH* 14 (May 1981): 219–31.
- "A Reconsideration of the State of Agriculture in Lower Canada in the First Half of the Nineteenth Century." *CPRH* 3 (1982): 9–49.
- "The Changing Structure of Canadian Agriculture, 1867–1897." *Journal of Economic History* 42, no. 1 (March 1982): 191–8.
- "A Further Look at French and Non-French Farming in Lower Canada." Paper presented to a conference on Canadian Rural History, Victoria, 1984.
- "Marketable Surpluses in Ontario Farming, 1860." *Social Science History* 8, no. 4 (autumn 1984): 395–424.
- "Ontario Agriculture, 1851–1901: A Cartographic Overview." *CPRH* 5 (1986): 290–301.
- "The Size Structure of Farming, Canada West, 1861." *Research in Economic History*, Supplement 5 (1989): 313–29.
- "Women, Work, and Childbearing." *HS/SH* 24, no. 48 (November 1991): 237–62.

Marr, William L. "Does Total Acres and Proportion of Farm Land in Specific Uses Vary by Size of Farm in York District, Ontario, 1871?" Research Report "#8583, Department of Economics, Wilfrid Laurier University, August 1985, 1–40.
- "Nineteenth Century Tenancy Rates in Ontario's Counties, 1881 and 1891." *Journal of Social History* 21, no. 4 (summer 1988): 753–64.
- "Family-Size Limitation in Canada West: Some Historical Evidence." *CPRH* 7 (1990): 273–92.
- "The Household Structure of Rural Canada West in 1851: Old Areas and Frontier Settlement." *CPRH* 9 (1994): 355–79.

Mays, Herbert and H.F. Manzl. "Literacy and Social Structure in Nineteenth-Century Ontario: An Exercise in Historical Methodology." *HS/SH* 7 (1974): 331–45.

Redish, Angela. "The Economic Crisis of 1837–1839 in Upper Canada: Case Study of a Temporary Suspension of Specie Payments." *Explorations in Economic History* 20 (1983): 402–17.

Williams, Michael. "Clearing the United States Forests: Pivotal Years, 1810–1860." *Journal of Historical Geography* 8, no. 1 (1982): 12–28.

PRAIRIES

Archer, John. *Saskatchewan: A History.* Saskatoon: Western Producer Books, 1980.

Armitage, Susan. "Women and Men in Western History: A Stereoptical Vision." *Western Historical Quarterly* 16 (1985): 391–5.

Bachelor, Bruce Edward. "The Agrarian Frontier near Red Deer and Lacombe, Alberta, 1882–1914." Doctoral dissertation, Burnaby: Simon Fraser University, 1978.

Backeland, Lucille and J.S. Frideres. "Franco-Manitobans and Cultural Loss: A Fourth Generation." *Prairie Forum* 2, no. 1 (May 1977): 1–18.

Bassler, Gerhard P. "Silent or Silenced Co-Founders of Canada? Reflections on the History of German Canadians." *Canadian Ethnic Studies* 22, no. 1 (1990): 38–46.

Baudoux, Maurice. "Le fait français dans l'Ouest." *Le Canada Français* 31, no. 8 (April 1944): 624–30.

Beaudoin, Alwynne B. "What They Saw: The Climatic and Environmental Context for Euro-Canadian Settlement in Alberta." *Prairie Forum* 24, no. 1 (spring 1999): 1–20.

Bellington, Ray A. (ed.). *Selected Essays of Frederick Jackson Turner – Frontier and Section*. Englewood Cliffs: Prentice-Hall, 1961.

Binnie-Clark, Georgina. *A Summer on the Canadian Prairie*. London: Edward Arnold, 1910.

Blouet, B.W. and F.C. Luebke (eds.). *The Great Plains Environment and Culture*. Lincoln: University of Nebraska Press, 1979.

Bradribb, Somer. "The Traditional Roles of Native Women in Canada and the Impact of Colonization." *Canadian Journal of Native Studies* 4, no. 1 (1984): 85–104.

Breen, David H. "The Canadian Prairie West and the 'Harmonious' Settlement Interpretation." *Agricultural History* 47 (January 1973): 63–75.

Britnell, George E. *The Wheat Economy*. Toronto: University of Toronto Press, 1939.

Bumstead, J.M. "Thomas Scott and the Daughter of Time." *Prairie Forum* 23, no. 2 (fall 1988): 145–70.

Burnet, Jean. *Next Year Country – A Study of Rural Social Organization in Alberta*. Toronto: University of Toronto Press, 1951.

Calderwood, William. "Religious Reactions to the Ku Klux Klan in Saskatchewan." *Saskatchewan History* 26, no. 3 (autumn 1973): 103–14.

Carroll, John Alexander (ed.). *Reflections of Western Historians*. Tucson: University of Arizona Press, 1969.

Carstensen, Vernon (ed.), *The Public Lands – Studies in the History of the Public Domain*. Madison: University of Wisconsin Press, 1963.

Chambers, Lori and Edgar-Andre Montigny (ed.). *Family Matters – Papers in Post-Confederation Canadian Family History*. Toronto: Canadian Scholars Press, 1998.

Chapman, Terry L. "Early Eugenics Movement in Western Canada." *Alberta History* 25 (autumn 1977): 9–17.

Cooper, Barry. *Alexander Kennedy Isbister: A Respectable Critic of the Honourable Company.* Ottawa: Carleton University Press, 1988.

Crowley, Terry "J.J. Morrison and the Transition in Canadian Farm Movements During the Early Twentieth Century." *AH* 71, no. 3 (summer 1997): 330–56.

Cruikshank, Julie. "Oral Tradition and Oral History: Reviewing Some Issues." *CHR* 75, no. 3 (1994): 403–18.

Dawson, Carl A. and Eva P. Younge. *Pioneering in the Prairie Provinces: The Social Side of the Settlement Process.* Toronto: Macmillan, 1940.

den Otter, A.A. *Civilizing the West: The Galts and the Development of Western Canada.* Edmonton: University of Alberta Press, 1982.

Dick, Evertt. *The Sod-House Frontier, 1854–1890.* Lincoln: Johnsen Publishing, 1954.

– *The Lure of the Land: A Social History of the Public Lands from the Articles of Confederation to the New Deal.* Lincoln: University of Nebraska Press, 1970.

Dregne, H.E. and W.O. Willis (eds.). *Dryland Agriculture.* Madison: American Society of Agronomy, #23 Agronomy Series, 1983.

Ens, Gerhard. "Kinship, Ethnicity, Class, and the Red River Metis: The Parishes of St François Xavier and St Andrews." Doctoral dissertation. Edmonton: University of Alberta, 1989.

Fite, Gilbert C. *The Farmers' Frontier, 1865–1900.* New York: Holt, Rinehart, and Winston, 1966.

– "The Pioneer Farmer: A View over Three Centuries." *AH* 50, no. 1 (1976): 275–89.

Flora, Cornelia Butler and Jan L. Flora. "Structure of Agriculture and Women's Culture in the Great Plains." *Great Plains Quarterly* 8 (fall 1988): 195–205.

Foster, John E. "Paulet Paul: Métis or 'House Indian' Folk-Hero?" *Manitoba History*, no. 9 (spring 1985): 2–7.

Frémont, Donatien. *Les Français dans l'Ouest Canadien.* Winnipeg: Les Editions de la Liberté, 1959.

Friesen, Gerald. *The Canadian Prairies: A History.* Toronto: University of Toronto Press, 1984.

– *River Road – Essays on Manitoba and Prairie History.* Winnipeg: University of Manitoba Press, 1996.

Friesen, John W. "Expansion of Settlement in Manitoba." In D. Swainson (ed.), *Historical Essays on the Prairie Provinces.* Toronto: McClelland and Stewart, 1970, 120–30.

Froeschle, Hartmut. "A Concise History." *German-Canadian Yearbook* 12 (1992): 13–29.

Furtan, W. Hartley and George E. Lee, "Economic Development of the Saskatchewan Wheat Economy." *Canadian Journal of Agricultural Economics*, 25, no. 3 (1977): 15–28.

Gallagher, Brian. "A Re-Examination of Race, Class and Society in Red River." *Native Studies Review* 4, no. 1-2 (1989): 25–66.

Geiger, John Grigsby. "River Lot Three: Settlement Life on the North Saskatchewan." *Alberta History* 44, no. 1 (winter 1996): 15–25.

Giraud, Marcel. "Les Canadiens français dans les provinces de l'Ouest." *La Revue de l'Université Laval* 3, no. 3 (November 1948): 215–32.

Gruending, Dennis (ed.). *The Middle of Nowhere, Rediscovering Saskatchewan*. Saskatoon: Fifth House, 1996.

Gunn, Donald. *History of Manitoba from the Earliest Settlement to 1835, and from 1835 to the Admission of the Province into the Dominion*. Ottawa: MacLean Roger, 1980.

Haites, Erik F. and James Mak. "Economies of Scale in Western River Steamboating." *Journal of Economic History* 36, no. 3 (September 1976): 689–703.

Hall, D.J. "T.O. Davis and Federal Politics in Saskatchewan, 1896." *Saskatchewan History* 30, no. 2 (winter 1977): 56–62.

Harrison, Dick. "Rölvaag, Grove and Pioneering on the American and Canadian Plains." *Great Plains Quarterly* 1 (fall 1981): 252–62.

Hartnett, Sean. "The Land Market on the Wisconsin Frontier: An Examination of Land Ownership Processes in Turtle and LaPrairie Townships, 1839–1890." *AH* 65, no. 4 (fall 1991): 38–77.

Hauser, George J. *The Swedish Community at Ericksdale, Manitoba*. Ottawa: National Museum of Man, Mercury Series #14, 1976.

Hay, Jim and Tom Isern. *Plains Folk – A Commonplace of the Great Plains*. Norman: University of Oklahoma Press, 1987.

Hessing, Melody et al. (eds.) *This Elusive Land: Women and the Canadian Environment*. Vancouver: UBC Press, 2005.

Hopkins, John A. *Changing Technology and Employment in Agriculture*. Washington: US Department of Agriculture, Bureau of Economics, 1941.

Ironside, R.G. and E. Tomasky. "Agriculture and River Lot Settlement in Western Canada: The Case of Pakan (Victoria) Alberta." *Alberta History* 24, no. 1 (April 1976): 3–18.

Jensen, Joan M. (ed.). *With These Hands, Women Working the Land*. New York: McGraw-Hill, 1981.

Johnson, V.W. and R. Barlow. *Land Problems and Policies*. New York: McGraw-Hill, 1954.

Kirkendall, Richard S. "A Professor in Farm Politics." *Mid-America* 41 (1959): 210–17.

– *Social Scientists and Farm Politics in the Age of Roosevelt.* Columbia: University of Missouri Press, 1966.

Knox, H. C. "Alexander Kennedy Isbister." *Manitoba Historical and Scientific Society Transactions,* 3rd series, no. 12 (1957): 17–28.

Kuznets, Simon. "Long-Term Changes in the National Income of the United States of America since 1870." In *Income and Wealth of the United States: Trends and Structure,* Income and Wealth, Series II. Cambridge: Bowes and Bowes, 1952, 196–204.

Lalonde, André. "L'intelligentsia du Québec et la migration des Canadiens français vers l'Ouest." RHAF 33, no. 2 (September 1979): 163–85.

Landale, Nancy S. "Opportunity, Movement, and Marriage: US Farm Sons at the Turn of the Century." *Journal of Family History* 14, no. 4 (1989): 365–86.

Lapointe, Richard and Lucille Tessier. *The Francophones of Saskatchewan – A History.* Regina: Campion College, 1988.

Liddell, Peter G. (ed.). *German-Canadian Studies: Critical Approaches.* Vancouver: Canadian Association of University Teachers of German, 1983.

Luebke, Frederick (ed.). *European Immigrants in the American West – Community Histories.* Albuquerque: University of New Mexico Press, 1998.

Lussier, Antoine S. and B. Bruce Sealey (eds.). *The Other Natives: The/les Metis, (1700–1885).* Winnipeg: Manitoba Metis Federation Press, 1978.

MacFarlane, R.O. "Manitoba Politics and Parties after Confederation." *Canadian Historical Association Historical Papers,* 1940, 45–55.

MacGregor, J.G. *Senator Hardisty's Prairies, 1849–1889.* Saskatoon: Western Producer Prairie Books, 1978.

McGowan, Don C. *Grassland Settlers: The Swift Current Region during the Era of the Ranching Frontier.* Regina: Canadian Plains Research Center, 1975.

McManis, Douglas R. *The Initial Evaluation and Utilization of the Illinois Prairies.* Chicago: University of Chicago Press, 1964.

Marchildon, Gregory P. (ed.). *The Early Northwest.* Regina: Canadian Plains Research Center, 2008.

Mitchell, Kenneth (ed.). *Horizon, Writings of the Canadian Prairie.* Toronto: Oxford University Press, 1977.

Moodie, D.W. "Alberta Settlement Surveys." *Alberta History* 18, no. 3 (summer 1970): 1–7.

Morton, W.L. "Two Young Men, 1869, Charles Mair and Louis Riel." *Historical and Scientific Society of Manitoba Papers,* 3rd series, no. 30, 1973–74, 33–44.

Mossmann, Manfred. "The Charismatic Pattern: Canada's Riel Rebellion of 1885 as a Millenarian Protest Movement." *Prairie Forum,* 10, no. 2 (autumn 1985): 307–26.

Noy, Gary (ed.). *Distant Horizon, Documents from the 19th Century American West*. Lincoln: University of Nebraska, 1999.

Pannekoek, Frits. "The Historiography of the Red River Settlement, 1830–1868." *Prairie Forum* 6, no. 1 (spring 1981): 75–86.

Patterson, G. James. *The Romanians of Saskatchewan: Four Generations of Adaptation*. Ottawa: National Museums of Canada, 1977.

Peterson, Jacqueline. "Ethnogenesis: The Settlement and Growth of a 'New People' in the Great Lakes Region, 1702–1815." *American Indian Culture and Research Journal* 6, no. 2 (1982): 23–64.

Phillips, W.G. *The Agricultural Implement Industry in Canada, A Study of Competition*. Toronto: University of Toronto Press, 1956.

Poelzer, Irene A. "Local Problems of Early Saskatchewan Education." *Saskatchewan History* 32, no. 1 (winter 1979): 1–15.

Potyondi, Barry. "Loss and Substitution: The Ecology of Production in Southwestern Saskatchewan, 1860–1930." Paper presented to the Canadian Historical Association, 1994.

– *In Palliser's Triangle, Living in the Grasslands, 1850–1930*. Saskatoon: Purich Publishing, 1995.

Primack, Martin L. "Farm Construction as a Use of Farm Labor in the United States, 1850–1910." *Journal of Economic History* 25, no. 1 (March 1965): 114–25.

Read, Colin. "The Red River Rebellion and J.S. Dennis, 'Lieutenant and Conservator of the Peace.'" *Manitoba History* no. 3 (spring 1982): 11–18.

Regehr, T.G. *Remembering Saskatchewan: A History of Rural Saskatchewan*. Saskatoon: University of Saskatchewan Extension Division, 1979.

Reinhardt, Nola and Peggy Barlett. "The Persistence of Family Farms in United States Agriculture." *Sociologia ruralis* 29 (1989): 203–25.

Rice, John G. "The Role of Culture and Community in Frontier Prairie Farming." *Journal of Historical Geography* 3, no. 2 (April 1977): 155–75.

Richtik, James Morton. "Manitoba Settlement: 1870–1886." Doctoral dissertation, University of Minnesota, Minneapolis, 1971.

– "The Policy Framework for Settling the Canadian West, 1870–1890." *AH* 49, no. 4 (October 1975): 613–28.

Ronaghan, Allan. "Charles Mair and the Northwest Emigrant Aid Society." *Manitoba History*, no. 14 (autumn 1987): 10–14.

– "The Confrontation at Rivière aux Ilets de Bois." *Prairie Forum*, 14, no. 1 (spring 1989): 1–8.

– "James Farquharson: Agent and Agitator." *Manitoba History*, no. 17 (spring 1989): 12–16.

Schoney, R.A. "The Impact of Price Stabilizing Policies on the Risk Efficient Crop/Fallow Decisions of Wheat Farmers in the Brown Soil Zone of Saskatchewan." *Canadian Journal of Agricultural Economics* 43 (1995): 259–70.

Simkin, Rubin. *The Prairie Farm Machinery Co-operative: Canadian Co-operative Implements Ltd.* Ottawa: Queen's Printer, 1970.

Smith, David E. (ed.). *Building a Province: A History of Saskatchewan in Documents.* Saskatoon: Fifth House, 1992.

Snow, John. *These Mountains Are our Sacred Places, The Story of the Stoney Indians.* Toronto: Samuel Stevens, 1977.

Socolofsky, Homer E. "Success and Failure in Nebraska Homesteading." AH 42 (1968): 103–7.

Spector, David. *Agriculture on the Prairies, 1870–1940.* Ottawa:History and Archaeology #65, National Historic Parks and Sites Branch, Parks Canada, 1983.

Stirling, Bob and John Conway. "Factions among Prairie Farmers." In G.S. Basran and D.A. Hay (eds.), *The Political Economy of Agriculture in Western Canada.* Toronto: Garamond Press, 1988, 73–83.

Strange, H.G.L. *A Short History of Prairie Agriculture.* Winnipeg: Searle Grain Company, 1954.

Taillefer, Jean-Marie. "Les Franco-Manitobains et l'Education, 1870–1890: Une Étude Quantative." Doctoral dissertation, University of Manitoba, Winnipeg, 1988.

Taylor, Jeffery. *Fashioning Farmers – Ideology, Agricultural Knowledge, and the Manitoba Farm Movement, 1890–1925.* Regina: Canadian Plains Research Centre, 1994.

Thomas, Greg and Ian Clarke. "The Garrison Mentality and the Canadian West." *Prairie Forum* 4, no. 1 (1979): 83–104.

Thomas, Lewis G. "The Umbrella and the Mosaic: The French-English Presence and the Settlement of the Canadian Prairie West." In J.A. Carroll (ed.), *Reflections of Western Historians.* Tucson: University of Arizona Press, 1969, 135–52.

Thomas, Lewis H. "A History of Agriculture on the Prairies to 1914." In R.D. Francis and H. Palmer (eds.), *The Prairie West.* Edmonton: Pica Pica Press, 1985, 221–56.

Thompson, John Herd. "Bringing in the Sheaves: The Harvest Excursionists, 1890–1929." CHR 59, no. 4 (December 1978): 467–89.

Tyman, John Langton. *By Section, Township and Range – Studies in Prairie Settlement.* Brandon: Assiniboine Historical Society, 1972.

Tyson Parson, Edna. *Land I Can Own.* Ottawa: Westboro Printers, 1981.

Vallee, Frank G. "Regionalism and Ethnicity: The French-Canadian Case." In
    B.Y. Card (ed.), *Perspectives on Regions and Regionalism*. Proceedings of the
    10th annual meeting of the Western Association of Sociology and Anthro-
    pology, 1968, 19–25.
– with Norman Shulman. "The Viability of French Groupings Outside Que-
    bec." In Mason Wade (ed.), *Regionalism in the Canadian Community,
    1867–1967*, CHA Centennial Seminars. Toronto: University of Toronto Press,
    1969, 84–99.
Vogelsang, Robin Russell. "The Initial Agricultural Settlement of the Morin-
    ville-Westlock Area, Alberta." Master's thesis, University of Alberta, Edmon-
    ton, 1972.
Voisey, Paul. "Rural Local History and the Prairie West." *Prairie Forum* 10, no.
    2 (autumn 1985): 327–38.
Waiser, W.A. *Saskatchewan: A New History*. Calgary: Fifth House, 2005.
Warkentin, John (ed.). *The Western Interior of Canada*. Toronto: McClelland
    and Stewart, 1964.
Wawrow, Les. "Nativism in English Canada: Attitudes of Anglo-Saxons to the
    Influx of 1896–1914 Immigration." In Benedykt Heydenkorn (ed.), *From
    Prairies to Cities*. Toronto: Canadian-Polish Research Institute, 1975, 68–80.
Weir, T.R. "Settlement of Southwest Manitoba, 1870–1891," *Historical and
    Scientific Society of Manitoba*, 3rd series, 1960-61, 17, 54–64.
– "Pioneer Settlement of Southwest Manitoba, 1879–1901." *Canadian Geog-
    rapher* 8, no. 2 (1964): 64–71.
Widdis, Randy William. *With Scarcely a Ripple, Anglo-Canadian Migration
    into the United States and Western Canada, 1880–1920*. Montreal & Kings-
    ton: McGill-Queen's University Press, 1998.
Wiesinger, Judith P. "Modeling the Agricultural Settlement Process of Southern
    Manitoba, 1872–1891: Some Implications for Settlement Theory." *Prairie
    Forum* 10, no. 1 (spring 1985): 83–104.
Wilcox, E.V. "Plan of the Department of Agriculture for Handling the Farm
    Labor Problem." *American Economic Review* 8 (March 1918): 158–70.
Wilson, Garrett. *Frontier Farewell, The 1870s and the End of the Old West*.
    Regina: Canadian Plains Research Center, 2007.
Wilson, Keith and J.B. Wyndels. *The Belgians in Manitoba*. Winnipeg: Peguis
    Publishers, 1976.
Wiseman, Nelson. "The Questionable Relevance of the Constitution in Advan-
    cing Minority Cultural Rights in Manitoba." *Canadian Journal of Political
    Science* 25, no. 4 (December 1992): 697–721.
Wonders, William C. "Scandinavian Homesteaders." *Alberta History* 24, no. 3
    (summer 1976): 1–4.

Woods, Laurence M. *British Gentlemen in the Wild West, The Era of the Intensely English Cowboy.* London (UK): Collier Macmillan, 1989.

Woywitha, Anne B. "A Roumanian Pioneer." *Alberta History* 21, no. 4 (autumn 1973): 20–7.

– "Waugh Homesteaders and Their School." *Alberta History* 23, no. 1 (1975): 13–17.

– "A Struggle for Survival." *Alberta History* 37, no. 3 (summer 1989): 1–6.

Wunder, John R. (ed.). *At Home on the Range, Essays on the History of Western Social and Domestic Life.* Westport: Greenwood, 1985.

THEORETICAL DEBATES

Barron, Hal S. "Rediscovering the Majority: The New Rural History of the Nineteenth-Century North," *Historical Methods* 19, no. 4 (fall 1986): 141–52.

Cook, Nancy. "The Thin with the Thick: Social History, Postmodern Ethnography and Textual Practice." *HS/SH* 32, no. 63 (May 1999): 85–101.

Curtis, Bruce. *The Politics of Population – State Formation, Statistics, and the Census of Canada, 1840–1875.* Toronto: University of Toronto Press, 2001.

Danbom, David A. *Resisted Revolution: Urban America and the Industrialization of Agriculture.* Ames: Iowa State University Press, 1979.

– *"The World of Hope": Progressives and the Struggle for an Ethical Public Life.* Philadelphia: Temple University Press, 1987.

Dewey, Clive J. "The Rehabilitation of the Peasant Proprietor in Nineteenth-Century Economic Thought." *History of Political Economy* 6 (1974): 17–47.

Dupre, Ruth. "Cliometrie, Économies et Histoire: un ménage à trios." *RHAF* 46, no. 4 (spring 1993): 645–60.

Engerman, Stanley L. "A Guide for the Perplexed." *Journal of Economic History* 36 (1976): 729–31.

Fogel, Robert W. and Stanley L. Engerman (eds.). *The Reinterpretation of American Economic History.* New York: Harper and Row, 1971.

Forster, Robert. "Achievements of the Annales School." *Journal of Economic History* 38, no. 1 (March 1978): 58–76.

Friedlander, Dov, Barbara S. Okun, and Sharon Segal. "The Demographic Transition Then and Now: Processes, Perspectives, and Analyses." *Journal of Family History* 24, no. 4 (October 1999): 493–533.

Furet, François. "Beyond the *Annales*." *Journal of Modern History* 55 (September 1981): 389–410.

Gerber, David A. "Cutting Out Shylock: Elite Anti-Semitism and the Quest for Moral Order in the Mid-Nineteenth Century American Market Place." *Journal of American History* 69, no. 3 (December 1982): 615–37.

Gurttler, K.R. (ed.) *Annals 5 Problem, Project, Perspective, Symposium 1985.* Montreal: Colloques DEAM 1986.

Iacovetta, Franca. "Post-Modern Ethnography, Historical Materialism, and Decentring the (Male) Authorial Voce: A Feminist Conversation." *Hs/SH* 32, no. 64 (November 1999): 275–94.

McClelland, Peter D. *Sowing Modernity, America's First Agricultural Revolution.* Ithaca: Cornell University Press, 1997.

McCloskey, Donald N. "The Achievements of the Cliometric School." *Journal of Economic History* 38, no. 1 (March 1978): 13–28.

Martin, David E. "The Rehabilitation of the Peasant Proprietor in Nineteenth-Century Economic Thought: A Comment." *History of Political Economy* 8, no. 2 (1976): 297–303.

O'Connor, James. "[Review] *The Twisted Dream.*" *Monthly Review* 26 (March 1975): 41–54.

Osberg, Lars and Fazley Siddiq. "The Inequality of Wealth in Britain's North American Colonies: The Importance of the Relatively Poor." *Review of Income and Wealth* 34, no. 2 (2005): 143–63.

Palmer, Brian. "Of Silences and Trenches: A Dissident View of Granatstein's Meaning." *CHR* 80, no. 4 (1999): 676–86.

– "Historiographic Hassles: Class and Gender, Evidence and Interpretation." *Hs/SH* 33, no. 65 (May 2000): 105–44.

Reay, Barry. "Kinship and the Neighbourhood in 19th century Rural England: The Myth of the Autonomous Nuclear Family." *Journal of Family History* 21, no. 1 (January 1996): 87–104.

Rudolph, Richard L. "The European Peasant Family and Economy: Central Themes and Issues." *Journal of Family History* 17, no. 2 (1992): 119–38.

Ruggles, Steven. *Prolonged Connections: The Rise of the Extended Family in 19th Century England and America.* Madison: University of Wisconsin Press, 1987.

Seavoy, Ronald E. "Portraits of Twentieth-Century American Peasants: Subsistence Social Values Recorded in *All God's Daughters* and *Let Us Now Praise Famous Men.*" *AH* 68, no. 2 (1994): 199–218.

Sherry, Robert. "Comments on O'Connor's Review of *The Twisted Dream.*" *Monthly Review* 28 (May 1976): 52–60 (with O'Connor's reply, 60–3).

Stanley, Tim. "Why I Killed Canadian History." *Hs/SH* 33, no. 65 (May 2000): 79–104.

Stone, Lawrence. "The Revival of Narrative: Reflections on a New Old History." *Past and Present* 85 (1979): 3–24.

Valverde, Mariana. "Some Remarks on the Rise and Fall of Discourse Analysis." *Hs/SH* 33, no. 65 (May 2000): 59–78.

Vinovskis, Maris A. "Socioeconomic Determinants of Interstate Fertility Differentials in the United States in 1850 and 1860." *Journal of Interdisciplinary History* 6, no. 3 (winter 1976): 375–96.

– "American Families in the Past." In J.G. Gardner and G.A. Adams (eds.), *Ordinary People and Everyday Life*. Nashville: American Association for State and Local History 1983, 115–35.

Wright, Donald. *The Professionalization of History in English Canada*. Toronto: University of Toronto Press, 2005.

Index